War, Strategy, and the Modern State, 1792–1914

This book is a comparative study of military operations conducted by modern states between the French Revolution and World War I. It examines the complex relationship between political purpose and strategy on the one hand and the challenge of realising strategic goals through military operations on the other. It argues further that following the experience of the Napoleonic Wars, military strength has been awarded a primary status in determining the comparative modernity of all the Great Powers; that military goals came progressively to distort a sober understanding of the national interest; that a genuinely political and diplomatic understanding of national strategy was lost; and that these developments collectively rendered the military and political catastrophe of 1914 not inevitable yet probable.

Carl Cavanagh Hodge is a Professor of Political Science at the University of British Columbia–Okanagan. He is a former Senior Volkswagen Research Fellow with the American Institute of Contemporary German Studies at the Johns Hopkins University and a former NATO-EAPC fellow. He is the author or editor of nine books and numerous articles on European and American politics and history. His titles include *The Age of Imperialism, 1800–1914* (Greenwood, 2008); *U.S. Presidents and Foreign Policy, From 1789 to the Present* (ABC-Clio, 2007); *Atlanticism for a New Century: The Rise, Triumph and Decline of NATO* (Prentice-Hall, 2004); *The Trammels of Tradition: Social Democracy in Britain, France, and Germany* (Greenwood, 1994).

T0394117

Warfare, Society, and Culture
Series Editors: Frank Tallett
David J.B. Trim

For a full list of titles in this series, please visit www.routledge.com.

War, Strategy, and the Modern State, 1792–1914

Carl Cavanagh Hodge

Routledge
Taylor & Francis Group

LONDON AND NEW YORK

First published 2017
by Routledge
2 Park Square, Milton Park, Abingdon, Oxon OX14 4RN

and by Routledge
711 Third Avenue, New York, NY 10017

First issued in paperback 2018

Routledge is an imprint of the Taylor & Francis Group, an informa business

British Library Cataloguing-in-Publication Data
A catalogue record for this book is available from the British Library

Library of Congress Cataloging-in-Publication Data
CIP data has been applied for.

ISBN 13: 978-1-138-33009-2 (pbk)
ISBN 13: 978-1-84893-613-3 (hbk)

Typeset in Sabon
by codeMantra

MIX
Paper from
responsible sources
FSC
www.fsc.org
FSC™ C013985

Printed in the United Kingdom
by Henry Ling Limited

To Senator D.D. Everett,
for the good conversations

Contents

List of maps

Acknowledgements

Of the many friends and colleagues who contributed with advice and criticism during the writing of this book, I would like to thank Frank Tallett and David Trim, series editors for the series *Warfare, Society and Culture* with Pickering and Chatto, along with Sofia Buono and Katherine Gilbert, respectively the production manager and copy editor for this volume. I am grateful in particular to Alan Dobson and Cathal Nolan for their informed criticism of the manuscript and Andrew Hibbert for his invaluable technical assistance. I would also like to thank colleagues with the Transatlantic Studies Association and Lori Bogle, along with the conferees at the 2013 McMullen Naval History Symposium of the United States Naval Academy for their comments on conference papers based in part on related material. Librarians and archivists with the University of British Columbia, the British Library, the Royal United Services Institute, and the Militärgeschichtliches Forschungsamt in Freiburg im Breisgau are too numerous to name, but they know who they are. Above all, I thank my wife, Jane Everett, for her advice, encouragement, and tireless patience.

A conceptual prologue

This book is concerned with the evolution of the use of arms to achieve the foreign policy goals of the Great Powers from the French Revolution to World War I. It is thus preoccupied with one aspect of a timeless art of statecraft during a specific phase of world history when the state developed a growing, indeed fateful, reliance on military power in its relations with other states. Statecraft, here defined as "the organised actions governments take to change the external environment in general or the policies and actions of other states to achieve the objectives that have been set by policy makers,"[1] is inherently multidimensional, drawing upon economic, diplomatic, cultural as well as military resources. The book's primary concern with strategy as a dimension of statecraft—more precisely, its application in the conception and prosecution of war—is intended first to explain the comparative success or failure of major states in the use of military force in major and minor wars during the nineteenth and early twentieth centuries. In addition, the book's purpose is to examine the phenomenon of militarism as an integral feature of the modern state as it evolved in the nineteenth century, that is: the progressive influence of military interests, values, personnel, and institutions in articulating the foreign policies of democratic and non-democratic states alike.

Samuel Finer's magisterial study of the history of government identified six constitutive features of the modern state: nationalism, an ethnic aspiration to independent self-governance; popular sovereignty, the notion that constituent power resides with The People; the nation-state, a fusion of nationalism and popular sovereignty in a political community within a given territory; secularism, the conviction that the state has conscious purposes that are this-worldly; industrialisation, the idea that among the conscious purposes the industrialisation of wealth production is a primary mission; and welfarism, an acknowledgement of the obligation to enable all citizens to be participants in the political community. To them can be added a seventh dimension that Finer deems "the syndrome of modernity," military power, an assumption that superior wealth and science entitled modern European states to expand influence and territory and that armed might represented a wholly legitimate instrument in the effort.[2] Consciously or not, the modernising states of the nineteenth century adhered to Machiavelli's dictum that "among other evils which being unarmed brings you, it causes you to be despised." Military power became the calling card of modernity; no matter how advanced its industry or sophisticated its sciences, a state of the nineteenth century risked the contempt of others unless it could demonstrate a formidable capacity for making war.

Where the political and the military intersect, moreover, the notion of modernity emerging from the eighteenth century was infused with a notion concerning its inherent dynamism. The fact that France's revolutionary leaders rarely used the word *modern* to characterise the regime change in which they were involved testifies to the fact that, in the first instance, they little understood what it implied. They marked dates such as July 14, 1789, and August 10, 1792, as milestones in replacement of the absolutist state with a republican order, yet they quickly realised that they stood at the beginning rather than the end of a process of change that in the short term implied little order at all. The way to the future therefore entailed an absolute duty to the mission of progress, lest the Revolution stall and betray its ideal. Reasoning in effect that the tree of liberty must be watered with blood, Saint-Just warned his contemporaries that to hesitate at the execution of Louis XVI was to fail the standard of Brutus and to concede that humanity in the eighteenth century was less advanced than in the time of Caesar.[3] In France and beyond, the Age of Revolution in Europe brought with it a sense that every stage of modernity inevitably yielded to the next, that accelerated change was to be welcomed and mastered, and that contempt for tradition was the passport to progress. What this political movement meant specifically for the arts and sciences of war at a time when European capitalism was only beginning to industrialise few could imagine. Although thoroughly respectable comparative studies of the relationship between the military and the modern take the second half of nineteenth century as their starting point, and others place military modernity with both feet in the twentieth century,[4] this book follows Finer's lead in proposing that the political upheaval of the French Revolution, "the most important single event in the entire history of government,"[5] begat the organisational changes to warfare as prosecuted by Napoleon Bonaparte in a largely preindustrial environment that later became common to wars conducted by all modern states. There is nothing especially original in this approach, but the author holds that if a state's formal and informal constitution is expressed in the way it employs military force, then the first manifestations of modern war were evident in Napoleonic warfare. Moreover, the mutation of the "syndrome of modernity," a preoccupation with military capacity, into the pathology of modern militarism finds its most striking iteration in Bonapartist France.[6]

The capacity for making war is only imperfectly related to the reasoning behind the used of armed force and the particular features of its application. Basil Liddell Hart's standard definition of *strategy*—"the art of distributing and applying military means to fulfill the ends of policy"—is only slightly less narrow than Clausewitz's definition of war itself as the *a continuation of political intercourse, carried on with other means,* from which he stipulates that strategy is *the use of engagements for the object of the war*.[7] Colin Gray's constructive rewording, "The bridge that relates military power to political purpose, *the use that is made of force and the threat of force for the ends of policy*,"[8] takes into account Liddell Hart's concern with the peace, or at least the circumstance, following upon war and whether it can be considered an improvement, or at least a more durable revision, of the circumstance that preceded it.

Moreover, the attention given to the *threat* of military force implies that a strategy crafted to achieve the object of war without in fact ever prosecuting a military conflict is either modest in its objective or particularly coherent and clever in its use of threat. Beatrice Heuser points out that the narrow, technical definition of strategy—in the extreme, that of Helmut von Moltke the Elder, for whom its essence was the preparations undertaken to get troops to the battlefield simultaneously—takes little account of the political objectives for which a strategy is deemed to be appropriate.[9] She therefore highlights the comprehensiveness of Henry Spencer Wilkinson's use of *policy* as "national action directed toward an end or purpose," a purpose moreover "that the nation values and appreciates, or else the Government will have no support in its efforts to attain it."[10] In other words, a definition of strategy that assumes military conflict and ignores strategy's affinity with diplomacy short of war ignores the fact that strategy is above all a conceptual instrument in the toolbox of statecraft in war and peace.

Although Wilkinson's definition is possibly overdetermined by a democratic context of political affairs, it rightly stresses the deterrent and persuasive potential of military power in lending credibility to diplomacy. The definitional evolution of the term "strategy" being in part a product of the errors, often catastrophic, of narrow understandings of strategy in the nineteenth century, the concept of *grand strategy* found common usage after two catastrophic world wars in the twentieth. By this was meant the use of "political, economic, psychological, and military forces as necessary in peace and war, to afford the maximum support to policies, in order to increase the probabilities and favourable consequences of victory and to lessen the chances of defeat."[11] This book assumes that nothing very useful about strategy in the conduct of war can be learned unless the comparative method is applied to historical case studies. It argues that strategy can never be a sufficiently coherent conception of the national interest in the international arena unless it strives for this last, grand strategic, perspective.

Another aspect of strategy indispensible to an understanding of war in any era is the fact of its mutability. In war and peace, a national strategy for prosperity, security, or regional or global power and influence is necessarily a process of adaptation to changing circumstance—much of which will be beyond the capacity of strategists to influence. The adaptation required *may* result from the initial application of a strategy and its apparent success or failure, but it is *always* the result of the actions of other players in the international arena—allies or adversaries—and their own adaptation, subject to chance, uncertainty, and ambiguity. Most useful writings on strategy have tended to stress even more than those of Clausewitz that when war is planned and prosecuted, strategy must be flexible in application, as well as comprehensive in conception, and that general rules, hardened principles, and detailed systems of military action often fall short in achieving the war's objectives. Just as political theorists are drawn to the tidiness of models and are baffled by the characteristic untidiness of political affairs, the building of general theories about war are intellectually or aesthetically satisfying to the theorist but of little use in understanding the complex reality of a past war for the purpose of applying its lessons to a future one. One of the best edited volumes on strategy rightly notes, following Clausewitz, that theory is beside the point, that it "deflects" inquiry toward objective factors, whereas strategy involves human agency and the intervention of passions and beliefs that elude rigorous measurement for an assessment of their effect.[12] This is perhaps especially true of the Napoleonic warfare that moved Clausewitz to put pen to paper in the first place, as there are few other instances of an entire era in history so thoroughly dominated by the agency of one individual. Certainly objective factors of late-eighteenth-century France facilitated his rise to prominence and celebrity in military leadership. Revolutionary France had enemies she was bound to fight; Napoleon's profession and skill in fighting alone possibly destined him to fame and power.[13] Still, fame and power do not equate with success. The book's first chapter offers a discussion of what was new and what was not new in Napoleon's way of war, with a mind to explaining why he "incarnated operational brilliance—and strategic lunacy."[14]

The book then turns to comparative discussions of the Great Powers at war, 1830–1905, in an attempt to demonstrate that, although certain common features of strategic thinking were clearly in evidence, national governments interpreted the Napoleonic experience according to national interests and national military capabilities. More often than not, how the national political regime was constituted and its relationship to its armed service branches were the dominant factors in its preferences for prosecution of armed conflict than was any objective accounting of national strategic strengths and weaknesses, costs and benefits.

Napoleonic France demonstrates more than most cases that states at war resist strategic reason as often as they yield to it. The book does not hold with Liddell Hart that strategy is "the very opposite of morality," or that "grand strategy tends to coincide with morality: through having always to keep in view the ultimate goal of the efforts it is directing."[15] Strategy is amoral in nature, but Liddell Hart is correct that it is properly animated by a concern for the peace that follows a war and therefore is integral to *statecraft*. In the eighteenth century, this idea of statecraft was less quaint, in so far as war—the threat, prosecution, and outcome thereof—served the goals of diplomacy and was often integral to them.[16] After Napoleon we encounter an international environment in which modern states often reversed that relationship to the extent that diplomacy served the objectives of war—in 1914 as much as in 1805.

A national strategy, of course, is not conceived in an international vacuum. In the period under study here, characterised by intensifying rivalry among the Great Powers of Europe and beyond, it is most obviously true that everyone's strategy to a significant extent depended upon everyone else's.[17] In the pressure cooker of European politics, moreover, the strategy of rival states could be known or deduced on the basis of familiarity and past experience. Beyond Europe, colonial and imperial wars were often as not the product either of unanticipated emergencies or of apparent and fortuitous opportunities—in which case, such strategy as applied was the product of hasty innovation rather than long-term planning. Comparing the conduct of wars in the nineteenth century involves above all a discussion of military *operations*, the field of action below *strategy*—and ideally governed by it—and above *tactics*, the actions of military forces in single engagements. *Operations* typically refer to the sequence of actions by large units such as armies, army corps or groups, or naval and maritime forces in accordance with a preconceived strategy or innovated strategic vision. Commonly referred to as "operational art" in deference to an understanding of national war-making developed by Soviet military theorists between the World Wars, military operations have an inherent though problematic relationship with strategy. Bluntly put, the one cannot exist without the other, but even the most thoroughly reasoned strategy contributes little to success in war until and unless the operations to put it into effect are properly conducted; conversely, the possession by any state of impressive operational capabilities in no measure means that its political and military leadership have a coherent, much less a prudent, strategy for guiding operations to achievable and politically worthwhile goals. This book assumes first that it is reasonable to hold that an art of operations began to emerge in the late-eighteenth and early-nineteenth centuries and was crucial to the success of Napoleonic war-making,[18] and second that the comparative study of military operations reveals much about the nature and goals of states prosecuting war.

Obviously, the ability to aspire to certain kinds of operations assumes on the part of the state conducting them certain attributes, from armies of a certain size and organisation to naval forces of adequate strength and reach; from communications to transportation; from scientific advancement to technological prowess; from the tedious details of logistics to the cutting edge of war: soldiers with weapons. The book deals with a period of revolutionary scientific and technological change in which the conduct of military operations was liable to an increasing complexity that challenged not only the technological capacity of the modern state and required a proportionate fiscal commitment to meet it but also an increasingly large and professionalised military establishment capable of understanding the nature of modern war.

The book includes an examination of the American Civil War, as well as the Spanish-American War and the Russo-Japanese War in comparative context. It is thus consistent with a school of thought for which responsible study of the military and its encounter with modernity must necessarily reach beyond Europe. Still, it is not a complete break with the Eurocentrism common to military history and security studies.[19] Nor can it be. This because its final chapter is concerned with the mutually reinforcing tendencies of the "new imperialism" in African and Asia, the effect of galloping changes in technology on naval power, and the willingness of political leadership to defer to a predominantly, then wholly, military interpretation of strategy. This process, clearly evident by the 1870s and accelerating after 1890, reduced not only geographical space and time considerations integrated into war planning but also the space and time of manoeuvre left to diplomacy in weighing the probable losses against the theoretical gains of a general war in Europe that quickly embraced much of the world.

The book turns lastly to the mutating relationship between statecraft and diplomacy on the one hand and military power on the other, a change in which the most fundamental aspect of strategy, national interest soberly assessed, was lost, and the "primacy of politics" was overthrown along with the peace.[20] This process varied significantly from one national context to the next, but is nonetheless hard to imagine the crisis of 1914 in the absence of broad public subscription to a militarist perception of world affairs. The reason that the term *militarism* applied to the period is so "vague and elastic" is that it is encountered on multiple levels, the highest and most important being the at the level of governmental policy and decision making, where purely or primarily military interpretations of the national interest, and hence of strategy, came to prevail.[21] The second and more elusive definition of the term, "the excessive permeation of civil society with the military outlook,"[22] is no less central to the book's argument concerning the evolution of war in the nineteenth century, from the cultural and political legacy of the French revolutionary army's *levée en masse* in the form of the *grognards*—post-Napoleon war veterans uncomfortable with parliamentary democracy and peace and for whom the Emperor was the authentic man of the people celebrated by Balzac, Hugo, and Stendahl—to the Prussian officers ubiquitous in Fontane's novels of the Second German Empire, or the popular identification of the army of late Meiji Japan with order, wealth, and power.[23]

After 1870, the influence of militarism on state and society alone became more difficult to measure, as competition among the major powers witnessed the cultivation of popular interpretations of the imperial mission that tended to equate loyalty to the state and nation with enthusiasm for its army and navy. The attendant Darwinist spirit of popular nationalism at the dawn to the twentieth century, likening competition among the powers to the natural selection of only the fittest for survival, extended alike to both those societies that endowed their armed forces with extraordinary esteem and to those that hesitated to do so.[24] Even in victory, the popular nationalism of Meiji Japan boiled with resentment to an extent that troubled the very oligarchy that had nurtured it. In the press and on the street, popular zeal in America for a splendid little war with Spain in 1898 ran well ahead of the McKinley administration's eagerness to prosecute it, while the popular jingoism in Britain that accompanied the final stages of the Boer War moved the prime minister to complain of the national inclination "to fight everybody, and to make a quarrel of every dispute."[25] The popular nationalism of the period under study here does not alone explain its disastrous finale, but the combination of factors that include it—from the baffling success of Napoleon's operational art to the subordination of statecraft to strategy and the reduction of strategy to a putative military science—together help to explain not only why a continent at the height of its material, intellectual, and cultural success chose to risk it all "in the lottery of a vicious and local internecine conflict" but also why the Great War that followed became a largely pointless slaughter.

Notes

1 K.J. Holsti. "The Study of Diplomacy," in *World Politics: An Introduction*, ed. James N. Rosenau, Kenneth W. Thompson, and Gavin Boyd (New York: Free Press, 1976), p. 293.

2 S.E. Finer. *The History of Government from the Earliest Times*. Vol. 3, *Empires, Monarchies, and the Modern State* (New York: Oxford University Press, 1997), pp. 1473–84.

3 Hans Ulrich Gumbrecht. "Modern," in *Geschichtliche Grundbegriffe*, ed. Otto Brunner, Werner Conze, Reinhart Koselleck, Vol. 4, *Geschichte, Historie* (Stuttgart: Klett-Cotta, 1978), pp. 102–3.

4 Michael Epkenhans and Gerhard P. Groß, eds. *Das Militär und der Aufbruch in die Moderne 1860 bis 1890: Armeen, Marinen und der Wandel von Politik, Gesellschaft und Wirtschaft in Europa, den USA sowie Japan* (Munich, Germany: R, Oldenbourg Verlag, 2003), pp. xv–xxix; Stephen Biddle. *Military Power: Explaining Victory and Defeat in Modern Battle* (Princeton, NJ: Princeton University Press, 2004), pp. 28–51.

5 Finer, *History of Government*, Vol. 3, pp. 1517–33; Michael Broers. *Europe under Napoleon* (London: I.B. Taurus, 2015), pp. 253–66.

6 Werner Conze. "Militarismus," in *Geschichtliche Grundbegriffe*, ed. Otto Brunner, Werner Conze, Reinhart Koselleck, Vol. 4, *Geschichte, Historie* (Stuttgart, Germany: Klett-Cotta, 1978), pp. 1–47; Alfred Vagts. *A History of Militarism, Civilian and Military* (New York: Free Press, 1937), pp. 116–28.

7 B.H. Liddell Hart. *Strategy* (New York: Meridian, 1991), p. 335; Carl von Clausewitz. *On War*, trans. and ed. Michael Howard and Peter Paret (Princeton, NJ: Princeton University Press, 1976), pp. 87, 128, 177.

8 Colin S. Gray. *Modern Strategy* (New York: Oxford University Press, 1999), p. 17.

9 Beatrice Heuser. *The Evolution of Strategy: Thinking War from Antiquity to the Present* (New York: Cambridge University Press, 2010), p. 7. See also Lawrence Freedman, *Strategy: A History* (New York: Oxford University Press, 2013), pp. 69–75.

10 Heuser, *Evolution of Strategy*, p. 7; Henry Spencer Wilkinson, *Command of the Sea and Brain of the Navy* (London: Archibald Constable, 1894), p. 21.

11 Heuser, *Evolution of Strategy*, p. 9; Edward N. Luttwak, *Strategy: The Logic of War and Peace* (Cambridge, MA: Harvard University Press, 1987), p. 240.

12 Williamson Murray and Mark Grimsley, "Introduction: On Strategy," in *The Making of Strategy: States, Rulers, and War*, ed. Williamson Murray, MacGregor Knox and Alvin Bernstein (New York: Cambridge University Press 1994), pp. 1–23.

13 Michael Broers, *Napoleon, Soldier of Destiny* (New York: Pegasus, 2014), pp. 2–14.

14 MacGregor Knox, "Continuity and Revolution in the Making of Strategy," in *The Making of Strategy: Rulers, States, and War*, ed. Williamson Murray, MacGregor Knox and Alvin Bernstein (New York: Cambridge University Press, 1996), p. 616.

15 Liddell Hart, *Strategy*, p. 220.

16 James Q. Whitman, *The Verdict of Battle: The Law of Victory and the Making of Modern War* (Cambridge, MA: Harvard University Press, 2012).

17 Kenneth N. Waltz, *Man, the State and War: A Theoretical Analysis* (New York: Columbia University Press, 1954), p. 201.

18 Claus Telp, *The Evolution of Operational Art, 1740–1813: From Frederick the Great to Napoleon* (London: Frank Cass, 2005); John Andreas Olsen and Martin van Creveld, eds. *The Evolution of Operational Art from Napoleon to the Present* (New York: Oxford University Press, 2011).

19 Hans-Ulrich Wehler, "Der Aufbruch in die Moderne 1860 bis 1890: Armee, Marine und Politik in Europa, den USA und Japan," in Epkenhans and Groß, pp. xxi–xxix; Jeremy Black, *Rethinking Military History* (Abingdon, UK: Routledge, 2004), pp. 66–103.

20 Wehler, "Aufbruch in die Moderne," p. xxiv.

21 Brian Bond, *War and Society in Europe, 1870–1970* (Montreal, PQ: McGill-Queen's University Press, 1998 [1984]), pp. 58–62; Stig Förster, *Der doppelte Militarismus: Die deutsche Heeresrüstungspolitik zwischen Status-quo Sicherung und Aggression, 1890–1913* (Stuttgart, Germany: Frank Steiner Verlag, 1985), p. 6; Gerhard Ritter, *Staatskunst und Kriegshandwerk: Das Problem des "Militarismus" in Deutschland*, 4 Vols. (Munich: Verlag R. Oldenbourg, 1968).

22 Bond, *War and Society in Europe*, p. 63.

23 Sudhir Hazareesingh, *The Legend of Napoleon* (London: Granta Books, 2004), pp. 234–59; Harry E. Cartland, "The Prussian Officers in Fontane's Novels: A Historical Perspective, *Germanic Review*, Vol. 52, No. 3, 1877, pp. 183–93; Edward J. Drea, *Japan's Imperial Army: Its Rise and Fall, 1853–1945* (Lawrence: University of Kansas Press, 2009), pp. 253–62.

24 Vagts, *History of Militarism*, pp. 390–91.

25 Andrew Roberts, *Salisbury, Victorian Titan* (London: Phoenix, 2000), p. 687; John Keegan, *The First World War* (1998: repr., Toronto: Vintage, 2000), p. 426; Jürgen Osterhammel, *The Transformation of the World: A Global History of the Nineteenth Century*, trans. Patrick Camiller (Princeton, NJ: Princeton University Press, 2009), p. 395.

1 Napoleonic warfare

"In the beginning there was Napoleon." This statement opens a study not of nineteenth-century France but rather of its neighbour and future mortal foe, Germany. In two decades of continuous war between the onset of the French Revolution and his final defeat at Waterloo in 1815, Napoleon I altered the nature of military conflict in terms of scale, speed, and carnage so radically that much of the rest of the century was a reaction to him. The ideological message of revolutionary upheaval in France was communicated to the lands east of the Rhine in the destruction by sword of its Holy Roman patchwork; with it came a sense of the power of the sovereign and centralised nation-state, felt in the speed and force of Napoleonic armies. The especially ambitious French imperialism of the Napoleonic age influenced, directly or indirectly, the great modernizing reforms of Prussia and of the German arts and sciences of war.[1]

France was capable after 1789 of revolution and conquest simultaneously, because in contrast to the infant American republic, the apparatus of the absolutist state was in place, highly developed, and more active and effective administratively than any other political entity on the European continent. From the fiscal crisis that became the catalyst for the revolution between 1787 and 1789 to the Republic and Terror of 1792–1794 and the Directory of 1795–1799, the French state underwent upheaval, reconstitution, and internal anarchy, yet emerged territorially intact, administratively even more centralised, and the ideal instrument for the ambitions of the politically astute and militarily gifted. When in 1791 the new National Assembly ordered all officers to sign a pledge of allegiance, Napoleon Bonaparte declared himself for the republic. When the patriots of his native Corsica called for liberation from the foreign yoke, Napoleon would not hear of separation from France; instead, he espoused the Jacobin cause, and "talked and wrote the revolutionary jargon with such success as to be called the little Robespierre."[2] The military and political career that followed thereafter has since moved even seasoned historians to rank Napoleon among the ancients.[3] This book renders no general verdict on Napoleon's place in history but rather an assessment of his legacy to war prosecuted by the modern states of the nineteenth and early twentieth centuries. The effort necessarily

begins by placing Napoleon in circumstantial context as a thoughtful student of the military arts and the most successful of the Revolution's soldiers.
Captain Bonaparte's revolution became a revolution in the European profession of arms.

The political revolution begat the military revolution. It was the
Girondins—a loosely knit group of deputies in the National Assembly who
clustered around Jean-Pierre Brissot, Pierre Victurnien Vergniaud, Jérôme
Pétion, and François Nicolas Léonard Buzot—who favored a war of expansion, while Robespierre continued to argue that war could only follow upon
the consolidation of republican rule. More immediate concerns motivated
the Girondins, as France's fiscal straits remained dire. In military expansion, followed by the exploitation of conquered territories and peoples, they
sought financial salvation, agreeing at least in part with the fiery journalist
Loubet that without war the republic could not survive.[4]

The revolutionary regime's war minister, Lazare Carnot, was meanwhile
tasked with defending the Revolution against the First Coalition of
monarchist powers arrayed against it, Austria and Prussia (who were later
joined by Britain and Spain).[5] Being at war with half of Europe required
that Carnot stop at nothing to forge the 800,000 men of France's twelve
field armies into a potent fighting force. This he accomplished by integrating
the green recruits raised by the *levée en masse* decreed in August 1793 with
veteran professionals, replacing aged commanders with generals eager for
action, and advocating aggressive tactics. Carnot's most consequential decision was to appoint Napoleon Bonaparte commander of the Revolution's
army in Italy in 1796, a command that initiated two decades of more or less
continuous conflict and a century in the militarisation of European society.[6]
The novelty of what became the Napoleonic way of war should nevertheless
not be overstated. Carnot and Napoleon inherited a good deal from the
military thought of the *ancien régime* and adapted it to France's radically
altered circumstance. Because seventeenth-century France had waged four
major wars,[7] a wealth of recently acquired experience was at their disposal.
France's poor performance in the Seven Years' War had the effect of divert-
ing some of the scientific enthusiasms of the Enlightenment toward military
matters, so that by the eve of the Revolution the prerevolutionary French
military was the most intellectually progressive in Europe.[8]

Captain Bonaparte's revolution

A graduate at sixteen of the *École Royale Militaire*, Second Lieutenant Bonaparte was assigned to Régiment de la Fère artillery and in 1787
posted to Auxonne in the Saône valley, where the regiment hosted the School
of Artillery commanded by Major-General Jean-Pierre du Teil, among the
most distinguished gunnery experts in the French army. Du Teil appreciated
Napoleon' s zeal for the latest technical and tactical advances and nomi-
nated him to serve on a committee tasked with determining how explosive

rounds might be fired from long-barrelled guns. Additionally, Napoleon absorbed the ideas of Marshal Count Maurice de Saxe on increasing the mobility and maneuverability of armies, creating self-contained, all-arms "legions" of troops, and using of swarms of skirmishers to precede the main infantry assault on an enemy force. Pierre-Joseph de Bourcet insisted that an attacking army should advance in parallel columns to converge at the critical time and place for advantage of weight in numbers; Jacques-Antoine-Hippolyte, Comte de Guibert, stressed maximum battlefield manoeuvrability and advised that a campaigning army must live off the country it occupied. Jean-Baptise de Gribeauval rationalised the distribution of the calibres of cannons according to their use for siege, infantry, or cavalry support. This reduced the weight of equipment without loss in firepower or range. Du Teil's younger brother, Jean "the Chevalier" du Teil, who was later Napoleon's immediate superior at Toulon, promoted the use of light and rapid horse artillery to support cavalry, an imitation and improvement of its use by Frederick the Great in the Prussian army during the Seven Years' War. Together, their conceptions of war were the foundation of Napoleon's formal military education, their application and adaptation in the Revolutionary campaigns of 1792–1795 the genesis of the Napoleonic system.[9]

What the Revolution inherited from Absolutist France was subjected during the Jacobin phase and the Terror (1793–1794) to politicised and anarchic restructuring, before the Directory (1795–1799) rationalised administrative structures to stress experience and efficiency over ideological conformity. Hence, much of what Napoleon thought appropriate in a governing system was in place before he rose to prominence and power; whereas the Old Regime had sought to renovate itself in line with the centralisation of authority in state-building, the Revolutionary and Napoleonic reforms reinforced state centralisation in nation-building. Absolutist centralisation fell to republican centralisation, before both fell to the popular autocracy that became the essence of Bonapartism.[10] In the meantime the Revolution had to fight for its life, repress opposition at home, and turn back its enemies abroad, an emergency in which "more men and more money was devoted to war than anything else."[11]

Because the Austro-Prussian Declaration of Pillnitz in August 1791 made the First Coalition officially a counter-revolutionary pact, it fired the ideological zeal of the Girondists in Paris.[12] The Brissotin faction in particular demonstrated an awareness of the historical moment by combining Austrophobia dating to the Seven Years' War with popular nationalism in an appeal to defend the revolution of the "most human people in the universe" against an implacable foe bent on its overthrow; Brissot brought the assembly to its feet with the swagger that not even Genghis Khan "with clouds of slaves in his train" could hope to master six million free soldiers.[13] In the event, the Battle of Valmy, fought September 20, 1792, one hundred miles east of Paris, witnessed 36,000 under General Charles Dumouriez against 34,000 under the Duke of Brunswick in an artillery duel ending in Prussian retreat.

Dumoriez thereupon launched an offensive against the Austrian Netherlands with 40,000 men reinforced by 10,000 under François Harville to clash with an Austrian force of 13,000 men under Duke Albert of Saxe-Teschen at Jemappes on November 6. Although the French army suffered greater losses, the Austrians were driven off and Dumouriez was able to advance to Brussels. The undisciplined levies of the Armée du Nord were able to harass the Austrians in skirmishing in open country while the more seasoned troops engaged them in set-piece battle. Not only were the Austrians compelled to fight in two kinds of battles, although they were trained for only one, conscription provided France with replacements for the Revolutionary army at a rate the professional armies of the Allies could not match.[14]

As 1793 brought the execution of Louis XVI, Britain, Naples, and the Netherlands joined the First Coalition, and a Royal Navy fleet under Admiral Samuel Hood seized of the harbour of Toulon on the French Mediterranean coast. To lift Toulon's occupation by British, Spanish, Sardinian, and Neapolitan troops, Napoleon, now a captain, pulled together thirteen batteries of artillery and proposed to his superiors a plan for the bombardment of the British fleet and an assault on the garrison's defences. He then took part in the infantry attack and sustained a wounded leg from a British bayonet. Paul Barras, the National Convention's *commissaire* of the south-eastern army, and Louis-Stanislas Fréron, *réprésentant en mission* to Provence, were at Toulon to witness the captain's performance. What they recognised was a rare commodity: a gifted soldier and a political animal who "thought more quickly, rose earlier, went to bed later, and talked more than anyone else."[15]

A promotion to Brigadier-General and assignment to the artillery of the Army of Italy followed. The success of his plan for the capture of the Piedmontese port of Oneglia encouraged Napoleon to draft something altogether more ambitious for the army's further advance into Italy for his commander General Pierre Dumerbion, accompanied by a memorandum assessing France's overall strategic circumstance. Whereas Robespierre sought to take the offensive on all fronts even as the Terror progressed to his own destruction, Napoleon observed that a nation at war not only with Piedmont but also with Austria, Britain, and Spain was in no position to advance on all fronts and proposed an attack by Dumerbion's army in combination with the Army of the Alps upon Piedmont to force it to peace. The army would then be free to march through the Tyrol to threaten Vienna, this time in combination with the French Army of the Rhine. This strategy looked to the past and the future simultaneously, the first campaign duplicating a plan Bourcet had prepared for Piedmont in 1744, the second anticipating Napoleon's military achievements between 1796 and 1805.[16] It also demonstrated an awareness of opportunity and limitation in equal measure, a balance that Napoleonic warfare ultimately abandoned.

Napoleon's career was briefly imperiled with the fall of Robespierre in July 1794, but his finesse with artillery in administering grapeshot into the face of the Royalist rising of the 13 Vendémiaire renewed his fidelity to the Republic. He thus sought and received command of France's beleaguered army in Italy, just as Carnot was pondering the campaigns of 1796 and recalled Napoleon's plan for a bold offensive.[17] Napoleon's campaign in Piedmont was less remarkable for its originality than for in its energetic execution and attention to detail. First he doubled the army's meat ration, stocked its ammunition parks, and detailed its transport columns. He then assembled a headquarters staff and placed at its head Louis-Alexandre Berthier, whose understanding of logistics was unrivalled and administrative energy endless. With an army of 63,000 men, only 41,000 of whom were available for field operations, he set out to execute his orders exactly as instructed by the Directory: swat aside the Piedmontese and thereafter inflict a compelling defeat on the Austrians.

Because at 53,000 their numbers exceeded his own, Napoleon sought to concentrate his forces against them sequentially before they could unite. He struck first against the junction of their armies at Montenotte and then turned west against the Piedmontese while pinning the Austrians; he then brought the Piedmontese to battle at Mondovi and forced them from the coalition. A victory against the Austrians followed at Lodi on May 10, enabling the French to occupy Milan. As they then laid siege to the fortress at Mantua, Austrian reinforcements arrived to retrieve the situation. These Napoleon defeated at Lonato and Castiglione in early August; as repeated Austrian attempts to relieve Mantua wore on into the winter, Napoleon was able to maul them again at Arcola in November, before the climactic engagement at Rivoli in January 1797, where 23,000 French met 28,000 Austrians and inflicted 10,000 casualties. When Mantua capitulated and Napoleon proceeded to invade Austria itself, Vienna sued for peace.[18] For his mastery of the rapid and coordinated movement and supply of ever-larger armies, Berthier was hence to be Napoleon's most vital human asset.[19]

The strategic goal of the campaign was thus achieved—breaking the coalition and imperiling Austria through Italy—but its political consequences were as important. As the Directory sought to keep its generals content by relieving them of the authority of the civilian commissioners, the generals acquired the role of armed diplomats, free to define peace terms as they pleased. Additionally, the Directory contributed a cult of personality by founding a military press in the *Journal des défenseurs de la Patrie*, for the purpose of unifying the armies against possible enemies of the Republic but with the effect of creating an organ that increasingly eulogised Napoleon as an "heir to the Enlightenment, a diplomat, a man of government, as well as an eminent strategist."[20]

Good propaganda is given to this kind of fiction; what the Directory had in Napoleon was a talented and studied soldier particularly adroit in the conception and execution of complex operations. In fact, the relationship between the Directory and its most celebrated general now inflicted strategic incoherence on France's struggle against the First Coalition.

Because British subsidies had been critical to maintaining the Coalition, the Directory found it convenient to cite Britain as the Revolution's most dangerous enemy and proposed a cross-channel invasion as the appropriate cause to unite the nation.[21] Never a proper enthusiast of the enterprise and worried that it might put his reputation at risk, Napoleon assembled troops and provisions along the Channel coast before informing the Directors that invasion was impractical. As success in Italy had given France new leverage in the Mediterranean, however, both the Directors and Napoleon saw alternative merit in attacking England indirectly by way of an invasion of Egypt in order to imperil British commerce in India. For all the alibis arguing its shrewdness, the Egyptian expedition was "fundamentally an aggressive impulse followed by a weak divided government for domestic more than foreign-policy reasons, without serious calculation of its feasibility and results."[22]

Those results were a major strategic defeat for France and a political debacle for the Directory. Following careful preparation for the expedition and the capture of Malta, Napoleon's 36,000 troops in Egypt won easy victories over Mameluke and Turkish forces but were then stranded, when on August 1, 1798, a British fleet under Horatio Nelson caught and destroyed the French Mediterranean fleet at anchor in Aboukir Bay. At the time the Royal Navy was emerging from a difficult period and had considerable difficulty in even locating the French formation, but the Battle of the Nile restored British naval supremacy in the Mediterranean.[23] The strategic impact was compounded by the fact that governments all over Europe were emboldening to ponder the formation of a new coalition against France. Within a year of Nelson's victory Austria, Naples, Russia, and Turkey had joined Britain.[24]

So the Egyptian campaign had an outcome quite the opposite of its intention. The Mediterranean was now open to British trade, along with that of other nations hitherto excluded by the French naval presence. Malta became a British base for the next 179 years, and the Mediterranean a British lake on France's southern coast. The French navy never recovered from the material and moral damage done to it, so that it involves little exaggeration to say that the Battle of the Nile was an early instalment in the much greater defeat at Trafalgar seven years later. Napoleon and his army were marooned for fifteen months, and French overseas colonies open to Royal Navy predations. The Egyptian campaign made Britain an implacable foe, whatever direction its diplomacy might have taken in the absence of a threat to India. Lastly, the prosecution of the campaign yielded early evidence that in Napoleon's case, limitless ambition led the sword. During the siege of Acre he claimed that Damascus would be the fruit of his expedition and that he would return to Paris by way of Constantinople. It is telling that he later cited Constantinople again, as the centre of a world empire.[25]

The Napoleonic state and the Grande Armée

Fatal politically to the Directors, the campaign was a coup, literally, for Napoleon. One month after his return to France, he overthrew the Directory on 18 Brumaire. Inflation had run out of control as the value of paper money plummeted; food shortages spread along with rumors of corruption; the executive and legislative agreed on almost nothing—to the Parisian public mind,this was a litany of abuses and failures. Napoleon was initially less the author than the object of the coup, planned jointly by the abbé Joseph Sieyès; the recently resigned foreign minister, Charles-Maurice de Talleyrand; and the minister of police, Joseph Fouché, who as provisional consuls declared administrative order, domestic tranquility, and international peace as their cause. Officially, Napoleon was to be First Consul along with Sieyès and Pierre-Roger Ducos, a protégé of Barras.[26] Unofficially, he was many things:

> He was not welcomed because he was a military man; he was welcomed because he could decide the crusade of liberty that had begun in 1792. For although Frenchmen certainly wanted peace in 1799, the constant linking of Bonaparte to military success showed that large sectors of opinion had lost none of their martial ardour. Most sinister of all, Bonaparte was popular in the army not only because of his successes but because officers and men had felt for years that years that civil society had let them down, that they were the last bastion of true revolutionary principles and that they were obliged to regenerate the nation as a whole.[27]

With the 18 Brumaire the Napoleonic era began, inaugurating a new and powerful unity of state, nation, and military. Put to the people in a rigged plebiscite, a new constitution established a Tribunate and a Legislature based on a complex formula of indirect election, yet vested all legislative initiative with the executive.[28]

That power was as yet insecure once the Austrian campaign of 1800 was underway and the French forces in the Italian Riviera were split, forced to take refuge in Genoa in one direction and driven westward along the Riviera in the other. In consultation with Carnot, again Minister of War, Napoleon marched his main army south through the Great Saint Bernard Pass of Switzerland to emerge from the Alps the rear of the Austrian army, cutting off its line of supply and retreat to Milan. The climactic battle of the campaign at Marengo was very nearly a disaster, but the campaign was shrewdly conceived and resulted in the collapse of the Austrian position in Italy. It demonstrated a maturing in Napoleon's approach to war by moving beyond Carnot's preference for occupying critical positions in favor of destroying the enemy army. This being the most direct means for both crippling the Second Coalition and securing the new regime in Paris, taking the greater risk was in fact the better part of prudence.[29]

Victories by the French army in Germany under Jean Victor Marie Moreau led to an Austrian suit for peace on Christmas Day 1800. With Austria again out of the Coalition, the sense conveyed by Pitt at Westminster that France, under the "child and champion" of the Revolution, was becoming something novel and menacing, offensive to republican and monarchist alike, was prophetic.[30] Even after the triumph of the Nile, Britain's strategy was a jumble of disparate objectives,[31] and successive governments came only by painful trial and error to invest the effort to defeat France with the requisite coherence. In 1800 that defeat lay fifteen years in the future. Until Napoleonic France met with an overwhelming coalition of countervailing force it was able to inflict upon its serial and separate victims war on a scale that redirected military thought and perverted European politics for the remainder of the century.[32]

Despite the triumph at the Nile, the British public wanted peace in 1802, and Pitt's government was unpopular as much for domestic politics as for its continuing belligerence toward France. Even if no more than a truce was ever realistic, Henry Addington, Pitt's successor, was genuinely interested in something durable.[33] For Napoleon the Treaty of Amiens brought popular prestige sufficient to bully the assemblies to do his will and complete his ascent to the apex of the state. The Concordat of 1801 sedated both Catholic and royalist sentiment, as the return of the priests, re-establishment of the bishops, and freedom of religious expression undermined popular will to oppose the regime. That King George III decided in May 1803 to return Britain to a war footing with France did not so much as interrupt this process. Whereas the ratification of Amiens bolstered Napoleon's popularity, such was the temper of national pride in him that its termination only enhanced the same. The Pope was invited to coronate Napoleon—more accurately, to anoint his self-coronation—as Emperor of the French at Notre Dame in December 1804. With the intermediary institutions between citizen and state co-opted or neutered, the French state was more brisk with its executive functions than it had been for a decade.[34] Fouché developed an elaborate network of spies and informants across the country. Disgruntled Jacobin officers who denounced the Concordat and France's new autocrat were swept up in Fouché's net to find themselves on expedition to Santo Domingo.[35]

The army was built into something more potent than the revolutionary prototype. The Jourdan conscription Law of 1798 had created a system for replenishing the army's ranks, possibly the greatest contribution toward strengthening bureaucratic authoritarianism under Napoleon.[36] Between 1800 and 1814 it put two million men, or about seven percent of the population, in uniform. Draft dodging was common, but Napoleonic infantry were generally obedient, brave, and zealous; officers could expect lavish rewards for success but were expected to demonstrate fearless efficiency.[37] At the head of large armies whose losses could be replaced, French generals employed aggressive tactics and took risks their adversaries initially took for suicidal. The social and political flux of the past decade had provided for this:

> Many had already been officers in 1789: senior non-commissioned officers, junior officers from the provincial nobility (like Napoleon) and *officiers de fortune* who had come up from the ranks were all common. What these men shared was the knowledge that under Louis XVI they would have been unlikely to make their name—that they would in the vast majority of cases have been condemned to a lifetime of obscurity, boredom and low pay. With the Revolution everything was transformed. All of a sudden everything was possible, and this bred a hunger for victory, an aggression and a vigour that was far less likely to be found in the ranks of their opponents.[38]

Where the Revolutionary armies had invented the organisational unit of the "division" as a product of their size, Napoleon refined their articulation into brigades and "corps" and promoted the "combined arms" concept of integrating infantry, cavalry, and artillery in order to achieve greater flexibility and speed in the delivery of decisive punch on the battlefield.[39] These were the organisational principles that enabled French armies to defeat all comers for the next decade, and the manner of their application in 1803 and 1805— where and against whom—determined the course of Napoleonic warfare. That course was decided by the Emperor himself and was determined by the combination of his unbounded ambition and its encounter with opportunity. Whatever might have happened had the army and Napoleon's command of it been less effective than they were, sober contemplation of Napoleon's serial campaigns forms a picture of a leader and a military instrument progressively addicted to aggression. A classic history of the period notes that within a decade France's fundamental advantages over its adversaries were sacrificed to his "inability to see a jugular without going for it, to forgo short-run opportunities for long-range goods."[40]

This was not readily apparent in the period between 1800 and 1805. But the army had evolved from the ragged formations of the Revolutionary defence to become an increasingly professionalised instrument of conquest. Its soldiers were survivors who had learned how to march, fight, and loot, its generals a "wolf-breed" whipped into a competitive meritocracy, first by the visceral egalitarianism of the Republic, then in hope of the Emperor's approval or fear of his wrath.[41] With the War of the Third Coalition, the contest of arms in Europe entered a new phase characterised above all by the *Grande Armée*'s extraordinary performance as a nation-in-arms. Britain became steadily more important as the foil to the French conquest, as its naval and maritime operations struggled to achieve harmony with Britain's continental allies. The two fed off each other, so that our understanding of the political and military impact of the Napoleonic Wars is enhanced when they are discussed together.

Trafalgar to Austerlitz

Specifically, an army of 167,000 men, raised and trained for an invasion of England in 1805, was excused from that mission following Britain's defeat of the combined French and Spanish fleets at Trafalgar in October. Trafalgar, a naval triumph equaled in strategic significance only by Japan's destruction of the Russian fleet a century later, was preceded by the Battle of the Nile in 1798 and the Battle of Copenhagen 1801—victories in Mediterranean, Baltic, and Atlantic waters that made the Nelsonian Royal Navy unrivalled and facilitated not only British maritime operations, along with the supply of British armies from European coasts, but also enhanced British prestige and diplomatic leverage in European capitals. The product of a commercial, maritime, and imperial political economy, the Royal Navy had claimed a share of Britain's fiscal resources during the eighteenth century sufficient to give it the world's best navy, commanded to a high professional standard, endowed with a sophisticated administrative structure and a considerable intelligence-gathering capability.[42]

Trafalgar was indirectly the result of Napoleon's attempt to draw the Royal Navy away from the English Channel so that his army could be borne safely to British soil by 2,000 landing craft. Because fighting France while striving to hold on to its overseas empire had been ruinously expensive, Spain had thrown its lot, and its navy, in with France in 1796. So it was a combined Franco-Spanish fleet under Admiral Pierre de Villeneuve that sailed for the West Indies in order to divert Royal Navy squadrons on post in the English Channel. When Villeneuve returned to European waters, he fought a confused engagement with a British squadron under Vice Admiral Sir Robert Calder one hundred miles west off Cape Finisterre and returned to Cádiz, where he was blockaded by the Royal Navy Channel Fleet under Vice Admiral Cuthbert Collingwood. Frustrated by the failure of his feint against the West Indies, Napoleon ordered the Combined Fleet into the Mediterranean, this time to cover troop movements in Italy in his campaign against Austria. By this time Nelson had resumed command off Cádiz, so it was after Villeneuve's sortie that Nelson intercepted him off Cape Trafalgar. Nelson's fleet of twenty-seven ships approached in two parallel columns and struck Villeneuve's line of thirty-three ships at right angles, after which superior morale, training, and gunnery told quickly in Nelson's favour. In five hours of fighting, eighteen of Villeneuve's ships were destroyed or captured, against no Royal Navy ships lost, and fewer than 500 British were dead, among them Nelson.[43] Trafalgar relieved threat of invasion and enabled the British government, in possession of lucrative colonies and secure sea lanes, to subsidise future continental coalitions against France. The enormous cost of more or less continuous conflict with France took the national debt to new heights, but Britain's worldwide assets were extensive enough that the effort made a major contribution to the development of a military-fiscal state whose origins reached back to the seventeenth century.[44] Like the

Directory's campaign against Egypt, the invasion of Britain thwarted by Trafalgar constituted a threat to Britain's security that was unnecessary to France's position in, and dominance of, Europe. In strategic terms, the mistake of 1805 compounded that of 1798, as together they transformed British perceptions of Revolutionary and Napoleonic France from an adversary to an existential threat and the national commitment to its defeat from circumstantial to absolute.

Moreover, Trafalgar paid a strategic dividend to any British government applying the resources and patience to redeem it by supporting offensive operations on the continent. Robert Stewart, Viscount Castlereagh, who assumed the responsibilities of secretary of state for war when Pitt returned to office in 1804, appreciated this more fully than any of his contemporaries. Whereas honors for developing and maintaining a durable British strategy are shared with his rival, George Canning, it was Castlereagh who took it upon himself "to counteract any belief that after Trafalgar a sense of urgency no longer attached to the navy and its role."[45] Castlereagh's later service as foreign secretary was especially fortunate in so far as nobody better comprehended the relationship between a maritime strategy in war and Britain's ability to influence a sustainable peace. Nelson and Wellington, the heroes of Trafalgar and Waterloo respectively, first met in the anteroom to Castlereagh's office.[46] If the strategic virtue of any effort in warfare is measured by its contribution to national security embedded in a durable international peace, then Castlereagh's vision of the struggle with Napoleonic France and its aftermath qualifies as among the most creditable episodes in statecraft of the nineteenth century.

Stoic patience was Castlereagh's governing virtue. Britain's circumstance demanded more of it than of any other, in light of France's demonstrated superiority over its continental foes. On the very day that Villeneuve sortied Cádiz, October 20, 1805, an Austrian army surrendered to Napoleon at Ulm on the Danube in Bavaria. The army that had been assembled for an invasion of Britain had turned on its heal and marched eastward when Austria, Russia, and Sweden formed the Third Coalition, and an Austro-Russian force threatened France through southern Germany. Beginning with Ulm French arms embarked on a series of extraordinary triumphs, due in large part to the *Grande Armée*'s improvements on royalist and republican army reforms. The establishment of army corps concentrated units of artillery and cavalry into reserves of fighting power capable of moving quickly, changing direction with flexibility while operating on a broad front, and striking very hard against even an enemy of superior numbers. The system facilitated the rapid and coordinated movement of separated army corps that could aspire to the envelopment of the adversary's forces.[47]

In the case of the Ulm campaign the French army entered Bavaria reinforced to 190,000 men in anticipation of an Austro-Russian invasion of France through southern Germany. Its mission was to come between an Austrian army of 72,000 under Karl Mack Freiherr von Leiberich, already moving west through Bavaria, and a Russian force of 100,000 commanded by Mikhail Kutuzov, marching to reinforce it at Ulm. Napoleon ordered a cavalry reserve under Joachim Murat to advance through the Black Forest and thus encourage Mack to assume a French line of advance by this traditional route, when in fact three much larger formations clustered around Marshal Jean Lannes' V Corps, Marshals Louis Davout's, Nicolas Soult's, and Michel Ney's III, IV, and VI Corps, and Marshals Jean-Baptiste Bernadotte's and August de Marmont's I and II Corps were deployed to the north-east along the Rhine from Strasbourg to Frankfurt. These marched separately on parallel routes to the south-east—the movement "resembled a door swinging on its hinges"[48]—and into Mack's rear, cutting of his communications with Austria even as he recognised Murat's advance to be a feint, while Kutuzov's army was still 160 miles to the east.

In order to save time, Bernadotte's corps ran the risk of provoking Prussia from its neutrality by marching through Ansbach. Forced back on Ulm and cut off from additional Austrian forces under Franz Freiherr von Werneck, Mack was then abandoned by Archduke Ferdinand d'Este and Karl Philipp Fürst zu Schwarzenberg as the noose of converging French corps tightened about him. By October 15, Napoleon's marshals had completed the envelopment of the city and commenced a bombardment. Mack surrendered five days later, delivering into captivity 50,000 of the men he had taken into Bavaria. In a series of engagements integral to the encirclement—at Wertingen, Günzburg, and Haslach-Jungingen—the *Grande Armée* had outmarched, out-manoeuvred, and out-fought the Austrians at every pass.[49] The Ulm campaign (See Map 1) was an operational masterpiece, demonstrating the rapid and coordinated movement of separate armies in the envelopment of their adversary. Prussian, American, Japanese would later attempt to duplicate its precision, with varying results.

However, the Ulm campaign did not incorporate the art of annihilation more typical of Napoleonic warfare. That status belongs to Austerlitz, prosecuted December 2, 1805. Austerlitz was the result Kutuzov's action following the news of Ulm, to retire to the east along the right bank of the Danube in order to join up with a second Russian army under Count Fedor Buxhöwden along with surviving Austrian units and augment his strength to a total of some 86,000. With another 80,000 Austrian troops across the Alps in northern Italy, having escaped the pursuit of Masséna and now marching north, Napoleon was able to muster immediately only 73,000 troops for a rapid advance eastward, yet felt compelled to land a decisive blow against the Allies before they presented him with overwhelming numbers. After resupplying in an undefended Vienna he left a garrison of 20,000 under Ney and Marmont in the city and proceeded north in search of a decisive engagement. Kutuzov was of a mind to deny him this but was overruled by Tsar Alexander I, who saw an opportunity to deal with a weakened French force. Napoleon himself contrived to confirm this impression by proposing an armistice he knew would be rejected. On both sides, moreover,

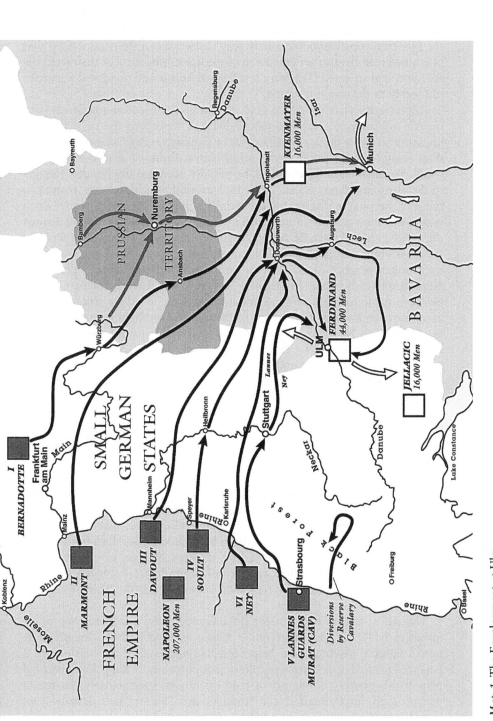

Map 1 The Envelopment at Ulm.

there was a compelling logistical reason to do battle sooner rather than later. Despite gargantuan feats in supplying and resupplying the *Grande Armée,* the French troops had come a long way eastward in a short period, so that Napoleon feared a further extension of the line of pursuit. For their part, the Russians had stripped Habsburg territory of horses and pondered a scarcity of food with the onset of winter.[50]

Appreciating that the Allied goal was to sever his communications with the Vienna garrison, Napoleon extended and weakened the right flank of his army so as to draw the Allies into a flanking assault against it, which, if successful, would position the Allies between himself and Vienna to the south. To enhance the temptation, he initially occupied the Pratzen Heights to the north and then conceded this high ground by withdrawing from it to the east, keeping a reserve force behind the line to the north-west, which was to deliver a counter-attack once the Allies were fully committed against the French right. Lastly, he issued detailed orders about tactical procedure. Whereas French battle drill was adequate for dealing with Austrian troops, the Russian practice of using dense columns in bayonet attacks prompted Napoleon to redistribute his artillery to wither any Russian infantry charge before it came to hand-to-hand combat.[51] When the Allies attacked, their every move conformed more or less to the trap laid for them, an assault led by Buxhöwden on Napoleon's right encountering stiff resistance from a smaller French force reinforced by Davout's III Corps, which had marched seventy miles to Austerlitz in forty-six hours, just as it was giving way. Kutuzov then committed more troops against the French right, drawing some of them from the Pratzen Heights. At this point Napoleon hurled a division of Soult's corps under Louis Saint-Hilaire and Dominique Vandamme up the Pratzen slopes to clear the heights and heave into the Allied centre. The pivotal engagement of the day, a brawl over control of the Heights once the Allies realised their peril and attempted to recover, told in favor of the French.

As the Allied counter-attacks stalled, their centre buckled under Soult's pressure, so that he was able swing around to the rear of the Allies engaged against Davout. Thus surrounded, the Allies attempted to flee across a frozen lake that came immediately under French artillery fire, smashing the ice. By 3:00 p.m. the issue had been settled; by midnight the Allies has suffered some 16,000 killed or wounded, 11,000 captured, and had lost 180 cannon, against 1,300 French killed and 7,000 wounded. Unable to continue operations, the Russian army retreated eastward, and the Third Coalition was a wreck.

The Allied troops had not fought incompetently, nor were they in all instances badly led. But the *Grande Armée* of 1805 had become a conditioned fighting machine, and Napoleon had approached the battle with a balanced tactical plan tuned to exploiting opportunity. Having demonstrated Napoleon's mastery of the art of land operations spectacularly, Austerlitz was promptly mythologised; the "thunderstroke victory that destroyed an enemy army in one clash of arms, ... remained inextricably intertwined with the worship of battle among European soldiers as the means to anni-hilation."[52] The Treaty of Pressburg, signed on December 26, 1805, ended hostilities with Austria yet did more to consolidate France's position than to expand Napoleon's empire at Austrian expense. Most significantly, the abandonment of the title of elector and surrender of the Holy Roman Emperor's right to call on military contingents from southern Germany signified the end of the thousand-year-old Holy Roman Empire. Napoleon established the satellite Confederation of the Rhine on July 18, 1806, and France's domination of Central Europe was recognised in exchange for a guarantee of Austria's territorial integrity—at the price of an indemnity of forty million French francs.

Michael Broers observes that the Ulm-Austerlitz campaign was pivotal, both for France and the future of Europe. Napoleon now had control not only of both banks of the Rhine but also of the Weser, and with it a strength-ened strategic hand against Austria, Britain, and additional potential adver-saries. Pressburg was crafted to "oust Austria from Germany, satisfy France's German clients with territory and independence, and ensure Napoleon direct control of Germany, military assets, and hard cash."[53] If the measure of strategic success is a peace superior to what preceded the conflict, then the Ulm-Austerlitz campaign measures up, as it enhanced France's security and its position from the Rhine to southern Germany and Bohemia funda-mentally. Had Napoleon been content with the outcome, it is hard to say how French hegemony in Western Europe would have been overthrown.[54]

Prussia: The apogee of Napoleonic operations

That he was not was evident from aspects of the peace terms contrived to be unbearable for the next object of aggression, Prussia. His government inwardly divided over the most prudent course to take following Austerlitz, King Friedrich Wilhelm III quickly came under pressure when Talleyrand informed Berlin that France would recognise Prussia's claim to Hanover only if Prussia forced the Russians and Swedes from northern Germany and closed its northern ports to British shipping. An attempt to modify the terms brought only new territorial demands—an insistence that Prussia occupy Hanover immediately and break relations with Britain along with a claim on Berlin's total support for any future French objective. When in August 1806 Berlin learned that France was holding out to Britain the return of Hanover as a peace offering, Prussia mobilised and in September invaded Saxony to draft it into an alliance.[55]

Napoleon had by now prepared detailed plans for a new campaign and modified them as he received intelligence about Prussian movements. Once underway the *Grande Armée* moved into Saxony from Bavaria in three multiple-corps columns to the north-east—Lannes and Augereau, Bernadotte and Davout, Soult and Ney—initially behind an aggressive cavalry screen under Murat to cover its actions. The infantry marched in a *bataillon carré* of almost 200,000 men through the Thuringian Forest, concentrating in ever-greater strength to the east of the Prussian line of advance into Saxony. Committed to taking the initiative, meanwhile, 145,000 Prussians under the overall command of the Duke of Brunswick did so more in principle than in application. Ever mindful of his line of communications with Berlin, the Duke advanced slowly and cautiously; wedded to eighteenth-century linear tactics and a depot system of supply, his army typically considered twelve miles a hard day's march. By contrast, Napoleon's corps carried ten days of supplies and otherwise lived off the land. They marched with such superior speed that the Prussian army was still extended in a cordon across Saxony and marching south-west toward country that was now largely empty of troops when the *Grande Armée* executed a gigantic wheel to the left, emerged from the Thuringian Forest, and on October 9 pitched into the Prussian flank.[56]

The first contact came on October 10, when Lannes corps routed a force of 8,000 Prussians and Saxons at Saalfeld under the Prussian Prince Louis Ferdinand, who was killed in the action. At this point Napoleon was unsure of the location and disposition of the main Prussian force and was to discover that its commanders fell short even of his low estimation of their ability. The Prussians at Saalfeld had in fact been the vanguard of a corps led by Friedrich Ludwig Fürst zu Hohenlohe-Ingelfingen, and the Prussian commanders were only just arriving at their positions and were divided over how to respond to what looked like a French breakout from an unanticipated direction. Hohenlohe now fell back on Jena, as the main Prussian force under Brunswick turned north-east toward Weimar. By this time, however, Davout's III Corps, now on the extreme right of the French army, had cut off the line of retreat and communications with Berlin so that the two armies collided at Auerstädt on October 18. To the south-west Napoleon had some 55,000 men to tackle at Jena what he assumed to the main Prussia army but was instead Hohenlohe's force of 38,000. Another 40,000 French troops arrived by noon, against which Hohenlohe could call upon only the 15,000 troops of Ernst Friedrich von Rüchel at Weimar for reinforcement.[57]

Ultimately Hohenlohe's force gave way to superior strength and retreated in a disorder that Napoleon's hot pursuit turned into a rout of 11,000 Prussian and Saxon dead and 15,000 captured against 5,000 French. Davout's 27,000 men at Auerstädt had meanwhile engaged Brunswick's 50,000 Prussians, moving at twice the speed into position in order to avoid being overwhelmed. Just at the point where sheer exhaustion threatened a French collapse, Brunswick was mortally wounded and the Prussian command effectively decapitated. Upon repelling the last serious Prussian assault, Davout's left wing went over to the attack while he ordered his right wing to pivot against the opposite Prussian flank. By day's end he had lost 8,000 men but accounted for 12,000 Prussian dead and 3,000 prisoners in "one of the signal achievements of all military history."[58]

The engagement had not evolved as Napoleon expected. But his operational conception of it was sound, and the corps system he had created was flexible enough to deal with surprises. For the Prussian army, sure of its reputation as the most professional formation in Europe, the rout of Jena-Auerstädt was the greatest crisis of its history. Initially, recriminations for the defeat treated it as a morality tale with Friedrich Wilhelm III in the role of ineffectual cipher for incompetent or traitorous cabinet advisors.[59] Friedrich Wilhelm's sympathetic biographer notes the melancholy king's habit of consulting with all his officers to the extent that all sense of hierarchy seemed to evaporate; no unity of purpose and direction emerged from their collective counsel, nor was it imposed by their sovereign.[60] Even when appropriate decisions were made the Prussian army shared with its Austrian counterpart an inability to circulate orders to its units crisply. Napoleon's staff system of communication was so superior in the circulation of orders that a typical French army corps might march twenty miles a day and be pushed to thirty-five against a mere ten miles covered by the Prussians—and yet retain coordination among dispersed corps. Without it the Jena campaign would have been impossible.[61] At Jena-Auerstädt, Napoleonic warfare achieved such a level of proficiency—in terms of the planning, direction, conduct, and coordination of military actions linking battlefield tactics to overall operational vision—that it rose to the level of what in the twentieth century came to be called "operational art."[62]

In that sense it was revolutionary in nature. It reflected the vigour of the state the Emperor had constructed from the intellectual and administrative legacy of French absolutism and wedded by force to the ideological claims and political flux of the upheaval begun in 1789. Like Frederick the Great whose countrymen he had just humiliated, he was at the heart of and centralised and autocratic structure, but on a vastly greater format. France's new way of war expressed in the most forceful way the central conceit of the modern state, that its rationalism alone both facilitated and entitled its victory over a less advanced state. At the core of its organisation, the *État Major de l'Armée* received regular situation reports from each corps, in response to which Napoleon drew up plans in broad strokes while Berthier articulated detailed orders and saw to it that they reached the corps in a timely fashion. Because his staff system appointed officers on a meritocratic system rather than according to social rank or ideological fidelity—and ensured that officers in staff duty were drawn from all branches of the army and had considerable practical experience in fighting—it achieved a high level of professional efficiency. It provided the *Grande Armée* with superior flexibility, speed, manoeuvrability, and terrific punch where and when it was needed. The new French nation provided the conscripts; its administration furnished the infrastructure and increased national production for military and civil functions. Because Napoleonic France centralised all control and meshed all policies for the purpose of war, Prussia's leadership never fully understood what was confronting it in 1806—and would struggle for decades to emulate it.[63]

With Jena-Auerstädt Napoleonic France reached the apex of its military supremacy. It might well have had a durable supremacy holding both Britain and Russia at bay, had Napoleon not chosen to afford a strategic windfall to the former while launching an annihilating attack against the latter. The combined assets of the world's greatest sea power and Europe's most populous land power were bound to exhaust France's war-making capacity if and when they could be brought to bear simultaneously. The issuing of the Berlin Decree, declaring the Britain under blockade and calling for the arrest of all Englishmen in the French Empire or its allies, amounted to a first diplomatic instalment in Napoleon's ultimate demise; equally, the advance of the *Grande Armée* eastward convinced Tsar Alexander I that a life-and-death struggle with France could be delayed but not avoided.[64] The 1807 Treaties of Tilsit, which temporarily made an ally of Russia following Napoleon's victory over the Fourth Coalition at Friedland, testified to an awareness of limitations, but intervention in Spain the same year against actual or imaginary British influence opened up a whole new front of conflict. The collapse of Tilsit would by 1812 see French armies extended from Madrid to Moscow.

For this reason of massive overreach it is an error to classify Napoleonic legacy to modern war as strategic, except in the sense that Napoleon's actions in the years from 1808 to 1812 taught less able but more prudent military and political leaders what strategic challenges ought to be avoided rather than embraced. Napoleon was an operational artist of extraordinary drive and imagination, yet his campaigns after 1807 have moved some historians to classify him as an anti-strategist. That the *Grande Armée* of his creation continued to fight so well beyond the limits of strategic reason and inflicted upon Europe years of carnage and desolation is the reason other historians classify his regime as a criminal enterprise.[65]

Even prior to Tilsit, France's capacity to sustain war on a continental scale was being taxed. The distance marched from the farmlands of Bavaria, Moravia, and Saxony, where the army had lived off the land, to the less plentiful Poland and East Prussia required that supply communications back to Saxony be maintained. Despite the availability of rivers and canals for transport during the mild winter of 1806, a military train of seven transport battalions with six hundred vehicles was needed to keep the army replenished. Reduced mobility and speed due to supply problems, poor roads, rough terrain, and winter cold meant that a Russian army under Baron Levin Bennigsen had sufficient time to concentrate 60,000 troops at Eylau, south of Königsberg, in December 1807 to link up with some 15,000 Prussians to present Napoleon's advance force of 30,000 with superior numbers and a two-to-one advantage in guns. In the face of a howling blizzard the two armies engaged in a two-day brawl that tilted gradually in Napoleon's direction as additional French corps arrived. But the Allies had taken 15,000 casualties while bleeding from the *Grande Armée* of some 25,000, so that Eylau posed the question whether the speed and sweep of

Ulm, Austerlitz, and Jena-Auerstädt could ever be duplicated.[66] It is true that Napoleonic battle redeemed itself with aplomb at Friedland in June 1807. But recovery of the initiative followed only upon the *Grande Armée*'s recuperation and refitting in winter quarters after Eylau, and it was only the early call-up the conscript classes of 1806 and 1807, along with intensified recruiting from France's satellite states, that enabled it to bring its numbers in Eastern Europe to 200,000 by spring.

France itself now consisted of 110 departments, but her vassal states and influence extended from Gibraltar to the Baltic, the shores of Normandy to the Nieman River where Napoleon signed the Treaties of Tilsit with Tsar Alexander I and Friedrich Wilhelm III of Prussia, ending the Fourth Coalition and making France supreme in Europe. The price of supremacy was high. The pounding pace of the *Grande Armée*'s operations had involved it in six major battles in two years at a cost of 65,000 of its seasoned soldiers. These losses had to be made up by contributions from the Netherlands, Poland, Spain, and Switzerland, along with the drafting of the conscription class of 1808 a full eighteen months in advance.

France's fiscal outlook was tolerable, and the army was flush with loot, stores, artillery, and equipment.[67] The period from 1799 to 1807 inside France and its vassals was in many respects one of regime consolidation and normalisation that could, over time, enhance Napoleonic France's security against foreign overthrow. The logic of the deal struck at Tilsit, however, was undermined by the Continental System designed to isolate Britain, because it demanded the increased attention to coastal defence that made Italy, and especially Spain, strategically salient.[68]

Britain was in a position to carry on the struggle at a lower level of domestic stress than that felt by Austria, Prussia, Russia—and France. The fiscal challenge drove British national expenditures to a four-fold increase between 1792 and 1806, a trebling of the debt, and even greater increases in taxes and stamp duties. But continuous hostilities also fostered stoic determination and nurtured a national Francophobia common to Tory and Whig alike; even among Napoleon's British admirers, he had become the most feared creature of the historical moment for whom the liberal spirit of the age was "simply a grindstone on which to sharpen his own blade."[69] The severing of British trade with the continent, moreover, put France's policy at odds with the material interest of Europeans who sought access to British manufactures and colonial goods imported through British *entrepôts*.[70] The Continental System was itself a product of carelessness warping Napoleon's actions following Jena-Auerstädt.

From Madrid to Moscow

It was Portugal's refusal to submit to the Continental System, after all, that prompted Napoleon to invade the country in 1807, the year of Friedland and Tilsit. In so doing he played directly into Britain's strategic strength, the capacity to initiate naval and land operations on a small scale and gradually expand them to the point where they tied down tens of thousands of French troops in an interminable struggle. The less-than-robust help from his ally Spain in the effort then moved Napoleon to replace the Bourbons on the Spanish throne with his brother Joseph. Popular rage at the removal of the king led to the rising of *Dos Mayo*, French columns marching to crush the revolt, and the punitive executions immortalised by Goya for Spanish national mythology.[71] Because Napoleon was sceptical that the Spanish army could long sustain resistance, the force he sent to Spain was numerically inferior—90,000—against 114,000 Spanish regulars, and qualitatively second-rate at best, featuring large numbers of raw recruits unaccompanied by a hard core of seasoned veterans who accelerated the training and assimilation of new conscripts in Germany and Poland. It thus met its first rebuff at Bailén in July 1808, where 17,000 French under Pierre Dupont were surrendered to an army of Spanish regulars under Francisco de Castaños, after a comic opera of incompetent manoeuvre by both generals, and then suffered defeat at Vimeiro in August by a British expeditionary force under Lieutenant General Sir Arthur Wellesley, the future Duke of Wellington.[72]

If the Peninsular War was the perfect theatre for British intervention on the continent, then Wellington was its perfect instrument. As a brigadier in India he had distinguished himself at the head of British and Indian troops, mastered the challenges of leading an expeditionary force: an eye for the implications of topography for tactics based on thorough reconnaissance and relentless attention to logistics and communications.[73] That Wellington was able to apply this experience in Spain was due to Castlereagh's understanding of the continental conflict, his appreciation of how British maritime operations could influence its outcome, and his dogged support of Wellington's command in Spain. A disastrous campaign under Sir John Moore in 1809 hardly wrinkled Castlereagh's conviction that Spain could be the pivot of the continental war. Indeed, he reformed the army to alleviate its chronic manpower problems and sought every opportunity to lever British naval power to advantage, going so far as to ponder operations in South America to challenge French strength overseas and risking an expedition against Walcheren on the Scheldt Estuary that temporarily cost him his position. A combination of naval and land forces against Denmark, the latter under Wellington's command, meanwhile prompted a domestic outcry when the Royal Navy fleet bombarded Copenhagen. But Castlereagh insisted that the operation improved Anglo-Russian relations by demonstrating British commitment to the cause. In the case of Spain he fought a cabinet war in support of Wellington against his rival Canning and lesser critics through the dark early days of Britain's commitment there.[74] To claim that Castlereagh saw the war in grand-strategic terms possibly goes too far, but his thinking tended in that direction, achieved remarkable coherence and became the patient foil to Napoleon's perversion of operational genius to support his serial aggressions.

Only continuous operations could gradually wear down France's war-making capacity, when combined with the ever-larger burden the *Grande Armée* shouldered fighting in Central Europe. The outbreak of the Fifth Coalition War with Austria in April 1809 drew Napoleon's attention eastward again and left Marshalls Ney, Soult, and Victor in charge of Spanish operations. After suffering his first significant battlefield defeat at Aspern-Essling in May, in July Napoleon defeated the Austrians in a two-day battle at the village of Wagram involving more than 300,000 men. In the first engagement, army reforms and an uncharacteristic seizure of the initiative permitted the Austrians to catch Napoleon flat-footed; in the second, the former celerity of operational and tactical execution characteristic of French arms from Ulm to Jena-Auerstädt showed signs of the wear of constant campaigning, with the result that Napoleon gained an artless victory at the cost of 32,500 casualties.[75]

Meanwhile Spanish regulars in Andalusia fought well against a renewed French offensive, while *guerrilleros* kept up a continual harassment, involving barbarous cruelties against captured French soldiers that elicited savage reprisals in response.[76] The initiative tilted toward the Allies with Wellington's return to Spain and the launch of an Anglo-Spanish offensive in the summer of 1809. After triumphs at Oporto and Telavera, in which Wellington's command skills shone through, the offensive stalled due to inadequate supply support from the Spanish. When Wellington then withdrew again to Portugal to reorganise and resupply his army, Soult promptly tore up a Spanish army of 60,000 at Ocaña while cavalry under François Kellerman destroyed a smaller force at Alba de Tormes. Wellington remained on the defensive in Portugal through 1810, due in no small part to the political strain caused by the costs of the Peninsular campaign back in Westminster. Indeed, a parliamentary motion to actually reduce the size of Wellington's army was defeated only after a bitter debate. Despite his lack of resources Wellington was able conduct an effective defensive campaign and to inflict a serious defeat on André Masséna, one of Napoleon's ablest commanders, at Busaco in September 1810, that signaled a turning point of the Peninsular War. Yet not until the autumn of 1811 was Wellington able to resume the offensive, after which the cause in Spain was aided by Napoleon's drawdown of French forces there in preparation for his greatest folly, the invasion of Russia in 1812.[77]

The error of 1812, moreover, compounded that of 1807. For even if the French troops taken from Spain could not have made much difference in Russia, it is hard to believe that a fraction of the men and material thrown against Russia would not have made all the difference in Spain. The two fronts were linked, in that the imposition of the Continental System was crafted to ruin British commerce yet was a more immediate and substantial threat to Russia and Spain. By 1810 it was doing much to ruin Russian overseas trade and commerce with the Baltic and North Sea coasts, especially following the French annexation of Holland, the Hanseatic cities, and the German states west of the Elbe. To this economic grievance Napoleon then added a more direct threat with the creation of the Duchy of Warsaw, nominally under the king of Saxony, the abolition of Polish serfdom, the introduction of the French civil code, and the incorporation of Western Galicia, won from Austria, into the Polish satellite. Finally, in January 1811 he added diplomatic insult to strategic menace by openly violating the Treaty of Tilsit with the annexation of the Duchy of Oldenburg, hitherto allied to Russia through Tsar Alexander's sister. Alexander had issued a decree taking Russia out of the Continental System the previous month, but he now faced an overthrow of the equilibrium on Russia's western frontier in which the potential fighting contribution of the Poles to the French cause was a factor. Yet in establishing the fact of hostilities with Russia, Napoleon's diplomatic bullying compromised the form in which they were to be prosecuted to Alexander's advantage. Initially wedded to the notion of taking the war to France—in the best scenario with the Austrians, Poles, and Prussians—the isolation Napoleon's diplomatic manoeuvres imposed on Russia, along with the sheer size of the army he was massing for action, forced Alexander into the defensive posture that offered the best odds for Napoleon's defeat. In the case of Russia it was less that Napoleon could not resist a strike at the jugular but rather that he imagined seeing a jugular at all.[78]

The army he assembled for the invasion—600,000 strong, composed of French, Austrian, Bavarian, Italian, Polish, Prussian, Saxon, and Spanish troops along with 1,372 field guns—was not at fault. Rather the very distances over which it was compelled to operate robbed the *Grande Armée* of the virtues of mass, speed, and manoeuvre that had brought it to Russia's frontier. More fundamentally, the catastrophe of the Russian campaign was the product of the waning military judgment of Napoleon himself, of a professional soldier who had become above all things a warrior in whom self-confidence had degenerated into rashness and an "unmeasured contempt of his enemies."[79] It is beside the point that he embarked on the Russian enterprise without having disposed of the Spanish one, as the very magnitude of the Russian challenge alone made the campaign a spectacular mistake in its own right. For it is not at all the case that Napoleon neglected the problem of supplying his army over marches of enormous distances so that it was able to fight major engagements far from home. To the contrary, he accomplished extraordinary and unprecedented feats in organizing magazines, supply depots, and horse-drawn trains of fully militarised personnel and equipment and devoted so much personal time to their coordination miles behind the army's spearheads that his care for logistics interfered with his conduct of the sharp end of operations.[80] Those operations called for the advance eastward of three army groups positioned along the Vistula River from Warsaw in the south to Königsberg on the Baltic with the objective of bringing Tsar Alexander's army to a decisive battle within the first twenty days of the campaign.[81]

It bears stressing that the refusal of the Russian forces to give battle accomplished the absolutely critical task of wearing down both the moral and the physical strength of *Grande Armée* until the trial of strength at Borodino, only 115 kilometres west of Moscow. Napoleon might have wintered at Smolensk and resumed the offensive in spring had not political and military factors combined to draw him with equal force to the same point on the map. The official cause of the campaign, to begin with, was to force Russia back into the Continental system with minimum delay. Secondly, a defeat of the Tsar's army so close to the very gates of the religious heart of his realm would surely bring Alexander to his knees. Lastly, the arrival of the news from Spain that Wellington had inflicted a crushing defeat on the army of Auguste Marmont at Salamanca convinced Napoleon that affairs in Russia must conclude immediately.[82] The wonder is not that the *Grande Armée* could bring only 133,000 men and 587 guns to bear against Kutuzov's 155,000 men and 640 guns at Borodino but rather that they fought as well as they did after the marches, deprivations, and disease of the preceding weeks—to which Napoleon now added the abandonment of tactical imagination.

Whereas Russian operations had used the vast space of the country to retreat and avoid encirclement, Kutuzov's plan was now to force the attacking French through small spaces in which his artillery would tear huge holes in their concentrated ranks. Prepared positions roughly in the centre of the Russian position—the storied Raevsky Redoubt and arrow-shaped earthworks or *fleches* at Borodino—made it static but also more defensible.[83] In the initial array of forces Kutuzov placed far too many men on his right to the north, where the terrain favored the Russians, and too few on his left to the south, where the natural advantages of terrain were fewer. Although Davout proposed to lead a force of some 40,000 men in a wide sweep around the Russian left, Napoleon uncharacteristically settled on a massive assault against the prepared positions of the Russian centre-left.[84] Borodino, fought at the farthest frontier of Napoleonic warfare, saw the French marshals and the Grande Armée rank-and-file grind out a decision in spite of their commander. The mostly Italian French IV Corps under Prince Eugène de Beauharnais captured the town of Borodino on the left, while Prince Józef Poniatowski's Polish V Corps took the village of Utitsa on the far right. Neither, however, was able to turn the Russian flank, so that over the course of the day the main action consisted of repeated French hammer blows against the *flèches* and the Raevsky Redoubt by Davout's I Corps, Ney's III Corps and Junot's VIII Corps in which massed artillery mowed down the packed formations of both sides and tens of thousands of infantrymen engaged in hand-to-hand fighting. By the time the Russians began a disciplined withdrawal, it had cost France 33,000 casualties to capture the ground and Russia roughly 44,000 to hold it for so long. Whereas the Russians had lost the battle, only in the strictest technical sense had the French won it, for Napoleon would not be able to make up his losses or replenish his supplies.

The *Grande Armée* had in effect prevailed without him, an instrument of war that had "stood up magnificently to the severest test it had yet undergone on a battlefield."[85]

It nonetheless now faced the beginning of its end. That end had been embraced by the very launch of the invasion of Russian, notes Paul Schroeder, less a typical European war than an imperial venture ending in disaster not unlike the destruction of the legions of Quinctilius Varus in the Germany in 9 CE.[86] Attrition had so winnowed the ranks of the *Grande Armée* even prior to Borodino that the campaign was in the strategic sense already a failure.[87]

Exhaustion and collapse

The storied retreat from Russia is rightly seen as setting the stage for ultimate collapse of the Napoleonic empire. That the schedule of the Russian campaign was influenced by Wellington's operations in Spain—and that prior even to that by the withdrawal of French troops from the Peninsular theater in order to augment the 1812 invasion force—testifies that in strategic terms Spain and Russia were parts of the same episode, the physical overextension and exhaustion of France's war-making capacity. Going over to the offensive on the tail of Napoleon's retreat, a Russian army now in the throes of accelerated reform was henceforth to be a major factor in the allied victory, especially in the struggle for Germany.

The term "allied" also began to take on a more substantial meaning, as Britain appointed William Cathcart as ambassador to St. Petersberg along with a subsidiary brief as London's representative in Northern and Eastern Europe with instructions to miss no opportunity to press Berlin and Vienna to coordinate their policies; Christoph Lieven, sent to London in January 1813, was meanwhile able to negotiate a British subsidy of £1.3 million with provision for an additional £3.3 million, projected at the time to cover Russia's expenses for campaigning in Germany through the end of the year. Although the Peninsular War had cost Britain £11 million, the forces landed in Portugal and Spain did not unduly strain national resources with demands for new capabilities, as Britain had been developing its skills in maritime operations since the Seven Years' War and the American War of Independence.[88]

In Germany even the most star-crossed of Jacobins had been disabused of their illusions about liberty by the reality of Napoleonic occupation; "instead of forming a federation of free States, Germany was becoming the parade-ground and commissariat department of French armies."[89] Nationalist resentment percolated first among historians, poets, and playwrights attached to the old German virtues. The Spanish resistance spoke to romantics such as Ernst Moritz Arndt and Heinrich von Kleist, the latter imprisoned by the French at Châlons-sur Marne for six months as a spy, but the pivotal event came with the Convention of Tauroggen, an unauthorised armistice reached by the Prussian general Johann David von Yorck with the command of an advancing Russian army in East Prussia. It was the first of a series of landmarks—from the Russo-Prussian alliance at Kalisch and Breslau to Prussia's declaration of war on France in March 1813—that led to Leipzig and the appropriately named "Battle of the Nations" in October of that year.[90] The same month, Wellington crossed the Bidossoa River onto French soil, so that the allied invasion of France actually began on its southern frontier. Nevertheless, with Britain, Spain, Portugal, and Sicily advancing from one end of Europe, Russian, Prussian, Swedish armies, along with a contingent from Mecklenburg-Strelitz, were gathering at the other.[91] They were soon to be joined by Austria in the middle.

There is a singular appropriateness to the climax of the Napoleonic battle falling upon Leipzig, a Saxon city between Berlin to the north-east and Jena to the south-west and thus accessible to Austrian, Prussian, and Russian armies that France had humiliated in this corner of Europe short years ago. Prussian hatred of Napoleon united adherents of its *ancien régime* such as Yorck, his king, Friedrich Wilhelm, and Gebhard von Blücher with reformers such as August Neidhardt von Gsneisenau, Karl August von Hardenderg, Baron vom Stein, and Gebhard von Scharnhorst. Their efforts began the transformation of semi-feudal Prussia into a market, society, and state of consequence—the abolition of serfdom, freedom of trade, tax reform, Jewish emancipation, and elected town councils—with a reconstituted and vastly stronger army at its disposal.[92] The basis for a general staff was laid, the *Junker* monopoly on the officer corps broken, the limit on the army's troop strength subverted, a *Landwehr* and *Landsturm* beside the regular army established, a new field manual incorporating Napoleonic combined arms doctrine published, a staff system founded, and an officer's war college opened. The 42,000-man troop limit imposed on the Prussian army was circumvented by the *Krumpersystem*, in which a percentage of men were sent on extended leave each year and replaced by new recruits, thus creating an ever-larger reserve force with some basic military training.[93] Although the Prussian army of 1813–14 remained in many respects that of a German *Kleinstaat* rather than a great power, the organisational seed of its growth into something vastly more formidable had been planted.[94]

The improvement of the Austrian army meanwhile had been in large part the work of Archduke Charles, who managed significant changes in two surges of reform between 1801 and 1804, then 1806 to 1809. These included both improvements in the terms of service and the deployment of troops on the battlefield in division formation, and skirmish training.[95] The creation of *Landwehr* home defence militias along with reserve battalions, whose training rotation enabled Austria to stay officially within the limit imposed by the Treaty of Schönbrunn, enabled it to field some 550,000 troops, the largest national contingent of the Allied forces. The Russian army too had undergone sweeping changes following the defeat of Austerlitz, particularly to its artillery, and after the defence of 1812 in the raising of new conscripts, improvements in their training, and logistics capable of sustaining hundreds of thousands of troops at great distance from the Russian heartland.

Augmenting Britain's role in leading the coalition advancing into France was Castlereagh, now foreign secretary, who secured an alliance with Sweden and enticed it with subsidies and a promise of sovereignty over Norway to commit an expeditionary force to operations in Germany. British subsidies of £2 million then helped to bring the Russian army in Germany to 160,000 men and the Prussian army to a strength of 80,000; additional British aid and money totaled £2 million to Prussia, £1.6 for Austria, £3.3 to Russia, and £2.3 for Sweden by the end of 1814—and was topped off by the equipping of a small British expeditionary force for northern Germany. Such was Castlereagh's contribution to the construction of the Sixth Coalition that his flexibility and "uncommon fund of good sense" of itself approximated the value of an army.[96]

As these forces converged on Saxony, Napoleon had abandoned the survivors of the Russian debacle and set about the work of raising an entirely new army. To his call for fresh recruits, initially an astounding target of 656,000, the nation responded positively by offering up its sons, husbands, and horses—possibly the best evidence, as Steven Englund puts it, that Napoleonic imperialism had "actually succeeded in imposing military service on the national mentality."[97] The army of 1813 was nevertheless short of everything, except guns and artillerists. Due to its depth of organisation and quality personnel artillery remained proficient and expertly commanded. French cavalry officers were also impressive despite inferior numbers, a shortage of mounts, and many novice horsemen. But the infantry arm had been terminally weakened by the scourges of 1812 and was dangerously short of veteran troops and qualified non-commissioned officers.[98]

In light of these facts, the degree of recovery achieved for operations in Germany in 1813 was remarkable. This was in part because the Allies did not have the unified command that could have made their applied strength proportional to their numbers. Poor staff communications among them meant that they achieved only an imitation of operational coordination.[99] Napoleon was thus periodically able to offset their numerical advantage by seizing the initiative. In the first major action of the campaign, the two armies did not so much engage as collide, at Lützen, south-west of Leipzig, each having miscalculated the enemy strength in front of it. Allied confidence took a blow when the confused system of high command was bested by Napoleon's flexibility and seasoned sense of the critical tactical moment. Still, Napoleon was impressed with the Prussian will to combat, observing that "these animals have learned something."[100] The follow-up engagement at Bautzen almost three weeks later witnessed a compounding of command problems on both sides. With 115,000 men and 150 guns, Napoleon pursued Wittgenstein's 96,000 men and 450 guns in the direction of Dresden.

Lützen, Bautzen, Dresden—each was in a different way a victory for French arms. They were nonetheless collectively irrelevant, because Napoleon could not afford to exchange high casualties with the Allies. For the Allies too, the fighting in Saxony had been somewhat futile, for unless and until they brought their collective strength to bear in a determined fashion they would not benefit significantly from their advantage in numbers. Neither would they have a measure of the effectiveness of their reforms. Just such a measure was applied at Leipzig over three days in October 1813, but not until the Allies had outmanoeuvred Napoleon was it possible. With the 130,000 Austrians, 270,000 Prussians, and 78,000 Russian troops present in Saxony in late 1813, now joined by 110,000 Swedes and a British rocket battery, Allied strategy was to avoid one-to-one battle with Napoleon's main army yet to continually prod those of his subordinates into minor engagements such that his continued efforts in marching and countermarching to reinforce them would oblige him ultimately to concentrate his forces as the Allies closed a ring around them. Prussian armies to the north and north-east, Russians to the east, and Austrians to the south-east could be kept apart only temporarily, as a confrontation with one, which nevertheless declined combat, permitted the other two time and space to continue their advance. The effort to engage Blücher in the north in particular enabled Schwarzenberg to close in from the south, until by October 16 some 335,000 allies with 1,500 guns had forced 190,000 French with 700 guns into a defensive position around Leipzig. Not only were their numbers superior, by 1813 many of the Allied rank-and-file had better training and more experience than Napoleon's raw recruits and had adopted the tactical capabilities that had distinguished French arms since 1792.[101] The Battle of the Nations was the largest engagement in European history but was bereft of tactical imagination, a brutal exercise in attrition. Napoleon was thrown back on a defence of north-eastern France, while the simultaneous abandonment of Spain and the presence of British forces in the south-west drew both Blücher and Wellington closer to the final drama at Waterloo.[102]

Against Schwarzenberg's Army of Bohemia invading through Switzerland, Blücher's Army of Silesia crossing from Germany, and Bernadotte's Army of the North moving through Belgium, Napoleon positioned the greater portion of his strength around Paris and with some 40,000 men fought a brilliant campaign of manoeuvre, chalking little victories among a series of running battles from Brienne on January 29 to La Rothière, Champaubert, Montmirail, Château-Thierry, Vauchamps, Montereau, Craonne, and Rheims on March 13. In theory, the point of the campaign was to keep Allied armies apart physically and in the process drive their governments apart diplomatically. To the extent that poor coordination among them played directly into his hands in one engagement after another, it worked; whereas Britain and Russia were bent on Napoleon's personal destruction, Metternich feared that too sweeping an Allied victory would not be in Austria's interest and sought to settle on a peace preserving France's borders of 1792.[103] In the northern countryside, moreover, Napoleon's army was welcome. War weariness had soured France's urban classes, but the peasants looked to the Emperor as the "crowned Jacobin," protector of the land rights won in 1789. It was an early indication that Bonapartism, a popular and romantic authoritarian interpretation of Napoleon's political legacy, was to haunt the politics of a restored monarchy or a democratic republic in France for a century after his death.[104]

Strategy and diplomacy

If the coalition of his foes was brittle, Napoleon nonetheless kept it united with the cynicism of his negotiation, changing his position with the subtlest shift in the military tide despite the general movement of the sea. Following his successes of Champaubert, Montmirail, and Montereau, he sent Armand-Augustin-Louis Caulincourt to the Châtillon Peace Congress with instructions to accept nothing less than France's "natural frontiers." Accepting the fiction of Napoleon's peaceful intentions, Castlereagh seized the opportunity to unify the Allies and harden their terms. The result, the Treaty of Chaumont, offered a ceasefire only in return for France's "ancient frontiers." In anticipation of a French rejection, the Allies swore, with the encouragement of a British subsidy of £5 million, not to seek a separate peace and to provide 150,000 troops each to a continuation of the war to a final decision and the restoration of the Bourbons to the throne. Because the treaty committed the signatories to remain allied for twenty years following France's defeat, it was the first act of the Congress of Vienna and the inauguration of the Congress System.[105] Before and after Leipzig the Allies had struggled to achieve greater unity of political purpose and more effective military coordination among themselves. By March 24 their convergence on Paris and a precipitant decline in French fighting power were nonetheless sufficient to move Napoleon's marshals to at last claim the initiative where it was needed most, by confronting their emperor at Fontainbleau with a demand for his abdication and exile. The day before, Marmont had surrendered the VI Corps to the Allies, while on the southern front Wellington's Army of Spain advanced on Toulouse.

Wellington's great contribution to Napoleon's defeat was in his command of British and Spanish forces through the thick-and-thin of the Peninsular War, but his fame as Napoleon's battlefield nemesis is eternally bound up with Waterloo. At the time of Napoleon's return from exile Wellington was in Vienna as a British delegate, first because the action was in now Vienna and second because his prestige together with Castlereagh's kept Britain involved in Europe and improved the odds of a sustainable continental peace. Although representatives of Napoleon's most intractable foe, both were sympathetic to Talleyrand's arguments on France's behalf. Castlereagh in particular shared the view that an even distribution of power and influence in Europe would make future aggression by any one power less likely; a secure island power as confident of its international position as Britain, moreover, could accept that what was good for France was good for Europe "as an ideal way to keep her rich possessions and enjoy her ease."[106] Less than a year after France's defeat Talleyrand had thus divided the Allies and negotiated a restorative settlement for France when Napoleon's landing at Fréjus dashed the pieces from the board and reunited them. Wellington departed immediately for Brussels feeling "the finger of God" upon him.[107]

The danger was not that Napoleon would turn the tide against the Allies. France's fighting power had suffered a crippling blow at Leipzig, and the collective strength of the Allies was in 1815 much too great as long as they remained united. They could mobilise 800,000 men, against whom France would strain to pull together half as many. In the event, Wellington defeated at Waterloo only what was left of the *Grande Armée* for immediate use, yet he accomplished this with only a fragment of the Allied forces, a mixture of British, Dutch-Belgian, and German troops to which a Prussian army under Blücher was added at the critical tactical moment. The task was to defeat Napoleon quickly and decisively, avoid thereby a drawn out struggle and a newly punitive animus toward France, and preserve as much as possible of the spirit and substance of Vienna. The Waterloo campaign is best understood by keeping these factors in mind.[108]

For Napoleon too, circumstance favored prompt action. In June 1815 only Wellington's army in western Belgium and Blücher's to the east on the Rhine were in any position to threaten France. A blow against them before the Austrians and Russians could cross the Rhine offered better numerical odds and a chance to deal with the latter pair in a separate engagement. Better still, mistrust between Britain and Prussia over the future of the Netherlands prompted their armies in Belgium to maintain separate communications systems, Wellington's through Brussels to the English Channel, Blücher's through Liège into Germany. Any blow that forced one or both to retire along these lines would push them apart and confound their effective coordination.[109] For operations against them in June Napoleon's *Armée du Nord* had 120,000 men and 366 guns. Blücher's Prussians totaled 108,000 men with 304 guns, whereas Wellington's Army of the Netherlands comprised 92,000 men and 174 guns.

The plan to drive north to occupy a central position between them and present each in turn with superior numbers was theoretically sound. As it turned out, the opening gambit of the Waterloo campaign achieved complete surprise, in part because Wellington's deployment of his own forces initially played straight into it. French concentration of five corps for the offensive was complete and undetected on June 6 and a general advance ordered for June 15, when Wellington received news of Prussian contact with the French near Charleroi and at first reacted badly. Mindful of his communications through Mons to the Channel coast and apprehensive of a French flanking manoeuvre from this direction, his first operational orders were to deploy two corps to the south and west of Brussels, thereby actually increasing the distance between his main force and Blücher and leaving the road junction between the Allied armies at Quatre Bras weak.[110] It was here that part of the left wing of the French army under Ney numbering 15,000 men fell upon 7,500 troops under William, Prince of Orange. That the Dutch troops were present to resist Ney's seizure of the crossroad was due only to an act of insubordination; Constant de Rebeque, William's chief of staff, and General Perponcher-Sednitzberg had ignored Wellington's order to concentrate to the west at Nivelles, because they sensed something serious afoot directly in front of them. Ney delayed his main assault unnecessarily, and the arrival of British reinforcements then forced him back. It may be too much to claim that Rebeque and Perponcher had saved the Waterloo campaign, but Wellington was suitably generous with his gratitude.[111] At any rate, the iron duke now gripped the bit. At Quatre Bras he exhibited the energy of the young Napoleon, riding tirelessly to reinforce threatened positions and narrowly escaping capture or worse by French cavalry.

The main French army of 77,000 men under Napoleon's direct command had meanwhile slammed into three of Blücher's four corps totaling 83,000 men at Ligny, six miles to the south-east. Ligny cost Napoleon 11,000 casualties, but the Prussians took a terrible mauling at 25,000. The collapse of the Prussian position at Ligny exposed Wellington's left flank and forced him to retreat toward Mont-Saint-Jean near Waterloo. While Blücher was incapacitated, his chief of staff, Gneisenau, ordered the Prussians at Ligny to retire not to Liège but rather toward Wavre, only seven miles east of Wellington's new position. Far from driving the Allies apart, therefore, the effect of the actions at Quatre Bras and Ligny had been to draw them closer together. Gneisenau's may have been the most important single decision of the campaign, as without Prussian aid, "Wellington would probably have been defeated if not utterly routed on the 18th."[112]

From this point Napoleon's decisions tilted the odds against him, while Wellington's were increasingly prescient. Of particular importance was Wellington's choice of ground to meet the next French attack. Of the 68,000 men at his disposal on June 18, less than half were British or of the King's German Legion, the remaining Belgian, Dutch, and German troops being inexperienced or politically suspect. Wellington had compounded this shortage of men by leaving no fewer than 17,000 men ten miles to the west at Hal and Tubize as a hedge against his initial worries over a French flanking move from that direction. Once events at Quatre Bras and Ligny had revealed the actual line of Napoleon's attack they should have been recalled. Thus condemned to a defensive posture, Wellington's deployments before Mont-Saint-Jean made perfect use both of the available strength and of the features of the terrain. In general terms the bulk of the Allied numbers was on the right, the left manned in anticipation of eventual Prussian reinforcement. Wellington's position was thus strong enough to make any frontal attack very daunting, whereas an attempt to envelope it from the east would have run the risk of colliding with a Prussian force of unknown strength.[113]

That its size and location were unknown was due to Napoleon's decision, once he had learned of Wellington's preparation at Mont-Saint-Jean, to detach his entire right wing under Grouchy and send it in pursuit of Blücher. He did not give the order promptly after the battle at Ligny, moreover, but rather late on the morning of the following day. In other words, some 33,000 men, who might well have been engaged at Waterloo on June 18, were committed not so much as to harry the Prussians and push them away from Wellington but, in effect, to find them. The only Prussians Grouchy was to encounter once he arrived at Wavre after a wide sweep to the east were 5,000 men of the III Corps under Freiherr Johann von Thielmann. Blücher had meanwhile turned the I Corps under Graf von Zieten, the IV Corps under Graf Bülow von Dennewitz, and the II Corps under General Pirch westward in the direction of Waterloo.[114]

These deployments weighed heavily against a French victory on June 18. Based on the assumption that the Prussian army would ultimately come to the aid of his own, Wellington had established a position at Waterloo that maximised the odds that Prussian intervention would be timely. Indeed, it is altogether appropriate to credit Wellington with "consummate judgement" in the selection of the ground on which he was to give—more accurately receive—battle and the disposition of his forces to minimising their exposure while maximising their defensive firepower.[115] Waterloo was essentially a succession of French assaults and Allied counterpunching. The first punch fell on the Allied left at Hougemont and was intended to look like the main assault so that Wellington would weaken his centre in order to reinforce the position. However, Hougemont was naturally such a strong position that by 1:00 PM it tied down more than two French divisions in return for a minimal response from Wellington.[116] Only if in the meantime the British infantry broke or Napoleon annihilated it as he had the Russians in the redoubts at Borodino would the arithmetic tell against Wellington. Whereas the bulk of Blücher's army was not engaged until late afternoon and evening, the first elements of the Prussian advance guard began to trouble the right flank of Napoleon's army as early as 1:30 PM.

Napoleon's efforts were thus increasingly based on a desperate need to deliver a fatal blow in short order. Much has been made of the charge of Ney's massed cavalry against the chequered squares of stalwart British infantry—not least by virtue of the spectacle of burnished steel and black horsehair bearing down on British soldiers preparing to receive the wrath of most storied army of the past twenty years—but Ney's request for more troops came to Napoleon just when the Prussian IV Corps under Bülow had captured the village of Plancenoit and threatened Napoleon's right flank in force. The French army was thus already being forced to look to its own preservation when the Emperor put its fate and his own in the hands of Ney to redirect the Guard for a last lunge against the Allied centre. Never short on courage but again short on acumen, Ney hurled it against the least shaken sector of the Allied line, where British and Dutch infantry rose from the grain and cut down the French infantry. At that point the *Armée du Nord* began to disintegrate. Only a determined defence by Lobau against Bülow and Pirch prevented its envelopment and permitted a retreat along the road south to Charleroi.[117]

The bicentennial of Waterloo produced a new flood of publications commemorating various aspects of the battle and agreeing on its epic symbolism.[118] In an essay reviewing the new Waterloo literature, Charles Esdaile stresses the more substantive thread connecting Waterloo in 1815 with Flanders in 1914 in the central legacy of Napoleon of to war and modern history, namely that in both instances the Allies fought "a militaristic imperialism that sought to turn the greater part of continental Europe into a power base serving the interests of a single state."[119]

Emperor Bonaparte's legacy: A century of militarism

It is in the pathology of militarism, the subordination of civil institutions and political leadership to military institutions and military priorities, that a sober reading of Napoleon's twenty years of war making locates his most durable impact. Captain Bonaparte mastered the tactical use of the weapons of his time, and General Bonaparte mastered the operational art of coordinating the rapid movement of army corps to surprise and overwhelm an adversary. After 1807 Emperor Napoleon continued to exhibit tactical and operational finesse superior to any of his enemies, yet no longer did so in a decisive manner that would enhance the security of France and secure it a durable dominance in Europe. War in the service of political survival was the challenge put to the Revolutionary army, whereas war in the service of strategic ends was, for a time, the vocation of the *Grande Armée*. After 1807 the continuous application of aggressive diplomacy and war could no longer serve any soberly calculated interest of France; indeed, the menace of Napoleonic France was after 1807 so much greater than that of Revolutionary France that it provoked ever-broader great-power coalitions of resistance. This is what is meant by the observation that Napoleon "incarnated operational brilliance—and strategic lunacy."[120] In the process he made war the primary mission of the French state and through twenty years of military conflict convinced Europe's other states to similarly orchestrated the purposes of modern government.

If the Vienna settlement inaugurated a period of more proactive and constructive diplomacy in which enlightened self-interest trumped fear and resentment—in so far as France was not reduced but rather returned to its pre-1789 role in Europe—it testified to an effort on the part of the diplomats to reshape the instruments of peace to the realities of war recently demonstrated. As representatives of that Ally unique for its sea power and maritime outlook, Castlereagh and Wellington sought a sustainable European equilibrium rather than the preservation of a victory. Because Britain was to have a vital role yet a limited liability, Castlereagh in particular viewed the requirements of peace as he had prosecuted the diplomacy of war: strategically. Indeed, it is no exaggeration that he applied what was later called in

Anglo-Saxon parlance "grand strategy": the application of all the capacities of his state, beyond the necessities of war, to the preservation of its advantages in peace. His reasoning was the polar opposite of Napoleon's, measuring national means against political ends in a fashion that the Emperor had abandoned after Jena-Auerstädt.[121]

After Vienna, British trade was able to expand unopposed and unrivalled, and commercial expansiveness was to provide an unequalled source of revenue for the expansion of sea power, while sea power protected further commercial expansiveness. The British Empire's foundations were broadened and deepened by the Napoleon Wars by a cycle of investment-expenditure-investment in which "the state in general and the Navy in particular were at the heart of this commercial and financial system."[122] The acquisition over the following decades of not only new colonial possessions but of far-flung island *entrepôts*, habours, and naval stations—Singapore in 1819, the Falklands in 1833, Aden in 1839, Hong Kong in 1841—inevitably gave British foreign policy a global strategic perspective with far-reaching consequences for the application of British power abroad for the rest of the nineteenth century. Indeed, toward the end of the century the British naval experience of Nelson's time exercised a formative influence on American and German naval ambition when the books of Alfred Thayer Mahan applied a compelling mixture of pragmatism, romanticism, and social Darwinism to their interpretation of the real and imagined advantages of naval power to Britain's past and the immediate future of any state aspiring to wield international influence.[123]

The legacy of the Napoleonic era for France was mixed, in the short-term ending the near anarchy of the Revolution by way of the Consulate, codifying French law, and transferring wealth to the middle classes by sweeping aside legal and economic feudalism. Many of the Revolution's liberal ideals and reforms travelled to German, Swiss, and Italian soil with the *Grande Armée*. After 1815 the surviving absolute monarchies were forced in the pursuit of popular legitimacy to undertake constitutional reforms that at least fenced certain liberties from abuse by the crown as a hedge against democracy. The positive aspects of Napoleon's reforms in France and abroad, however, were largely confined to the period of consolidation, 1799–1807. Thereafter, he transformed a nominally democratic form of government first into an oligarchy of officials and ultimately an unconstrained personal tyranny legitimated by its popularity.[124] Thus, Napoleon's most durable legacy was political as much as military, based on a malleable ideological tradition about the relationship of the state to the nation, democracy, and political leadership—balanced on the fragment of truth in Napoleon's own statement that he had not usurped the crown of France but rather plucked it from the gutter and permitted the people to set it on his head. For the remainder of the nineteenth century, Bonapartism represented a mixture of popular sentiments, deeply subversive both of the restored monarchy and to republicanism. We can stop short of declaring Bonapartism responsible for the monstrous totalitarian progeny of the twentieth century and still acknowledge that the romantic vapor surrounding it was politically disorienting and produced in France an ambivalence about the legitimacy of democratic representation and a recurrent yearning for state intervention.[125]

The connection between the regime and militarism was in the romantic popularisation of martial values. With it prospered the notion that the *patrie*—any *patrie* worthy of the name—was built around a community of warlike men leading a whole nation trained in the vocation of arms. The moment that made Waterloo necessary, after all, was Ney's choice to join Napoleon when sent by the restored Bourbon dynasty to arrest him; for no matter how rightly unpopular the Bourbons remained, Ney had taken an oath of allegiance to Louis XVIII and betrayed both it and the principle of civilian rule when he defended his choice for treason with the claim that "it is only by a soldier like the Emperor that the soldiers of France will ever be treated with respect."[126] More legitimate regimes than the Bourbons treated the soldiers of France with suspicion for the remainder of the nineteenth century, and republicans in particular saw in the military an enemy of democracy they sought alternately to purge or domesticate to civilian rule.

Because after 1807 Napoleon refused to confine his military ambition to strategically defensible limits, his gathering host of adversaries was forced to reform militarily to meet the challenge, adopt Napoleonic methods, and adapt them to national circumstance. His revolution in military affairs had enabled a single country, France, to overrun most of Europe in a few short years, thereby waking all of its foes to the perils, and possibilities, of the future. The Austrian army had undergone reforms following upon the War of Austrian Succession and the Seven Years' War, when after 1792 the Napoleonic storm broke. Its continuous exposure to war with France prompted its reorganisation into the corps structure that had enabled it to manoeuvre on a broad front and undertake operational campaigns rather than isolated engagements. It was the Austrian army executing a concentration of five corps columns that first inflicted a significant reverse on the *Grande Armée* at Aspern-Essling in 1809 after a string of defeats at Rivoli, Marengo, and Austerlitz. Although Napoleon promptly corrected the setback by prevailing at Wagram, he failed to appreciate fully that the Austrians of 1809 had begun to narrow their qualitative disadvantage. He was witnessing a further step in the emergence of modern war, a dynamic he had set in motion yet no longer fully understood.[127]

Armies as dissimilar as the British and the Russian had also been able to make significant contributions to Napoleon's defeat by adopting and adapting. Reforms of the Russian army, especially its infantry, were primarily the work of Barclay de Tolly, who instituted a corps system and divisional structure on the French model yet never achieved the same flexibility or speed of concentration. Conservatives like Kutuzov were always willing to fight but rarely willing to change, with the result that by 1813 the Russian army had sustained appalling casualties and was in much worse shape than a fully modernised force would have been.

At the opposite strategic frontier, the British army in Spain had recovered quickly from its early disasters and forced the French from the Iberian Peninsula; under Wellington it had then stood up to Napoleon's hammer blows at Waterloo and counter-attacked to smash his Imperial Guard. Being more consistently at the cutting edge of the British army's travails, it was Wellington who in 1809 first organised it into divisions. In this sense Napoleon was a success in transforming war yet a failure in prosecuting it in a fashion that would give France a lasting advantage from it. Not only did the strategic illogic of his policy after 1807 strain France's capabilities, the operational and tactical edge the *Grande Armée* had enjoyed too was progressively eroded.

But it was in Prussia and with its army that the predatory nature of Napoleonic imperialism in Europe had its most important legacy politically, so that the era, above all in the humiliation of Jena, justifies the claim for Napoleon as constituting a beginning. Hegel's *Verfassung Deutschlands* explained the loss of the statehood of the old German Reich in large part due to its revealed incapacity for the unified conduct of war against the French Republic and Empire.[128] Following Jena-Auerstädt the Prussian army reformers moved quickly in the direction of meritocracy, removing older officers and promoting talent at such a rate that by 1818 half of the officer corps was no longer of the nobility. They used the rotation system and the creation of the *Landwehr* to augment the size of the army's reserve, broaden the ambit of military training, and move personnel through the ranks. It was a general, Yorck, who at Tauroggen and in defiance of his king, made the army corps under his command the avant-garde of a national uprising against France. The *Wehrgesetz* of 1814 then announced that all male Prussians were to be liable for military service upon their twentieth birthday, so that by the time of Waterloo, Prussia alone had adopted almost completely Napoleon's system in order to be rid of French imperialism. And in 1815, it was Prussia who was "pulling the Duke of Wellington's chestnuts from the fire of Waterloo and transforming 'a damn near-run thing' into a decisive victory."[129] Jena-Auerstädt was rightly viewed as a crisis of the Prussian state and later led to reforms that, along with an awakening of German national consciousness, in the next century produced an army that "bestrode nearly all Europe and long held most of the world at bay."[130]

The broader reforms of the Prussian bureaucracy, economy, and society ultimately provoked a conservative backlash against the fear of fundamental constitutional change, but the army had made a start toward becoming not only the most effective military in Europe but also the symbol of a nation and of a state-within-a-state.[131] Despite the enormity of these changes, the Prussian army had barely begun to digest intellectually the meaning for itself and its state of the struggle concluded at Waterloo. That task was undertaken over the following decades by the military theorists, the Baron de Jomini and Carl von Clausewitz, both of whom saw action in the Napoleonic Wars and now grappled with their meaning. Initially, Jomini's writings were more influential, but over the course of the nineteenth century Clausewitz did more to define the Napoleonic paradigm for future generations. What the Napoleonic experience meant for Prussia and Germany—rather, what Clausewitz and others said it meant—did much to legitimate the popularity of the social Darwinist streak in German nationalism later in the century.[132] The period had given the army a unique place in Prussian society, and the Prussian army's reading of Clausewitz was to give war a uniquely baleful place in its politics.[133]

The Napoleonic era, then, is notable for the reorganisation of large armies to prosecute complex operations, ambitious enough to imply the strategic dividend of renovated dominance for France on the European continent. That France ultimately suffered a further erosion of its status by 1815 cannot be blamed on a failure of Napoleon's operational art and is to be found instead in his neglect of and apparent contempt for the limits inherent in France's strategic circumstance. It is tempting to conclude that the excellence of Napoleon's operational innovations and the resilient fighting power of the *Grande Armée* together tempted him after 1807 to campaigns that could only undermine the potential for a peace with France's adversaries that would have strengthened her security from foreign occupation. It may be that such restraint was never in the deoxyribonucleic acid of Napoleon or the predatory regime he created, but that does not concern us here. It suffices for now to observe that extraordinary military capabilities in a modern state—and under Napoleon France was the cutting edge of military modernity—do not provide for success when strategic thought is absent. Sadly, many of France's adversaries over the Napoleon era—Prussia most prominent among them—were much too impressed with what Napoleonic France had achieved to care sufficiently about what else it entailed. Although it was not wholly apparent until the latter half of the nineteenth century, Napoleon's curse on modern military conflict was that wars "consistently ended up raising basic revolutionary questions about the organisation of society and the legitimacy of states."[134]

After 1815 and before Great Power warfare returned to Europe in the Crimea in the 1850s, the lessons of the Napoleonic Wars influenced only at the margins the smaller conflicts fought beyond European shores. Nonetheless, technological progress and imperial competition among the Great Powers in Africa and Asia produced expeditionary campaigns, which, when considered together, reveal much about the nature of the political regime waging war and the strategic reasoning it employs.

Notes

1 Thomas Nipperdey, *Deutsche Geschichte, 1800–1866: Bürgerwelt und starker Staat* (Munich, Germany: C.H. Beck, 1984), pp. 11–31; Azar Gat, *A History of Military Thought: From the Enlightenment to the Cold War* (New York: Oxford University Press, 2001), pp. 314–81.
2 J. Holland Rose, *The Revolutionary and Napoleonic Era, 1789–1815* (Cambridge, UK: Cambridge University Press, 1935), p. 97.

3 Andrew Roberts, *Napoleon the Great* (London: Allen Lane, 2014).
4 J. Holland Rose, *Revolutionary and Napoleonic Era*, p. 78; David Kaiser, *Politics and War: European Conflict from Philip II to Hitler* (Cambridge, MA: Harvard University Press, 2000), pp. 214–16.
5 Kaiser, *Politics and War*, p. 217. See also S.J. Watson. *Carnot* (London: Bodley Head, 1954); Robert S. Quimby. *The Background of Napoleonic Warfare: The Theory of Military Tactics in Eighteenth-Century France* (New York: Columbia University Press, 1957); Émile G. Léonard, *L'Armée et ses problèmes au XVIIIe siècle* (Paris: Librairie Plon, 1958).
6 Jean-Paul Charnay et al., *Lazare Carnot, ou le savant citoyen: Actes du colloque* (Paris: Presses de l'Université de Paris-Sorbonne, 1990), pp. 135–43; Michael Howard, *War in European History* (New York: Oxford University Press, 1976), pp. 75–115.
7 The Wars of the Spanish Succession (1702–1713), Polish Succession (1733–1738), Austrian Succession (1741–1748), and the Seven Years' War (1756–1763).
8 Patrice Bret. *L'État, l 'armée, la science: L'Invention de la recherche publique en France (1763–1830)* (Rennes, France: Presses universitaires de Rennes, 2002); Jeremy Black, *European Warfare, 1660–1815* (New Haven, CT: Yale University Press, 1994), pp. 168–74; Gat, *History of Military Thought*, pp. 27–55.
9 James Marshall-Cornwall, *Napoleon as Military Commander* (London: B.T. Batsford, 1967), pp. 24–31; Hew Strachan, *European Armies and the Conduct of War* (London: Routledge, 1983), pp. 23–59.
10 S.E. Finer, *The History of Government from the Earliest Times*. Vol. 3, *Empires, Monarchies, and the Modern State* (New York: Oxford University Press, 1997), pp. 1517–66; Jack Hayward, *Fragmented France: Two Centuries of Disputed Identity* (New York: Oxford University Press, 2007), pp. 108–9; D.M.G. Sutherland, *The French Revolution and Empire: The Quest for Civic Order* (Oxford, UK: Blackwell, 2003).
11 Sutherland, *French Revolution and Empire*, p. 181.
12 T.C.W. Blanning, *The Origins of the French Revolutionary Wars* (London: Longman, 1986), pp. 86–89; Paul W. Schroeder, *The Transformation of European Politics, 1763–1848* (New York: Oxford University Press, 1994), pp. 100–3; Christopher Clark, *Iron Kingdom: The Rise and Downfall of Prussia, 1600–1947* (Cambridge, MA: Belknap, 2006), pp. 284–87.
13 Blanning, *Origins of the French Revolutionary Wars*, pp. 100–8.
14 Jean-Paul Bertaud, *Valmy: La démocratie en armes* (Paris: Éditions Julliard, 1970); John A. Lynn, *The Bayonets of the Republic: Motivation and Tactics in the Army of Revolutionary France, 1791–94* (Champaign, IL: University of Illinois Press, 1984), p. 278; Claus Telp, *The Evolution of Operational Art: From Frederick the Great to Napoleon* (London: Cass, 2005), pp. 44–45.
15 Steven Englund, *Napoleon: A Political Life* (Cambridge, MA: Harvard University Press, 2004), pp. 63–65; Marshall-Cornwall, *Napoleon as Military Commander*, pp. 36–39.
16 Marshall-Cornwall, *Napoleon as Military Commander*, p. 41.
17 S.J. Watson, *Carnot*, pp. 121–22.
18 Marshall-Cornwall, *Napoleon as Military Commander*, pp. 45–78; Günther E. Rothenberg. *The Napoleonic Wars* (London: Cassell, 1999), pp. 37–47.
19 David G. Chandler, *The Campaigns of Napoleon* (New York: Scribner, 1966), p. 56.
20 Jean-Paul Bertaud, *The Army of the French Revolution: From Citizen-Soldiers to Instrument of Power*, trans. R.R. Palmer (Princeton, NJ: Princeton University Press, 1989), pp. 330–32.
21 Georges Lefebvre, *The Directory*, trans. Robert Baldick (London: Routledge & Kegan Paul, 1964), pp. 110–25; Martyn Lyons, *France under the Directory*

(London: Cambridge University Press, 1975), pp. 200–3; David Lawday, *Napoleon's Master: A Life of Prince Talleyrand* (London: Jonathan Cape, 2006), pp. 105–13.

22 Schroeder, *Transformation of European Politics*, pp. 177–79; Charles Esdaile, "De-Constructing the French Wars: Napoleon as Anti-Strategist," *Journal of Strategic Studies* 31, no. 4 (2008): 524–28; J. Holland Rose, *Revolutionary and Napoleonic Era*, pp. 106–7.

23 N.A.M. Rodger, *The Command of the Ocean: A Naval History of Britain* (New York: Norton, 2005), pp. 454–60; Arthur Herman. *To Rule the Waves: How the British Navy Shaped the Modern World* (New York: Harper Collins, 2004), pp. 356–62.

24 Blanning, *Origins of the French Revolutionary Wars*, pp. 183–84; Lefebvre, *The Directory*, pp. 166–69; Lyons, *France under the Directory*, p. 213.

25 Roger Knight, *The Pursuit of Victory: The Life and Achievement of Horatio Nelson* (New York: Basic Books, 2005), pp. 288–303; Georges Lefebvre. *Napoleon: From 18 Brumaire to Tilsit, 1799–1807*, trans. Henry F. Stockhold (New York: Columbia University Press, 1969), p. 275; Noël Mostert, *The Line upon a Wind: The Greatest War Fought at Sea under Sail, 1793–1815* (London: Vintage, 2008), pp. 341–42.

26 J. Holland Rose, *Revolutionary and Napoleonic Era*, pp. 114–23.

27 Sutherland, *French Revolution and Empire*, p. 298. See also Patrice Gueniffey, *Bonaparte*, trans. Steven Rendall (Cambridge: Belknap Press, 2015), pp. 543–74.

28 J. Holland Rose, *Revolutionary and Napoleonic Era*, pp. 119–24; Finer, *History of Government*, Vol. 3, pp. 1562–63.

29 Russell F. Weigley. *The Age of Battles: The Quest for Decisive Warfare from Breitenfeld to Waterloo* (Bloomington: Indiana University Press, 1991) pp. 365–71; Robert Warschauer. *Studien zur Entwicklung der Gedanken Lazare Carnots über Kriegsführung, 1784–1793* (Berlin: Verlag E. Eberling, 1937), pp. 142–43.

30 Speech in the House of Commons, February 17, 1800 in *Principles and Problems of International Relations*, ed. Hans J. Morgenthau and Kenneth W. Thompson (New York: Alfred A. Knopf, 1950), p. 349; J. Holland Rose, *Pitt and Napoleon: Essays and Letters* (London: G. Bell, 1912), p. 14.

31 Knight, *Pursuit of Victory*, p. 331.

32 Heinrich August Winkler, *Geschichte des Westens*. Vol. 1, *Von den Anfängen in der Antike bis zum 20. Jahrhundert* (Munich, Germany: C.H. Beck, 2012), pp. 374–85.

33 Schroeder, *Transformation of European Politics*, pp. 225–30; Rodger, *Command of the Ocean*, p. 472; Boyd Hilton, *A Mad, Bad, and Dangerous People: England, 1793–1846* (Oxford: Clarendon Press, 2006), pp. 91–98.

34 Englund, *Napoleon: A Political Life*, pp. 252–62; Sutherland, *French Revolution and Empire*, p. 321.

35 D.M.G. Sutherland, *France 1789–1815: Revolution and Counterrevolution* (New York: Oxford University Press, 1986), pp. 360–61.

36 Howard G. Brown, *War, Revolution, and the Bureaucratic State: Politics and Army Administration in France, 1791–1799* (Oxford: Clarendon Press, 1995), pp. 124–49, 235–64.

37 Sutherland, *France 1789–1815*, pp. 376–80; Englund, *Napoleon: A Political Life*, pp. 271–72.

38 Charles Esdaile., *Napoleon's Wars: An International History, 1803–1815* (London: Allan Lane, 2007), p. 169.

39 Ibid., pp. 168; Rothenberg, *Napoleonic Wars*, pp. 24–28.

40 Schroeder, *Transformation of European Politics*, p. 225.

41 Ibid., pp. 229–30; Gueniffy, *Bonaparte*, pp. 803–5; Esdaile, *Napoleon's Wars*, pp. 151–53; John R. Elting, *Swords around a Throne: Napoleon's Grande Armée* (New York: Free Press, 1988), pp. 27–53, 123–55, 589–603; J. Holland Rose, *The Personality of Napoleon* (New York: Putnam, 1912), pp. 86–87.

42 John Brewer, *The Sinews of Power: War, Money and the English State, 1688–1783* (Cambridge, MA: Harvard University Press, 1990), pp. 197–99; Roger Morriss, *The Foundations of British Maritime Ascendancy: Resources, Logistics and the State, 1755–1815* (New York: Cambridge University Press, 2011), pp. 396–403.

43 Rodger, *Command of the Ocean*, pp. 536–43; Roy Adkins, *Trafalgar: The Biography of a Battle* (London: Little, Brown, 2004); Robert Gardiner, ed., *The Campaign of Trafalgar, 1803–1805* (Annapolis, MD: Naval Institute Press, 1997); Oliver Warner, *Trafalgar* (London: B.T. Batsford, 1959).

44 William H. McNeill, *The Pursuit of Power: Technology, Armed Force and Society since A.D. 1000* (Chicago, IL: University of Chicago Press, 1982), pp. 206–15; Colin Gray, *The Leverage of Sea Power: The Strategic Advantage of Navies in War* (New York: Macmillan, 1992), pp. 136–73; P.J. Cain, *British Imperialism, 1688–2000*, 2 vols. (London: Longman, 1993).

45 Peter Padfield, *Maritime Power and the Struggle for Freedom: Naval Campaigns That Shaped the Modern World, 1788–1851* (New York: Overlook Press, 2003), p. 259; Mostert, *Line upon a Wind*, p. 575.

46 Schroeder, *Transformation of European Politics*, p. 458; Knight, *Pursuit of Victory*, p. 497; John Bew, *Castlereagh: A Life* (New York: Oxford University Press, 2012), pp. 207–9.

47 Esdaile, *Napoleon's Wars*, p. 218; Weigley, *Age of Battles*, pp. 378–82.

48 Chandler, *Campaigns of Napoleon*, p. 392.

49 Ibid., pp. 390–402.

50 Weigley, *Age of Battles*, 384–86; Martin van Creveld, *Supplying War: Logistics from Wallensetin to Patton* (New York: Cambridge University Press, 2004), pp. 56–61.

51 Marshall-Cornwall, *Napoleon as Military Commander*, pp. 141–42; Robert Goetz, *1805: Austerlitz; Napoleon and the Destruction of the Third Coalition* (London: Greenhill, 2005), pp. 85–119.

52 Goetz, *1805: Austerlitz*, p. 208; Chandler, *Campaigns of Napoleon*, pp. 413–39; Weigley, *Age of Battles*, p. 389; Frederick W. Kagan, *The End of the Old Order: Napoleon and Europe, 1801–1805* (Cambridge, MA: Da Capo Press, 2006), pp. 62–25.

53 Schroeder, *Transformation of European Politics*, pp. 282–83.

54 Michael Broers. *Europe under Napoleon* (London: Hodder Education Publisher, 1996: London; I.B. Taurus, 2015), pp. 40–42.

55 Schroeder, *Transformation of European Politics*, pp. 284–85; Weigley, *Age of Battles*, p. 392; Brendan Simms, *The Impact of Napoleon: Prussian High Politics, Foreign Policy and the Crisis of the Executive, 1797–1806* (New York: Cambridge University Press, 1997), pp. 269–303; Clark, *Iron Kingdom*, pp. 301–5.

56 Chandler, *Campaigns of Napoleon*, pp. 466–70; Weigley, *Age of Battles*, pp. 392–93; van Creveld, *Supplying War*, p. 61.

57 Chandler, *Campaigns of Napoleon*, pp. 479–85.

58 Idid., p. 488; Weigley, *Age of Battles*, pp. 396–97; Robert M. Citino, *The German Way of War: From the Thirty Years War to the Third Reich* (Lawrence: University of Kansas Press, 2005), p. 119.

59 Wilhelm Leopold Colmar, baron von der Goltz. *Von Roßbach bis Jena und Auerstedt: Ein Beitrag zur Geschichte des preussischen Herres* (Berlin: Ernst Friedrich und Sohn, 1906), pp. 497–98; Simms, *Impact of Napoleon*, pp. 18–28.

60 Thomas Stamm-Kuhlman, *König in Prueßens großer Zeit: Friedrich Wilhelm III. der Melancholiker auf dem Thron* (Berlin: Siedler Verlag, 1920, p. 234.

61 Neil M. Heyman, "France Against Prussia: The Jena Campaign of 1806," *Military Affairs* 30, no. 4, 1966–1967, pp. 186–98; Frederic N. Maude, *The Jena Campaign 1805* (London: Swan Sonnenschein., 1909), pp. 46–47.

62 Claus Telp, *Evolution of Operational Art*, pp. 1–4, 69–97.

63 Ibid., pp. 62–63; Chandler, *Campaigns of Napoleon*, pp. 367–78; Martin van Creveld. "Napoleon and the Dawn of Operational Warfare," in *The Evolution of Operational Art: From Napoleon to the Present*, ed. John Andreas Olsen and Martin van Creveld (New York: Oxford University Press, 2011), pp. 22–29.

64 Schroeder, *Transformation of European Politics*, pp. 307–10, 383–92; Dominic Lieven. *Russia Against Napoleon: The True Story of the Campaigns of War and Peace* (New York: Viking, 2009), pp. 38–59.

65 Broers, *Europe under Napoleon*, pp. 42–47; Charles J. Esdaile, "De-Constructing the French Wars," pp. 515–52; Paul W. Schroeder, "Napoleon's Foreign Policy: A Criminal Enterprise," *Journal of Military History* 54, No. 2 (1990), pp. 147–62.

66 Weigley, *Age of Battles*, pp. 400–4; Esdaile, *Napoleon's Wars*, pp. 284–86.

67 Sutherland, *French Revolution and Empire*, pp. 361–62.

68 Broers, *Europe under Napoleon*, pp. 49–96.

69 Schroeder, *Transformation of European Politics*, pp. 383–84; Stuart Semmel, *Napoleon and the British* (New Haven, CT: Yale University Press, 2004), p. 250.

70 Schroeder, *Transformation of European Politics*, pp. 385–86; McNeill, *Pursuit of Power*, p. 202; Louis Bergeron, *France Under Napoleon*, trans. R.R. Palmer (Princeton, NJ: Princeton University Press, 1981), pp. 159–90.

71 Charles Esdaile, *The Peninsular War: A New History* (London: Penguin, 2003), pp. 37–61; Talleyrand-Périgord, Charles Maurice de, prince de Bénévent, *Memoirs of the Prince de Talleyrand*, Vol 1, ed. Albert de Broglie; trans. Raphaël Ledos de Beaufort. (New York: Putnam, 1891), pp. 291–92.

72 Esdaile, *Peninsular War*, pp. 62–108.

73 Michael Glover, *Wellington as Military Commander* (London: B.T. Batsford, 1968) pp. 33–48; Jac Weller, *On Wellington: The Duke and his Art of War* (London: Greenhill, 1998), pp. 29–46.

74 Bew, *Castlereagh: A Life*, pp. 224–26; Esdaile, *Peninsular War*, pp. 143–44, 214–16; Rory Muir, *Britain and the Defeat of Napoleon, 1807–1815* (New Haven, CT: Yale University Press, 1996), pp. 14–16, 22–23, 37–41; Charles Oman, *A History of the Peninsular War*. 2 vols. (London: Greenhill Books, 1903), II, pp. 286–311; Peter Snow, *To War with Wellington: From the Peninsula to Waterloo* (London: John Murray, 2010), pp. 9–11; Joshua Moon, *Wellington's Two-Front War: The Peninsular Campaigns at Home and Abroad* (Norman: University of Oklahoma Press, 2011), pp. 15–16, 24–25, 46–48.

75 Chandler, *Campaigns of Napoleon*, pp. 677–736; Weigley, *Age of Battles*, pp. 425–32.

76 Esdaile, *Peninsular War*, pp. 250–80; Ronald Fraser, *Napoleon's Cursed War: Popular Resistance in the Spanish Peninsular War* (London: Verso, 2008); John Lawrence Tone, *The Fatal Knot: The Guerilla War in Navarre and the Defeat of Napoleon in Spain* (Chapel Hill: University of North Carolina Press, 1994).

77 Esdaile, *Peninsular War*, pp. 499–509; Gates, pp. 304–5; M. Glover, *Wellington as Military Commander*, pp. 188–89; Marshall-Cornwall, *Napoleon as Military Commander*, pp. 216–27; Donald D. Horward. *The Battle of Bussaco: Masséna vs. Wellington* (Tallahassee: Florida State University, 1965).

78 Schroeder, *Transformation of European Politics*, pp. 416–29.

79 J. Holland Rose, *Personality of Napoleon*, p. 122.

80 Marshall-Cornwall, *Napoleon as Military Commander*, p. 227; van Creveld, *Supplying War*, pp. 61–74.

81 George F. Nafziger, *Napoleon's Invasion of Russia* (New York: Ballantine, 1988), pp. 110–11.

82 Chandler, *Campaigns of Napoleon*, pp. 790–99.

83 Ibid., pp. 794–96; Lieven, *Russia Against Napoleon*, pp. 192–95; Christopher Duffy. *Borodino and the War of 1812* (New York: Scribner, 1973), pp. 71–93.

84 Chandler, *Campaigns of Napoleon*, p. 798; Lieven, *Russia Against Napoleon*, pp. 199–200; Duffy, *Borodino and the War*, pp. 84–85; Weigley, *Age of Battles*, pp. 448–49; John G. Gallaher. *The Iron Marshal: a Biography of Louis N. Davout* (Carbondale: Southern Illinois University Press, 1976), pp. 247–49.

85 Duffy, *Borodino and the War*, p. 139.

86 Schroeder, *Transformation of European Politics*, p. 447.

87 van Creveld, *Supplying War*, pp. 61–74.

88 Muir, *Britain and the Defeat*, pp. 226–27; McNeill, *Pursuit of Power*, p. 204.

89 J. Holland Rose, *Revolutionary and Napoleonic Era*, p. 191.

90 Rainer Wohlfeil, *Spanien und die deutsche Erhebung* (Wiesbaden, Germany: Franz Steiner Verlag, 1965); Schroeder, *Transformation of European Politics*, pp. 452–53; Nipperdey, *Deutsche Geschichte, 1800–1866*, pp. 82–83; Clark, *Iron Kingdom*, pp. 358–60; Gordon A. Craig. *The Politics of the Prussian Army, 1640–1945* (New York: Oxford University Press, 1964), pp. 58–65.

91 Ian C. Robertson, *Wellington Invades France: The Final Phase of the Peninsular War, 1813–1814* (London: Greenhill, 2003), pp. 123–36; Esdaile, *Napoleon's Wars*, pp. 498–500.

92 Nipperdey, *Deutsche Geschichte, 1800–1866*, pp. 44–59.

93 Curt Jany, *Geschichte der Preußischen Armee vom. 15 Jahrhundert bis 1914*, 4 vols. (Osnabrück, Germany: 1967) Vol. 4, pp. 12–14, 40–41; Dierk Walter. *Preußische Heeresreformen 1807–1870* (Paderborn, Germany: Ferdinand Schöningh, 2003), pp. 253–57, pp. 322–24; Dennis E. Showalter. "Manifestation of Reform: The Rearmament of the Prussian Infantry, 1806–13," *Journal of Modern History* 44, No. 3 (1972), pp. 364–80; Craig, *Politics of the Prussian Army*, pp. 47–48; Clark, *Iron Kingdom*, pp. 345–87.

94 van Creveld, "Napoleon and the Dawn," p. 38.

95 Manfried Rauchensteiner, *Kaiser Franz und Erzherzog Carl: Dynastie und Heerwesen in Österreich, 1796–1809* (Munich: R. Oldenbourg Verlag, 1972, pp. 58–110.

96 Esdaile, *Napoleon's Wars*, pp. 500–1; Schroeder, *Transformtion of European Politics*, pp. 458–59.

97 Englund, *Napoleon: A Political Life*, p. 393.

98 Scott Bowden, *Napoleon's Grande Armée of 1813* (Chicago: Emperor's Press, 1990), pp. 204–6.

99 Dennis Showalter, "Prussian-German Operational Art, 1740–1943," in *The Evolution of Operational Art: From Napoleon to the Present*, ed. John Andreas Olsen and Martin van Creveld (New York: Oxford University Press, 2011), p. 38.

100 Chandler, *Campaigns of Napoleon*, pp. 882–87; Weigley, *Age of Battles*, pp. 464–65.

101 Weigley, *Age of Battles*, pp. 476–81, Chandler, *Campaigns of Napoleon*, pp. 912–22; Archer Jones, *The Art of War in the Western World* (Urbana: University of Illinois Press, 2001), p. 356.

102 Weigley, *Age of Battles*, pp. 483–512; J. Holland Rose, *Revolutionary and Napoleonic Era*, pp. 288–92.

103 Schroeder, *Transformation of European Politics*, pp. 496–97.

104 J. Holland Rose, *Revolutionary and Napoleonic Era*, pp. 303–4; Sudhir Hazareesingh, *The Legend of Napoleon* (London: Granta, 2004); Theodore Zeldin, *France 1848–1945: Politics and Anger* (New York: Oxford University Press, 1979), pp. 140–205.

105 Schroeder, *Transformation of European Politics*, pp. 501–5; Henry Kissinger, *A World Restored: Metternich, Castlereagh and the Problems of Peace, 1812–1822* (London Weidenfeld & Nicolson, 1957), pp. 131–32; Gregor Dallas, *The Final Act: The Roads to Waterloo* (New York: Henry Holt, 1996), pp. 47–64.

106 Lawday, *Napoleon's Master*, pp. 272–75; Schroeder, *Transformation of European Politics*, pp. 529–30.

107 Lawrence James, *The Iron Duke: A Military Biography of Wellington* (London: Weidenfeld & Nicolson, 1992), p. 241.

108 Schroeder, *Transformation of European Politics*, pp. 550–53.

109 Chandler, *Campaigns of Napoleon*, p. 1016; Marshall-Cornwall, *Napoleon as Military Commander*, p. 264.

110 Chandler, *Campaigns of Napoleon*, pp. 1020–29; Weigley, *Age of Battles*, pp. 516–17; M. Glover, *Wellington as Military Commander*, pp. 193–97; Andrew Roberts. *Waterloo: Napoleon's Last Gamble* (New York: Harper Perennial, 2005), pp. 38–39.

111 Chandler, *Campaigns of Napoleon*, pp. 1031–32; M. Glover, *Wellington as Military Commander*, pp. 196–97.

112 Chandler, *Campaigns of Napoleon*, pp. 1057–58. See also Weigley, *Age of Battles*, pp. 535–535; Peter Hofschröer. *1815, The Waterloo Campaign: The German Victory* (London: Greenhill Books, 1999).

113 Chandler, *Campaigns of Napoleon*, pp. 1064–66; M. Glover, *Wellington as Military Commander*, pp. 200–3; John Keegan, *The Face of Battle* (London: Jonathan Cape, 1976), pp. 122–23.

114 Chandler, *Campaigns of Napoleon*, pp. 1058–72; Marshall-Cornwall, *Napoleon as Military Commander*, pp. 273–76; Weigley, *Age of Battles*, pp. 526–27.

115 William Siborne, *The Waterloo Campaign, 1815* (Westminster, UK: Archibald Constable, 1900), p. 353; M. Glover, *Wellington as Military Commander*, p. 201.

116 Roberts, *Waterloo: Napoleon's Last Gamble*, pp. 52–53; Weigley, *Age of Battles*, p. 529.

117 Siborne, *Waterloo Campaign*, pp. 443–46; Roberts, *Waterloo: Napoleon's Last Gamble*, pp. 92–94; Weigley, *Age of Battles*, pp. 530–31.

118 Most notable among them: Brendan Simms, *The Longest Afternoon* (New York: Basic Books, 2015); Gregory Fremont-Barnes, *1815: The British Army's Day of Destiny* (Stroud, UK: History Press, 2014); Gordon Corrigan, *Waterloo: A New History of the Battle and its Armies* (London: Atlantic Books, 2014); Gareth Glover, *Waterloo: Myth and Reality* (Barnsley, UK: Pen & Sword Books, 2014); Paul O'Keefe, *Waterloo, The Aftermath* (New York: Overlook Press, 2014).

119 Charles Esdaile, "The Battle of Waterloo in Bicentennial: A Review of Seven Books on Waterloo," *British Journal of Military History* 1, no. 3 (2015), pp. 157–58.

120 MacGregor Knox. "Conclusion: Continuity and Revolution in the Making of Strategy," in *The Making of Strategy: Rulers, States, and War*, ed. Williamson Murray, MacGregor Knox, and Alvin Bernstein (New York: Cambridge University Press, 2009), p. 616.

121 Bew, *Castlereagh: A Life*, pp. 576–87; Schroeder, *Transformation of European Politics*, pp. 458, 557–58, 580–82; Muir, *Britain and the Defeat*, pp. 334–42; H.M. Scott, *The Birth of a Great Power System, 1740–1815* (London: Pearson, 2006), pp. 354–57; B.H. Liddell Hart. *Strategy* (New York: Meridian, 1991), pp. 353–60.

122 Rodger, *Command of the Ocean*, pp. 578–81; P.J. Cain and A.G. Hopkins, *British Imperialism, 1688–2000* (London: Longman, 1993) pp. 76–81.
123 Paul Kennedy, *The Rise and Fall of British Naval Mastery* (New York: Prometheus, 1976), pp. 154–155; Philip A. Crowl, "Alfred Thayer Mahan: The Naval Historian," in *Makers of Modern Strategy from Machiavelli to the Nuclear Age*, ed. Peter Paret (Princeton, NJ: Princeton University Press, 1986), pp. 444–77.
124 Broers, *Europe Under Napoleon*, pp. 49–96; Finer, *History of Government*, vol. 3, pp. 1562–66.
125 Finer, *History of Government*, Vol. 3, p. 1560; Englund, *Napoleon: A Political Life*, p. 462; Hazareesingh, p. 260–268; Zeldin, pp. 140–205; Paul Johnson, *Napoleon* (New York: Penguin, 2002), pp. 182–87.
126 Quoted in Raymond Horricks, *Marshal Ney, The Romance and the Real* (London: Archway, 1982), p. 197; Hughes, pp. 110–35.
127 Martin van Creveld, "Napoleon and the Dawn of Operational Warfare," pp. 29–30; Robert M. Epstein, *Napoleon's Last Victory and the Emergence of Modern War* (Lawrence: University of Kansas Press, 1994), pp. 171–77; Gunther E. Rothenberg, *The Art of Warfare in the Age of Napoleon* (Bloomington: Indiana University Press, 1978), pp. 170–73.
128 Herfried Münkler, *Im Namen des Staates – Die Begründung der Staatsraison in der Frühen Neuzeit* (Frankfurt am Main: S. Fischer Verlag, 1987), p. 326.
129 Dennis E. Showalter, "Prussian-German Operational Art, 1740–1943," in John Andreas Olsen and Martin van Creveld, eds., *The Evolution of Operational Art: From Napoleon to the Present* (New York: Oxford University Press, 2011), p. 38.
130 Weigley, *Age of Battles*, p. 398; Nipperdey, *Deutsche Geschichte, 1800–1866*, pp. 31–82; Simms, *The Impact of Napoleon*, pp. 338–43; Craig, pp. 34–42.
131 Craig, pp. 59–69; Strachan, *European Armies*, pp. 57–58.
132 Gat, *History of Military Thought*, pp. 238–46; Beatrice Heuser, *The Evolution of Strategy: Thinking War from Antiquity to the Present* (New York: Cambridge University Press, 2010), pp. 113–36.
133 Peter Paret, *Clausewitz and the State: The Man, His Theories, and His Times* (Princeton, NJ: Princeton University Press, 1985), p. 166.
134 James Q. Whitman, *The Verdict of Battle: The Law of Victory and the Making of Modern War* (Cambridge, MA: Harvard University Press, 2012), p. 251.

2 Far-distant aggression
Anglo-French expeditionary warfare

Clausewitz's interpretation of Napoleonic warfare, along with Jomini's critique of it, emerged only slowly as influential strains of military thought in Europe and beyond. The overriding concern of Clausewitz's thought—the vitality, stability, and power of the state—was a concern shared by Prussian and other European reformers and quickened by Clausewitz's insights. These were not published in coherent and comprehensive form until 1832, and until 1871 Clausewitz was seldom read outside Prussia. Thereafter, Prussia's victory over France and the translation of *Vom Kriege* into *On War* gave the book its prominence among military professionals.[1]

In the meantime, the nineteenth century witnessed an incremental reduction in Anglo-French antagonism. The two Western European powers remained rivals in overseas colonial expansion but only intermittently came into conflict and were more usually diverted to separate imperial vocations until they converged in common cause against Tsarist Russia in the 1850s.

The military dimension of colonialism exerted little influence on the evolution of military thought in Europe, and even the scholarship that takes due note of this fact tends to lay stress on colonial warfare in the second half of the nineteenth century.[2] At mid-century Britain and France were nonetheless involved in colonial wars in Northern Africa and Central Asia of significant political, military, and strategic consequence. In these, as in the Crimean War, Clausewitz's dictum that war amounts *to the continuation of political discourse by other means* is immeasurably useful in appreciating the political mediation of wars prosecuted far from home.

The variable commitment to distant wars exerted profound impact on the outcome and strategic dividend paid to France in Algeria and Britain on the frontier of India. Fighting in coalition against Russia in the Crimea in a fashion made possible by the fruits of advanced industry, the two powers then demonstrated the superiority of Western European arms and operations over Russia, yet also displayed an extraordinary ignorance of the potential cost of what they had undertaken. The Crimean War featured all the problems of divided command in military alliances. Equally, different national motivations in going to war with Russia, in which the military defeat of its armies was one among a number of impulses, in the course of the conflict influenced national perspectives of its strategic benefit following the armistice.

A desert named peace:[3] The French conquest of Algeria

France, for example, perceived a political and operational connection between the Napoleonic occupation of Spain after 1807 and the establishment of colonial rule in Northern Africa beginning in 1830. The Peninsular War begat the use of the term *la guerrilla* referring to the struggle of irregulars practicing harassment and sabotage of the Napoleonic army—*guerrilleros* being the appropriate Spanish term for the fighters themselves. Romanticised as the champions of a "people's war" against foreign occupation, they were notorious for extraordinary cruelty to the French soldiers they captured and were blamed by the victims of the harsh French reprisals that ensued. A related vocabulary of insurgency had been coined by the Revolution, beginning with Louis Lazare Hoche, who commanded the efforts to defeat counter-revolutionary revolts in the Vendée and drafted a seventeen-page instruction manual based on his experiences.[4] Adolphe Thiers, later the father of the Third Republic, applied the term *insurgent* in his history of the French Revolution to any rebellious entity, referring throughout to "insurgent provinces" but also labelling as "insurgents" those who rebelled against the National Convention of the 13 Vendémiaire and were later torn up by Napoleon's grapeshot.[5]

As France's minister of the interior in 1835, Thiers prevailed upon his government to intervene militarily on behalf of the constitutional right of Isabel II to the throne against the Carlist revolt in Spain, which was led by the staunch royalist and Catholic faction of the Spanish court seeking to counter liberal and anticlerical influences.[6] Thiers viewed French intervention as a form of diplomacy, a service to European stability with which France could begin to rehabilitate its legitimacy among the major powers. France's minister of war, Nicolas Soult, was a veteran of the Peninsular War and saw only another endless and ugly struggle with Spanish peasantry. The compromise settled upon was to intervene without invading, to deploy to Spain the *Légion étrangère*, newly created in 1830. The Foreign Legion's foremost historian explains how the force suited the both the circumstance of 1835 and any number of unknown contingencies of the future:

> By sending the Legion, France could affirm diplomatic support short of a binding commitment. If things turned sour in Spain, Paris would not confront the difficult problem of extracting her forces while at the same time struggling to save face, for, after all, wars are often easier begun than terminated. Once France turned over the Legion, its fate would be in Madrid's hands. For its part Isabel's government may have preferred French support to come in the form of regular regiments. But this simply was not realistic given the political situation in Paris. And

besides, the Legion offered tangible evidence of French interest, with no strings attached. A substantial commitment of French forces most certainly would have required French interference in the political and military affairs of Spain. But the Legion was a different matter—it was a gift, a disposable item, and so appealing to the politicians and diplomats precisely because it was expendable.[7]

The Legion's utility as a military force to be "placed between politics, diplomacy and the cannon,"[8] made it ideal for deployment overseas in theatres of conflict deemed of secondary importance though significant interest. It was therefore in Algeria, France's most consequential colonial acquisition of the nineteenth century that the Legion found its spiritual home in the mission that shaped its character—and that of all French army forces overseas—for the next century.[9]

France's initial seizure of the Algerian coast in 1830 in no way testified to an appetite for a permanent presence. And yet Algeria became an obsessive colonial project that the shifting shoals of French domestic politics in the mid-nineteenth century did not reverse. The national commitment to it waxed and wavered but mostly intensified, and the army became the principal agent of this process. Throughout, French forces struggled with the logistical problems encountered by all European armies deployed at great distance from their homeland and developed many practices for campaigning against nature as much as against an armed enemy.[10] France had lost many of its old pre-revolutionary overseas colonies to Britain in 1815, and Algeria was an early acquisition of the new colonial empire. Whereas the seventeenth- and eighteenth-century empires had been traders' and settlers' empires, the nineteenth-century empire was one of military men and missionaries.[11]

Algiers had been a tributary of the Ottoman Empire since Süleyman I consolidated the command of Muslim pirates and the Ottoman navy under the pirate leader Hayrettin as Grand Admiral in 1533. In 1827 French debts incurred by the Revolutionary regime to the merchants of Algiers for grain shipments to France's armies were the source of a diplomatic incident in which the dey of Algiers struck the French consul with his fly-whisk and later destroyed trading posts at Bastion de France. When Charles X attempted conciliation through an emissary and Algerian ships fired upon the emissary's ship after failed negotiations, Charles shifted to a belligerent stance in the name of a national honour but in pursuit of public approval to redeem the prestige of his flagging regime.[12] His prime minister, Jules de Polignac, sent an expeditionary force of 635 ships, some 34,000 troops and 3,400 non-combatants to whom Algiers fell in July 1830. Polignac's ministry expressed its willingness to return Algiers to Ottoman control in exchange for an increase in French territory elsewhere, but the commander of the French forces in Algiers, General Louis-Auguste de Bourmont, sought to force his government's hand by declaring that his army had come to drive out the Turks and had no intention of returning Algiers to Ottoman tyranny.[13] Algeria thus became the first war of many in the evolution of French "military imperialism" in Africa.

De Bourmont was relieved of the Algerian command when Charles was ousted in the July Revolution of 1830 that brought Louis-Philippe to power, yet Polignac's successor, Casimir Périer, asserted that France would extend its occupation to the whole of the regency. Delay in the implementation of this plan until a French governor-general could be installed in July 1834 then subjected the hinterland beyond Algiers to period of anarchy.[14] Bourmont's successor, Bertrand Clauzel, was ordered to reduce the cost of the expeditionary force and to absorb a cut of its total strength to 10,000 men. Uncertain about whether he meant to make the occupation permanent, Louis-Philippe dithered, and Clauzel made local decisions by default. In response to his manpower dilemma he raised new units locally from Berbers of the Zouaoua tribe in the Djurajura country south-east of Algiers, later named *Zouaves*, and in 1831 organised the *Chasseurs d'Afrique* with volunteers from the French settlers and metropolitan France. All three of the new military units—the Legion, *Zouaves*, and *Chasseurs*—suffered from discipline problems in the early phases of the Algerian mission, as the priority of getting undesirables out of France or inducting potential insurgents into French service merely mixed them all together in the colonial army.[15] Still, Clauzel's reorganisations established the foundation of the future *Armée d'Afrique*, and many were later applied to other regions of the French domain in Northern Africa.[16]

The next noteworthy *commandant en chef*, General Savary, Duc de Rovigo, routinely applied a measure of humiliation in the day-to-day policing of the townspeople of Algiers, ordered summary executions on the slimmest of incriminating evidence, and indulged brutality to its absolute in the extermination of the small el Ouffia tribe near Maison Carrée.[17] Under Colonel Michel Combe, an early commander who innovated light infantry tactics, the Legion was put to work on engineering and construction works in the area around Algiers. This work was accompanied by small actions in which the Legion began to learn the art of colonial warfare. But the learning curve was initially very steep and the Legion a victim of defeats bred both of incompetence and the listless course of French policy.[18] That policy produced successors to Rovigo, including the return of Clauzel, but none were equal to the Algerian resistance, now increasingly united and competently led by the charismatic Abd el-Qadr, who organised the tribes of western Algeria and began a campaign of harassment of French forces, from which he emerged triumphant in a number of small engagements. The Scottish poet Thomas Campbell, who visited Algeria in 1837, noted that el-Qadr had achieved mythic status among his people[19] of the kind perilous to France's hold on the country.

Not until Marshal Thomas-Robert Bugeaud arrived in 1836 and served as governor after 1840 was the military effort in Algeria overhauled to meet this challenge. A veteran of the Peninsular War, where he had developed techniques of counter-insurgency,[20] Bugeaud was a archetypical figure both of political conservatism and French militarism in the nineteenth century. He was elected to the Chamber of Deputies in 1831 and was nonetheless an implacable foe of France's democratic tradition, made infamous in Paris for his repression of the insurrection of 1834. Concern for France's domestic social peace and political cohesion had initially led Bugeaud to oppose military ventures abroad. This was reinforced by awareness that France's geography deprived it of Britain's luxury of maintaining only a small standing army and the conviction that 500,000 men would be needed to defend the country against threats from beyond its Rhenish frontier.[21] Yet Bugeaud invariably responded to any assignment with ferocious energy. By 1837 he had concluded that Algeria might be a useful training theatre for the French army while continuing to offer appropriate exile for radicals disrupting the domestic tranquility of the metropole. Although his conscience told him that the Algerian venture was a mistake, the military professional in him saw three practical options going forward: withdrawal, the control of Algeria's coastline, or conquest of the interior. The challenge alone drove him to recommend the third option. He informed the government that the Algerian war would be interminable unless and until France committed forces sufficient to "strike at the morale of the Arab everywhere."[22] If Bugeaud was to complete a mission he deemed peripheral to the national interest, he was determined that Algeria should benefit the army even if the army could not benefit Algeria.

Bugeaud's first order of business was the improvement of the morale of troops fighting both an implacable enemy and the rigors of the desert, which, Campbell reported, involved "more than one instance of the infantry soldier, driven to madness by thirst and agony, putting his head to the mouth of his musket, and his foot to the trigger, and committing suicide."[23] Additionally, Bugeaud found the army to be repeating the errors of the Peninsular War, involving the defence of fixed points and the burdening of troop columns with artillery and convoys of supplies. Concentrating his reforms on mobility, morale, leadership, and firepower, he stressed that only the vigorous application of unconventional tactics could recover the initiative and take the fight to el-Qadr's insurgents:

> In place of fortifications, which had been the principal French method of controlling the countryside, he emphasized the value of scouting parties and intelligence reports in locating enemy forces against which troops could be readily deployed. Mobile columns numbering from a few hundred to a few thousand men, shorn of artillery and heavy wagons, could fan out over the countryside to converge from different directions on a previously selected objective. In this way, Bugeaud was able to penetrate into areas that had been immune to attack, carry the fight into the very heart of the Kabylia Mountains, and give his enemies no rest.[24]

Action and initiative answered both the problem of morale and the challenge of the insurgency. In large part a decision to adopt the tactics of the insurgents in defeating them, these methods made Bugeaud a master of irregular warfare and generated principles and methods that were to characterise colonial campaigning ever after.[25] At their core in Algeria was the practice of raiding adapted from the *razzia* or *ghaziya* employed by pre-Islamic Bedouin for the seizure of livestock or goods from rival tribes. Bugeaud developed surprise attacks in overwhelming force against lightly defended settlements into a doctrine of devastation against tribal sustenance—involving burnt villages, blackened fields, and ravaged orchards—to crush the inurgents' will to resistance.[26] Integral to the legitimacy of such methods was the argument that they were the invention, after all, of the Algerians themselves and adapted by Bugeaud to fight in a grammar they would understand. General Eugène Daumas, who served with Bugeaud, observed dryly that "the most frequent and almost daily deed in Arab life is the *razzia*,"[27] versions of which he described in detail before ending with the summation that "these *razzias*, most of the time, turn into shocking carnages."[28] Under Bugeaud the *razzia* achieved a new order of shock altogether. Once unleashed, discipline among soldiers waging war on silos, cattle, sheep, and women was often so difficult to maintain that a *razzia* could easily degenerate into an orgy of excess. For Bugeaud the risk was justified, as any sign of indecision or weakness in Algeria would be fatal to France's dominion there. His successes in Algeria ultimately earned Bugeaud and Algeria large entries in C.E. Calwell's primer on colonial warfare, published in 1906.[29]

The influence Bugeaud exerted on his government with this reasoning was enhanced by victory in a pitched battle in the European style. This he accomplished in August 1844 at the Isly River, when his advancing army threatened Abd el-Qadr's sanctuary in Morocco. Although France's foreign minister, François Guizot, had issued an ultimatum to Morocco that the Algerian leader be ejected from its territory while French warships bombarded Tangier and Mogador to underscore the point, Bugeaud stampeded events on land by advancing a small army westward toward the Moroccan frontier and was attacked by Moroccan cavalry from every direction. Cool heads in the French ranks prevailed, so that that a disciplined defence by 8,500 infantry and 1,200 cavalry infantry routed a combined Algerian-Moroccan force of some 45,000. Bugeaud called the victory "the consecration of our Algerian conquest" and his own consecration in France followed hotly upon it. Louis-Philippe elevated him to the Duc d'Isly, launching a binge of national celebration that climaxed with Bugeaud's address to the Chamber of Deputies in January 1845. For the arousal of Parisian audiences Hector Berlioz orchestrated two piano compositions by the Austrian pianist Leopold De Meyer, the *Marche marocaine* and the *Marche d'Isly*, that subsequently were taken on tour to foreign cities as an act of musical public relations for French imperialism.[30] Horace Vernet immortalised Isly in oil on canvas in 1846. A policy that France's soldiers in Algeria had done as much to articulate as its foreign minister was thus promptly woven into the tapestry of national greatness.

The prestige of Isly encouraged Bugeaud to speak often and forcefully about that policy, especially as new rebellions occasioned repeated application of "cruel necessity" repugnant to metropolitan France. Less than a year after Isly a revolt among the Kabyle tribes of the Dahra Mountains led to a *razzia* under the command by Colonel Amable Pélissier, resulting in the unnecessary murder of some five hundred men, women, and children. When news of the horror reached Paris, parliamentary fury ensued. Although Bugeaud had not ordered the atrocity, he noted that any punishment for it should fall upon himself and offered that the "philanthropic" instincts of the deputies blurred their appreciation of the reality of Algeria. Although Bugeaud sought commerce and trade for the colony, he advocated a special role for the military—habituated to the extremes of climate and hardened to the requirements of maintaining order—likening the civilian population of the Algerian coast to badly reared children. Bugeaud added that the assimilation of Algerians to French rule, a project that would take many years to "weaken that spirit of revolt which has animated them under all their leaders," made it good policy to replace all the Arab chiefs with French officers.[31] Bugeaud reminded the Chamber of Deputies that he had personally opposed the possession of Algiers, but warned that those who sought the ends must not shrink from the means. If the national conscience required the salve of historical allusion, Bugeaud was prepared to compare his campaign to the Roman conquest of Northern Africa and hail it as the recovery of Latin civilisation in the Mediterranean.[32] His defence of the army referred explicitly to its central role in Algeria and awarded it a capacity to define the national interest as responsibly as any civilian authority. The civilian sensibilities of the deputies he usually countered with derision, and such reforms to increase civilian authority as were forced upon him he implemented only haphazardly.[33]

France thus permitted the military to set the terms and tone of its colonial policy to an unusual extent. This policy originated in Algeria and under Bugeaud first reached a stage in which the French army operated as a semi-autonomous force, officially subordinate to, yet practically independent of, metropolitan France. In Algeria the army laid the foundation of colonial administration and staffed its positions, excluding civilians from meaningful participation in political affairs.[34] Service in Algeria afforded officers both supplements to their pay and more varied opportunity for distinction and promotion than the tedious climb through the seniority system. The experience shaped two generations of officers not only in the methods colonial warfare, for which the *razzia* formed the core, but also in their more general outlook on war and the army's relationship to the state:

They were supremely confident of their military capacities and convinced they alone knew how to wage war. They had a profound suspicion of anything that smacked of military science. For civilians they felt nothing but contempt. Through them this mystique came to pervade the whole Army, ultimately with terrible consequences; most of the Generals who showed themselves so lamentably ignorant of modern warfare in 1870 were graduates of the Algerian school.[35]

France colonised Algeria in four stages. Between 1830 and 1839 it occupied the urban centres and their hinterlands. In the second phase, from 1840 and 1847, the colonial army extended the conquest inland to the fertile plains of the Tell in northern Algeria. This seventeen-year period witnessed the struggle with Abd el-Qadr. The third and fourth stages, from 1848 to 1872 and from 1873 to 1954 respectively, involved the subjugation of the mountain communities of the Tell and thereafter of the oasis communities and pastoral nomads of the Sahara.[36] The culture of military imperialism was carried from Algeria to later conquests in West Africa, especially the Western Sudan. The great irony is that the imperialism of the Restoration, July Monarchy, and Second Empire was often hesitant and opportunistic, whereas that of the Third Republic after 1871 was a more determined enterprise driven by intensifying competition from other European powers. Part of the explanation for this is that for metropolitan France, Algeria ranked low among political priorities, while for the army it had become uppermost. Another part of the explanation is that the government in Paris, monarchy or republic, largely accepted the army's definition of the national interest.

Eventually, the Third Republic was to experience heightened conflict between civil and military authority that climaxed at the end of the nineteenth century in the Dreyfus Affair, yet it actually afforded the military wide latitude in colonial matters that only deepened the army's sense of entitlement. The idea of a commercial presence in the Western Sudan in which the size of the territorial expanse was a secondary concern to economic benefit gave way to the priority of seizing territory that might otherwise be lost to British penetration when imperial competition in Africa intensified starting in the 1880s. Because the French military in Africa experienced less supervision from Paris whenever engaged in military operations, it could enhance its immunity to civilian control by remaining hyperactive. The conquest of ever-greater territory therefore became a goal of itself, regardless of the economic dividend, or cost, to France. Military administration did little to alter, much less improve, the economic foundation of the Sudan, and may have hastened its decline. French imperialism in Africa was military imperialism, therefore, because it benefited primarily the military conquerors. "Not so much by being French as by being military" the Third Republic's imperialism "gave France title to territories more impressive for their size than for their wealth," and the French army secured for itself in Africa a sanctuary where it was its own sovereign.[37]

It is a measure of the spell of imperialism over the national imagination that an intellect as acute as that of Alexis de Tocqueville's was drawn to it.

During a visit to Algeria in 1841, he interviewed a French colonel who was happy to relate the details of a *razzia* in which he had participated, including his interrogation and execution of an Arab suspect brought before him and whose severed head was on public display. De Tocqueville found the colonel's casualness about the episode deeply upsetting and wondered at the fate of a country at the mercy of such men, yet his biographer notes that he "could not or would not make the inferences which leap to the modern eye."[38] Although he found much otherwise to criticise in the French government, the Algerian venture spoke both to his national pride and a deep envy of the British Empire. He held to Pericles' formula that an empire is held by force; though it have been wrong to take it, "it is certainly dangerous to let it go."[39] Algeria demonstrates that the spirit of France at mid-century was predominantly Bonapartist, the most powerful interest group of the state and society being the swords around the throne.[40]

For Britain in the 1830s, rivalry with Russia over Central Asia led indirectly to a disastrous military intervention in Afghanistan that has instructive similarities and dissimilarities to the French experience in Algeria. An important difference in national context is that France in the mid-nineteenth century was sufficiently insecure about its status in Europe as to afford the army a disproportionate role in politics and policy, whereas Britain's fundamental confidence in its international preeminence afforded its army no such role and was often perilously casual about the policy and resources it applied to the defence of the Empire.

The Army of the Indus

In the case of British India, much of the effort was shouldered by a private chartered enterprise, the East India Company. In the serial wars of the Company against the Maratha Confederacy of south-central India many British officers received their education in combat, the Duke of Wellington being the most celebrated among them. The general rule for Company soldiers was that they served, like the French Foreign Legion, one step removed from their government and fought some of Britain's dirtiest wars in the Company's interest but in Britain's name, so that any government in Westminster retained the prerogative to intervene in their activities.[41] Because Britain was primarily a naval power, furthermore, its army was clearly the subordinate of its service branches and enjoyed little of the lobby leverage of its French counterpart.

The First Anglo-Afghan War of 1838–1842 illustrates the costs that this status entailed, especially when the strategic reasoning behind the use of armed force far from home bases was uncertain. Britain found no cause to covet Afghanistan as France coveted Algeria; the country's value was purely derivative of its proximity to India, an overseas possession vital to the global system of commerce Britain sought to consolidate and expand following the Napoleonic Wars. As with France in Algeria, Ottoman decline was a factor drawing Britain into Afghanistan. In the 1820s, Russian penetration of the territory from the Kazakh Khanates to the north and west of India posed the hypothesis of incursions into Persia and Afghanistan. A Tsarist presence in the lands west of the Indus River threatened, in the worst scenario, either a military campaign across Afghanistan against the Indian frontier or an attempt to cultivate rebellion among Indian princes under British rule. Russian victories over Persia in 1826 and Ottoman Turkey in 1829 heightened this concern, felt most acutely by Company officialdom in India.[42]

The international horizon surveyed from London linked Britain's European diplomacy to the goal of supporting the Ottoman Empire as an obstacle to Russian expansion into the swath of territory between the Bosporus Strait and India's northwest frontier. In the 1850s Ottoman weakness in the face of Russian pressure prompted a costly Anglo-French military intervention in the Crimea, but in the 1830s British policy in India was by contrast to "maintain an ill-defined paramountcy over a vast area at little or no cost to the metropolis."[43] Two attempts at establishing commercial relations with Persia, directly to the west of Afghanistan, were ventured in pursuit of this objective. When they failed and Persian forces laid siege to the city of Herat in western Afghanistan with Russian encouragement, British policy shifted toward making Afghanistan a buffer against Russo-Persian encroachment.[44]

George Eden, the Earl of Auckland and British governor-general of India from 1835, initially expressed interest in Afghanistan both as "outwork" to India and as a target for expanded commerce along the Indus through Sind and the Punjab to Kabul.[45] Yet he chose military preemption over commercial penetration and, with the encouragement of his political secretary, William Macnaghten, developed a plan to topple the reigning Khan in Kabul in favour of a regime friendly toward Britain. For this scheme Auckland sought support from the Melbourne government in London and received it in particularly robust form from its foreign secretary, Henry Temple (Lord Palmerston), and John Hobhouse, president for the Board of Control for India. This quartet—Auckland and Macnaghten in India, Palmerston and Hobhouse in London—saw to it that a corner on the broad canvass of Britain's empire was momentarily given a priority by Whitehall and Westminster greater than sober thought could justify.[46]

Russophobia, a neurosis based as much on revulsion at the Tsarist regime itself as on Russian competition in Central Asia, united British politicians of all persuasions, not least of all because Palmerston was so skilled in its public articulation with a mixture of liberal principle and imperial interest. A Russian threat to India was just plausible enough to make Afghanistan the theatre for a demonstration of national will, yet not urgent enough to move the various impulses behind it toward a policy for achieving something durable.[47] Hobhouse sought the annexation of Sind and the Punjab to British India in principle, professing to be convinced that a Russian invasion was imminent and advising Palmerston at one point that unless Britain was prepared for a great struggle in Central Asia "we had better quit the field, and await for the attack, which will assuredly not long be delayed, upon our Indian frontier."[48] As the theatre for a show of strength, Afghanistan had a political advantage; action in Persia would require some financial commitment from the home government and entail close scrutiny by parliament, whereas a campaign in Afghanistan financed by the East India Company would not attract equivalent attention.[49]

The target of this line of calculation, Dost Muhammad Khan, had opposed previous British attempts to place Shah Shuja-ul-Mulk on the Afghan throne and by 1824 had managed to put himself in power in Kabul. In 1837 he defeated Ranjit Singh (1780–1839), the Sikh ruler of the Punjab, in battle at Jamrud but was unable to stop Ranjit's annexation of Peshawar. Consequently, British policy now looked to an alliance with Ranjit Singh and its extension into a tripartite pact to include Shah Shuja. The Treaty of Simla, signed in June 1838 by Shah Shuja and Ranjit Singh under British auspices in the person of Macnaghten, settled or compensated outstanding claims among the three parties and formed the diplomatic basis for the Simla Manifesto. In substance the manifesto was a declaration of war against Dost Muhammad, an enemy of Ranjit Singh and Britain, on behalf of Shah Shuja's claim to the Afghan throne. The manifesto made no mention of Russia yet was nonetheless the "first military card" of what came be known in history and fiction as the Great Game.[50]

That it turned out to be a weak suit and a calamity for British arms was the product of three factors. The first was political: the choice of Shah Shuja for the throne in Kabul. Shah Shuja had been allied since 1833 with Ranjit Singh in his effort to regain the throne; because the Sikhs had been acquiring parcels of Afghan territory since 1813, the pact of 1833 could be interpreted by as a charter for Sikh territorial aspirations, with Shah Shuja as its stooge and the British Empire its sponsor.[51] A second factor was also political, the fall of Melbourne's ministry in August 1841 in favour of a Tory cabinet headed by Sir Robert Peel. Prior to the change of government, the Tory critic of Melbourne's India policy, Edward Law, Lord Ellenborough, had in March 1839 demanded papers leading up to the decision for war and moved quickly to the preliminary conclusion that the expedition was folly while reserving judgement, pending the perusal of more papers, as to whether it constituted a crime.[52] When Peel's government took over responsibility for a venture the new prime minister deemed "the most absurd and insane project that was ever undertaken in the wantonness of power," the expedition was deprived of the support of those who had conceived it. The final factor was military. The Army of the Indus, the expeditionary force tasked to oust Dost Muhammad, was poorly constituted and badly led. Under the command of Sir John Keane, it was composed of troops from Bengal, Bombay, and Shah Shuja's army of 6,000 mercenaries.

The operational complexity of the Afghan mission compounded these flaws of its conception. The Bombay force of 5,600 men travelled by ship from the coast of Sind to the port of Karachi at the mouth of Indus, from which it proceeded upstream by boat. The 9,600-strong Bengal army assembled at Ferozepore. In the tradition of all Indian armies on the move, Keane's command had a long wake of camp followers and servants sustained by a baggage train; indeed, the Army of the Indus was exceptionally swollen, initially accompanied by some 38,000 Indian servants and 30,000 transport camels.[53] On December 10, 1838, the Bengal force began a circuitous march of 850 miles from Ferozepore to Kandahar. The Bombay force moving north while the Bengal army marched south-west, the two converged at Shikarpore. This plan, argues Fortescue's *History of the British Army*, wins the "palm of imbecility," for "if we imagine a German army marching through France to the invasion of Spain, and effecting, north of the Pyrenees, a junction with a weak force landed at the mouth of the Adour, we can take some measure of the enterprise."[54] From Shikarpore the combined force proceeded northwest through the Bolan Pass to Quetta. This route was taken because the Sikh leader, Ranjit Singh, had not only declined to participate in the expedition but had also refused passage for the Army of the Indus through the Punjab, thereby forcing the army to detour through Sind to the south and thence north-east through Baluchistan to Kandahar and north again to Kabul.

At Quetta the army faced a supply-and-command crisis. Local Baluchi tribesman viewed the British columns, with their provisions and livestock, as a godsend to be plundered. There was friction between Keane and Major General William Nott, whom Keane overlooked for command of the Bombay division, despite Nott's seniority, in favour of Major General Thomas Willshire. Nott was an able and aggressive soldier, and Keane's decision was to have serious consequences.[55] Keane's advance on Kandahar witnessed a slow bleed of his army's strength, principally through the want of forage and the predations of the tribesmen. The army's artillery horses began to collapse from daytime heat and were shot where they fell on the line of march, but the greatest sufferers were the camels, of which some 20,000 perished.[56]

The army first encountered frontal resistance to its advance at the fortress of Ghazni, some 320 miles further along the road to Kabul. After Keane determined that the his six- and nine-inch artillery would not suffice to reduce its walls—he had left his 18-inch guns behind in Kandahar—he ordered the fortress taken by storm in a night action that produced scenes worthy of Hieronymus Bosch, of the "dead and dying, both Europeans and natives, were lying in heaps amidst the smoking ruins of the gateway" of animals "galloping wild in every direction, fighting, kicking and plunging over each other.[57] When Dost Muhammad heard the news, he prepared to come to terms with the conquerors. Offered honourable asylum in India, he declined in favour of a retreat from Kabul first to Urgundeh and then to the hill country of Bamian. Keane's force advanced on Kabul, arriving on August 6, 1839. The next day Shah Shuja entered the city at the head of a great martial spectacle that wended its way to the gates of the Bala Hissar.

If the pageant aroused no fervour from his restored subjects,[58] the Army of the Indus could at least congratulate itself on achieving its stated objective.

From this point very little went well. Willshire left Kabul with the Bombay division on September 18 with orders to punish Mehrab Khan of Kalat on his march southward. Keane ordered Nott to put his troops at Willshire's disposal if and when they were needed. Nott flatly refused to obey any orders issued by Willshire and presented his superiors with mutinous behaviour at a time when Auckland had intended to place him in command in Kabul in the place of Sir Willoughby Cotton, once Keane had returned to India. Instead, Cotton would now have to remain in command in Kabul. The most thorough scholarly treatment of the war to date speculates that "it might be argued that the whole course of events in Afghanistan in 1840 and 1841 would have been different if Nott had taken command at the end of 1839."[59] After a skirmish with a brigade under Major General Sir Robert Sale at Parwan Durrah Dost, Muhammad rode into Kabul and surrendered personally to Macnaghten.[60] Cotton, having previously worried that Shah Shuja could never hold his crown if regular troops were withdrawn, now concluded that the surrender "completely knocked on the head the plans of the disaffected" as "they are deprived of the great rallying point."[61] Afghan resentment of Shah Shuja varied in nature and intensity from one region to another, but Dost Muhammad's followers eventually settled upon religion as a great rallying point against a puppet prince of the British Empire whom Afghans had aided at the cost of forsaking Islam for worldly gain.[62]

In November 1840 Cotton was compelled by ill health to retire from command in Kabul and was replaced by Major General William Elphinstone. Elphinstone was chosen by virtue of a mild and conciliatory manner deemed to balance the qualities of a soldier with those of a diplomat. Nott was again passed over.[63] The contradiction in Auckland's policy—that Shah Shuja required British troops to consolidate his regime, while their very presence eroded his local legitimacy—also crossed the purposes of the garrison Elphinstone took over. The strongest defensive position at Kabul was the Bala Hissar, an ancient fortress dating to the fifth century BCE. Yet for the sake of appearances Shah Shuja and his retinue were installed there, while the British constructed a cantonment two miles away at a site chosen prior to Elphinstone's assumption of command.[64] A small army of occupation garrisoned in a weak tactical position at Kabul in support of an unpopular ruler thus faced an Afghan tribal population on the eve of *jihad*.

By the end of 1840 the Afghan mission was costing £1 million per annum, an aggravating factor in the annual deficit in the exchequer of British India.[65] When Melbourne's government in Westminster fell to a confidence motion in June 1841, its successor under Peel convinced itself that Afghanistan could be held with Shah Shuja's forces, stiffened by one European regiment each in Kabul and Kandahar, for a total outlay per annum of £300,000. This meant that the occupation force was to be stripped down to 4,500 fighting men saddled with 12,000 camp civilians.[66] Shah Shuja's regime in Kabul was now a frontier outpost of British India, a creature of one government in London now slipping from the attention of its successor.[67] Captain Colin Mackenzie observed that, "the idea of withdrawing our troops for the next ten years, *if ever,* is perfectly chimerical," adding more prophetically that "our gallant fellows in Afghanistan must be reinforced or *they will all perish.*"[68]

Cuts to tribal subsidies set off a rebellion by Ghilzais in the Khurd Kabul region east of the capital in October. Because the rising in Kabul was not promptly suppressed, disaffected tribes in the surrounding countryside joined in and confronted the garrison with a tribal coalition in open revolt.[69] A riotous mob surrounding the residency of Alexander Burnes, the British consul on Kabul, on November 2 numbered some three hundred at most, but it generated the first flicker of a revolt that over the next five hours murdered Burnes along with the guards, servants, women, and children at the residency and the adjacent treasury and its mansion. Shah Shuja attempted to come immediately to Burnes' rescue, but in moving his troops through the narrow streets of the city, he was repulsed with heavy losses. Elphinstone ordered Colonel John Shelton to advance to the Bala Hissar from his encampment in the Seah Sung Hills, but Shelton made no move against insurgents and elected instead to cover the retreat of the Shah's bloodied troops to the fortress.[70] As the riot of November 2 evolved into an insurrection on a broader scale, the British garrison lacked the numbers to contest it across the country. Nor was the garrison deployed properly in the capital to defeat the revolt before it acquired momentum.

On one occasion a force of seventeen companies of British and native infantry led by Shelton launched an attack against the village of Baymaroo. Unaware of the presence of horsemen, the force found itself pinned down by *jezail* fire and was ordered into squares for defense against cavalry when Akbar Khan's horsemen appeared. The horsemen, however, declined to attack. Instead, Afghan snipers picked off the men of the assault force at their leisure. In range and accuracy the Afghan *jezail* was superior to the British Brown Bess musket for the sniping tactics of the tribesmen.[71] The *jezail*'s effective range of 500–800 yards, as against 150 yards for the Brown Bess, meant that there was really no small arms response available to British troops as long as the Afghans remained at long range. British army doctrine in the age of Wellington held that the faster British infantry closed with the bayonet in offense, the sooner the day would be won.[72] In defense the squares that in 1815 had confounded Ney's cavalry at Waterloo were a pact with suicide in Afghanistan, as the most mediocre of the Afghan marksmen could hardly fail to score a hit from a safe position firing a ball into a mass of British troops standing shoulder to shoulder.[73]

The Afghan chiefs made an offer to negotiate, which Macnaghten felt compelled to accept. But the meeting with Akbar Khan on December 23 ended in a riot in which Macnaghten, among others, was murdered. It thereupon fell to Eldred Pottinger, the senior political agent after Macnaghten, to negotiate a treaty for the withdrawal of the British garrison from the country. On New Year's Day 1842 he secured their agreement to a safe and unmolested passage from Kabul to the frontier.[74] The host that marched from the cantonment on January 6 consisted of about 4,500 armed men, of whom about 600 were Europeans, 2,840 native soldiers on foot, and 970 native cavalrymen. Two days after its departure, it met with massacre in the Khurd Kabul Pass. At the time of his arrival at Jalalabad on January 13, Dr. William Brydon was thought to be the sole survivor of the Kabul garrison, commemorated as the *Remnants of an Army* by Elizabeth Butler's painting. The misadventure of the Army of the Indus had weakened the security of the frontier of British India by provoking a population to armed hostility while conveying an image of British military weakness. The Duke of Wellington, now minister without portfolio in Peel's second government and its leader in the Lords, chalked the defeat to "inconceivable imbecility" and railed that the capture of the cantonment's women in particular would have a "moral effect injurious to British influence and power throughout the whole of Asia."[75] Subtler strategic concerns would now have to be set aside and efforts bent to the immediate objective of retribution.[76]

Nott was still in Kandahar and had concentrated his forces there ever since his attempt to get a relief column to Kabul had been halted by winter weather in the passes. The critical military question in the north was the reinforcement or withdrawal of the garrison at Jalalabad. Although an attempt to relieve it by marching a force from Peshawar through the Khyber Pass had been defeated by local Afridi tribesmen, the garrison under Sir Robert Sale conducted a successful defense and even risked offensive thrusts against the camp of Akbar Khan's besieging army. So in April 1842, a second attempt to run the Khyber Pass and march on Jalalabad, this time under Major General George Pollock, held out the prospect of joining with Sale's force. Ellenborough was determined that these armies withdraw as soon as practicable to positions where they would have easy communications with India, but Pollock explained that he did not yet have enough carriage to support a retirement. For his part, Nott, having been ordered by Ellenborough to retire in the direction of Quetta, responded that such a route would be impracticable until the autumn but that a march by way of Ghazni and Kabul to Jalalabad would be a viable alternative. When Pollock recommended to Ellenborough that he be permitted to join up with Nott at Kabul and received approval, the two generals had in effect reworked the governor-general's plan for withdrawal into one for a pincer offensive against Akbar Khan's remaining forces positioned between them.[77] Nott had 6,000 men, Pollock 8,000, a combined strength now under leadership capable of ugly revenge.

Even in advance of orders to advance on Kabul, Pollock began to ravage the Shinwari country south of Jalalabad. Nott meanwhile advanced quickly to the north and east and encountered little resistance until Mukur, about halfway to Kabul. The key engagements for the combined forces of the Army of Retribution took place between Pollock and Akbar Khan at Jagdalak and

Tezin on September 8 and 12 respectively, in the latter instance involving an Afghan force some 16,000. By September 16 the Union Jack flew again from the Bala Hissar, and Kabul was at Pollack's mercy. As the crowning tribute to Britannia's wrath, Pollock settled on the complete destruction of Kabul's central bazaar, a centuries-old roofed plaza famous over all of Central Asia, because it had been the site of display for Macnaghten's mutilated body. Although Pollock stationed detachments of men to avert chaos, the city was nonetheless the victim of plunder, rape, and murder. On October 12, by which time military discipline had been restored, the combined armies left Kabul for India.

The invasion of Afghanistan had been a waste of life and prestige. Far from securing the north-western Indian frontier of the Empire, the fiasco demolished Britain's reputation for invincibility and emboldened the rebellious spirit in the Sind and Punjab. Three years after the punitive expedition of 1842, British India found itself in the first Anglo-Sikh War.[78] Dost Muhammad returned to power in Kabul and in 1846 found it convenient to ally himself with the rebellious Sikhs; after the defeat of the rebellion he consolidated his position inside Afghanistan, remained neutral during the Indian Mutiny, and eventually aided Britain against Persia. This outcome raises the issue as to whether the campaign to oust Dost Mohammed had ever been necessary, as the recovery of Britain's military prestige against the Sikhs alone shunted him to adopt a pro-British position.

At Westminster a stampede of political dissociation from military failure was the immediate consequence of the First Anglo-Afghan War, it being easier in such circumstances to charge that a war that was impolitic was also unjust—and therefore a product of duplicity. Palmerston's foreign policy and Auckland's Indian policy were caricatured as monuments of treachery hustled past an innocent parliament by a doctoring of the official record.[79] In truth the war had been a mistake, its prosecution closer to a crime. It committed extensive military resources to a cause of secondary foreign policy importance to the Melbourne government, and after its initial success quickly lost its place in that government's rank order of priorities, among them the First Opium War in China in which Mars again followed Mammon in the Company's pursuit of markets.[80] Never having enjoyed the interest of the successor Peel government, the occupation of Afghanistan was subjected to economies that sapped its strength. Yet none of this doomed the Kabul garrison to annihilation. In purely military terms, noted Sir Henry Durand, the campaign violated every manner of precaution; "never before, during the history of the British power in India, had so wild, ill-considered, and adventurous a scheme of far-distant aggression been entertained."[81]

The British and French campaigns in Algeria and Afghanistan ultimately shared the application of brutality, a feature common to all colonial wars. The point of the comparison here is to stress the differing domestic political circumstances conditioning overseas military campaigns. The French intervention in Algeria began casually yet evolved into a project conquest by

France in Africa, in which the army became an author of policy. The importance of Afghanistan to the British Empire was by contrast secondary, the worry that it might provide a strategic approach to India from Russia's position in Central Asia. The British army in Afghanistan never had the full attention, much less the full support, of the government at home and possessed none of the lobbying leverage enjoyed by its French counterpart. Participants in and witnesses to colonial wars usually explained away much of what they saw with the observation that what moved Asians and Africans to obedience was demonstrated ruthlessness. Without delving into the multiple factors that move human beings to cruelty, in colonial wars terror and atrocity are often the main event, as an integral aspect of policy advocated by Bugeaud or the bi-product of it applied by Pollock.[82] The smaller numbers of the forces engaged in colonial wars threw acts of cruelty into high relief, and for many of the imperial powers of the nineteenth century the gradual development of the liberal conscience of parliamentary democracy often meant that news about how political discourse was being pursued in Africa and Asia could be deeply troubling to domestic politics. France established the Foreign Legion in part to insulate the French state from the domestic political cost of France's action abroad; until the India Act of 1858 the Honourable Company provided much the same service for Britain. The one reflected the statist nature of French imperialism, the other the commercial spirit of British imperialism.

The advance of democracy in nineteenth-century Europe, and with it the increased importance of public opinion to the prosecution of even distant conflicts, nonetheless cut both ways. In a time of increasingly competitive imperialism, the cultivation of popular nationalism in support of an assertive foreign policy could be more critical to the political survival of elected governments that to autocrats. A liberal imperialist such as Palmerston understood this. During the parliamentary debate on Afghanistan, in which Palmerston defended the Melbourne government's policy, he taunted the Tories both for their silence in 1839 and their prudery in retrospective, then switched over to the offensive with aplomb by laying all blame at the feet of the army's ineptitude. Such as it was, Palmerston went on to explain, the neglected British Army was unequal to a threat far closer than Afghanistan in the form of France's standing army of 340,000.

In this he was half-right. Britain's army was indeed ill equipped and unprepared, but it was to demonstrate its shortcomings not against but rather in alliance with France in the Crimean conflict of 1854. For Palmerston, contesting Russian power in Afghanistan had been a side-show; its complete humiliation in the Crimea was a taller order of business, a Great Power conflict in South East Europe. For Napoleon III in France it acquired similar importance, not least of all to restore French prestige and overturn the settlement of 1815 with British cooperation.[83] The combined efforts of British and French governments in directing their nations toward war with Tsarist Russia over the Crimean Peninsula testify to these parallel yet not entirely convergent interests. The challenge integral to expeditionary warfare in Algeria and Afghanistan, that of the logistics of deploying and supporting armies in a distant theatre for an uncertain length of time,[84] was the central military and political challenge for all the belligerents of the Crimean conflict at mid-century. As in Northern Africa and Central Asia, the decline of the Ottoman Empire moved the Western powers to adopt a strategic perspective on south-eastern Europe that led them to war-in-coalition against Russia.

Modern militaries at mid-century: The Crimean conflict

Heinrich August Winkler maintains that the Crimean War anticipated the twentieth century in two respects. It was an East-West conflict, in that it pitted Britain and France against Tsarist Russia, in the first instance in support of the Ottoman Empire but additionally to contain Russian expansion and secure their own interests in the Eastern Mediterranean arising from the colonial wars that Algeria and Afghanistan exemplified. In 1849 London and Paris forced St. Petersburg to back away from its ultimatum that the Porte hand over Polish and Hungarian fugitives given sanctuary in Turkey following the defeat of the Hungarian revolt. When in 1853 St. Petersburg returned to diplomatic extortion—this time demanding that the Porte recognise the Tsar as the defender of the faith for the Christian subjects of the Ottoman realm in the Holy Land—the two Western powers backed the Porte's refusal by sending their Mediterranean fleets to the entrance of the Dardanelles. Additionally, the Crimean War began as a classic "cabinet war," generated by political leaders in pursuit of specific strategic goals involving no issue of vital national security, yet became a "media war," above all in Britain, by virtue both of the ideological tone struck in its justification and of the public attention it eventually drew for its duration and cost.[85] The Crimean War was not a colonial conflict but rather an expeditionary campaign against another European power, the primary target of which was Russian naval power based at Sevastopol on the Crimean peninsula.

The Whig-Peelite government of George Hamilton-Gordon, the Earl of Aberdeen, took Britain into the war despite the efforts of Aberdeen to avoid it. As home secretary in that government, Palmerston could do little directly to influence foreign policy within the cabinet, so he engineered his own resignation, ostensibly over a reform bill, and influenced it profoundly from without. From that position Palmerston argued that British Eastern policy should be based on the conviction that the Ottoman Empire served as an obstacle to Russian territorial expansion and that France shared this view.[86] The fluidity of parliamentary support for a firm British line with Russia, however, required that Palmerston adjust his argument to a public sentiment that was anti-Russian yet still haunted by the Napoleonic Wars. He therefore advocated fortification of England's coast against invasion by Napoleon III's army in one instance and praised cooperation with France in confronting

Russia in the next.[87] Hard calculations of *Realpolitik* did not render the liberal principles of freedom and constitutionalism he invoked to appeal to middle-class opinion a cynical fiction. On the contrary, Palmerston's speeches inside and outside parliament stroked the competing liberal and imperial impulses of informed public opinion masterfully. "He contrived," notes one biography, "to make the honest passivism of the Manchester school, which some hold to have been noble, sound like cheap and blinkered commercialism, and chauvinism sound noble and unselfish" and in the effort "emerged as the accredited champion of the national mood."[88]

France was at this time was headed toward a domestic crisis, as Louis Napoleon confronted the constitutional bar the Second Republic set against his right to run for a second term as its president. His solution, a coup d'état sprung on the December 2 anniversary of the Battle of Austerlitz and his uncle's coronation, sought and secured a measure of popular legitimacy through a plebiscite revealing the resilience of Bonapartist sentiment. After consolidating his position through the arrest of opposition leaders and critical journalists and imposition of martial law in the provinces, Napoleon III drew up a new constitutional document giving himself the authority to remain president with near dictatorial powers for ten years. He then looked to the Russo-Turkish crisis as the occasion to free France of the limitations imposed at Vienna in 1815 and recover its continental preeminence at the expense of Russia. For, whatever the nature of Napoleon III's regime, metropolitan France was an increasingly liberal society in which indictments of Tsarist absolutism did a good deal to stroke national self-esteem. *Letters from Russia*, by the Marquis de Custine, was first published in 1839. Its vision of the Tsar's empire as one vast prison was hugely popular and took the book to multiple reprints and translations. It was not difficult in such an atmosphere to cultivate support for reestablishment of an autonomous Polish state while promoting a war in alliance with Britain in support of the Ottoman cause that promised to divide Russian energies between Central Europe, the Balkans, and the Eastern Mediterranean.[89] In July 1853 Nicholas I ordered Russian troops to occupy the Danubian principalities, and a Turkish declaration of war followed in October of the same year. The Turks had already chalked a minor victory at Oltenitza when France and Britain dispatched naval forces to Constantinople. Not until the Russian fleet took revenge by destroying an Ottoman squadron at Sinope on the Black Sea, however, were Anglo-French strategic interests truly engaged and was popular opinion duly enraged. Napoleon III thereupon proposed that the British and French fleets enter the Black Sea and force all Russian warships to return to their base at Sevastopol, adding that France was prepared to act alone.[90]

Sincere or not, the French leader spoke to Britain's status as the preeminent global power, a status that could be eroded if Ottoman power were so ground down that Russia enjoyed undisputed control of the Black Sea and the Sea of Marmara.[91] Additionally, Palmerston thought Russia's position in the Baltic Sea and Northern Europe sufficiently problematic to warrant an approach to Sweden to ally itself with the Western powers as "a long line of circumvallation to confine the future extension of Russia."[92] In parliament Palmerston ventured that "no doubt, Russia speculated upon differences— irreconcilable, as it thought—between England and France. It never imagined that there could be a cordial union between these two Powers."[93] The Crimean War was thus a wider conflict than its name suggests, with the Black Sea and Crimean Peninsula representing its primary theatre. Its opening engagements were joined in the Ottoman provinces of Wallachia and Moldavia in 1853; joint naval and maritime operations by Britain and France were undertaken in the Baltic in 1854 and 1855, while minor naval and marine battles were fought in the far north of the White Sea and the far east of the Pacific Ocean.[94]

The literature on the war has long been negligent of its naval dimension. Recent scholarship has given appropriate attention to sea and maritime operations in the Baltic Sea while integrating them fully into an understanding of the conflict of the conflict as whole.[95] This is a welcome development, highlighting in the case of the Crimean War the relationship between naval strategy in the Napoleonic era and that of mid-century industrialising Europe. For Britain in particular the Treaty of Tilsit and the ensuing blockade of Britain, to which France had compelled Russia, Prussia, and Denmark to join, imperilled commercial access to Baltic waters and ports. The Concert System, according to which a brittle peace was maintained, began to break down not least of all due to Russia's intervention in the liberal and nationalist movements in Central Europe in defense of monarchy and Tsarism's European sphere of influence, posing the prospect of conflict between Russia and the Western powers.

For the most commercially cosmopolitan of those powers, Britain, Russian actions renewed concern for the Baltic almost as much as for the Mediterranean. Compared to the Napoleonic era, Britain in the 1850s was more confident of its power, so that the simultaneous naval and maritime campaigns against Russia in the Baltic and Crimean theatres—without which the Crimean War could never have been prosecuted as it was—offered to Britain a chance to relegate Russia to the status of a second-rate power incapable of troubling European peace and British supremacy.[96] Britain sought the destruction of Russian naval power at Sevastopol, thereafter to drive the Tsar's armies out of the Crimea and the Caucasus, and ultimately to strip Finland and Poland from his empire. France accepted the necessity of the campaign against Sevastopol, but considered a Russian defeat there sufficient to destroy the Holy Alliance and restore France as the primary power on the continent. Both intended a short, sharp war. What the Turks wanted was unimportant.[97]

On March 28, 1854, the Allies declared war on Russia and in early April had sufficient naval assets in the Black Sea, including new steam-powered vessels that relieved navigation from the chance of wind and current, to bombard the coastal city of Odessa, between the Dnieper and Dniester estuaries, with only light damage to their ships. The action set the seal on naval operations for the war, as time and again Allied squadrons attacked Russian ports to destroy defensive works, shipping and supply, establishing such naval dominance as to render Russian coastlines anywhere in the world open targets for aggressive naval action.[98] The naval campaign in the Baltic had only a limited impact on Russian coastal defences yet exerted a significant influence for the larger conflict. The Royal Navy fleet commanded by Admiral Sir Charles Napier was composed of high-seas warships, ill-suited to the shoal waters off the formidable coastal fortress works of Sveaborg and Kronstadt. Even the lesser defences of Hangö and Åbo, aided by their gunboats, were able to drive off the British attack. Bomarsund in the Åland Islands was another story. Bomarsund was captured after the ships of the Allied fleet bombarded it and then supported a combined land and sea assault of some 3,000 French troops landed four miles south of the harbour and an Anglo-French force of roughly equal strength put ashore two miles to the north of it. Despite the difficulties inherent in allied operations, the capture of Bomarsund demonstrated to the Russians that "small, isolated garrisons could not resist allied, amphibious power."[99]

As conceived by First Lord of the Admiralty, Sir James Graham, the Baltic campaign was never intended to be a decisive contest of arms. Although blockading operations involved little glory, the presence of British and French war ships in the Baltic seized up Russian trade in the region. Moreover, the campaign's indirect contribution to the Allied war effort went beyond the scale of its operations. Because the St. Petersburg-Kronstadt region was the heart of the Tsarist government, the Anglo-French naval presence compelled the deployment of 200,000 troops in the region a portion of which might otherwise have been available for the Crimea.[100] Additional Allied naval operations in the White Sea and the Pacific had little impact on the war's progress. The Allied performance in the Pacific was miserable in every instance; following bombardment of Petropavlovsk on the Kamchatka Peninsula two successive assaults by sailors and marines were beaten off and operations terminated.[101] But the disappointments of the 1854 Baltic campaign meanwhile led in 1855 to a second and fundamentally superior effort.

Replacing Napier in command of the British fleet, Rear Admiral Sir Saunders Dundas had 105 ships at his disposal, including battleships, mortar boats, gunboats, and steam frigates, supplemented by a French formation of much smaller size under Rear Admiral André Édouard Penaud. The most significant action of the new campaign was the bombardment of Sveaborg in the Gulf of Finland. The Allied navies used their gunboats and mortar ships to pound the Sveaborg fortress works with more than 6,000 shells, yet attempted no landing and capture of the town of Helsingfors. The Sveaborg operation was thus less ambitious militarily than Bomarsund. Still, if it was contrived to create an impression, it succeeded. It convinced the Russians that Kronstadt might be vulnerable and compelled the Tsar's army to maintain or augment the troops stationed in the area. Sweden and Norway were moved to enter into an alliance with Britain and France, while Austria and Prussia now questioned their position of neutrality.[102]

The stationing of forces around the perimeter of Russia's sprawling interior lines of defence made proportionally fewer available for the Crimean theatre. Here too the Anglo-French naval advantage was decisive. British and French ships, some of them steam-driven, were able to land and supply troops on the Crimean Peninsula from West European ports more efficiently than Russian troops and material were able to cover the distance over land on the Tsar's primitive roads and wholly inadequate railway network.[103] Infantry divisions ordered south from Yaroslavl and Moscow took months to reach the Crimea, so that by September 1854 Prince Alexander Menshikov, commander-in-chief in the Crimea, had at his disposal only 38,000 soldiers and 18,000 sailors of some two million men in Russia's armed forces. Against these the Allies ferried from Varna on the Bulgarian coast of the Black Sea and landed at Eupatoria 61,000 men between September 7 and 13. In his classic study of maritime strategy Julian Corbett later wrote that "as a combined operation its opening movement was perhaps the most daring, brilliant and successful kind of thing of the kind we ever did."[104]

These operations also featured all the difficulties of coalition warfare, as the French were not prepared for the ferrying of troops to from Varna to the Crimean coast. Corbett's claim that "we had in fact, besides all the other difficulties, to carry an unwilling ally upon our back,"[105] is valid for ferrying of troops for Varna to Eupatoria landing, but thereafter it was the often French who had cause to wonder at their ally. Ironically, this was because the British had expected to have to fight their way ashore and had made no plans for an unopposed landing. For five days after the French had established a camp, British troops, horses, pack animals, and baggage struggled ashore under variable surf conditions only to spend their first nights on shore with no shelter and few provisions. Once the Allies were able to march south toward Sevastopol, many of the soldiers weakened by the cholera contracted at Varna, their columns became ragged as men fell out under the punishment of heat and thirst.

Yet the war was at this point an issue of comparative weakness. The fact of the march alone put the Allies at an advantage, partly compensating their enfeebled condition, as Russian forces in the Crimea had not yet been adequately reinforced. When informed of the Eupatoria landing, Menshikov declined to challenge Allied naval power with his own fleet and opted instead for a defence on land. He marched his troops to the Alma River north of Sevastopol and deployed them along a naturally strong position on the high ground on the river's south bank. He then waited for the Allies to come on, without either making extensive defensive improvements to his position or launching harassing attacks during the most vulnerable phase of their operations, during and after the landing. The latter might have hobbled the Allied march before it achieved any momentum; a competent execution of the latter might have stopped them cold. Either would have constituted a disaster from which the war might not have recovered politically in London and Paris.[106]

The more so as any Anglo-French unity of purpose was absent at the Alma. Because neither of the Allied armies would accept a commander-in-chief from the other, they now advanced on Alma side by side but with little coordination. Worse still, neither of their respective commanders was wholly fit for action in the Crimea. Lord Raglan, was at sixty-six a veteran of the Peninsular War and Waterloo, where he had an lost arm; Marshall Jacques Leroy de Saint-Arnaud was more than ten years his junior and had fought with the Foreign Legion in Algeria but was frequently laid low by the effects of stomach cancer during the Crimean campaign. Theirs was a relationship of mutual suspicion and slight regard. The Allies approached the Alma River marching parallel to the coastline, the French and Turks forming the right of the army supported by naval gunfire from the sea, the British its left on the inland side astride the Sevastopol Road.

On September 20, as the two armies advanced simultaneously on the Alma, the Russian guns opened fire at a range of 1,800 metres. Although Raglan and Saint-Arnaud had agreed that they would attempt to roll up the Russian flank on the left, Raglan hesitated to send his men over the river pending developments on the right. Happily for the Allied cause, the far right was composed of *zouaves*, seasoned veterans of mountain fighting in Algeria. They set about scaling the cliffs and inspired other French troops to follow, hauling artillery behind. Because Menshikov had assumed his left flank secure by virtue of the terrain alone, the *zouaves'* presence immediately posed a dire threat, especially as the greater range and accuracy of the French Minié rifles' fire kept the Russian artillery at a distance until Bosquet's guns reached the heights. Initially, Menshikov refused to believe that his left flank was imperilled, but as other French units began to advance against the Russian left, Menshikov's guns pinned them down and the French flanking movement stalled with only a tentative hold on the heights. It was Major General George de Lacy Evans who conveyed to Raglan a message from the French command that now was the time for the British army attack. Only after overcoming resentment at his subordinate apparently taking orders from the French did Raglan order the British infantry to strike at the Russian centre. From Menshikov's perspective the Allied actions must have appeared far more coordinated than they were.

Initially the attack went badly for the British infantry, but officers stiffened the courage of the ranks against the contagion of panic, while superior weaponry again told against the Russian army. The British 1851 pattern Minié rifle, produced by the Enfield factory in London, fired a .702-inch round and had four times the range of the Russian smooth-bore musket. Because a single round could tear through several men, its effect was to neutralise any advantage the Russian infantry had in position and numbers in the Great Redoubt of the Russian defences.[107] The Russian military engineer, Edouard Totleben, later observed that "left to themselves to perform the role of sharpshooters, the British troops did not hesitate under fire and did not require order or supervision."[108] As other units joined the fusillade, Russian resistance withered, and the British uphill advance steadied. By late afternoon the engagement was over. Russian casualties numbered 5,000; British 2,000; French 1,600. Apart from Bosquet's initiative against the Russian left, the Allied command had left much to be desired. British infantrymen on the slopes above the Alma "won a battle which the men who led them might have lost."[109] The superiority of the Minié rifle over the Russian muskets, combined with the initiative of middle and lower ranks, had made the difference.

The Allies were later criticised for their failure to pursue Menshikov's army as it fled in disorder, on the assumption that Sevastopol was now all but defenseless and would have fallen in few days.[110] The primary error of the Allies in the Black Sea theatre, however, was not in failing to attack Sevastopol immediately but rather in besieging the city from the wrong side. The original plan had been to attack from the north—where the Russian star fort, naval barracks, and supply depots were located—supported by naval bombardment. The main part of the city in the south, separated from the north by Sevastopol Harbour, would be at the Allies' mercy once the north had been captured. It had been Saint-Arnaud's understanding that the Allies would proceed to Sevastopol and take in from the north quickly before it could be reinforced, ending the war on Allied terms by October. Moreover, Russia's territorial expanse continued to tell against its chances. Menshikov had bivouacked his battered army north of the city following his retreat, but on September 24 marched it north-east from Sevastopol in order to maintain a link through Simpferopol to southern Russia. The remaining garrison in Sevastopol numbered no more that 17,800, while its poorly fortified north side had only 4–5,000 soldiers and sailors. Totleben, Admiral Vladimir Kornilov and Vice Admiral Nakhimov all thought it unlikely that the Sevastopol garrison could withstand a determined Anglo-French land assault from the north.[111]

In this they overrated their adversaries. Not only did the Allies march south on Sevastopol without sufficient advance reconnaissance—and thus managed to miss Menshikov's army moving to the north-east—they were also seized by an excess of caution upon arrival. The chief engineer of the British army, Sir John Burgoyne, prevailed upon Raglan with the view that the south side of Sevastopol would be more lightly defended than the north, while the Russian blockade of the harbour entrance precluded Allied cooperation in a naval bombardment of the north. Raglan was far too deferential to Burgoyne's point of view, while Saint-Arnaud lacked the stamina and possibly the mental acuity to oppose this change of plans.[112] The choice for an attack from the south, assumed to offer the better part of prudence, was a gamble with strategic implications:

> As it was the sense of dependence on the sea predominated and the indecision which was shown suggests that the two commanders-in-chief

had forgotten the original aim of the Crimean expedition. Undertaken late in the season, without preparation for a winter campaign, its object—less military than political—had been to administer a sharp blow to Russia which would compel her to cut short the war and leave Turkey alone. And no doubt if Sebastopol had been captured in October 1854 that might have been the effect. As it was a protracted defence of their Crimean base gave the Russians' prestige a welcome boost and provoked in Central Asia a new respect for Russia's innate vitality.[113]

If the war's initial strategic logic in London and Paris had indeed been more political than military the military virtue of the political timetable was soon to become obvious, as the lengthy siege of Sevastopol caused by hesitation was to be politically costly in both capitals but militarily calamitous for their armies in the Crimea. The apportioning of blame for fateful decision to besiege the city from the south varies according to interpretation,[114] but the fact remains that the movement of the Allied armies to the east, then south, and finally west around Sevastopol Harbour began on September 25, and that the bombardment of the Russian defences did not begin until October 17. The lull in Allied action was exploited brilliantly by Totleben and Kornilov for building new defensive earthworks, and Kornilov pressured Menshikov with a threat of a complaint to the Tsar to reinforce the 16,000-man garrison with an additional 28,000 troops.[115]

Those Russian warships that had not been scuttled to blockade the harbour and were now safe within it could contribute their guns and crews to the artillery dual. In this the Russian garrison had the much better part of the action dishing out far more damage to the Allied batteries and warships than it sustained in return. Although the combined Allied fleets posed an impressive threat, strung out in a line two miles long on a south-west to north-east axis across the mouth of habour with a collective broadside of 1,100 guns, Dundas drafted a letter to First Lord of the Admiralty, Sir John Graham—never completed, never posted—asserting that "the length of time in pressing the siege operation has caused the enemy to take courage after his defeat at the Alma," so that "the sea front is now far stronger than ever, very commanding and I cannot see much probability of our making any impression his works."[116] The command of the combined armies in the Crimea turned a plan for short and decisive naval and maritime operations into a land war of uncertain duration.

Neither the naval nor the land bombardment did damage to the Russian positions sufficient to embolden the Allies to an infantry assault. Of greater importance than the failure of the bombardment itself was the blow it gave to the Anglo-French mystique, its proportional boost to Russian morale, and the spur it delivered to initiative of the Russian command. Menshikov now moved his field army from Bakhchiserai to the north-east of Sevastopol to the Chernaia Valley south-east of Sevastopol, there to be reinforced by troops from the Danubian front to a total strength of some 60,000. From that position it posed a threat to the British supply base a Balaklava. Raglan had thought Balaklava's small harbour adequate when the decision for siege operations was taken, as these he assumed would be a brief rather than a year-long ordeal. The French supply habours were meanwhile well to the north of the coast at Kamiesch and Kazatch, so Menshikov's offensive not only imperilled the British army's supply base but also positioned a Russian army to come between the Allies.[117]

Every feature of the defence of the British base on October 25, 1854, had to be innovated in short order. Once the Russians had captured four of the six redoubts north of Balaklava, their cavalry was repulsed by the "thin red line" of the 93rd Highlanders commanded by Colin Campbell. Brigadier James Yorke Scarlett then led the 900 sabres of the 5th Dragoons of the Heavy Brigade against 3,000 Russian cavalry in a slashing attack, as devastating morally as physically to Russian resolve. Finally, there was the suicidal charge of Lord Cardigan's Light Brigade. While magnified by Tennyson for its heroic symbolism, the cavalry charge came in response to a poorly communicated order against a Russian position held on the front and flanked by artillery; it was actually a small and indecisive engagement.[118] Still, it was instructive. It was now apparent to all that the superiority of British cavalry at Balaclava and Allied infantry at Alma had shown that a campaign against the Russian army in open terrain, rather than an extended siege of Sevastopol, had always been the best way to force a military decision. Because the move on Balaclava came up short, Menshikov sought a larger engagement to relieve pressure on Sevastopol.[119]

The politics of protracted conflict

In this goal at least he succeeded, as the Allies had set the date of November 6, before the onset of winter, for a new assault. The Battle of Inkerman demolished this timetable. The cost for the Russian army was nonetheless a tactical defeat with a horrific toll in casualties. Circumstance gave Menshikov little choice in taking the offensive. By November additional reinforcements had arrived from the Danube front, bringing total Russian troop strength to 107,000 men against 71,000 allies; additionally, the Tsar involved himself personally in planning the attack and had dispatched his sons, the Grand Dukes Michael and Nicholas, to impress upon Menshikov the urgency of the situation, as the Tsar had intelligence of Emperor Napoleon's plan to send three additional French divisions to the Crimea. Again, Russia's immense territory connected by primitive communications was a factor: France could deliver reinforcements by sea to the war more quickly than Russia could deploy them over land.[120]

The plan for a move against the British position on Inkerman Ridge was logical enough. Located on the southern side of the easternmost extremity of the Bay of Sevastopol, the ridge was a weak point in the Allied siege disposition, because Raglan had chosen not to occupy it in strength. If Russian troops could capture its high ground and establish artillery upon it, the threat then posed along the Allied line could undermine the whole siege position. The plan was for 19,000 men under General Fedor I. Soimonov on the Russian right to take Sapper's Road from Sevastopol and then to turn on the British position through the Careening Ravine; the Russian left of 16,000 men under Lieutenant General Prokofij Pavlov would meanwhile cross the Tchernaya River and filter into the Georgievsky, Volovia, and Quarry Ravine to converge atop Inkerman Ridge with Soimonov's thrust upon the right flank of the British position. Pavlov was to be accompanied by General Peter Dannenberg, newly arrived with two divisions from the Danube. An additional feature was that a third force of 22,000 under General Piotr Gorchakov was a feint against the French under Bosquet on the Sapun Heights to the south of the British to prevent them from rushing to the aid of the overwhelmed British.[121]

Yet the plan was knocked sideways from the outset. Pavlov's men were unable to cross Tschernaya on schedule, as the bridge over it was under repair. By the time they attacked, Soimonov's troops were already fully engaged. From the start Bosquet recognised Gorchakov's demonstration against the French position as pure theatre and was prepared to divert troops to aid the British. Lastly, rainy weather and thick mist confounded the efforts of both sides to know where they were or what was happening. Clausewitz had written on the multiple factors in war that lead to uncertainty and wrap actions "in a fog of greater or lesser uncertainty."[122] The tragic farce at Inkerman was that the adversaries had been bumping about the Crimea since the Allies landed at Eupatoria in a fog of uncertainty due to poor reconnaissance and were now confronted with the real meteorological phenomenon.

In its opening phase Inkerman was therefore not an integrated action but rather "a series of undirected encounters, fought by groups of men" in a "rolling vapour of ghostly incoherence."[123] Dense Russian columns emerged from the mist to be mowed down by Minié rifles. Although every inch of the British position was doggedly defended, at the height of the action fatigue began to play upon the British troops as the Russian strength came to bear. At this point the arrival of three batallions of *zouaves* and Algerians bolstered British spirits and withered Russian resolve in proportion. Alexander Kinglake of the *Illustrated London News* reported that Allied volleys into the Russian columns wrought "perfect carnage" yet "the enemy kept their order, retreating almost at slow time, and every five or ten minutes halting and charging desperately up the hill."[124] For its failure to overthrow the British position at Inkerman the Russian army paid with 11,000 casualties, a loss of one-third of the men in action, in six hours of fighting. British losses totaled 2,500, while the French sacrificed approximately 1,700. Even more so than Alma, Inkerman was a "soldier's battle" in so far as its outcome was the product individual initiative extending from the foot soldier to the regimental commander rather than of generalship; Menshikov, Raglan, and Francois Canrobert were effectively absent without leave, none of them having issued an effective order while their respective armies engaged in the largest engagement of the war. In London and Paris momentary satisfaction over the heroism of Inkermen quickly gave way to the realisation that a siege of Sevastopol over the Crimean winter was now unavoidable.

The overture to the Crimean winter in the form of a hurricane-force storm was the source of misery in the short term; over the longer term it was the product of human incompetence. All three armies suffered serious privations, but the British army was by far the most sorely damaged physically and morally. Its docking facilities were unequal to the traffic in goods even in the best conditions, so that "the only industrialised country in the world was filling its merchant fleet with untold millions in supplies and depositing them with great precision in Balaclava where undeliverable clothing, vegetables, medicines, and weapons piled up alongside a harbour choked with filth."[125] Florence Nightingale arrived in November 1854, just in time to receive the wounded of Balaklava. The British army hospital was located at Scutari on the Asian shore of the Bosporus Strait, where facilities included a main barrack building with more than four miles of beds, as few as twenty chamber pots shared by as many as 2,000 men, the sick and the wounded in common wards side by side in the company of lice, maggots, and rats.[126] The suffering encountered here was inflicted for the most part by the British army on its own men, as Miss Nightingale recognised from the start. It was her expertise in hospital organisation and principles of sanitation rather than of nursing itself that were most critical at Scutari; it was her personal friendship with Secretary of War Sidney Herbert, moved to action by the reporting of the *Times* on the state of affairs at Scutari, that facilitated their application against the army's strenuous and idiotic resistance.[127] Because by the winter of 1854 the French had laid a telegraph connection to Varna, to which the British added an underwater cable linking Varna to Balaklava, the misery of the troops in Crimea the could be communicated to Western European cities within hours. Telegraphic communications were intended for military use and enhanced the link between the Allied governments and their armies in the field; the reverse of the coin was that newspaper correspondents could now as never before enhance the public measure of how both were performing.[128] Although William Russell became the prototype of the war correspondent, it was his colleague at the *Times*, Thomas Chenery, who broke to the British public the condition of their boys at Scutari.

There was a measure of justice to the agonies visited upon the Aberdeen government. Aberdeen was himself wholly unequal to the rigors of political leadership in war; because he deemed war a failure of politics rather than an integral aspect of them, he had delayed preparations for the conflict even as the diplomacy hurdled toward it. Early in 1855 parliamentary furor over the war led to the establishment of an investigative committee and ultimately to the fall of Aberdeen's government in favour of one under Palmerston. He, Gladstone, Graham, Herbert, Russell, and Newcastle were prominent among the ministers blamed as the sheep of a weak executive, above all in together deciding on an invasion of the Crimea without making provisions for a protracted struggle. Palmerston was as responsible for the state of affairs in the Crimea as any of his colleagues at Westminster, yet he not only survived but benefited from the scandal, his triumph the product of an understanding of the new importance of public opinion and his skill in navigating is shoals.[129]

While it goes too far to conclude that the Crimean War killed Nicholas I, the Tsar's last act before succumbing to pneumonia in February was one of exasperation, in at last replacing Menshikov with the Prince Mikhail Gorchakov.[130] Equal impatience from Napoleon III—the emperor could orchestrate press commentary, yet remained highly sensitive to flux in public opinion—prompted increased intervention in the conduct of the siege. This came first through the dispatch of the emperor's aide Adolphe Niel to Sevastopol with orders to reorganise so that the numerically stronger French army might take over the right sector of the siege ring; second in the division of Canrobert's 80,000 troops into two army corps commanded by Bosquet and Aimable Pélissier, recently arrived from Algeria; third in a change in the tactical target of the siege, now to be the Malakov bastion, the focal point of the Russian fortifications at Sevastopol. When the telegraph line linking Varna to Balakava was established, the command interventions from Paris intensified, imposing a plan to send two armies against Simferopol in the south-central Crimea upon another plan, already underway, for naval and land operations against Kertsch on the coast of its eastern extremity. Conflict between Canrobert and Raglan over the competing priorities inherent in the two plans convinced Canrobert that he had had enough of both his government and his ally. On May 16, 1855, he resigned his command.[131] Pélissier took over the following day.

In the spring and summer of 1855 this meant three things. First, because the French army in the Crimea now far outnumbered the British army— 120,000 against 32,000 troops—Pélissier was in position to dominate future planning. Second, although Pélissier was mindful to stay on good terms with Raglan, he was, as Andrew Lambert writes, "the most determined advocate of simple, direct methods"[132] resolved above all to resume siege operations with redoubled vigor. Lastly, the siege was now to become an uglier affair. Pélissier's principal virtue, energetic initiative, was also his vice. A veteran of Algeria where his responsibility for the Dahra Massacre earned him a reputation for barbarous ruthlessness, he ignored telegraphic communications containing still more of the emperor's thoughts on Simferopol in order to decide the issue at Sevastopol. Following an initial success on June 7 in which the Allies captured positions critical for the assault on the main fortifications—for the British the Great Redan, for the French the Malakhov— Pélissier chose June 18, the anniversary of Waterloo, for the main assault. The Allies were beaten back after the French suffered 3,600 and the British 1,500 casualties; even though Totleben counted 1,500 out of action on June 18 and an additional 4,000 due to the bombardment, Sevastopol held.

Napoleon was livid that his order for field operations had been ignored and demanded that Pélissier be replaced by Niel, an order that his minister of war, Jean-Baptiste Vaillant, judiciously transmitted by post rather than telegraph.[133] Hence, Pélissier was still in place to lead the capture of Sevastopol but not before prudence of his emperor's instructions was demonstrated in one final Russian offensive foray. This came on August 17 when Gorchakov ordered an attack against French and Sardinian positions along the Tchernaya. The specific goal of the Tchernaya action was never defined, but in the event it was a repeat of Inkerman: a commander-in-chief pressed by St. Petersburg to do something; sound tactical reasoning nullified by poor execution; a Russian butcher's bill of 8,000 casualties against some 1,800 French and Sardinians.[134]

So the final act of the war returned to Sevastopol. By September 1855 the Allied siege works approximated the thoroughness of a Roman circumvalla-tion, with a bullet-proof shelter for generals and a subterranean conference room; French trenches crept to within twenty-five yards of the Malakhov, and batteries on the Mamelon were able to fire short-range ordnance against it. Tchernaya gave Pélissier such a whiff of Russian vulnerability that he ordered an artillery barrage for August 17 that continued day and night until August 27. After a war council on September 3, at which it was agreed that a renewed bombardment on September 5 would continue uninterrupted in preparation for the for the assault on September 8, the weight and con-centration of firepower thrown against Sevastopol anticipated the artillery infernos of World War I, as did the men huddled in trenches against it. To increase the Russian casualties, short pauses in the artillery fire encouraged the defenders to emerge from their trenches, whereupon the storm of steel would suddenly renew. Bosquet was given the task of capturing the city's Korabelnaya suburb, while General Patrice MacMahon, another Algerian veteran recently arrived, was tasked with the capture the Malakhov. The on-off rhythm of Allied firing made it difficult for the Russians to anticipate the moment of the Allied infantry assault, just as the actual moment of its onset, midday, came when least expected.

Thus, when MacMahon's *zoauves* lept from their trenches and covered the distance to the Malakhov in seconds they achieved a critical measure of surprise over Russian gunners who were, often as not, bayoneted where they sat. The capture of the Malakhov was the signal for the attack against other bastions to begin. The French assault on the Little Redan failed, even after six hours of fighting in which Bosquet committed his reserves and was himself wounded by canister fire. The British attack on the Great Redan was likewise repulsed, possibly because the British trenches were more than two hundred yards of open ground from the Russian defences. Neither failure influenced the issue of the day, as Gorchakov's obsession with retaking the Malakhov sent wave after wave of Russian infantry against MacMahon's *Zouaves,* who would not be moved. Under cover of darkness Gorchakov began to withdraw his battered garrison from Sevastopol even as the city was swept by fire and shaken by explosions. When news of Sevastopol's fall reached London and Paris, celebratory cannon fire rocked St. James's Park and Les Invalides—but under the ecstatic racket the prevailing mood had to have been one of exhausted relief.[135]

Strategic purpose and political consequence

At mid-century the comparative condition of the British and French militaries reflected the aspirations and neuroses of the governments presiding over them as well as those of the changing societies supporting them. The three conflicts under review here represent national responses to the perceived challenge posed to British and French security interests by the decline of the Ottoman Empire in Northern Africa, the Eastern Mediterranean and Black Sea, and Central Asia. To say that those perceptions changed even as the conflicts were underway is an understatement.

The impact of domestic politics on an imperial enterprise is most vividly illustrated by the French acquisition of Algeria. Indeed, the casualness with which Charles X embarked on an overseas enterprise he thought would enhance the image of restored royalist rule is quite remarkable. Initially a gesture to assert a French interest in North Africa without provoking response from the dominant naval power of the time, Britain, Charles decided to convert a punitive expedition into an invasion once it became apparent that British intervention was unlikely and Algerian resistance stiffened. The public justifications for this—ranging from just punishment for an insult to French dignity to ending Mediterranean piracy and reclaiming Algeria for Christianity—amounted neither to a strategy nor a promising political basis for one. It amounted to an open-ended imperial expenditure that troubled French politics into the mid-twentieth century; "what the French must have hoped was nearly the end of their work," notes one classic on colonial wars, "was only the beginning."[136] Worse still, the invasion did not buttress the Bourbon throne. The July Revolution that brought Louis-Philippe to power, a popular and comparatively liberal monarchy, had wholly domestic causes and consequences, so that Algerian policy was for a time neglected to an extent that the French military had to make it up on the fly, if not to achieve a mission dictated from Paris, then at least to shore up morale with a sense of purpose.

The French army never developed a strategy for Algeria more articulate than the pacification the people of the coast and interior. What it worked out in its place was a *doctrine* derived in part from the experience of the Peninsular Wars that suited both the practical imperatives of that mission and the self-image of the *Armée d'Afrique*. The *razzia* was at its core. The intervention of 1830 that became an invasion thus evolved incrementally over the remainder of the century into the incorporation of Algeria into the French body politic. Although for obvious reasons Algeria could never be a department of metropolitan France, its status among French colonies was always head and shoulders above any other overseas possession. It became part of such a strategy over the course of the nineteenth century, the goal of which was to maintain France's status among the first rank of great powers by conceding Britain's preeminent status and advancing such French overseas interest as did not challenge that status. Among the initiatives that gave coherence to this strategy was the alliance France sought, and found, confronting Tsarist Russia in the Crimea.

The army's experience in Algeria became constitutive not only for its approach to other colonial ventures but also for the strategic perspective of the French state more generally, whatever its current political colouring. This is the furthest reaching implication of what scholars of French colonialism label "military imperialism."[137] Whatever its unattractive aspects, it was resilient enough to survive the passing of the Second Empire and prosper under the Third Republic's democracy. The combination of Bugeaud's misty notion of the revival Latin culture in Northern Africa, combined with the brutal reality of the the *razzia*, was popular enough to anticipate the social Darwinism animating European imperialism in the second half of the nineteenth century. *The Origin of Species* was first published in 1859, so that by the time a republican of Jules Ferry's stature rose in 1884 to speak in parliament of the *mission civilisatrice*, "the duty to civilise inferior races,"[138] he expressed both the ethos of the French army in Africa and a vogue of public opinion across Great Power Europe. Although Socialists such as Jean Jaurès doubted the cost and morality of colonial ventures in one instance, they thought them a vehicle for the promotion of French culture, liberalism and the principles of 1789 in the next.[139]

The contrasting experience of Britain in Afghanistan was not conceived in a strategic vacuum, yet neither did it engage the attention of the British government in anything like the fashion that Algeria came to obsess France. On the one hand, the small post-Napoleonic British army could not exert anything like the foreign policy influence over civilian politicians that became routine for the French army after the 1850s. On the other, the size and influence of the Royal Navy, combined with the flourishing of a truly global overseas empire, meant that British foreign policy was always grand-strategic if not explicitly so. Indeed, the origins of Britain's global strategic perspective predated the Napoleonic period, but by mid-nineteenth century, a triumphant and wealthy Britain could "have its cake and eat it too," afford substantial commitments on land without risking its dominance of the sea.[140] The British strategic concern that led to the Afghan initiative of 1838—global naval reach combined with extensive overseas territories—was the same that led to the Crimea in 1854: the containment of Russia territorial expansion in Europe, the Caucasus, and Central Asia. Still, the complacency that followed upon Waterloo and the parsimony restricting expansion or modernisation of the army meant that organisation, equipment, and tactics were slow to change, so that British imperialism experienced periodic military disasters that only Britain could afford.[141]

But relative to France, Britain was a significantly more democratic society and state in which "policy choices continued to reflect the ebb and flow of partisan government."[142] The quartet that initially sent the Army of the Indus on its march to Kabul—Auckland, Macnaghten, Palmerston, and Hobhouse—reflected a mixture of motives typical of any imperial military scheme at the frontiers of empire. In adjusting its military plan to local sensibilities, it ultimately produced an operational plan of bizarre complexity and imposed upon it a force of doubtful composition and a campaign of physical hardships more daunting than the military defeat of the enemy. And these were all eccentricities of the Afghan campaign in the first instance, when Palmerston's Russophobic arguments were sufficient to fashion a semblance of a policy in the Melbourne government. In the next political instance, that government fell and was replaced with another that planned no withdrawal yet imposed austerities that weakened resistance to a rising of the population against the puppet prince and the British garrison sustaining him. That it was a garrison—one at great distance from support from British India— was itself possibly the first instalment on disaster. That it was a garrison configured primarily by diplomatic protocol and only secondarily by military necessity meant that even a force superior to what remained of the Army of Indus by the end of 1841 would have had difficulty facing down the full-blown insurgency that emerged. Only after the withdrawal and slaughter of the garrison did an army of retribution resort to its own *razzia*, withdraw to India, and accept Dost Mohammed on the Afghan throne.

In the face of extraordinarily grim odds, many British soldiers and officers in Afghanistan gave a good professional account of themselves. True, they resorted to tactical infantry methods such as defensive squares that were near suicidal in the presence of Afghan tribesmen, but many officers and men adapted effectively to a near hopeless situation. It was at the higher instances of British civilian and military authority in Afghanistan that leadership was poor. One of the most striking features of British army efforts against the rebels was the initiative shown by Nott and Pollack in improvising a counteroffensive in the absence of authority from above. That said, there was no British counterpart to French military imperialism and the tail-wags-dog fashion with which generals in Algeria not only led campaigns but fashioned colonial and foreign policy. The British army remained small, utterly subordinate to civilian control and secondary in importance to the Royal Navy. Experiences like the Anglo-Afghan War of 1838–1842 and the Sikh Rebellion of 1846 led London to impose more rigorous control over the Anglo-Indian colonial elite and its merchant-warrior ethos.[143] But reforms of the army itself were slight. The fact was that the Afghan frontier was of strategic interest but also that London wanted it defended on the cheap; defeats such as that of 1842 were humiliating, but Britain was strong enough to shake them off with only slight offence to national confidence.

The radical element at Westminster was meanwhile critical of what it saw as Palmerston's recklessly aggressive foreign policy and increasingly scathing in its critique of the cruelties inherent in colonial rule. But the liberal spirit of the age cut both ways; the free trader who professed to hate colonial wars still wanted foreign markets opened to British trade and might be convinced by Palmerston to hate Tsarist Russia even more, based on the same liberal principles.[144] As a consequence Britain again went to war in the 1850s in a distant theatre when its strategic perspective on Russia aligned with that of France—and did so with an army scarcely more modernised than that of the 1840s. This is most apparent when one recalls how easily the combined Anglo-French naval forces penetrated Russian waters in the Baltic and Black Seas, blockaded Russian harbours, and landed expeditionary forces on the Crimean Peninsula, yet how ill-equipped the British army was to campaign thereafter. The British army's Crimean experience was a stiff jolt to complacency and a catalyst for significant reforms.[145] The modernised quality of the Allied naval forces was in part the product of a naval arms competition between them, a competition in which Britain was clearly ahead yet had neglected its army for maintenance of naval supremacy. The complementarity of British naval capacity and the gathering strength of the French army in the Crimea over the course of the campaign meant that the Allies were able to inflict a humiliating defeat on Tsarist Russia on its own soil and at great distance from their home bases. France's army had been compelled to do the greater share of the fighting on land, but the Allied strategy of simultaneous naval operations in the Baltic was only possible with British naval capacity.

In contrast to the Algerian and Afghan conflicts, the Crimean War was prosecuted during an early phase in the technological transition of arms from the Napoleonic era to more lethal, rifled weapons made available by mid-century technological change. Even from a strong tactical position, the defensive firepower of the Russian army at Alma did not prevail, because the Allies had weapons of longer range and accuracy. Yet the defensive firepower of the British did prevail at Inkerman, because those better weapons were in the hands of the side occupying just such a position.[146] The greatest defensive position of the war, indeed its whole object of contention by 1856, was the Russian fortress at Sevastopol. Advances in artillery technology, such as rifled breech-loading ordnance, along with the application of heavier guns from land and naval positions, certainly spoke to the future of industrialised firepower, but so too did the fact of trenches from which Allied assault troops emerged with little or no cover to the future of cannon fodder.[147]

And yet the length of the war and ravages of disease ultimately did more damage than the fighting itself. Political leadership in London in particular demonstrated neglect and incompetence that "might have been concealed if the Allies had occupied Sebastopol by the beginning of November, as they could have done by bold strokes which seemed to Raglan and Canrobert too reckless."[148] Such bold strokes had been absent, because the British and French commanders used each other, in selective communication with their governments, as alibis for their own native caution, Canrobert at one point offering overall command to Raglan on certain conditions and Raglan rejecting the offer for the want of certain other conditions. Once London and Paris applied more determined attention to the war—Napoleon III and Palmerston advocating a field campaign to draw the Russians into decisive battle—their generals alternately ignored, evaded, or refused orders from their political masters, "who did not have the courage to dismiss them."[149] Hence strategy, coherent in conception, became the victim of operational drift, and military leaders compounded the effect of government errors. Examples of independent initiative going so far as to shape the conflict— Nott and Pollack in Afghanistan, Bugeaud in Algeria—were absent in the Crimea, except at the tactical level where lower ranks repeatedly decided the issue. "Raglan and Pélissier between them," notes Hugh Small "had made it impossible for the two strongest powers in the world to impose a joint military strategy,"[150] so that the first great power conflict in Europe since 1815 was less consequential than was intended. The provisions of the Treaty of Paris and Triple Treaty of Austria, Britain, and France, both signed in 1856, were both wholly inadequate for containing Russia, with the result that "a huge effort in a just cause with wide international backing had yielded a minimal and fragile result."[151] France lost some 95,000 men to the conflict, Britain 21,000, with the ratio of combat deaths to deaths from disease at roughly 1:4.

In France the outcome consolidated the regime of Napoleon III and enhanced France's position in Europe. The objective of overturning the status of 1815 at Russian expense with British cooperation had been secured yet at the price of a generalised European nervousness about future French revisionism. The east-west form of European order that Winkler identifies was thus in its initial iteration hardly stabilising; the French army emerged with a self-confident cockiness over its successes from Algiers to Sevastopol. Those who opposed the war as a plot to restore the blood-soaked eagles of Bonapartism had a valid point. The public controversy of the war in Britain in the end benefited Palmerston, its primary public enthusiast, as the irresolute leadership of Aberdeen government seemed to demand both a stronger prime minister and a diminished political influence of the crown. But Palmerston's zeal for hobbling Tsarism was not an unqualified success, while the new flux in European stability was undeniable.[152] For Russia and Nicholas I the war had been a great humiliation, yet the crisis was only the beginning of the long process that overthrew Tsarism in 1917. Reforms under Alexander II made better use of the country's massive resources, while the siege of Sevastopol was later elevated as a moment of national heroism, like Borodino, and incorporated into a generalised fear and loathing of the West.[153]

None of the conflicts studied here featured the systematic application of theories and principles developed by either Jomini or Clausewitz based on Napoleonic method, as reference to either philosophy of war awaited their academic vogue later in the century. The Crimean War did anticipate features of much larger and more consequential conflicts later in the century, namely the American Civil War and the Franco-Prussian War, the nature of which merit comparative discussion in the following chapter. In the latter case we encounter a military leader, Helmut von Moltke, avowedly committed to Clausewitz's theory of war. But the Franco-Prussian and American conflicts exhibited the emergence of so many common aspects of modern war, in settings so geographically and culturally different, that strategy and its operational realisation seem to have developed as much from common features of the challenges involved—and the practical application of new technologies to them—as from any shared strategic theory. Indeed, one is tempted to generalise that military leaders proceeded operationally from what the available resources implied and resorted to strategic theory after the fact to legitimate intellectually what their actions had achieved.

Whereas the three mid-century conflicts examined here exhibit aspects of the evolution to modern from Napoleonic war, those aspects are much more pronounced in the Prussian and American wars. Equally more pronounced in both cases—though in contrasting constitutional settings—are common aspects in the tension between political and military leadership in modern war.

Notes

1 Hew Strachan, *Carl von Clauswitz's On War: A Biography* (London: Atlantic Books, 2007), pp. 1–27; Azar Gat, *A History of Military Thought: From the Enlightenment to the Cold War* (New York: Oxford University Press, 2001), p. 247; Peter Paret, *Clausewitz and the State: The Man, His Theories and His Times* (Princeton, NJ: Princeton University Press, 1985), p. 341.

2 For example, Hew Strachan, *European Armies and the Conduct of War* (New York: Routledge, 1983), pp. 76–89; Bruce Vandervort, *Wars of Imperial Conquest in Africa, 1830–1914* (Bloomington: Indiana University Press, 1998); Thomas Pakenham, *The Boer War* (New York: Random House, 1979; New York: Perennial, 2001); Byron Farwell, *Queen Victoria's Little Wars* (New York: Norton, 1972); Saul David, *Zulu: The Heroism and Tragedy of the Zulu War of 1879* (New York: Penguin, 2005); Ian Castle. *Zulu War, 1879.* Westport, CT: Greenwood, 2005); A.S. Kanya-Forstner, *Conquest of the Western Sudan*; Douglas Porch, *The Conquest of Morocco* (New York: Farrar, Strauss and Giroux, 1982).

3 Benjamin Claude Brower, *A Desert Named Peace: The Violence of France's Empire in the Algerian Sahara* (New York: Columbia University Press, 2009).

4 Jonathan North, "General Hoche and Counterinsurgency," *Journal of Military History* 67, No. 2 (2003), pp. 529–40; Jacques Godechot, *The Counter-Revolution, Doctrine and Action, 1789–1804*, trans. Salavdor Attanasio (New York: Howard Fertig, 1971), p. 213; Charles Tilly, *The Vendée* (Cambridge, MA: Harvard University Press, 1964), pp. 5–6, 27–28; Anthony James Joes, "Insurgency and Genocide: La Vendée," *Small Wars and Insurgencies* 9, no. 3 (1998), pp. 17–45.

5 M. Adolphe Thiers, *History of the French Revolution*, trans. Thomas W. Redhead (London: A. Fullarton, 1845), p. 543.

6 E. Holt, *The Carlist Wars in Spain* (London: Putnam, 1967).

7 Douglas Porch, *The French Foreign Legion: A Complete History of the Legendary Fighting Force* (New York: Skyhorse Publishing, 2010), p. 25.

8 Porch, *French Foreign Legion*, p. 49.

9 Porch, *French Foreign Legion*, p. 11.
10 Vandervort, *Wars of Imperial Conquest*, pp. 56–70; Robert Aldrich, *Greater France: A History of French Overseas Expansion* (London: Macmillan, 1996), pp. 24–28; C.E. Calwell, *Small Wars, Their Principles and Practice* (London: H.M.S.O, 1906; repr. Lincoln: University of Nebraska Press, 1996) pp. 57–70. Page references are to the 1906 edition.
11 Denis Brogan. *The Development of Modern France, 1870–1939* (London: Hamish Hamilton, 1967), pp. 217–54; Frederick Quinn, *The Overseas French Empire* (Westport, CT: Praeger, 2000), pp. 121–27.
12 Brower, *Desert Named Peace*, pp. 9–10; Roger Magraw, *France 1815–1914: The Bourgeois Century* (London: Fontana, 1983), pp. 35–42; Pierre Montagnon. *La Conquête de l'Algérie: Les Germes de la discorde, 1830–1871* (Paris: Pygmalion–Gérard Watelet, 1986), pp. 57–98; Justin McCarthy, *The Ottoman Turks, An Introductory History to 1923* (New York: Longman, 1998), p. 89, p. 125.
13 Charles-Robert Ageron, *Modern Algeria: A History from 1830 to the Present*, trans. Michael Brett (London: Hurst, 1991), p. 7; Guillaume de Bertier de Sauvigny, *The Bourbon Restoration*, trans. Lynn Case (Philadephia: University of Pennsylvania Press, 1966), pp. 434–39.
14 Ageron, *Modern Algeria*, p. 9; Charles-André Julien, *Histoire de l'Algérie contemporaine*, Vol. 1: *La conquête et les débuts de la colonisation, 1827–1871* (Paris: Presses universitaires de France, 1964), pp. 62–105; On the miscalculations behind the fall of Charles X, see John R. Hall, *The Bourbon Restoration* (London: Alston Rivers, 1909), pp. 422–96.
15 Porch, pp. 13–14.
16 H.A.C. Collingham, *The July Monarchy: A Political History of France, 1830–1848* (London, Longman, 1988), pp. 246–47; Anthony Clayton, *France, Soldiers and Africa* (London: Brassey's Defence Publishers, 1988), p. 53; Paul Azan, *L'Armée d'Afrique, de 1830 à 1852* (Paris: Librairie Plon, 1936), pp. 41–101; Dieter Braunstein, *Französische Kolonialpolitik, 1830–1852: Expansion-Verwaltung-Wirtschaft-Mission* (Weisbaden, Germany: Steiner, 1983), p. 107.
17 Julien, Vol. 1, p. 92.
18 David Jordan, *The History of the French Foreign Legion, from 1831 to the Present Day* (Guilford: Lyons Press, 2005), p. 12–14.
19 Thomas Campbell, *Letters from the South*. 2 vols. (London: Henry Colburn, 1837), Vol. 2, pp. 196–99.
20 Douglas Porch "Bugeaud, Galliéni, Lyautey: The Development of French Colonial Warfare," in *Makers of Modern Strategy from Machiavelli to the Nuclear Age*, ed. Peter Paret (Princeton, NJ: Princeton University Press, 1986), pp. 378–82.
21 Barnett Singer and John Langdon, *Cultured Force: Makers and Defenders of the French Colonial Empire* (Madison: University of Wisconsin Press, 2004), pp. 48–49; Anthony Thrall Sullivan, *Thomas-Robert Bugeaud, France and Algeria, 1784–1849: Politics, Power and the Good Society* (Hamden, CT: Archon Books, 1983), pp. 56–66.
22 Singer and Langdon, *Cultured Force*, pp. 65–67; Quoted in Sullivan, *Thomas-Robert Bugeaud, France and Algeria*, p. 67.
23 Campbell., II, pp. 210–211.
24 Porch, "Bugeaud, Galliéni, Lyautey," pp. 378–79.
25 Calwell, *Small Wars*, p. 188; Vandervort, *Wars of Imperial Conquest*, p. 63.
26 Porch, "Bugeaud, Galliéni, Lyautey," pp. 380–81; Thomas Rid, "Razzia: A Turning Point in Modern Strategy," *Terrorism and Political Violence* 21 (2009), pp. 617–35.
27 Eugène Daumas [General], *The Ways of the Desert*, trans. Sheila M. Ohlendorf (Austin: University of Texas Press, 1971), p. 10.

28 Ibid., pp. 12–13.
29 Porch, "Bugeaud, Galliéni, Lyautey," pp. 380–81; Singer and Langdon, *Cultured Force*, pp. 75–76.
30 Singer and Langdon, *Cultured Force*, pp. 73–74; R. Allen Lott, "A Berlioz Premier in America: Leopold De Meyer and the *Marche d'Isly*," *19th-Century Music 8*, No. 3, (Spring, 1985), pp. 226–30.
31 Vandervort, *Wars of Imperial Conquest*, pp. 62,–70; Sullivan, *Thomas-Robert Bugeaud, France and Algeria*, pp. 106–7.
32 Patricia M.E. Lorcin, "Rome and France in Algeria: Recovering Colonial Algeria's Latin Past," *French Historical Studies 25*, No. 2 (2002), pp. 299–301.
33 Collingham, *July Monarchy*, p. 254; Paul Azan, ed., *Par l'épée et par la charrue: Écrits et discours de Bugeaud* (Paris: Presses universitaires de France, 1948), pp. 90–202.
34 A.S. Kanya-Forstner, *Conquest of the Western Sudan*, pp. 8–9; Leland Barrows, "The Impact of Empire on the French Armed Forces," in *France and Africa in the Age of Imperialism*, ed. G. Wesley Johnson (Westport, CT: Greenwood Press, 1985), pp. 53–91.
35 Kanya-Forstner, *Conquest of the Western Sudan*, pp. 9–10.
36 Mahfoud Bennoune, *The Making of Contemporary Algeria, 1830–1987* (New York: Cambridge University Press, 1988), pp. 35–43.
37 Kanya-Forstner, *Conquest of the Western Sudan*, p. 273.
38 Hugh Brogan, *Alexis de Tocqueville, A Life* (New Haven, CT: Yale University Press, 2006), p. 398.
39 Ibid., p. 399.
40 Collingham, *July Monarchy*, p. 256; Sudhir Hazareesingh, *The Legend of Napoleon* (London: Granta, 1988), pp. 151–83.
41 John Keay, *The Honourable Company* (London: Harper Collins, 1991); V.G. Kiernan, *Colonial Empires and Armies, 1815–1960* (London: Fontana, 1982; Montreal, PQ: McGill-Queen's University Press, 1998), pp. 17–32, 134; John Darwin, *The Empire Project: The Rise and Fall of the British World System, 1830–1970* (New York: Cambridge University Press, 2009), pp. 1–53; Lawrence James, *Raj: The Making and Unmaking of British India* (New York: St. Martin's Griffin, 1997), pp. 13–60; P.J. Cain and A.G. Hopkins, *British Imperialism, 1688–2000* (Harlow, UK: Pearson Education, 2002), pp. 97–99; Philip Lawson, *The East India Company: A History* (New York: Longman, 1993).
42 T.A. Heathcote, *The Afghan Wars, 1839–1919* (Staplehurst, UK: Spellmount, 2003), pp. 7–31; E. Ingram, *The Beginning of the Great Game in Asia, 1828–1834* (Oxford, UK: Clarendon, 1979), pp. 74–117.
43 Paul W. Schroeder, *The Transformation of European Politics, 1763–1848* (New York: Oxford University Press, 1994), p. 757; M.E. Yapp, *Strategies of British India: Britain, Iran and Afghanistan, 1798–1850* (New York: Oxford University Press, 1980), pp. 1–20.
44 Schroeder, *Transformation of European Politics*, pp. 757–58; Peter Hopkirk, *The Great Game: On Secret Service in High Asia* (London: John Murray, 1990), pp. 42–43, 175–87; Suhash Chakravarty, *From Khyber to Oxus: A Study in Imperial Expansion* (New Delhi: Orient Longman, 1976), pp. 24–25; Rose Louise Greaves, *Persia and the Defence of India, 1884–1892* (London: Athlone Press, 1959), pp. 2–3.
45 Quoted in J.A. Norris, *The First Afghan War, 1838–1842* (New York: Cambridge University Press, 1967), p. 91.
46 Schroeder, *Transformation of European Politics*, pp. 758–59; Yapp, *Strategies of British India*, pp. 290–91. Charles Webster, *The Foreign Policy of Palmerston, 1830–1841*, 2 vols. (London: G. Bell & Sons, 1951), Vol. 2, pp. 841–43.
47 James, *Raj*, pp. 88–89.

48 Robert E. Zegger, *John Cam Hobhouse: A Political Life, 1819–1852* (Columbia: University of Missouri Press, 1973), p. 257; David Brown, *Palmerston and the Politics of Foreign Policy, 1846–55* (Manchester, UK: Manchester University Press, 2002), pp. 1–17; James Chambers, *Palmerston, The People's Darling* (London: John Murray, 2004), pp. 185–86; Yapp, *Strategies of British India*, pp. 290–91.

49 Yapp, *Strategies of British India*, pp. 289; Schroeder, *Transformation of European Politics*, pp. 758–59; Harold N. Ingle, *Nesselrode and the Russian Rapprochement with Britain, 1836–1844* (Berkeley: University of California Press, 1976).

50 Heathcote, *Afghan Wars*, p. 31. See also Karl E. Meyer and Shareen Blair Brysac, *Tournament of Shadows: The Great Game and the Race for Empire in Central Asia* (Washington, DC: Counterpoint, 1999); James Hevia, *The Imperial Security State: British Colonial Knowledge and Empire-Building in Asia* (New York: Cambridge University Press, 2012), pp. 9–12.

51 Nancy Hatch Dupree, "The Question of Jalalabad during the First Anglo-Afghan War," *Asian Affairs* 6, No. 1 (1975), pp. 45–60.

52 Norris, *First Afghan War*, p. 352; David Cecil, *Lord M. or the Later Life of Lord Melbourne* (London: Arrow Books, 1962), pp. 234–35; Webster, Vol. 2, pp. 740–47.

53 Charles Rathbone Low, ed., *The Afghan War, 1838–1842: From the Journal and Correspondence of the late Major-General Augustus Abbott* (London: Richard Bentley, 1879), p. 73.

54 J.W. Fortescue, *A History of the British Army*. 13 vols. (London: Macmillan, 1859–1930), Vol. 12, pp. 38–39; Henry Marion Durand, *The First Afghan War and Its Causes* (London: Longmans, Green, 1879), pp. 84–85.

55 Norris, *First Afghan War*, pp. 259–65.

56 James Outram, *Rough Notes on the Campaign in Sinde and Afghanistan in 1838–9* (Bombay, India: American Mission Press, 1840), pp. 57–58, 69, 77.

57 "Assault of Ghuznee: From the Letter of an Officer in the Army of the Indus," *United Services Journal and Navy and Military Magazine*, 1840, Part I, pp. 145–48.

58 Archibald Forbes, *The Afghan Wars, 1839–42 and 1878–80* (New York: Scribner, 1892), p. 30.

59 Norris, *First Afghan War*, pp. 296–97.

60 Ibid., pp. 330–35.

61 H/546 Letter Book of Major-General Sir Willoughby Cotton, commanding at Kabul, Sept. 1840–Feb.1841, pp. 51–52, 82.

62 Yapp, *Strategies of British India*, pp. 346–47; See also M.E. Yapp, "Disturbances in Eastern Afghanistan, 1839–42," *Bulletin of the School of Oriental and African Studies* 25, No. 1–3 (1962), pp. 499–523.

63 Norris, *First Afghan War*, pp. 338–39.

64 J.W. Fortescue, Vol. 12, pp. 103, 145.

65 Norris, *First Afghan War*, p. 346.

66 Ibid., pp. 359–60.

67 James, *Raj*, p. 95.

68 Quoted in: Fortescue, Vol. 12, pp. 132–33.

69 Yapp, pp. 419–21.

70 Durand, *First Afghan War*, pp. 352–53; Norris, *First Afghan War*, p. 367.

71 D.F. Harding, *Small Arms of the East India Company, 1600–1856*. 4 Vols. (London: Foresight Books, 1997), Vol. 3, pp. 377–78.

72 Ibid., Vol. 3, p. 275.

73 Vincent Eyre, *Journal of an Afghan Prisoner* (London: Routledge & Kegan Paul, 1976; original edition published 1843 under the title *The Military Operations at Cabul*), p. 115.

74 Norris, *First Afghan War*, p. 378.
75 Quoted in Norris, *First Afghan War*, pp. 395–96.
76 Yapp, 442–54.
77 Stephen Tanner, *Afghanistan: A Military History from Alexander the Great to the Fall of the Taliban* (Cambridge, MA: Da Capo Press, 2002), pp. 196–97.
78 Schroeder, *Transformation of European Politics*, pp. 761–63; James, *Raj*, pp. 98–101.
79 Norris has refuted the charge. See Norris, *First Afghan War*, pp. 224, 423. See also: G.J. Alder, "The 'Garbeled' Blue Books of 1839—Myth or Reality?" *The Historical Journal* 15, No. 2 (1972), pp. 229–59.
80 Cain and Hopkins, *British Imperialism*, p. 282; Douglas M. Peers, "Between Mars and Mammon: The East India Company and Its Efforts to Reform Its Army, 1796–1832," *Historical Journal* 33, No. 2, (1990), pp. 385–401.
81 Durand, *First Afghan War*, p. 92.
82 Kiernan, *Colonial Empires and Armies*, pp. 160–63; Roger Beaumont, "Thinking the Unthinkable: On Cruelty in Small Wars," *Small Wars & Insurgencies* 1, No. 1 (1990), pp. 54–73.
83 Norris, *First Afghan War*, pp. 417–23; 441–42; Chambers, *Palmerston, The People's Darling*, pp. 211–14; Roger Price, *The French Second Empire: An Anatomy of Political Power* (New York: Cambridge University Press, 2001), p. 407.
84 Martin van Creveld, *Supplying War: Logistics from Wallenstein to Patton* (New York: Cambridge University Press, 2004).
85 Heinrich August Winkler, *Geschichte des Westens*, 2 vols. (Munich, Germany: C.H. Beck, 2009) Vol. 1, pp. 690–98; Schroeder, *Transformation of European Politics*, pp. 637–63.
86 David Brown, *Palmerston, A Biography* (New Haven, CT: Yale University Press, 2010), pp. 215–17; Schroeder, *Transformation of European Politics*, pp. 756–63; Hermann Wentker, *Zerstörung der Großmacht Rußland? Die britischen Kriegsziele im Krimkrieg* (Göttingen, Germany: Vandenhoeck & Ruprecht, 1993), pp. 23–38, 68–73.
87 Brown, *Palmerston*, pp. 389–92, 487–489.
88 Donald Southgate, *The Most English Minister: The Policies and Politics of Palmerston* (New York: St. Martin's, 1966), p. 334, 337; Orlando Figes, *The Crimean War, A History* (New York: Metropolitan Books, 2010), pp. 148–49; Antony Taylor, "Palmerston and Radicalism, 1847–1865," *Journal of British Studies* 33, No. 2 (1994), pp. 157–79.
89 Winkler, *Geschichte des Westens*, p. 692; Price, *French Second Empire*, pp. 41–94, 407; Hazareesingh, *The Legend of Napoleon*, pp. 234–59.
90 Figes, *Crimean War, A History*, p. 147.
91 Winkler, *Geschichte des Westens*, p. 691.
92 Winfried Baumgart, *The Crimean War, 1853–1856* (New York: Oxford University Press, 1999), p. 29; Sudhir Hazareesingh, *From Subject to Citizen: The Second Empire and the Emergence of Modern French Democracy* (Princeton, NJ: Princeton University Press, 1998), pp. 29–95; Jost Dülffer, "Vom autoritären zum liberalen Bonapartismus: Der politische Systemwechsel in Frankreich, 1858/60," *Historische Zeitschrift* 230, No. 3 (1980), pp. 549–75; Christian Sigrist, *Das Rußlandbild des Marquis de Custine: Von der Civilizationskritik zur Rußlandfeindlichkeit* (Frankfurt/Main: Peter Lang, 1990).
93 *HC Deb 31 March 1854 vol 132 cc198–308*.
94 Baumgart, *Crimean War*, pp. 93–92; David M. Goldfrank, *The Origins of the Crimean War* (London: Longman, 1994), pp. 219–68.

95 Andrew D. Lambert, *The Crimean War: British Grand Strategy against Russia, 1853–56* (Farnham, UK: Ashgate, 2011); Basil Greenhill and Ann Giffard, *The British Assault on Finland, 1854–1855* (Annapolis, MD: Naval Institute Press, 1988).

96 Greenhill and Giffard, *British Assault on Finland*, pp. 3–46.

97 John Shelton Curtiss, *Russia's Crimean War* (Durham, NC: Duke University Press, 1979), pp. 308–9.

98 Peter Duckers, *The Crimean War at Sea: The Naval Campaigns against Russia, 1854–56* (Barnsley, UK: Pen & Sword, 2011), pp. 50–51.

99 Lambert, *Crimean War: British Grand Strategy*, p. 200; A.J. Barker, *The War Against Russia, 1854–1856* (New York: Holt, Rinehart and Winston, 1970), pp. 272–72.

100 Curtiss, *Russia's Crimean War*, p. 287; C.I. Hamilton, "Sir James Graham, The Baltic Campaign and War Planning at the Admiralty in 1854," *Historical Journal* 19, No. 1, 1976, p. 92.

101 Baumgart, *Crimean War*, 185–92.

102 Greenhill and Giffard, *British Assault on Finland*, pp. 327–36; Lambert, *Crimean War: British Grand Strategy*, pp. 302–3; Curtiss, *Russia's Crimean War*, p. 550.

103 Curtiss, *Russia's Crimean War*, pp. 337–41, 558.

104 Julian S. Corbett, *Principles of Maritime Strategy* (London: Longmans, 1911), p. 292.

105 Ibid., 293.

106 Figes, *Crimean War, A History*, pp. 203–4; Lambert, *Crimean War: British Grand Strategy*, p. 150; Curtiss, *Russia's Crimean War*, pp. 305–8.

107 Peter Gibbs, *The Battle of Alma* (London: Weidenfeld & Nicolson, 1963), p. 107; Figes, *Crimean War, A History*, pp. 213–15; Barker, *War Against Russia*, pp. 89–90.

108 Quoted in Figes, *Crimean War, A History*, p. 215.

109 Gibbs, *Battle of Alma*, pp. 173–74, 178–79; Barker, *War Against Russia*, pp. 307–8.

110 Barker, *War Against Russia*, pp. 120–22.

111 Baumgart, *Crimean War*, pp. 121–23.

112 Barker, *War Against Russia*, pp. 125–26.

113 Ibid., p. 124.

114 Ibid., pp. 124–26; Baumgart, *Crimean War*, p. 121; Lambert, *Crimean War: British Grand Strategy*, pp. 153–54.

115 Curtiss, *Russia's Crimean War*, pp. 318–19.

116 Quoted in Lambert, *Crimean War: British Grand Strategy*, p. 159; Duckers, *Crimean War at Sea*, pp. 60–68.

117 Lambert, *Crimean War: British Grand Strategy*, p. 155; Duckers, *Crimean War at Sea*, p. 58; Figes, *Crimean War, A History*, pp. 240–41; Barker, *War against Russia*, pp. 150–53.

118 Mark Adkin, *The Charge: The Real Reason Why the Light Brigade Was Lost* (London: Leo Cooper, 1996); Michael Barthorp, *Heroes of the Crimea: Balaclava and Inkerman* (London: Blandford, 1991); Terry Brighton, *Hell Riders: The True Story of the Charge of the Light Brigade* (London: Henry Holt, 2004); John Sweetman, *Balaclava 1854: The Charge of the Light Brigade* (London: Greenwood Publishing, 2005); Cecil Woodham-Smith, *The Reason Why* (London: Penguin, 1991).

119 Barker, *War Against Russia*, pp. 150–74.

120 Albert Seaton, *The Crimean War, A Russian Chronicle* (London: B.T. Batsford, 1977), p. 159.

121 Ibid., pp. 157–64; Baumgart, *Crimean War*, pp. 131–34; Barker, *War Against Russia*, pp. 176–79; Patrick Mercer, *Give Them a Volley and Charge! The Battle of Inkerman, 1854 (*Staplehurst, UK: Spellmount, 1998), pp. 43–75.
122 Carl von Clausewitz, *On War*, ed. and trans. Michael Howard and Peter Paret (Princeton, NJ: Princeton University Press, 1976), p. 101.
123 Barker, *War Against Russia*, p. 182.
124 Quoted by Mercer, *Give Them a Volley and Charge!*, p. 172; Barker, *War Against Russia*, pp. 182–90.
125 Hugh Small, *The Crimean War: Queen Victoria's War with the Russian Tsars* (London: Tempus, 2014), p. 102; John Sweetman, "Military Transport in the Crimean War, 1854–56," *English Historical Review* 88, No. 346 (1973), pp. 81–91.
126 Barker, *War Against Russia*, pp. 212–15.
127 Ibid., pp. 216–17; Figes, *Crimean War, A History*, pp. 292–304.
128 Figes, *Crimean War, A History*, pp. 302–6; Trevor Royle, *Crimea: The Great Crimean War, 1854–1856* (New York: St. Martin's Griffin, 2000), pp. 254–59.
129 Wentker, *Zerstörung der Großmacht Rußland?*, p. 320.
130 W. Bruce Lincoln, *Nicholas I, Emperor and Autocrat of all the Russias* (Bloomington: Indiana University Press, 1978), pp. 348–49.
131 Baumgart, *Crimean War*, pp. 145–49; Alain Goutmann, *La Guerre de Crimée: La Première Moderne* (Paris: S.P.M. 1995), pp. 387–91.
132 Lambert, *Crimean War: British Grand Strategy*, pp. 239–50.
133 Gouttman, *La Guerre de Crimée*, pp. 412–14.
134 Baumgart, *Crimean War*, pp. 150–59.
135 Barker, *War Against Russia*, pp. 266–68.
136 Kiernan, *Colonial Empires and Armies*, p. 73; Martin Evans, *Algeria: France's Undeclared War* (New York: Oxford University Press, 2012).
137 A.S. Kanya-Forstner, *Conquest of the Western Sudan*, pp. 1–21; Barnett Singer and John Langdon, *Cultured Force*, pp. 47–116.
138 Paul Robiquet, ed., *Discours et Opinions de Jules Ferry*. 7 vols. (Paris: Armand Colin, 1897), Vol. 5, pp. 199–218;.
139 James J. Cooke, *New French Imperialism, 1880–1910: The Third Republic and the Colonial Mission* (Hamden, CT: Archon Books, 1973), pp. 14–20.
140 William S. Maltby, "The Origins of a Global Strategy: England from 1558 to 1713," *The Making of Strategy: Rulers, States, and War*, ed. Williamson Murray, MacGregor Knox, and Alvin Bernstein (New York: Cambridge University Press, 1994), pp. 151–77.
141 Richard Hart Sinnreich, "About Turn: British Strategic Transformation from Salisbury to Grey," in *The Shaping of Grand Strategy: Policy, Diplomacy, and War*, ed. Williamson Murray, Richard Hart Sinnreich, and James Lacey (New York: Cambridge University Press, 2011), pp. 111–17; Farwell, *Queen Victoria's Little Wars*.
142 Maltby, p. 177.
143 Darwin, *The Empire Project*, p. 61.
144 Ibid., p. 30.
145 Jay Luvaas, *The Education of an Army: British Military Thought, 1815–1940* (Chicago, IL: University of Chicago Press, 1964), pp. 65–99.
146 Hew Strachan, *From Waterloo to Balaclava: Tactics Technology, and the British Army, 1815–1854* (New York: Cambridge University Press, 1985), p. 41.
147 Ibid., p. 135.
148 Gen. Francois Canrobert, successor to St. Arnaud. Small, *Crimean War*, p. 107; Southgate, *Most English Minister*, p. 343.

149 Small, *Crimean War*, pp. 126–36; 132–33; 195.
150 Ibid., p. 186.
151 Ibid., 193, Baumgart, *Crimean War*, pp. 211–17.
152 Price, *French Second Empire*, pp. 340–41, 406–7; Southgate, *Most English Minister*, pp. 401–3; Small, *Crimean War*, 195–96; Wentker, *Zerstörung der Großmacht Rußland?* p. 320.
153 Seton-Watson, pp. 332–77; Figes, *Crimean War, A History*, pp. 484–93.

3 Second Republic, Second Reich

American and Prussian wars of national unity

Prosecuted within six years of each other, the American Civil War and the Franco-Prussian War gave birth to two powers critically important to the course of modern warfare. The one war an existential struggle of the American republic, the other clearly an exercise in predatory opportunism by autocratic Prussia, they nonetheless had the common feature of reconstituting their respective political systems as powerful modern states. Although no war can be deemed inevitable, the American war came as close as any conflict of modern times. The Prussian war was eminently avoidable, a work of cold and even cynical calculation. And yet it rates equally both as a war of national consolidation and as an apparent verdict of history on the special legitimacy of the state it hammered out.[1]

The American Civil War was fought between the forces of the Federal Government of the United States against those of the Confederate States of America, made of eleven states that announced their secession from the Union in early 1861. More than 600,000 American soldiers lost their lives during a conflict involving more than three million military personnel. After four years of bloodshed, the unity of the United States was preserved, slave labour abolished, and a newly assertive national government was poised to complete territorial expansion across the American continent. In the process, the war advanced the industrialisation of military conflict in several ways, the most obvious among them the extensive use of telegraph communication following its introduction in the Crimean War, the transportation of troops and supplies by railway, and the introduction of an early version of the machinegun. In the war's final stage the command of the Union army also found it expedient to target the civilian population and private property of the South in a systematic fashion that anticipated in a limited fashion some of the horrors of war in twentieth century.

So too did the final and most significant of the wars of German unification, the Franco-Prussian. The war's political source was Prussia's ambition to bring about the unification of the German states of Central Europe under its leadership, and its outcome was also a triumph for Prussian authoritarianism and militarism. The French Second Empire collapsed in military debacle and Prussia welded the German states into a German Empire with a rapidly industrialising economy at the continent's core. The political leadership of the Prussian chancellor, Otto von Bismarck, initially bore similarities to that of President Abraham Lincoln, in so far as he set the diplomatic conditions for war with France as adroitly as Lincoln forced the Confederacy into the role of aggressor in 1861. Bismarck, however, was not involved in an existential struggle but rather a limited war with ambitious though restricted goals. Having established the war's goals, he turned its prosecution over to the Prussian General Staff and exercised nothing approximating the authority over military operations wielded by Lincoln. What matters above all is the play of politics and policy on the conduct of the conflicts—each in its own way, to use Bismarck's words, a trial of blood and iron.

Yankee leviathan[2]

Political conflict among the United States was a product of the young republic's very success, set against the hallowed myth of its founding that a truly free people could be effectively self-governing in the absence of a strong central authority. From its very infancy the United States, advantaged enormously by its geographical isolation from European conflict, was nonetheless extraordinarily precocious about its place in the world. By 1823 it had articulated the Monroe Doctrine, a sweeping hemisphere-of-interest declaration, and by the 1840s had developed in Manifest Destiny a popular nationalist ideology of expansion that American power was only circumstantially capable of redeeming.[3] At every stage territorial expansion heightened the tensions between the plantation South and the industrial North over the extension of slavery to lands beyond the Mississippi River. The most astute observer of American democracy, Alexis de Tocqueville, noted in the 1830s that the United States was two countries, inhabited by the Northerner, "patient, calculating, tolerant, slow to act, but persevering in his designs," and the Southerner, given to "greatness, luxury, renown, excitement, enjoyment, and above all, idleness."[4] He might have added "criminal adventurousness" to the qualities of Southerners such as William Walker, who led freebooting expeditions to Central America with the vision of conquering territory and adding new slave states to the Union. Closer to home slave owners looked to Texas for the expansion of the cotton economy.

President James Polk linked the annexation of Texas to his 1844 reelection campaign at a point where pressure in its favour within the Democratic Party was becoming irresistible. As abolitionists warned it would, the annexation of Texas led to war with Mexico.[5] In a short but decisive conflict, the United States prevailed and in the peace treaty with Mexico acquired a vast, expanse of territory roughly comprising the present-day states of California, Nevada, and Utah, much of New Mexico and Arizona, as well as parts of Wyoming and Colorado. The question mark over the socioeconomic future of states formed from this frontier brought terminal pressure to a national political system straining under the weight of its contradictions, as the Free Soil

Party eclipsed the congressional Whigs and brought forth its own progeny, the Republican Party. No less a figure than Ulysses Grant later judged the annexation of Texas as the product of "a conspiracy to acquire territory out of which slave states might be formed" and the Civil War largely an outgrowth of the Mexican conflict.[6]

The first skirmishing of the Civil War took place in Congress, where the Republican Party was the most recent partisan manifestation of Northeastern and Western sentiment about further expansion. The republic had outstripped the political community governing it and the apparatus of the state regulating it; the nation's political economy was so self-contradictory by 1860 that it hardly constituted a nation at all. And yet Northern industrialists sought the expansion of central authority into two interrelated matters, the establishment of a unified market across the nation, and the suppression of the southern secessionism that could thwart it.[7] Abraham's Lincoln's election to the presidency of itself brought that secessionism to a fever. During the 1850s Lincoln had found his voice in the new Republican Party on the slavery issue, citing it as the source of the national crisis and simultaneously expressing a willingness to employ force to preserve the American federation. Southern planters correctly viewed Lincoln's opposition to slavery's expansion into the new territories in the West as a creeping declaration of war on their peculiar institution. Who could doubt that such a declaration would be made official after Lincoln's Cooper Union speech of February 27, 1860, in Brooklyn, wherein he turned the attention of his fellow Republicans to that institution with the plea that they not be diverted by some belabored "groping for some middle ground between the right and wrong"?[8]

National disintegration did not wait for his inauguration. South Carolina seceded on December 10, 1860; Mississippi, Florida, Alabama, Georgia, and Louisiana in January 1861; Texas in February. After Lincoln took the oath of office on March 4, Virginia seceded in April; Arkansas, Tennessee, and North Carolina in May. Lincoln sought to gather moderate opinion to the Federal cause by placing his administration's policy on firm constitutional ground and declining to initiate military action. His inaugural address therefore posed the question whether "the United States be not a government proper, but an association of States in the nature of contract merely" that could be "unmade by less than all the parties who made it," before assuring the southern states that "in *your* hands, my dissatisfied fellow-countrymen, and not in *mine,* is the momentous issue of civil war. The Government will not assail *you.* You can have no conflict without being yourselves the aggressors."[9] When the militia of South Carolina opened fire on Fort Sumter on April 12, 1861, Lincoln began a career of war leadership that routinely informed the conflict's prosecution, "an exceptionally unforgiving commander" who "not only tolerated but fostered the ruthlessness needed to wage a total war."[10]

Yet the most remarkable aspect of the early stages of the war was the more rapid and effective mobilisation of the Confederacy and its success in early engagements set against the Union's inability to bring its strength to bear. In the spring of 1861 each side expected a short war, based on a faith in the martial inferiority of the other, an odd expectation in light of the fact that the two military commands had taken much the same curriculum at either the West Point Military Academy or the Virginia Military Institute—heavily influenced by interpretations of the Napoleonic experience—and had fought together in the war with Mexico.[11] Lincoln responded to Northern public sentiment in favour of smashing the secession before the Confederate Congress could convene for the first time in Richmond, when in late June he approved a plan to take the war into Virginia with 35,000 Union troops under General Irvin McDowell, West Point class of 1838. The Confederate commander opposing him at Manassas was General Pierre G.T. Beauregard, also West Point class of 1838, who had himself been planning a short, sharp offensive when McDowell stole a march on him.[12]

McDowell's offensive advanced too slowly and afforded time for the Confederates to reinforce their numbers with three brigades under Joseph E. Johnston, transported from the Shenandoah Valley by railway, the first of many contributions of rail steam power in the prosecution of the conflict. McDowell nevertheless very nearly prevailed at Manassas when he sent a flanking attack of some 12,000 men six miles around the Confederate left to its rear while 8,000 men held Beauregard's attention in the center. This feint in the center unconvincing, and the Union attack stalled against stiffened resistance. The Confederate counter-attack then turned a Union retreat into a rout. Simply put, the use of railway transportation to redeploy forces along the northern defensive perimeter of Virginia enabled the Confederate army to make a stand at Manassas, while tactical astuteness turned a disaster for Beauregard back upon McDowell.

Although the character of the engagement "did not differ from those of the French Revolution and Napoleon,"[13] Manassas was the first of many battles in which an attacking side that failed to achieve either surprise or advantage of position with a flanking movement was repulsed by a defending side that kept its head. Additionally, Confederate and Union forces alike took to digging entrenchments in preparation for the encounter, a tactical habit that was generally to increase over the course of the war and which departed significantly from the Napoleonic period's greater use of cavalry and artillery in offensive roles. Manassas in 1861 was highly representative of subsequent engagements, the primary change being in the efforts of both sides to overthrow the dominance of defensive manoeuvre with greater numbers of attacking infantry.[14] European military observers at the time gave mixed reviews on the importance of entrenchments, but highly influential European military scholars of the war were later to observe that "in 1861–65 the rifle bullet was lord of the battlefield as was the machinegun bullet in 1914–18" and that both forced infantry to dig in order to survive.[15] The immediate impact of Manassas was to feed Confederate confidence, although in the spring of 1861 the logistics of the Confederate army were as yet so undeveloped that it was incapable of a sustained advance. Two days after Manassas Lincoln drafted a memorandum on future strategy that stressed the importance of an effective naval blockade of the south, firm Union control of the border state of Maryland, reinforcement of Union troops in Virginia, and an offensive by Union forces in the Western Theater of the war with special attention to Missouri. Thus, for different reasons both sides came to the sobering acknowledgment that there would be no ninety-days war. The first major clash of arms "blew away illusions like rags of fog."[16]

The Union survives

The rebel victory threw up the issue of international recognition of the Confederacy. Lincoln's naval blockade complicated matters further, as under international law this made the war no longer a purely domestic affair and raised the possibility of a confrontation with Great Britain over the rights of maritime commerce. Beyond the fact that the Union did not at this point have the naval capacity to blockade Southern ports effectively, the Palmerston government in London was now in a position to make mischief by standing on the rights of neutrals on the one hand while building ships for the Confederacy on the other. Although damage inflicted on American commerce by products of British yards such as the raider *CSS Alabama* were significant, Britain's position on the war inevitably took a more ominous turn when a Union warship intercepted the British mail steamer *Trent* on its way from the Bahamas to Europe and arrested two Confederate envoys bound for Europe. As the Confederates were sailing under a neutral flag, the offence to international law was clear. Every European power of consequence sided with Britain. Still, Foreign Secretary Lord John Russell persuaded Palmerston to moderate the language of his diplomatic notes to Washington, while the British representation there delayed formal presentation of Palmerston's ultimatum to give passions a chance to cool. Lincoln backed down and agreed to the release of the prisoners to British custody with the explanation to cabinet hotheads that "we must have no war with England now; we cannot afford it." It was an unpleasant diplomatic humiliation, yet was more than compensated by the fact that British satisfaction with it was a bitter disappointment to the Confederacy. In January 1863 the Confederate envoys were released; the one went to London, the other to Paris, but neither accomplished anything.[17] In 1861 any degree of British intervention represented a threat to the Union's survival, so the diplomatic resolution of the Trent Affair was of strategic benefit to the United States greater than any early battlefield engagement.

The Union nonetheless found itself at a loss for a way forward. Winfield Scott, at the time of Manassas brevet lieutenant general in charge of all military affairs for the Union, was seventy-four and incapable of commanding an army in the field. He took full responsibility for Manassas, yet had in fact opposed both the idea of an early Union offensive in conception and execution. His own plan, rejected in the fevered political climate if 1861, envisioned a strangulation of the Confederacy with a naval blockade of its seaports and seizure of its inland waterway, the Mississippi River. Scott was at least half-right in his understanding of the Confederacy's weaknesses, and the memo penned by Lincoln was a variant of Scott's concept. The primary instrument of its execution, Ulysses Grant, was at the time a mere colonel of the 21st Illinois Volunteers.[18]

The comparative fortunes of the war alone favoured his rise. The failure of the Union to make significance progress against the Confederacy in the east, despite its overall advantage in numbers, was compensated by Grant's southward advance through engagements large and small into Tennessee and toward the Mississippi. The Western Theater nonetheless remained a secondary theatre, and Grant a peripheral figure, as in 1862 General George McClellan was given the troops and supplies necessary to launch a campaign he judged would bring an end to the war. His Peninsular Campaign, intended to relieve Confederate pressure against Washington by landing an army from Chesapeake Bay and then to use the roads and rivers south and east of Richmond to threaten the Confederate capital, was a strategic manoeuvre into the enemy's rear. For the campaign he was given 121,500 men, forty-four batteries of artillery, 14,592 animals drawing 1,224 wagons and ambulances, all transported and supported by Union naval superiority and secure water communications. McClellan underestimated the plan's inherent logistical problems and executed it with such inordinate caution that he added to them. Worse still, the Confederate army declined to provide him the decisive battle he sought until he approached the vicinity of Richmond, whereupon the campaign did not so much climax as peter out in the six running engagements of the Seven Days. The failed offensive was a watershed, moving Lincoln, in the face of press charges that his administration was timid and ignorant, to request of Northern state governors another 300,000 men for a long war.[19]

While the squandering of resources and time continued in the east, Union forces under Major General Henry Halleck in the west were wasting neither. Confederate Forts Henry on the Tennessee River and Donelson on the Cumberland River became targets for Union attacks in preparation for advances up both rivers to collapse the rebel position in the region. Halleck estimated that such a campaign would require 60,000 men for mid-February, but his subordinate, Grant, asked Halleck in mid-January for permission to move against the forts with only 15,000 men. When Halleck consented after an initial refusal, Grant's little army combined its effort against Fort Henry with navy gunboats to bring the rebel garrison to surrender on February 6. Fort Donelson then fell to Grant's demand of unconditional surrender nine days later. It was in an attempt to retrieve initiative and territory that Albert Johnston, together with Benjamin Prentiss and P.G.T. Beauregard, marched 40,000 men north to fall upon

Grant's army camped on the west bank of the Tennessee River. Johnston was initially successful in overrunning Union positions, but Grant's troops settled into firm resistance and held on until Don Carlos Buell's arrived to reinforce them and join in a counter-attack the following day. By the time Johnston had withdrawn, the ferocious fighting around Shiloh Church had cost the Union 13,047 and the Confederacy 10,694 men.[20]

It was this scale of the carnage that brought forth Northern public indignation against Grant and his immediate subordinate, William Tecumseh Sherman, for having been surprised at Shiloh. The criticism of Grant's generalship rose through the Republican congressmen to Lincoln, where it ended with the famous riposte that the President of the United States could not spare a man who fights. At the time, McClellan was only beginning his lavishly supplied misadventure on the Peninsula, so the contrast between enterprise and caution may have been on Lincoln's mind. Grant's defence at Shiloh paid a strategic dividend despite the fact that it was in the wrong theatre, as the Confederate army was forced to abandon Corinth and never again regained the initiative in the West.[21] President Lincoln and General Grant were beginning to understand the conflict better than anyone. For a time yet Halleck was to run administrative interference in the emerging understanding between them, but his ultimate removal opened the way to one of the greatest partnerships of political reason and military command in modern history.[22]

In 1862 the combination of those two dimensions ended the first phase of the Civil War and changed its nature altogether. Late in the year the Union's use of railroad was beginning to demonstrate its advantage in logistics, and the Confederate offensive that climaxed at Antietam was in part inspired by the need to strike against Northern rail lines with strategic effect.[23] Following Manassas the Confederacy began what Jefferson Davis called an "offensive-defensive" strategy, according to which its armies would, with interior lines of communication, defend the South against a Northern invasion yet would also hazard offensives into Union territory as opportunity afforded. Confederate success with raiding generally and adroit manoeuvring defensively against the Union army of John Pope in northern Virginia that climaxed in a second Confederate victory at Manassas in August 1862 prompted a switch to the offensive with a march north of the Potomac into western Maryland.

The Confederate army under General Robert E. Lee would temporarily sever railway lines connecting the Union's eastern and western armies and confound their coordination. Although the operation was to involve 40,000 men, Lee conceived of it essentially as a raid that would force a defensive posture on the Union Army of the Potomac without involving a battle. The fact that the campaign climaxed on September 17, 1862, in the bloodiest single day in American history alone testifies to the folly of this calculation. An appreciation of the juncture of the Northern political scene, with congressional elections looming and antiwar sentiment growing, was also a factor in the decision to strike at a moment of psychological opportunity. Still, Lee's Army of Northern Virginia had just completed an exhausting, if successful, fighting season and was plagued by straggling and desertion. The capture of Lee's Special Order No. 191, outlining the goals of the operation, by soldiers of McClelland's XII Corps, completed for the Union commander a picture of Lee's intention already roughed in by the reports of Union informants along the Confederate line of advance.[24] This these factors, combined with Lee's decision to send part of his army against the crossing at Harper's Ferry, meant that initially the Confederate forces deployed north of Sharpesburg west of Antietam Creek totaled 26,000 opposite the 70,000 Union troops McClelland was in a position to concentrate against them.[25]

McClellan's caution prevented him from taking full advantage of Lee's errors in judgement. Joseph Hooker, in command of the Union I Corps, opened the battle at 5:00 AM with a determined assault on Lee's left, which might have rolled up the Confederate line had it been directed over weakly defended high ground further to the west. Instead it slammed into the main body of the Confederate left under Thomas Jackson, degenerated into a bloodbath, and ground to a tactical stalemate. By the time McClellan then ordered an attack by Ambrose Burnside's IX Corps over the stone Rohrback Bridge against Lee's right, the Confederate force from Harper's Ferry under A.P. Hill had come to Lee's aid and promptly tore into Burnside's flank. Thereafter, Lee held his ground, shifting attention and troops along his line against piecemeal Union attacks. By the end of the day Lee's army had received a mauling of 13,724 casualties it could ill afford, while the Union sacrifice of 12,410 was squandered when McClellan declined to pursue Lee on the night of September 18. Lee had bested McClellan tactically, while McClelland had forced Lee back to Virginia. Both were losers, Lee because the Antietam campaign was ill-conceived and costly, McClellan because "he had failed to seize the greatest opportunity handed on a plate to a federal general to destroy a Confederate army."[26]

When Lincoln could not convince his general to take the offensive following Antietam, he looked for a replacement.[27] In the meantime he launched an offensive of his own, extracting a maximum of benefit from the blood sacrifice of Antietam to issue a preliminary proclamation formally freeing the slaves of the secessionist states. The Emancipation Proclamation was intended to damage the economy of the Confederacy without alienating slave states loyal to the Union. Although Lincoln had first broached the issue with his cabinet in July, the issuance of the Proclamation on September 22, five days after Antietam, declared the battle a Union victory and burned all imaginary bridges of compromise or tender peace with the Confederacy. "When Lee came over the river," he explained, "I made a resolution that if McClellan drove him back I would send the Proclamation after him."[28] The act was as important as any other of the war, politically the most revolutionary action taken since the Declaration of Independence; it was to be coupled with the suspension of the writ of habeus corpus, the imposition of conscription, the seizure of Confederate civilian property, and a newly aggressive conduct of the war. It chimed with the public temper in the Northern states in the summer and autumn of 1862, now newly darkened by Antietam and recommending not only the freedom of the slaves but, from more than one mouth, the extermination of the slaveholders.[29] Its timing and articulation thread the needle:

> Lincoln had acted constitutionally. Emancipation was an act of "military necessity," he insisted, permissible under his powers as commander in chief to take whatever steps were necessary to win the war. The action was legal; it did not affect the slaves in areas loyal to the Union and did not violate the due process guarantee in the Constitution. Politically, the move averted confrontations with the border states, the Southern Unionists, and conservative Northerners who had no interest in blacks. Finally, the proclamation had diplomatic implications that would undermine the South's professed claim of fighting oppression by converting the war into a humanitarian crusade.[30]

Abroad, it spoke to popular anti-slavery sentiment in Europe and complicated the calculation of European governments who looked upon the dissolution of American republic with predatory interest.[31] At home Lincoln had seen off cabinet and congressional disunity over emancipation with guile and persuasion, consolidating the authority of the executive branch even as the proclamation's promise to amend the constitution promised new power and prestige for the central government.[32] The coherence of the strategy emerging at this point was remarkable. Lincoln had insisted that he would not make war on the secessionist states unless and until they made war against the Union. Once they had crossed the threshold from secession to war, he was far less constrained in the means he could employ to defeat secessionism. Antietam then marked the hinge of the war, as the Emancipation Proclamation further revised the strategy: the Confederacy was not simply to be defeated but destroyed—as a political entity, economy and society, and a way of life.

The symphony of Vicksburg, Tullahoma, and Gettysburg[33]

In 1862 that remained a distant prospect. Geography and limited resources forced the Confederacy into a fundamentally defensive war, involving a strategic concentration in space of its strength. Interior lines of defence and the astute use of railroads facilitated the timely redeployment of troops sequentially for engagements such as beat-off, delayed, or thwarted Union penetration. In other words, the South's best chance of winning the war was by not losing it. The Union's challenge was inherently offensive and vastly more complicated. In square miles the territory of the Confederacy was as large as Russia west of Moscow, the theatre of war that had consumed

Napoleon's army in 1812. The advantage of the Union's greater manpower and industrial resources was offset—as Lincoln understood better than most of his generals—by the problem of bringing them to bear in a coordinated fashion. The sea blockade in the East, the seizure of the Mississippi in the West, and battlefield engagements in both theatres meant that the Union's strength was spread across a greater number of commitments; only its concentration in time, involving the simultaneous operations and a harmony of purpose in two theatres or more, would suffice to strain the South to the breaking point.[34]

Lincoln implored his generals to campaign aggressively. McClellan's insistence that he would act only according to purely military principles is most revealing. Unanticipated setbacks were to come not only from maps that promised roads where there only sodden tracks but also from a civilian leadership responding to a roused public. He never appreciated that a soldier is not a free agent and that this is doubly true in a democracy; the United States was at war with itself, and its capital was awash in fear and suspicion. The president was in fact shielding McClellan from much of it, but, in the absence of results, "nobody was going to be reasonable about anything."[35]

The impatience that eventually cost McClellan his command became active earliest in the Western Theater. Lincoln appointed John McClernand, an Illinois Democrat born in Kentucky, to head a campaign down the Mississippi, because, like Lincoln, McClernand understood popular sentiment in the Middle West and had the connections to mobilise it in support of an aggressive campaign into the Confederacy by the back door. As McClernand also had a plan for a Mississippi campaign that Lincoln thought sound, politically and militarily, the general's zeal was something Lincoln was anxious to employ in the autumn of 1862. He therefore gave him command of the river expedition without consulting either his chief of staff, Henry Halleck, or the best soldier of the Union in the West, Ulysses Grant.[36] Grant emerged as both the leader of the western army and the hero of the Vicksburg campaign, a tribute to his political acumen in navigating the triangle of Lincoln, Halleck, and McClernand, even as he strove to direct Union strength against Vicksburg.[37]

More than once Grant committed costly errors due to poor information or even personal scepticism about sound information. The virtuous side of this coin was that he would not let the uncertainty bred of incomplete information excuse him from action. His apprenticeship in the Western Theater of the war, its secondary theatre, forced him to see its relationship to the larger conflict. The campaign down the Mississippi involved planning the movements and coordinating the marches of more than one army for sequences of interrelated minor and major engagements, such that Grant developed a policy of relentless campaigning in pursuit of the destruction of the Confederate armies while developing a grasp of the operational coordination of his own. Mastery of these manifold difficulties ultimately made

Grant, in the judgement of J.F.C. Fuller, "the greatest general of his age, and one of the greatest strategists of any age."[38]

In the early stages of the advance down the Mississippi, he was repeatedly thwarted by a combination of logistical challenges and Confederate counterinitiatives. Johnston's move against Grant at Shiloh was the first of these. Because Grant held his ground and kept the initiative, rebel thrusts at Iuka and Corinth in September and October 1862 were likewise intended to wrong-foot the Union advance but achieved only a delay. Roughly simultaneous with the eastern offensive into Maryland that climaxed at Antietam, they were merely supplementary to the Maryland campaign, and their failure shifted Confederate attention in the West to Kentucky, where support for the rebel cause was comparatively strong, as more promising terrain from which to trouble the flank of Union armies in the West.[39] Converging marches by two Confederate armies under Braxton Bragg and Kirby Smith failed to concentrate before they collided with Union troops under Buell at Perryville. In an early demonstration of promise Brigadier Philip Sheridan first stiffened the Union defence, then shifted promptly to a counter-attack. Because Bragg chose not to slug it out, in Lee's style at Antietam, the Kentucky offensive dissolved in anticlimactic withdrawal.[40] Vastly more effective were raiding operations of Confederate cavalry under Nathan Bedford Forrest and Earl Van Dorn against Union transportation and supply depots as Grant concentrated men and material for a march against Vicksburg on the Mississippi. The rebel generals used the geography east of the river to advantage, pillaging Grant's depot at Holy Springs and tearing up track on the Central Mississippi Railroad stretching south from western Tennessee. Sherman, in command of the Union forces above Vicksburg, was cut off by these operations well to his rear, so that the first Vicksburg campaign collapsed from want of life support.[41]

Still, it is not hard to see why Lee was tempted to view major engagements as the key to winning the war, when successive Union commanders in the east handed him lopsided victories in major battles in late 1862 and early 1863. In the first of these McClellan's replacement at the head of the Army of the Potomac, Ambrose Burnside, initially slipped by to the east of Lee's army and threatened the Confederate capital, his intent being to draw Lee into a hasty defense of it on open ground on Union terms of superior numbers. When Burnside was delayed crossing the Rappahannock River awaiting pontoon bridges, Lee was afforded time to take up strong defensive position on high ground south-west of Fredericksburg. Burnside now accepted battle on Lee's terms and launched a series of frontal assaults against Confederate troops behind walls and breastworks until darkness halted the massacre, taking 12, 653 against 5,309 casualties.[42]

Fredericksburg precipitated a crisis in Lincoln's party and cabinet. The war was consuming lives and resources at a rate never anticipated, while a cause many thought at odds with the preservation of the Union, emancipation, seemed to be redefining its very purpose. The alternative view held by radical Republicans was that the price being paid in blood necessarily joined the moral issue with military measures to demand that the war be a crusade for liberty. While the latter view was ascendant among Republicans in Congress, Lincoln's cabinet was split. Secretary of State William Seward was Lincoln's ablest and most trusted advisor, but his lack of passion for emancipation angered Salmon Chase, Secretary of the Treasury, as the position of an amoral manipulator. At the height of their rivalry for presidential favour over the matter each resorted to brinksmanship by offering his resignation, but Lincoln managed to retain both while accepting the radical interpretation. In the process he undercut criticisms from Congress that cabinet government was failing the challenge of war leadership and bolstered the unity of the executive while making himself the clear master of it. He declared to the cabinet after exhaustive consultation that "I do not wish your advice about the main matter—for that I have determined for myself."[43]

Conscription too underwent a qualitative change in the pivotal months of late 1862 and early 1863. Although the Militia Act of 1862 was the first assertion of the power of conscription by a government of the United States, in practice state governors resented the recruitment quotas and were delinquent in their implementation. The Enrollment Act of March 1893 therefore resorted to an outright draft of all able-bodied males between twenty and forty-five years of age. It is one of the great paradoxes of the Union army that, although the draft provoked violent protest in Northern cities—in New York attacks on soldiers, policemen, firemen, and any black person the mobs could find—only six percent of the 2,666,999 men who ultimately served in it were pressed by the 1863 act.[44] The act meanwhile extended both the reach of federal power and that of executive authority within it, as it brought to a head the question of legalising the suspension of the writ of habeas corpus. Whereas the early stages of the war had witnessed an executive proclamation suspending the writ to pursue anyone running from the draft, the Habeas Corpus Act now authorised the president to suspend the writ when "in his judgment the public safety may require it;" it gave immunity to federal officials acting under a presidential suspension in enforcement of the draft and permitted cases to be removed from state to federal courts.[45]

The need for a constant replenishment of Union manpower was demonstrated again at Chancellorsville only weeks after the Enrollment Act. After succeeding Burnside in the command of the Army of the Potomac on January 6, Joseph Hooker's crisp administration of the army and dedication to its cause quickly won support for its reinforcement to 134,000 men in April, plus approval of a plan to apply its superior numbers immediately against Virginia. Such was Hooker's advantage in number and position that he might still have crushed Lee, if the execution of his plan had not failed its theoretical boldness. But when the advanced Union columns collided with two Confederate divisions, he fell back on the defensive around Chancellorsville and surrendered the initiative. At this point Lee divided his army, compensating for his modest numbers with speed and aggression by sending Jackson's corps to the south and west on a wide sweeping march to fall upon the vulnerable Union flank with devastating effect. Chancellorsville was thus transformed from a probable Confederate disaster into Lee's greatest feat of arms.[46] Yet it could not reverse the tide of military fortunes.[47]

Following Chancellorsville the strategic options available to North and South began to tip in the former's favour, above all due to the progress and ultimate success of Grant's Vicksburg campaign. Lee threw the prestige of his recent victories and his powers of persuasion into approval from President Davis for a new offensive into Maryland or Pennsylvania as the best means at least of maintaining some initiative and at best of inflicting another rout on the Union. Vicksburg and Mississippi enjoyed lower rank of priority than Virginia to Southern generals, in part because they underrated its utility to the Union but also because they despaired of being able to reinforce and hold it. They were therefore willing to concede the fall of Vicksburg in order to concentrate efforts in the Eastern theatre where they hoped that operations north of the Potomac would draw Union strength away from Virginia and North Carolina and possibly relieve pressure Vicksburg as well.

Present in Lee's reasoning and his conversations with Davis was the chance that the continuing cost of the stalemate in the East would tilt Northern public opinion in favour of a negotiated peace.[48] Yet Lincoln, though frustrated by the reversal at Chancellorsville, was otherwise increasingly confident, even as Lee's Pennsylvania campaign got underway. He could accept the stalemate in the Eastern Theater while insisting that Union concentration in the more fluid and promising Western Theater remain inviolate; conscription would supply enough men to fight effectively in both, so that he did not have to choose to be numerically inferior in either. Thus by the summer of 1863 the South's vision of possible victory depended upon Confederate military success depressing Northern morale, whereas the North's vision of material advantage was at last beginning to weigh heavily.[49]

There is an elegant appropriateness in one of the great studies of the Civil War referring to this phase as "the symphony of Vicksburg, Tullahoma, and Gettysburg,"[50] in which Union operations in three theatres of the conflict achieved a near-perfect unity. Thwarted in his earlier effort to capture Vicksburg from the north, Grant sifted through the strengths and weaknesses of no fewer than seven alternative plans before settling on a decision to approach Vicksburg from the south and east. This plan—not Grant's alone but rather a synthesis with Halleck's and Lincoln's—spoke to the growing maturity of the Union war command. Its execution was nonetheless Grant's alone, and it involved the coordinated manoeuvre of armies of Sherman, McClernand, and McPherson to direct the attention of Confederate garrison in the city toward another threat from the north while Grant's main force marched down the west bank of the river to be ferried to the eastern bank south of the city and proceed north into the Confederate rear. This involved the coordination of marches with the movement of steamers downriver on the river to run the bombardment by the Vicksburg batteries and link up with the Union Army of the Gulf, under General Nathaniel Banks, moving upstream. Once his army had arrived on the eastern bank of the Mississippi, moreover, Grant abandoned his supplies temporarily, the better to take the fight to Confederate armies in Mississippi before they could concentrate against him, defeating one force under Joseph Johnston at Jackson and driving off another under John Pemberton from Champion's Hill before turning to the siege of Vicksburg itself. Grant's operations against Vicksburg involved not only an understanding of the use of rail but also of an appreciation of the superior utility of river transport in dealing with supplying larger armies over the enormous distances to be covered in a strategic turning movement against the south. Slow and short trains carried much less cargo than large river steamers, and the sabotage of track disrupted rail transport. With Vicksburg in Union hands, the Mississippi, wonderfully impervious to being blown up, became the artery of transport for Union armies and supplies deep into Confederate territory.[51] The campaign was a masterpiece of strategic manoeuvre, as sweeping as Napoleon's at Ulm yet executed against much greater logistical difficulties and achieved with the bold embrace of greater risk (See Map 2).

The attendant risk that Confederate forces at Vicksburg might be reinforced with troops drawn from Tennessee moved Lincoln and Halleck to prompt a limited Union offensive there, bold enough to command the attention of Braxton Bragg's Army of Tennessee yet not so aggressive as to drive it from the state prematurely in the direction of Mississippi. General William Rosecrans tailored the campaign to order, manoeuvreing his Army of the Cumberland superbly against Bragg at Tullahoma.[52] This was accomplished just as Lee's offensive in Pennsylvania was about to climax in disaster. Jefferson Davis authorised the Gettysburg campaign against his own personal doubt and the lone vocal dissenter in his cabinet, Postmaster General John. H. Reagan, who argued that no victory anywhere could compensate the loss of Mississippi.[53] Beyond the impact a major rebel victory north of the Potomac might have on public opinion in the Union, Lee reasoned, his army could sustain itself materially in the farmland of Maryland and Pennsylvania—possibly for the whole summer of 1863—more easily than in the ravaged countryside of Virginia. The first Confederates to engage Union forces near Gettysburg on July 1, after all, were in search of shoes from a local factory.

They came upon and were promptly rebuffed by the 1st Division of the Cavalry of the Army of the Potomac under John Buford, who was first to arrive in the vicinity of Gettysburg and appreciated the importance of the crossroads and the surrounding defensible ridges. The encounter may have been one of only a few in which technology made a critical difference, as Buford's dismounted cavalrymen gave battle from behind fences and trees and were able to hold off three times their number for two hours, in large part because they were equipped with the seven-shot Spencer repeating carbine, capable of a sustained rate of fire of fifteen rounds per minute. Although Lee

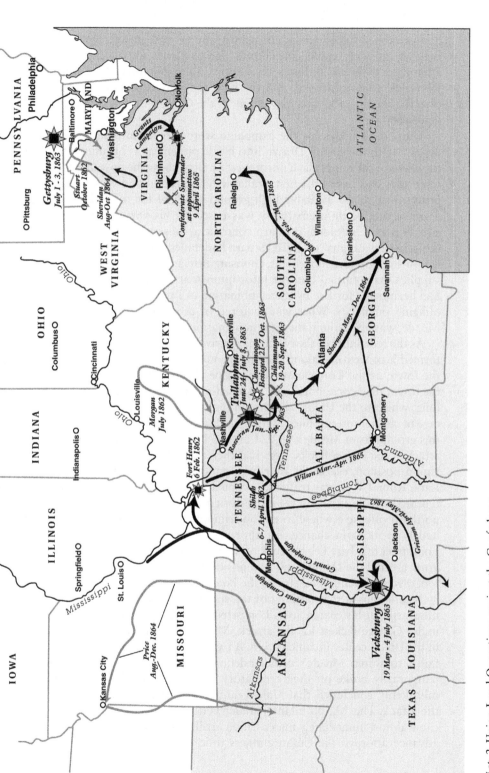

Map 2 Union Land Operations against the Confederacy.

had cautioned his commanders against any general engagement until such time as his army could concentrate, the Confederates under Harry Heth attempted to break Buford's resistance. Union reinforcements from John Reynolds' I Corps arrived, and the fight took on a life and appetite of its own that became the three-day agony of the Confederacy in the farmland of Pennsylvania.[54]

Thus, Lee's hopes for the campaign were turned on their head at first contact with the enemy. Drawn into battle piecemeal as his units arrived in the wake of the initial clash north-west of Gettysburg, he now faced a Union force that had seized the first available high ground and then extended its position to all the available high ground south of the town. Lee's caution about giving battle prematurely was based on his hazy knowledge of his situation as it unfolded; in sharp contrast to its service at Chancellorsville, the scouting cavalry of J.E.B. Stuart had failed to keep Lee informed of Union strength and movement, choosing instead to raid the countryside for supplies. As it turned out, the most important choices of when and where had been made for Lee by the combination of Buford's initiative and Heth's obliging pugnacity. What was required of the Union commander, George Meade, was neither initiative nor imagination but prudence and backbone.[55]

As the remainder of the two armies arrived on the scene the Union position formed a convex line along the high ground extending three miles south of the town; as the Confederate corps came up after the initial clash north of the town, they correspondingly assumed a concave configuration four miles long, which to the Union strength on high ground added the further advantage of shorter interior lines. With 71,699 men and 272 guns Lee was to take this ground from Meade's 93,921 and 354 guns. On July 2 Lee nevertheless attacked the Union flanks. This had the effect of actually consolidating the Union position, especially after importance of a hill to the extreme south, Little Round Top, was realised, occupied by Union troops and held against repeated attacks in one of the most storied engagements of the war.[56] If Lee's northern offensive where to end in triumph, the second day at Gettysburg had been its main chance. An appreciation of this moved General James Longstreet to advise Lee to break off from Gettysburg and to march his entire army around the Union flank to a position it between Meade and Washington, thereby forcing the Army of the Potomac from its secure position.

Meade sensed that nothing of the sort was at hand and that Lee would now strike at his center. So as Longstreet prepared a newly arrived division under George Pickett for the attack, Meade had concentrated his II Corps in the Union center in anticipation. A two-hour preparatory artillery barrage failed to soften Meade's center adequately, yet when the Union gunners temporarily broke off their retaliatory barrage the Confederate command mistakenly concluded that Union cannon had been silenced and ordered the attack. The 13,500 infantry under Pettigrew, Pickett, and Trimble thus came almost immediately under Union artillery fire, and the distance of their advance afforded the Union gunners time to change at their leisure from shell to case shot and canister before musket volleys joined in the choir of carnage. Whole units were mowed down until almost two-thirds of the Confederate infantry were out of action. The three days of Gettysburg that cost the Confederacy 28,063 casualties were the product of an offensive conceived in haste and likely to end in disaster if it encountered merely competent command from the Army of the Potomac.[57] Lee's army retreated from Pennsylvania on July 4, the same day Vicksburg surrendered to Grant. On Independence Day the Union's armies thus drew together the Eastern and Western Theaters and achieved a concentration in time and space every bit as valuable strategically at it was symbolically.

The end of measured combat

Named general-in-chief of all Union armies only in March 1864, Grant had already assumed the role in everything but title. In response to a near rout of Rosecrans's Army of the Cumberland at Chickamauga on September 20, 1863 he orchestrated the resupply rescue of the Union forces evacuated to and besieged in Chattanooga. This involved the theatre-wide coordinated concentration of troops from both the Army of Tennessee and the Army of the Potomac both to save the Army of the Cumberland and redeem the promise of the Union's position won by Vicksburg, Tullahoma, and Gettysburg. Although the Confederacy gained a serious tactical triumph at Chickamauga, Grant's crisis-management of the Chattanooga campaign robbed it of any strategic dividend. The retrieval of the federal position in Tennessee severed one of the Confederacy's few east-west railway links and opened the door for a Union advance on Atlanta.[58]

That advance was governed now by political factors in anticipation of the fall and reconstruction of the Confederate States of America. One of the more remarkable documents of the war, drafted by Sherman in response to a request from Halleck for his thoughts on Reconstruction, advocated the application of the physical power of the United States to "every part of the national domain," and the destruction of every obstacle to that end, if need be "every life, every acre of land, every particle of property."[59] It observed that among the social classes of the South its young bloods—"sons of planters, lawyers about town, good billiard players and sportsmen, men who never did work and never will"—were the best cavalry in the world and "the most dangerous set of men that this war has turned loose upon the world;" it recommended that "these men must all be killed or employed by us before we can hope for peace."[60] Sherman's winter raid from Vicksburg against Meridian, Mississippi in February 1864 was in many respects a rehearsal for ambitious projects of destruction to be launched in the spring. It demolished one hundred miles of railway track, ravaged the crop and stock, and "made a swatch of desolation 50 miles wide across the state of Mississippi."[61] The lack of significant rebel resistance also indicated that parts of the Confederacy amounted to a hollow military shell.

Other parts, in particular Virginia, were still very far from that condition. As the Union armies encircled Lee's beloved Commonwealth following Vicksburg and Gettysburg, the rebel commander was compensated with strong interior lines of defense and shortened ligatures of communications. This, in combination with Lee's generalship, meant Union forces would be given scant opportunity for the masterpiece of manoeuvre with which Grant had swept up Vicksburg. But neither could Lee escape battle with superior Union numbers. The centerpiece of the Union invasion of the Confederacy was a series of large-scale engagements in which Grant struck against the rebel defense like a battering ram and bled the Confederacy of fighting power. In the Battle of the Wilderness west of Fredericksburg of May 5–7 Grant and Meade brought to bear 101,895 troops against Lee's 61,025; at Spotsylvania, May 8–21, 100,000 against 52,000; at Cold Harbor, May 31-June 12, 108,000 against 59,000. While Grant's casualties totaled a horrific 48, 792, Lee's came to an unsustainable 29,141. Grant managed to maintain such constant contact with and pressure on Lee's exhausted army. Losses made no dent in his resolve, his famous dispatch from Spotsylvania promising to slug it out "if it takes all summer" typifying a serene stoicism about the outcome.[62]

This relentless pressure was supplemented by Sheridan's efforts in the Shenandoah Valley and Sherman's in Mississippi and Georgia. Grant had since Shiloh struggled to develop ever-greater operational coherence—to articulate between battle tactics and war strategy "plans for defeating the confederates not only along their entire defensive perimeter but also in theater wide settings, by coordinating the maneuvers of several forces in each major theater."[63] To this he now added an additional increment of comprehensiveness:

> Superior force had been put in his hands, and it was to be used not so much to win strategic victories as to destroy a nation. The richness of the Mississippi land had been taken to feed his army, during the march away from Grand Gulf, but it would have been well to take it even if his army had not been hungry, because its richness was a military target in itself: it helped to support the fabric of a nationhood which the North was sworn to obliterate.[64]

In this policy Grant enjoyed the unblinking support of President Lincoln despite their shared horror at the carnage. This was in large part because his attempts to drive down on the Confederacy at as many points and as continuously as possible accorded with Lincoln's inexpert but astute understanding of the conflict from as far back as 1862. But it was also because the war had evolved to point where only unconditional Confederate surrender could begin to redeem the sacrifice made.[65] The mounting human cost of war and weariness of the Northern public placed Lincoln in a vulnerable position in the electoral year of 1864. His chances of reelection were troubled by the moral absolutism of critics who saw the war as a crusade against slavery yet recoiled at its carnage and sought—with the Confederacy at last reeling under Grant's blows—"any peace consistent with national integrity and honour."[66] Critical to Lincoln's understanding of national integrity included the authoritative reach of its federal government. Lincoln considered provisions for the reconstruction of the South that would maximise popular acceptance of the Union following a Confederate surrender to be as vital to the prospects of a timely military decision as Sherman's capture of Atlanta or Grant's grinding siege of Petersburg, where Union forces had found it necessary to construct thirty miles of trench works. Lincoln had to fight simultaneously a rearguard defense against malcontents in the Republican Party—denouncing the "imbecile and vacillating policy of the present Administration in the conduct of the war," even as Union armies laid waste to the heartland of the Confederacy—while simultaneously looking to the sentiments of pro-Union Democrats as might flesh out his voting coalition. In the event he carried the country handily with the support by an increased margin of the same groups who had voted for him in 1860. It was in Grant's opinion a "victory worth more to the country than a battle won," to Lincoln proof "that a people's government can sustain a national election in the midst of a great civil war."[67]

The Emancipation Proclamation had been simultaneously a pledge to the dead of Antietam and an article for the uncompromising continuation of the war; it had strengthened executive prerogative and raised the profile of the executive branch against that of Congress. The Thirteenth Amendment to the Constitution, debated in Congress following the 1864 election, now raised that profile further. Firm in his conviction at the time of Proclamation of his legal authority to free slaves wherever the war was being fought, as it now continued toward a Union victory he etched emancipation into the marble of the Constitution. The change was simultaneously a major victory for the authority of the federal government over the states, as it in effect nationalised regulation of black labour with the very act of freeing the slaves everywhere in the republic. The hard war, emancipation, reconstitution and federal authority were all of a piece.[68]

The advance of Sherman's army on Atlanta and the march to the sea demonstrate in particular the blurring of purely military-operational considerations with the political goal of impressing the meaning of the war on the Southern population. Determined to reach Atlanta and willing to sustain casualties proportionally as large as those of Grant at Cold Harbor, Sherman became increasingly dependent on railway lines stretching from his main depot in Louisville to Nashville in Tennessee and from there on to Chattanooga and Atlanta. Because the railway was exposed to rebel guerrilla and cavalry predations over much of its length, the momentum of advance was maintained by the skills of the army construction corps, the elimination of all unnecessary baggage, and the exclusion of all civilian passengers and freight.

Once he had captured Atlanta, moreover, Sherman could not sustain offensive operations while devoting a large garrison to the city's occupation, so he forced the evacuation of its entire population, "the harshest measure taken against civilians by Union authorities during the entire Civil War."[69] The evacuation was regarded as militarily expedient above and beyond the destruction of property, its secondary purpose being the devastation of Southern morale. The latter was already in advanced application by Sheridan's army in Virginia's Shenandoah Valley when Sherman left a smoldering Atlanta and began his march across Georgia to Savannah on the Atlantic coast. In 1865 he headed north into the Carolinas, saving a special vengeance for South Carolina, the original home of secession.[70]

Sherman's slicing raids and their destruction of rail and rolling stock cut Confederate units off from one another, while the ravishing of livestock and crops left many rebels "marooned in a wasteland," making the choice for desertion eminently reasonable. The dramatic decline of Confederate morale following the fall of Atlanta in September 1864 and the descent of much of the Confederacy's territory into anarchy took the Civil War into its endgame.[71] It is revealing that as Lee's army retreated westward from Richmond and Petersburg, elements of Grant's cavalry actually arrived at Appomattox ahead of Lee. At this point the president of the dying Confederacy called upon the "unconquerable hearts" of its population to provide general resistance but was told by Generals Johnston and Beauregard that after Lee's surrender at the Appomattox Court House, guerrilla warfare was as futile as organised resistance.[72]

William Sheridan at Châteaudun: The Franco-Prussian war

If one accepts the notion that the American and German wars of national unity shared some of the features of the "total" wars of the twentieth century,[73] the treatment of the civilian population by conquering armies is a convenient point of connection. General Philip Sheridan—present with President Grant's blessing as an observer of the Prussian army's operations in northern France in 1870—advised his hosts that the predations of *francs-tireurs* should be countered with the utmost severity, so that French civilians would "be left with nothing but their eyes, to weep with over the war."[74] That Helmut von Moltke, the chief of the Prussian General Staff in command of operations against France, took little heed of the advice testifies to the comparative lack of official interest taken by German observers in the American Civil War. In 1862 the Prussian General Staff had completed a detailed study of events closer to home, the Austro-French-Piedmontese War of 1859, because the contending Austrian and French armies were of immediate and specific interest to its plans for the balance of power in Europe.[75] Just as the conflict in Piedmont and the cause of Italian unification served as a catalyst to the political forces in Prussia favouring the unity of the German states, so too was the year 1859 catalytic to the Prussian military's understanding as to how such unity was to be achieved.[76] Although the prosecution of Prussia's war in 1870–1871 was to share many of the features of America's of 1861–1865, the circumstances of its outbreak were entirely different. Prussia in 1870 embarked purposefully and wholly prepared for a short war of conquest in order to overthrow the European balance of power yet preserve at its centre the absolutist state for which the army was and would remain the central pillar.

Otto von Bismarck, the principal architect of Prussian ascendancy, was appointed prime minister of Prussia in September 1862. A "white revolutionary," his life's achievement was to bring the German states under Prussia, thereby creating the greatest power in Europe while delaying, and deforming, its political development.[77] From 1851 to 1859, Bismarck served as chief Prussian delegate to the Frankfurt Diet of the German Confederation, where he came to understand the economic and social forces active in the German states and concluded that Prussia could never thrive in any political constellation dominated by Austria and must exploit the neuroses of the smaller German states to emerge the hegemon among them. The opportunistic pursuit of the vital interests of the Prussian state—for Bismarck a mission transcendent of interest or ideological enthusiasm—thus was from this point onward the mainspring of Bismarck's statecraft. He wrote in 1853 that great crises would provide "the weather" for Prussia's growth.[78] It was thus entirely appropriate that in 1853 the liberal journalist and publicist Ludwig von Rochau drafted an essay under the title, "The Foundations of *Realpolitik* Applied to the Public Circumstances of Germany."[79]

Bismarck's partner in unification of the German states, Helmut von Moltke, since 1858 chief of the Prussian General Staff and architect of the army's reform and modernisation, was possibly the most consequential student of war since Clausewitz and Jomini. Moltke had an intellect of broad scope capable of serious historical study that helped him to master organisational and strategic planning, as well as to excel at operational command with an appreciation for the advantages of railway transport and telegraph communications. To Moltke, France's triumph over Austria in 1859 indirectly exposed a weakness in Prussia's capacity to mobilise and deploy its strength. At the time he had been petitioning the War Ministry for additional double-track railway line to the West. Yet by the time Prussia had been able to mobilise six corps in support of a role of armed mediation, France had prevailed in Italy and come to terms with Austria. Moltke therefore convened discussions of civil and military officials and proposed that they establish standing commissions for speeding mobilisation procedures. This was accomplished not only with additional track and rolling stock but also by keeping army units intact during transport, army corps travelling in their war order-of-battle, with the units most distant from the theatre of war being moved first.[80] Moltke's role in the unification of the German states under Prussia was second only to Bismarck's, not least because like Bismarck he saw the project as necessarily a politico-military venture for which the great struggle with France was the capstone. Despite this shared perspective, their relationship was more troubled than the coordination of civil and military authority worked out by Lincoln and Grant—indeed, increasingly so as the project approached its culmination in 1871.

The orchestration of strategic leverage

The opening phase of the wars of unification, an Austro-Prussian combination against Denmark over Schleswig-Holstein in 1864, was a by-product both of the 1815 European settlement and of the liberal and nationalist movements of the 1850s. Holstein had been given to the German Confederation in 1815 as punishment for Denmark's alliance with Napoleon. During the revolutions of 1848, Denmark sought to annex the Jutland duchies, but the local population resisted and was supported by Prussian troops. A conference in London in 1852 achieved a compromise among competing claims, but after the death of Frederick VII of Denmark in 1863, his successor, Christian X, whipped up Danish national enthusiasm for annexation against Austrian and Prussian counterclaims. The Austrian foreign minister, Bernhard von Rechberg, saw in the crisis an opportunity to fashion a durable Austro-Prussian condominium to buttress the German Confederation against the advance of liberal nationalism. Bismarck sought to take the duchies for Prussia, a goal for which Austria was no more than an ally of convenience. Hiding his intentions for the duchies while cooperating with Austria, Bismarck sought the optimum diplomatic moment to strike. This came when Denmark rejected an Austro-Prussian ultimatum, and troops under Friederich Graf von Wrangel crossed into Schleswig.[81]

The early progress of the war was distressingly slow and Austria a difficult ally. The mobilisation of 65,000 Prussian troops consumed too much time, in part due to badly coordinated rail transport and supply that broke up divisions over too many trains. Additionally, reserve troops accounted for some sixty-six percent of Prussian strength, a handicap aggravated by the fact that the army as whole was spread thinly over a growing number of garrison cities. In light of the Danish war, Moltke's ideas for improvements in mobilisation gained traction. Specifically, he proposed that the peacetime corps headquarters be made the organisational centers for mobilisation, that district commands be established with authority over reserves, *Landwehr*, and substitute reserves, and that their offices be located with a mind to accessing railway lines and telegraph communication. Because the supervision of this work fell to the General Staff, these changes became an important step in advancing its authority, one of Moltke's greatest contributions to the Prussian state and to the German art of war. Within nine months Denmark ultimately sued for peace and abandoned its claim to the duchies to Berlin and Vienna. Bismarck was vague about their future, the better to bring about a dispute with his ally. Prussia was far better prepared for the war to which Bismarck steered it, in large part due to the lessons Moltke had drawn from the Danish experience.[82]

Bismarck's diplomacy now moved seamlessly toward a crisis with Vienna, in which the Austrian government, since 1859 preoccupied with the negotiation of a new legal status for Hungary that terminated in the *Ausgleich* of 1867, was wrong-footed at every turn.[83] First, Rechberg was thwarted in his effort to get Prussian support for the reconquest of Austria's Italian territories in return for acknowledgement of Berlin's influence over Schleswig-Holstein. This eroded domestic support for Rechberg's policy of rapprochement with Berlin, a reverse he attempted to compensate by taking up the matter of Austria's possible membership in the German *Zollverein*, only to be thwarted yet again.[84] Rechberg resigned, and his successor, Count Mensdorff-Pouilly, was tasked by Emperor Franz-Josef with adhering to cooperative line with Prussia. Bismarck promptly rendered cooperation impossible by demanding that Saxon and Hanoverian troops leave Schleswig while the Prussian garrisons remained; that the armed forces of the duchies be folded into the Prussian military; that Prussia have coastal fortifications and the right to build a canal across the territories linking the Baltic with the North Sea; and that the duchies join the *Zollverein*. The Gastein Convention of 1865, according to which the administration of Schleswig and Holstein was to be divided between the two powers, represented only a way-station on the path to war. Most critically, Bismarck proposed the abolition of the German Confederation's Diet and its replacement by a popularly elected German parliament, thereby coquetting with both liberal and national sentiment in many of the smaller German states while conjuring the nightmare of manhood suffrage for the Habsburg monarchy and the kings of Hanover and Bavaria. This time Mensdorff pushed back by referring the dispute over the duchies to the German federal Diet in Frankfurt, technically a violation of the exclusively bilateral Gastein agreement and a sufficient excuse for Prussia to declare war to expel Austria from the Jutland Peninsula. Having secured French neutrality with vague promises of territorial concessions west of the Rhine and negotiated an alliance with Italy, Bismarck was in a position to confront an isolated Austria with military force. The division of labour evident here between diplomacy and military force is particularly tidy. Once the diplomatic campaign had been completed, Moltke could turn to military operations with mobilisation procedures he had worked obsessively to accelerate since the victory over Denmark.[85]

By 1866 the General Staff had been enlarged and reorganised, while the army was articulated into regiments, divisions, and corps, with each corps stationed in the district from which it drew its reserves. Mobilisation preparations within army commands were directed by officers with staff training delegated according to the district command system, a change critical in 1866, as Prussia had now to mobilise not 65,000 but 280,000 men against a more formidable opponent, with whom a number of the smaller German states were likely to ally, and defeat it before France had time to rethink its neutrality and call its own forces to action. Bismarck's diplomacy had created an interval of opportunity in which Moltke's army was to achieve in short order a decisive military rout of Habsburg Austria.[86]

As Austria in 1866 could field 400,000 men in ten corps against Prussia's grand total of 300,000 in eight, Moltke faced an adversary of nominally greater strength. Adding to this challenge was the fact that Austrian forces in Bohemia would have shorter interior lines, while Prussia would have to deal with the smaller German states and divide his army into four groups transported by widely separated rail lines to the Austrian, Hanoverian, and Saxon frontiers. Still, Austria faced 200,000 Italian troops on a secondary front, to which it had to commit three infantry corps and two cavalry brigades, leaving 245,000 troops against 254,000 Prussians in the North. Most critically, Austria had only one rail line leading to the main theatre, while Prussia had five.[87] Moltke's plan for their use envisaged moving troops as far and on as many rail lines as possible, then from rail termination points that formed a wide arch from the west to the north of the area of Austrian deployment to have them re-converge for the ultimate concentration of strength.[88]

The Prussian advantage in meeting Moltke's all-important stress on speed of mobilisation and deployment was enhanced by the Austria's arrangements for command. At its apex was Ludwig August von Benedek, a Hungarian Protestant of lesser nobility, with a common touch that made him popular among enlisted men. Militarily, Benedek's appointment to the command of Austria's Northern Army was calamitous. In the first instance this was because Benedek saw the Prussian monarch's initial hesitation to declare war on Austria not as an opportunity to concentrate forces but as an interval of uncertainty that merited a wait-and-watch response.[89] This meant that an Austrian-German concentration of forces in what was to be the main theatre of the war, Bohemia, did not occur even as Moltke was shifting troops about to answer a possible Austrian invasion of Silesia. Kaiser Wilhelm I's patience meanwhile ran out first with Austria's allies among the German states. After demanding on June 15 that Hanover, Kassel, and Saxony abandon their alliance with Austria—a demand they rejected, correctly assuming that Prussia planned to absorb them in any event—Prussia invaded all three.[90] With the surrender of the Hanoverians, Prussian railway access to Saxony and Bohemia was secure and Austria increasingly vulnerable from the west and north-west. The convergence the Prussian I Army (93,000 men) and Elbe Army (46,000 men) to the west brought engagements at Podol and Münchengrätz and forced a withdrawal of Austrian forces to Gitschin in the south-east, where another reversal made it clear to Benedek "that he was being caught in a remorselessly closing ring of steel."[91] At the center of the ring some 450,000 Austrians and Prussians then converged for the climactic battle of the war on less than eight square miles of terrain south-east of Sadowa and north-east of Königgrätz.

The compact Austrian position has been likened to that of the Union army at Gettysburg.[92] The integrity of the position was nonetheless compromised when the Austrian IV Corps allowed itself to be drawn into a fight with the Prussian 7th Division over possession of the Swiepwald forest. The Prussians were eventually driven from the forest, but at the cost of thousands of casualties for the possession of ground that did nothing to strengthen the Austrian position. Over the morning of June 3, Benedek's army nonetheless performed respectably, its artillery besting the Prussian batteries and its infantry offering heroic resistance to the initial Prussian attack led by a hesitant Prince Friedrich Karl on Moltke's insistence that the Prussian First Army pin Benedek in place until the Second Army could fall upon his right flank. A combination of hesitant command on Benedek's part let pass the chance to take the initiative against Friedrich Karl at the point in late morning when his troops neared exhaustion. The arrival of the Prussian Second Army, 100,000 strong under the command of Crown Prince Friedrich Wilhelm, from the north and on the Austrian right flank, thereafter decided the matter. The Prussians promptly carried the high ground around the village of Chulm and held it against a desperate Austrian counter-attack. Thereafter, numbers and technology tipped the scales quickly and radically against the Austrians. Fresh Prussian infantry armed with breach-loading Dreyse "needle guns," capable of five rounds per minute and exceeding the Austrian muzzle-loaders in range, winnowed Benedek's infantry ranks and brought isolated artillery batteries too under murderous fire. At mid-afternoon Moltke sent word to Karl Herwath von Bittenfeld, in command of the Prussian Elbe Army on the Austrians' opposite flank, that he should now press forward to complete the envelopment.[93]

Just as Napoleon had destroyed the Third Coalition in a single engagement in 1805, Austria in 1866 accepted the verdict of a pitched battle. At a cost of 360 officers and 8,812 other ranks, the Prussian army had killed or captured 1,372 officers 43,500 men of the combined Austrian and Saxon forces. Königgrätz stands out an exception to the rule of mid-nineteenth-century conflict that the era of decisive battles was coming to an end. The campaign of 1866 was for Moltke in many respects a model of how modern war should be prosecuted: a coherent plan for the mobilisation of superior force, involving the coordinated operation of multiple armies for the purpose of their sudden concentration in time and space to deliver a killing blow to the adversary. Moltke retained throughout an unruffled confidence in the integrity his plan, so that the spectacular victory it ultimately produced took on in retrospect the aura of inevitability commanded by genius. "If one considers the economy with which Moltke employed material forces in order to achieve results according to a preconceived plan," observes Gordon Craig, "then the victory at Königgrätz deserves to be regarded as a work of art."[94]

Königgrätz brought to an end Austria's influence over the lesser German states—transforming the Habsburg realm into a strudel of nationalist conflict—and increased the radiance of Prussia in proportion. The impact on Prussian domestic affairs was to delay progress toward genuine parliamentary sovereignty, royal absolutism cashing a military triumph abroad as a political triumph at home and making Bismarck, in the words his biography, into a "genius-statesman" credited with mythic powers of judgement. Lastly, the relatively lenient peace terms Berlin worked out with Vienna reflected the immediate shift of Prussia's attention and ambitions westward, where the federation of North German states now came into Prussia's orbit, and the independence of South German states was exposed to terminal pressure, the occupation of Frankfurt-am-Main by Prussian troops signaling the end of the independence of Rhenish Germany that Talleyrand had sought for France as a hedge against Prussia in 1815.[95] Königgrätz came to occupy a place in the mythology of Prussian arms that was ultimately an immense disservice to Prussia and the German state it created. Its apparent lessons were applied for the next and greatest masterpiece in Bismarck's orchestration of diplomatic crisis leading to military conflict, a war with France as disturbing to the victor as to the vanquished.[96]

Preparation for that war, the most important war in Europe between the Napoleonic era and World War I, began immediately. Bismarck's objective of a new German Empire under Prussian leadership inevitably pointed toward the southern German states, embarrassed by the ease of their defeat in common cause with Austria and now isolated and confused as to their future.[97] For France this was ominous. With nothing approximating his legendary ancestor's abilities, Napoleon III had counted on an Austro-Prussian balance in Germany for France's security, or, failing that, a lengthy conflict in 1866, in which French intervention or mediation would accomplish much the same object. He was not in principle opposed to German unity, although Prussia's lightning victory and the terms agreed upon with Austria moved some of his countrymen to observe that in fact France had been defeated at Königgrätz.[98]

The emperor's domestic enemies on the political left were quick to exploit France's embarrassment, although many of them were naïve about the nature of the state taking shape beyond the Rhine. An appreciation of that, combined with the knowledge that the victory over Austria had brought Napoleon III under pressure and might move him to imprudent action in order to shore up the legitimacy of his flagging regime, informed Bismarck's opening diplomatic gambit in the diplomacy that led to war with France. This was occasioned by the overthrow of Spain's Queen Isabella II by a junta and the scramble to find a suitable successor from among the royal families of Europe. When Bismarck advised the foreign office that any candidate acceptable to France was not likely to be useful to Prussia, he meant that a German candidacy to the Spanish succession might be sufficiently provocative to bring about a crisis—in the best scenario a war—that would prompt the southern German states to accept unity under Prussian leadership and thereby complete the work begun in 1864 at Denmark's expense.

He worked diligently but discreetly to overcome the initial resistance of the Swabian house of Hohenzollern-Sigmaringen and of Wilhelm to a Spanish offer. Prince Leopold's acceptance of the Spanish throne, made public in July 1870, then delivered a sufficiently hot-headed response from the French Foreign Secretary, the Duc de Gramont, that France's honour and interests were at stake. Because Wilhelm intervened as this point to bring about Leopold's withdrawal, war might have been avoided had Gramont not pushed the French ambassador to extract from the Prussian king a promise that the issue would not be revisited in the future. Wilhelm's offence at the demand was genuine enough, but a consultative telegram he sent from Bad Ems to Bismarck over the matter gave the chancellor his best chance to slam the door on a peaceful outcome. Bismarck, Moltke, and Roon condensed the telegram to make Wilhelm's account of the exchange with the French ambassador appear especially heated and released it, with Wilhelm's permission, to Prussian embassies and the press. Bismarck later claimed to have provoked the war with the Ems telegram, but the French government and public sentiment was in fact well inflamed prior to his editing effort. France declared war on July 19. In light of the absurd premium already placed on "honour," the war might have come in any event, but the chancellor's biographer notes that it is impossible to avoid the conclusion "that Bismarck engineered the crisis and that the French reacted exactly has he had imagined they would."[99]

A promise of many tears

The "mastadon trumpeting" of parliamentary deputy Antoine Guyot-Montpayroux that Prussia had forgotten the France of Jena was exactly wrong; the Prussian military had since 1806 carried the memory of Jena-Auerstädt into every reform.[100] Rather, the French state and army had long since lost sight of what had made Napoleon irresistible for so long: unity of command, efficient staff work, rapid deployment, and concentration of force. The French Second Empire lived ideologically off a Bonapartist tradition that made something of a national religion of war, yet with the exception of the Italian campaign of 1859, its army had not seen major action in Western Europe since Waterloo and was constituted to support operations in Africa, China, the Crimea, Mexico, and Spain.[101]

The regime this army served was meanwhile less and less adapted to the society it governed. Having taken power in an election and consolidated it in a coup, Napoleon III was himself a caricature of the conflicting impulses roiling France since the Bourbon restoration. Although he was willing to adapt to a more liberal political system, the very people he might have pleased with this, the middle classes, were hostile to his sensible ideas for the army's reform, above all its enlargement by any conscription that included service by the educated classes. After 1815 France had turned away from the nation-in-arms and sought an army less frightening to recovered aristocratic privilege; over time bourgeois France too regarded the army with suspicion as the praetorian guard of an insecure regime rather than the instrument of national defense. In this they were justified, as events following the war with Prussia were to demonstrate, but by the time the shock of Königgrätz shifted the ground in favour of reform, it was too late for France to fully appreciate, much less meet, the peril it faced.[102] This peril was in direct proportion to Prussia's embrace of the nation-in-arms tradition France had abandoned, as by 1870 Prussia and the German states had vastly greater reserves at their disposal. Together they were able to mobilise 850,000 men, 300,00 of whom went to the field armies, whereas France had some 567,000 available and only 200,000 for the field.

The army of the Second Empire also suffered from a split personality, because so much of its command experience and tactical doctrine had been drawn from service overseas, especially Algeria. Following the defeat of 1871, however, the *Africains* were too often made the scapegoat for the more fundamental weakness of French command generally, the erosion of professionalism in an army where rank had come to depend more on social position and connections than on demonstrated competence.[103] Although gaining entry to staff college was highly competitive, a successful application amounted to the first stage of professional security; the best graduates claimed desk positions in Paris and evolved from there into uniformed civil servants, ever more remote from the grime of the martial arts. Marshal Adolphe Niel, the Empire's war minister, struggled mightily in the eleventh hour before disaster, 1867–1869, to reinvigorate the rank-and-file with a French version of the Prussian *Landwehr*, but in the legislature, republican fear of Bonapartist militarism did everything possible to draw the teeth from even this reform.[104] Undeniably, France had superior sea power. Even as the conflict raged, shiploads of war materials from overseas flowed freely into French ports, against which Prussia could do nothing. Still, for neighbouring continental powers at war, naval capacity could have only a peripheral influence on a contest of great armies.[105]

Not only was the strength of these armies unbalanced, the faster concentration and deployment of the Prussian forces by railway endangered the strategic position of the French Army of the Rhine massing around the axis of a road running between Metz in France to Saarbrücken across the German border. The delivery of Prussian and German troops to the French frontier was not unlike a factory assembly line, using nine rail lines of a system of 11,000 miles of track, two-thirds of which was double-tracked, to deliver the first Prussian troops to the French ten days after the start of mobilisation and running their number to 300,000 within eight more days. The French command had expected the Prussians to take seven weeks to concentrate at the front, possibly because their own management of railway mobilisation approximated a riot. Regiments left their garrison for concentration areas, while reservists left their homes for regimental depots, and supplies and munitions came from central magazines or depots to their regiments. A regiment stationed in Dunkirk was supplied by a depot in Lyons, another stationed at Lyon was supplied from Saint-Malô.

To the weaknesses of France's military system was added imprudent leadership at the apex of its command on display in the opening phase. Napoleon's faith in the fundamental superiority of France's professional soldiers encouraged him to appeal to the cult of the offensive, even as war enthusiasts quoted only the most bellicose voices of the Parisian press to argue that the nation's will was engaged. Indeed it was. Even newspapers that opposed the war as a ploy to strengthen the emperor's support among the people failed to anticipate its calamitous outcome, "especially as they shared with all Frenchmen an inability to believe in the possibility of their defeat."[106] The Ems telegram had the effect on French public opinion that Bismarck had anticipated; once the newspapers printed it, giant public demonstrations broke out on July 14, and crowds charged to the gates of the Prussian embassy. It was a popular war. Bismarck had willed it, and France had declared it, but French public opinion "had been an ever-present accessory before the fact."[107]

The emperor urged upon Marshal Achille Bazaine, a veteran of service in Algeria, the Crimea, and Mexico, an attack his army was incapable of sustaining against any coherent response.[108] The emperor's insistence that General Charles Frossard lead the seizure of Saarbrücken against Bazaine's seniority, and doubts as to what would follow it, gave the attack the quality of a gesture to stoke public enthusiasm. Once Moltke overcame initial confusion about Frossard's thrust into the very teeth of gathering Prussian strength to the north and south, he coordinated massive counterstrokes at Wissembourg, Spicheren, and Froeschwiller. The battle at Wissembourg, in fact, became something a paradigm for the remainder of the war. It featured the concentration of superior German numbers against poorly positioned French troops vulnerable to envelopment; deadly defensive firepower from the French Chassepot rifle overcome by massed German artillery; and the acceptance of high casualties by both sides.[109]

The defeat of Patrice MacMahon's I Corps at Froeschwiller put Moltke in a position to invade Lorraine from the north with the 50,000 men of the First Army, from the north-east with 134,000 of Second Army, and from the east with 125,000 of the Third Army—in much the same fashion as his invasion of Bohemia in 1866—coming around either side of the forward elements of the Army of the Rhine. The threat to supply lines and communications forced a French withdrawal. Running engagements were fought at Colombey-Borny and Mars-la-Tour/Vionville until the fronts of the war had reversed with Bazaine's army falling back on Gravelotte-Saint-Privat to face the Prussian First and Second Armies coming now from the west. This situation was brought about in part by the fact that Moltke was better informed about his adversary than was Bazaine. Because he had found cavalry almost useless in the war with Austria, he had since stripped its regiments of the capacity for independent action and reformed them for reconnaissance, escort, rear and advanced guard duty—in short, to be the eyes of the army everywhere at once—and ordered them to learn French, read maps, and interpret terrain.

Organised in the traditional role as mass shock units, Bazaine's cavalry told him nothing about the size and progress of Moltke's converging forces.[110]

He could hardly thwart Moltke's attempts at encirclement if he could not see the pattern emerging. By the time Bazaine drew up for battle at Gravelotte, Moltke had positioned two Prussian armies between him and the rest of France. An encounter engagement at Mars-le-Tours had brought this about. Lieutenant General Konstantin von Alvensleben had launched the Prussian III Corps in an attack against what he took to be the Bazaine's rearguard but which was in fact the main body of the Army of the Rhine. He averted the disaster his rashness deserved, because the French rebuffed the assault yet failed to follow through with a counter-attack. More Prussians arrived, so that the fighting dragged to a tactical draw in the evening, with the important difference that Prussian forces now straddled the road west to Verdun. The Prussian armies had in effect turned from their advance westward, wheeled north-east, and then east to press Bazaine back against the fortress frontier town of Metz. It was at this point, moreover, that Napoleon III recognised his own failings and turned supreme command over to Bazaine on the eve of the war's largest engagement.[111] It turned out to be the first episode in the surrender of his crown.

Gravelotte might have become a turning point in the deterioration of French fortunes, notwithstanding the fact that Moltke's war to this point had been an operational reprise of 1866. Bazaine chose favourable ground on which to fight a disciplined defence in the war's first set-piece battle, in which the superiority of French small arms could be brought to bear against Moltke's superior numbers; Gravelotte was "the most artless" battle of the Prussian's career, because headstrong subordinates compromised his plan for the engagement just as they had at Königgrätz.[112] Bazaine deployed his 160,000 men and 520 guns along a north-south line of hills running from Gravelotte-Saint-Privat at one end to Rozérieulles at the other, the latter anchor much stronger than the former. With 200,000 men and 730 guns Moltke intended to pin the French center and left so that the Saxon XII Corps could come around the right at Saint-Privat and initiate a roll-up of the entire French line. Premature and unauthorised assaults, however, ruined coordination among the Prussian units and led many of them into pointless slaughter under the fire of the Chassepot and the Mittrailleuse, an early version of a machine gun similar to the Gatling. At one point a French counter-attack might have won the day, but Bazaine remained throughout in his command post, Plappeville, like his namesake brooding in his tent at Troy, answering every plea for direction with an order to adhere to a static defence. Once the staggered Prussians had regained their equilibrium, 270 of their mass guns lobbed some 20,000 shells onto Saint-Privat and obliterated entire units. In the end Moltke's army paid with nearly 20,000 casualties to push Bazaine's army off the ridge.[113]

Bismarck began to feel the pressure for peace even as Bazaine withdrew to the fortress at Sedan. The carnage at Gravelotte was horrifying, and the Iron Chancellor's reaction to the corpse-strewn field, Sheridan reported in his memoir, was squeamish. Foreign governments that no longer thought the military outcome at issue began to urge negotiations, the Italian foreign minister inviting Austria and Britain to join a league of neutrals to save France from dismemberment and Europe from future war.[114] Already, the worry that the dividends of a Prussian victory might be diminished by the involvement of other powers began to trouble Bismarck's nights, so that an early ceasefire and the restriction of peace negotiations to an exclusively Franco-Prussian affair became of supreme importance even before the war's climactic clash at Sedan.[115] The war was already a much less fastidious affair than the duel with Austria.

As Bazaine's Army of the Rhine withdrew from Gravelotte to the fortress of Metz, France's last hope of redeeming the situation rested with MacMahon's Army of Châlons. After joining MacMahon's force on August 16, a despondent emperor remarked that he seemed to have abdicated his responsibility to his soldiers and was advised that his responsibility to his regime dictated withdrawal to the west in the direction of Paris. Convinced that he must reassert himself as commander-in-chief, yet knowing neither his own military mind nor his own political interest, Napoleon nonetheless decided that a withdrawal toward Paris would look like an abandonment of Bazaine. So MacMahon and the Army of Châlons marched eastward— actually some 130,000 men and 400 guns cobbled together now involved in more of a gesture than a campaign—to relieve Metz.

Moltke hesitated to believe his good luck. He nonetheless left the First and Second Prussian Armies to pin Bazaine in Metz, and ordered the Third Army and the Army of the Meuse of the North German Confederation— almost 200,000 men with 774 guns—in separate marches north with the goal the of blocking both the relief of Metz and all possible roads back to Paris.[116] These two armies were able to catch up with MacMahon and, after a preliminary skirmish at Beaumont, force the Army of Châlons back on the town of Sedan on August 31; they were thus able to trap the Army of Châlons within a great triangle against the Belgian border and, with a final night march on Sedan, bring it to annihilation. That business began in earnest at dawn on September 1, when the Bavarian I Corps moved against the French position at Bazeilles, so that by 5:00 in the afternoon, "the shattered remains of what had been an army of 130,000 men was a mere chaos of fugitives crowded around the walls and approaches of Sedan."[117] (See Map 3)

Early in the action of the final Prussian assault on September 1, MacMahon was severely wounded. There immediately followed a quarrel concerning who, Auguste Ducrot or Emmanuel Wimpffen, should assume command. As Prussian artillery controlled the heights above Sedan on all sides, this was in effect a struggle over the honour of presiding over the greatest debacle of French arms since the retreat from Moscow. There were instances of extraordinary heroism. As all French forces were pressed back on the fortress in the town of Sedan, Moltke's artillery coordinated gunfire of unprecedented precision by setting its guns at every possible elevation so that "there was no quarter of this last shelter of the French army which was

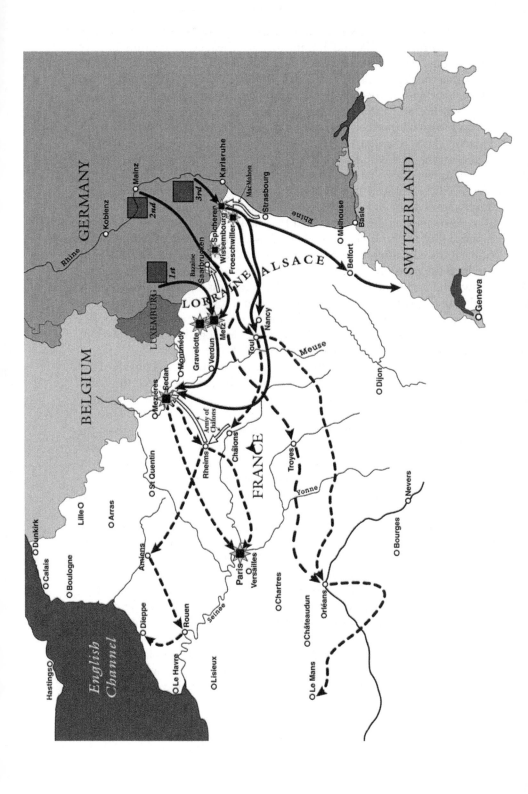

not saturated."[118] From this hopeless position the emperor ordered a white flag hoisted over the fortress walls.

The Battle of Sedan was thus consequential vastly out of proportion to the tactical verdict. Moltke's last great envelopment of the war had killed 3,000 French, wounded another 14,000, and bagged 103,000 prisoners, among them MacMahon and Napoleon III himself. It therefore had three immediate effects. Militarily, Prussia had lost only 9,000 men killed or wounded in eliminating the last French army that could block the road to Paris. Politically, the capture of the emperor had decapitated the French Second Empire and tipped France into internal turmoil. Diplomatically, the emperor's fall diminished the danger of intervention by third powers and enabled Bismarck to claim both that European monarchies must stand together against republicanism now rousing itself in Paris and that Germany would have to annex Alsace and Lorraine as a buffer of protection. It is therefore a valid claim that Bismarck not only founded the Second German Reich but also did more than any other single figure to father the French Third Republic.[119]

But if France's political regime had fallen, the nation would not quit. Léon Gambetta—son of a grocer from Cahors, barrister, orator, deputy from Marseille, and dedicated enemy of the Empire—took possession of the Ministry of the Interior and de facto political leadership of the defence of Paris. The republican deputy for Paris, Jules Favre, in effect re-declared war in the name of the Republic on September 6. Any notion of a reversal of military fortunes was clearly delusional—Paris was isolated by September 19—but Gambetta's Jacobin determination to save the national honour with genuine resistance was infectious enough to make the endgame of the war a troubling experience for both Bismarck and Moltke.[120]

France still commanded the seas around its coasts, so that Gambetta's orders of rifles and artillery from British and American arsenals were delivered safely to French ports. Many of the weapons found their way into the hands of *francs-tireurs*, civilian combatants from rifle clubs or amateur military societies who operated independently in small units against German troops, railway, and telegraph lines. As the French countryside refused to acknowledge the nation's obvious defeat, German reprisals escalated; at the old Jacobin town of Châteaudun, Philip Sheridan advised Bismarck to do to the French countryside what he had done to Shenandoah Valley and advised harsh retaliation against the local population.[121] This brought out the worst in the chancellor. Angered at having his careful plan spoiled, he threatened to have all villages harbouring *francs-tireurs* burned to the ground, all men, women, children thought to have fired on German troops shot out of hand, and the population in particularly defiant areas carted off to prison camps in Germany. The last threat was never implemented, but there was a good deal of shooting and burning, while Bismarck's public fury "did much to inflame and sustain the passion of hatred and contempt for all things French that swept through Germany."[122]

As Bismarck's concern to conclude hostilities gravitated between anxious and frantic, Moltke was proportionally reticent that his operational masterpiece not be hurried.[123] He sought the goal of the annihilation of France's war-making capacity in a strategic vacuum, as if political and diplomatic factors could not—certainly should not—influence it. The chancellor sought an early armistice that precluded the revived interest of any third power in diplomatic intervention. Moltke's resistance to Bismarck's urgings was based as largely on the practical and concrete demands of war leadership, but it is important to stress that Moltke and the entire General Staff resented them in principle as the interference of a military amateur. Bismarck's biographer identifies Paul Bronsart von Schellendorf as a particularly dedicated enemy of the chancellor on Moltke's staff; "the civil servant in the cuirassier jacket," fumed Bronsart in his diary, "begins really to be ready for the mad house."[124] Wilhelm I was unequal to the task of reconciling the conflict but tilted ultimately in favour of the implacable will of his chancellor, appreciating that the behaviour of Moltke and the Prussian higher command was nonetheless "a promise of many tears in the years to come."[125]

Wilhelm's interest in a settlement was helped by the balance of political forces in France among conservatives drawn to the sober judgement of Louis Adolphe Thiers, for whom a prolonged war promised either a consolidation of Gambetta's radical regime or a total collapse of the French state. His history of as a foe of the Empire in the Chamber of Deputies and opposition to the war with Prussia gave Thiers the prestige of international legitimacy at this critical juncture; his refusal to join the Government of National Defence added independence. Legitimists, Orleanists, and moderate republicans were drawn to Thiers more in fear of a radical dictatorship under Gambetta than in enthusiasm for what terms could be negotiated with Bismarck. When the bombardment of Paris began January 5, 1871, and the city's eventual starvation loomed, the preliminary armistice negotiated with Bismarck by Favre tilted political circumstance decisively against Gambetta. When elections to a new National Assembly were concluded— the irony being that Gambetta opposed them while Bismarck insisted upon them—Thiers finally won the argument with his countrymen. His name had been placed on the electoral list of twenty-six departments and had carried the day in every one; the assembly met on February 13 and voted him Chief of the Executive Power of the French Republic.[126]

With significant portions of France occupied, Thiers' mission was to make the best of a weak hand. The conflict between Prussian civil and military authorities had been temporarily resolved by the crown's insistence that the General Staff report to the chancellor,[127] but Bismarck's own peace terms were tough enough: French territory was to be annexed to the newly created German Empire and a financial indemnity of five billion francs was to be paid to keep France from financing rearmament. The territory included all of the province of Alsace and most of Lorraine, including the fortress town of Metz. Although the German occupation of Paris was symbolic, that of the eastern part of France was in effect a hostage-taking to be maintained until the indemnity had been paid. Thiers' primary achievements were to stand up to Bismarck, in principle to save a morsel of dignity by negotiating concessions, in substance to come to grips with the political crisis shaking France at its centre. In the first instance Bismarck conceded French retention of the fortress of Belfort in return for a humiliating German parade into Paris; in the second Thiers was able to minimise German interference in dealing with the insurrection seizing that same city, calling itself the Commune in evocation of the Jacobin assembly of 1793, and to convince Bismarck to release sufficient numbers of troops of the French army to take their capital back. Once within the gates of the city, they spent their rage on the Communards.

In a sense the suppression of the revolt was the Empire's revenge on Parisian radicalism. Napoleon III may not have prepared France to fight Prussia, but in Paris he had taken elaborate measures to fight Frenchmen with the modernisation of the capital under Georges Haussmann from 1853 to 1870. Broad and long tree-lined avenues and boulevards that cut through the tangled mass of narrow streets and old urban neighborhoods made it impossible for insurrectionists to erect barricades, while the system of converging avenues at *étoiles* and the location of the main railway stations made it possible to transport large numbers of troops from the provinces and to deploy them quickly throughout the city. Aesthetically, the classicism of avenues radiating out from the *Arc de la Triomphe* gave Paris the look of an imperial capital. Functionally, it facilitated the state's grip on the throat of insurrection; some 20,000 Communards perished to the forces of order under Thiers in street fighting, drumhead courts-martial, and summary executions.[128] The Third Republic's violent repression of the Commune was both a reaction to defeat and a further evolution in French militarism.

American and German ways of war

A final peace, the Treaty of Frankfurt, signed May 10 1871, had to await the defeat of the Communards, but a new German Empire was in the meantime declared at the Palace of Versailles on January 18. The diplomatic crisis Bismarck had orchestrated had through force of arms brought about what he had sought since 1864: the unity of the German states under Prussia. The delirium of victory would dissipate quickly, so the metal had to be struck before the whole circus of German princes and soldiers returned to their provincialisms. A union that owed nothing to parliamentarians and conceded still less of democracy to popular nationalism had to be wrought while Bismarck himself was still in place to direct its affairs. His contempt for titular fripperies and monarchical protocol showed on more than one occasion as he stage-managed his king and bribed the princes into an ill-tempered ceremony of unity in the Hall of Mirrors.[129] Remembering that the ceremony at Versailles represented the political capstone of not one but rather three wars of increasing scale—the diplomatic circumstance of each meticulously calculated to isolate the foe and limit the length of the conflict—underscores the significance of Bismarck's achievement and explains his anxiety over the terms of its completion. At the time possibly only Benjamin Disraeli, the leader of Gladstone's opposition at Westminster, appreciated the enormity of what had happened: German Central Europe unified into one state and two centuries of French dominance on the continent overthrown.

It takes away nothing from Helmut von Moltke's planning and execution of the military operations, moreover, to acknowledge that the victory of Prussian arms in three successive wars was as much Bismarck's handiwork as his own, above all in the arranging of optimal political and diplomatic conditions for the prosecution of limited war. In the diplomatic gambit leading to conflict with France, if not after, Moltke himself appreciated the consummate skill of "Europe's last cabinet warrior."[130] The conviction that strategy should logically be subordinate to policy—and therefore military expertise to civilian authority—was at the core of his conflict with Moltke. In the end he prevailed due to the intervention of his sovereign, yet he learned in the process that Moltke considered the Chief of the General Staff and the Federal Chancellor to be co-equal agencies under the crown and that even Moltke's staff rejected in principle civilian encroachment on its domain. This was a selective reading of Clausewitz for a military that had made *Vom Kriege* its bible; it exiled civilian authority and went some distance to making strategy no more than a composite of operations and tactics. Because the wars of German unification had been sharp and decisive, Moltke saw in them the Napoleonic and Clausewitzian ideal and hove to an exclusively, not to say perversely, military philosophy of war.[131]

In this he was a world removed from Grant's understanding of the command of Union armies and the relationship with the civilian authority of Lincoln. For a start, the latter was constitutionally mandated by the president's role of commander-in-chief, a position that in war combined the titular role of the head of state with substantive powers not unlike that of a prime minister. In the emergency of civil war Lincoln was prepared to define these powers as broadly as the necessities of victory over secessionism required. The paradox was that between 1861 and 1865 the president of the American republic wielded more war-making authority than Wilhelm I, Bismarck, or Moltke. In the exercise of that authority Lincoln heightened the contrast still further with a growing involvement in the military aspects of the war from the outset. Lincoln's policy—the defeat of secession and preservation of the Union—flowed naturally from his oath of office, and the abolition of slavery became politically and strategically conjoined to it. Beyond all these factors, however, Lincoln's war leadership involved a genuine fascination with the military arts. W.F. Smith, at the head of the Union XVIII Corps until July 1864, claimed that by the end of the war the president was the superior of his generals, and even one of the more critical assessments of Lincoln's military intellect concedes that he "had a deep and constructive involvement in initiating and executing Union strategy."[132]

Lincoln's extraordinary patience with the serial commanders of the Army of the Potomac may have kept him from putting Grant at the head of the Union armies much earlier than March 1864. However, the Grant of 1862 had not yet developed the strategic vision that ultimately crushed the Confederacy. He did so in commanding the campaigns of western and secondary theatres from a position on the periphery of war that compelled him to appreciate fully its relationship to the larger struggle. The Vicksburg campaign testifies to the coherence of his learning, and his capture of the city became the pivot of the conflict. Grant's reciprocal appreciation that his commander-in-chief was fighting a war not only against the Confederacy but also with procrastination from his generals, pressure from public opinion in the North, and above all, Congress, "which was always with him," also did a good deal toward developing a collaborative sense of common purpose.[133] A comparison of Grant with Moltke underscores in the latter an academic and theoretical bent tested with extraordinary success against the chaos of conflict in three short wars; indeed, the balance of Moltke's intellect and command skills made him unique among modern military leaders in his understanding of the connection between strategy and operational conduct.[134] Although Grant was above all a practitioner, his leadership reveals a studied warrior who rarely repeated an error and who, in a long war of national survival, articulated clear military objectives in support of a sweeping strategic plan and mastered the simultaneous direction of armies in its execution. The master of the short war, Moltke's stress on rapid deployment and telling blows against his adversary's vulnerable point made him in some respects the grandfather of the *Blitzkrieg*. Grant prosecuted a longer war over greater distances. Its complexity and the fact that his task was not to bring the Confederacy to terms but to destroy it led him to the application of continuous battle. Both are major figures in the unification of their states and in the development of modern warfare, but Grant's relationship with civil authority and his coordinated communication between military and political leadership over a larger numbers of theatres made him the more sophisticated strategist.[135]

Neither the world-political significance of the American Civil War nor of Grant's role in it were fully appreciated, either in the United States or beyond, in the decades immediately following. Much of the war's constitutional and political legacy was subverted in the former Confederacy by a society determined to deprive emancipated slaves of the constitutional rights of citizenship and poisoned by the vengeful incompetence of Reconstruction inflicted on the South after Lincoln's assassination. The system of command worked out in trail-and-error by Lincoln, Stanton, Halleck, and Grant was abandoned for prewar habits. Meanwhile, an army of over a million men at the moment of Confederate surrender was cut to 200,000 by December 1865 and to 37,240 by 1870. The U.S. Navy too underwent a radical reduction of its strength after 1865, yet began to recover in the 1880s; when in 1898 a vastly stronger American republic went to war with

Spain, the navy's performance reflected the national confidence of a commercial colossus, while its personnel testified to growing professional confidence. The army's capacity, by contrast, felt well short in the rigors of modern war.[136]

In the near term, the great dividend of the triumph of the Union in 1865 was the resumption and acceleration of the political economy that had engendered it. With the completion of a transcontinental railway in 1869, the American economy had at its disposal some 40,000 miles of track, more than the rest of the world combined, both a product of and a factor in the explosion of steel production from 1.4 million to 11 million tons between 1880 and 1900 alone. Party politics and patronage matured, but a combination of ideological commitment to limited government and a sheer inability to keep pace with the scale and complexity of business meant that American state-building prior to 1900 had an improvised, patchwork quality. A sense of its inadequacies in grappling with regulatory and social problems of industrial capitalism helped to produce the Progressive movement. Progressivism and a gathering sense of nationalism—commercial and optimistic by nature—threw up an economic and political leadership strata that "felt the urge to match itself against others."[137] This iteration of the United States embarked on the only genuinely imperial war of American history against Spain in 1898—at a time when most Americans were hardly aware of their collective strength.

The same could hardly be said of the German Empire that emerged from the war with France. The political unification of the German states, certainly, delivered on the economic down payment of the *Zollverein*, facilitating a rapid expansion and diversification of the German economy. Yet although Bismarck's introduction of a social insurance system in the 1880s testified to a determination to address the socioeconomic impact of mature industrialism, its inspiration was a desire to immunise German wage-laborers against the political appeal of the socialism. Whereas the dominant Republican Party in the United States was forced to compete with a resurgent Democratic Party for the reformist vote under the spell of the Progressive movement, the constitution of the German Empire short-circuited the connection between elections and public policy. The emperor alone retained the constitutional authority to conduct foreign affairs and had the authority to declare war. Parliament was convened or dissolved at his pleasure, and imperial officials served at his appointment independent of parliamentary oversight. As chancellor, Bismarck enjoyed broad executive and legislative powers; although the lower house or Reichstag was elected by universal manhood suffrage, it had no ministerial responsibility and its decisions had to be approved by an upper house or *Bundesrat* dominated by the delegation from Prussia. The system provided for mass political action, in other words, but denied it political consequence. In 1891 the Social Democratic Party declared officially Marxism as its doctrinal base, but the first demand of its program was a sovereign parliament based on universal suffrage. Elections became a barometer of the crisis between Prussian authoritarianism and Germany's dynamic but subject people.[138] The victory of 1871 had created a powerful but insecure German state. Its nationalism was not confident but paranoid; after Bismarck's departure, its army was "a monarchical household force rather than an instrumentality of the state."[139] By the 1890s, the General Staff could aspire to revise even this arrangement. During the war with France it had resented the very existence of a War Ministry, and in the 1880s the weakness of Germany's parliamentary system offered no resistance to a reform giving the General Staff direct access to the emperor.[140] Any monarch lacking Bismarck's character—which is to say all monarchs—was likely to find himself the instrument of the household force.

That force overrated itself. As early as the 1880s observers could acknowledge the remarkable feat of Prussian arms under Moltke's command yet caution that it did not have the mark of original genius witnessed at Marengo or Ulm and wonder, perhaps, whether the pursuit of a science of war might neglect its art.[141] Moltke had conceded the constitutive role of policy in defining the aims of war but rejected the notion that the prosecution of conflict too was a creature of policy—or that policy itself could change in the course of war. Whether Moltke and the General Staff believed that their army had mastered the short war, or in the alternative feared that short wars alone offered the prospect of decisive victory, is of secondary importance.[142] Of primary importance—and this was the essence of German militarism— they knew that they knew best. Liddell Hart wrote in 1948, after Germany's second great disaster of the twentieth century, that the German General Staff was a "collective substitute for genius."[143] In Moltke's time the German military was only beginning a progression that was ultimately calamitous. The very nature of the General Staff, bureaucratic and hierarchical, cramped the growth of genius "but in compensation it sought to raise the general standard of competence to a high level."[144] When genius was in short supply it was a good substitute, but a substitute nonetheless.

That Moltke could apply his theories to war with France and see them vindicated led successive generations to believe he had made a science of the art. The Franco-Prussian War was another step in the march toward total war, "for in none of the preceding mid-century wars in Europe had the state and people of one society been locked in a fight to the death with the state and people of another."[145] The war's shortness was misleading, because, although it chalked a lower absolute casualty rate than the American Civil War, it witnessed a higher rate of killing; in just six months of combat, France suffered 150,000 killed and wounded; Prussia and its allies lost 117,000. The slow grind of Grant's war taught him lessons that eluded Moltke in his lightning triumph over France. Grant was the first practitioner of an operational art that achieved the objectives of a coherent strategy through the coordinated movement of multiple armies and corps in campaigns of remorseless attrition. We do not need to establish that either Grant or Moltke waged a systematic war against civilians to acknowledge that their actions presaged the shock of total war in the next century.[146] For his part, Lincoln understood the qualities of a modern state in ways Bismarck never guessed at.

Notes

1 James Q. Whitman, *The Verdict of Battle: The Law of Victory and the Making of Modern War* (Cambridge, MA: Harvard University Press, 2012), pp. 225–26, 243–44, 251; J.F.C. Fuller, *War and Western Civilization, 1832–1932: A Study of War as a Political Instrument and the Expression of Mass Democracy* (London: Duckworth, 1932), pp. 84–128. Günter Moltmann, "Ansätze zur totalen Kriegführung im amerikanischen Bürgerkrieg (1861–65) und im deutsch-französischen Krieg (1870/71)" in *Politischer Wandel, organisierte Gewalt und nationale Sicherheit: Beiträge zur neuern Geschichte Deutschlands und Frankreichs*, ed. Hansen, Schreiber, and Wegner, (Munich, Germany: R. Oldenbourg Verlag, 1995), pp. 29–45.

2 Richard Franklin Bensel, *Yankee Leviathan: The Origin of Central State Authority in America, 1859–1877* (New York: Cambridge University Press, 1990).

3 Walter Russell Mead, *Special Providence: American Foreign Policy and How It Changed the World* (New York: Knopf, 2001), pp. 180–204; Peter S. Onuf, *Jefferson's Empire: The Language of American Nationhood* (Charlottesville: University Press of Virginia, 2000); Frederick Merck, *The Monroe Doctrine and American Expansionism* (New York: Knopf, 1966); Gordon S. Wood, *Empire of Liberty: A History of the Early Republic, 1789–1815* (New York: Oxford University Press, 2009), p. 358.

4 Alexis de Tocqueville, *Democracy in America*, trans. George Lawrence (1966; repr., Garden City: Anchor Books, 1969) Vol. 1, Part II, Chapter 10, p. 375.

5 Sam W. Hays, *James K. Polk and the Expansionist Impulse* (New York: Longman, 1997); Brian Holden Reid, *The Origins of the American Civil War* (New York: Longman, 1996), pp. 110–11.

6 Eric Foner, *Free Soil, Free Labor, Free Men: The Ideology of the Republican Party before the Civil War* (New York: Oxford University Press, 1995), pp. 40–72, 92–93; Ulysses S. Grant, *Personal Memoirs of U.S. Grant*, Vol. 1 (Hartford, CT: C.L. Webster, 1885), pp. 37–38. See also Jean Edward Smith, *Grant* (New York: Simon & Schuster, 2001), pp. 34–69.

7 Bensel, *Yankee Leviathan*, pp. 1–57; Reid, *Origins of the American Civil War*, pp. 228–33.

8 Michael Burlingame, *Abraham Lincoln, A Life.* 2 vols. (Baltimore, MD: Johns Hopkins University Press, 2008) Vol. 1, pp. 410, 586.

9 Lincoln's First Inaugural Address, March 4, 1861, in *Documents of American History*, ed. Henry Steele Commager, (New York: Appleton-Century-Crofts, 1949), pp. 385–88.

10 Eliot A. Cohen, *Supreme Command: Soldiers, Statesmen, and Leadership in Wartime* (New York: Free Press, 2002), pp. 15–51, 20–21.

11 Russell F. Weigley, *The American Way of War: A History of United States Military Strategy and Policy* (Bloomington: Indiana University Press, 1973), pp. 82–89.

12 James M. McPherson, *Battle Cry of Freedom: The Civil War Era* (New York: Oxford University Press, 1988), pp. 331–38.

13 Ibid., pp. 339–44; Byron Farwell, *Stonewall: A Biography of General Thomas J. Jackson* (New York: Norton, 1992), pp. 172–96; George Edgar Turner, *Victory Rode the Rails: The Strategic Place of Railroad in the Civil War*

(Lincoln: University of Nebraska Press, 1992), pp. 86–95; Archer Jones, *Civil War Command and Strategy: The Process of Victory and Defeat* (New York: Free Press, 1992), p. 31.

14 Jones, *Civil War Command and Strategy*, pp. 26–38; John K. Mahon, "Civil War Infantry Assault Tactics," *Military Affairs* 25, no. 2 (1961) pp. 57–68.

15 Jay Luvaas, *The Military Legacy of the Civil War: The European Inheritance* (Lawrence: University of Kansas Press, 1988), pp. 214–15.

16 McPherson, *Battle Cry of Freedom*, pp. 345–50; Allan Nevins, *Ordeal of the Union*, 4 vols. (New York: Collier Books, 1992), Vol, 3, p. 223.

17 Burlingame, *Abraham Lincoln, A Life*. Vol. 2, pp. 221–29; Howard Jones, *Union in Peril: The Crisis over British Intervention in the Civil War* (Chapel Hill: University of North Carolina Press, 1992), pp. 80–99; Gordon H. Warren, *Fountain of Discontent: The Trent Affair and the Freedom of the Seas* (Boston: Northeastern University Press, 1981).

18 Burlingame, *Abraham Lincoln, A Life*. Vol. 2, p. 180–89; Bruce Catton, *Grant Moves South* (Boston: Little, Brown, 1960), pp. 3–43.

19 Burlingame, *Abraham Lincoln, A Life*. Vol. 2, pp. 325–326; Reid, *Origins of the American Civil War*, pp. 144–59; Archer Jones, *Civil War Command and Strategy*, pp. 60–71; Stephen W. Sears, *To the Gates of Richmond: The Peninsula Campaign* (New York: Ticknor and Fields, 1992). Phillip Shaw Paludan, *The Presidency of Abraham Lincoln* (Lawrence: University of Kansas Press, 1994), p. 142.

20 Russell F. Weigley, *A Great Civil War: A Military and Political History* (Bloomington: Indiana University Press, 2000), pp. 108–15; Wiley Sword, *Shiloh: Bloody April* (New York: William Morrow, 1974); James Lee McDonough, *Shiloh—in Hell before Night* (Knoxville: University of Tennessee Press, 1984).

21 McPherson, *Battle Cry of Freedom*, pp. 413–14; T. Harry Williams, *Lincoln and His Generals* (New York: Knopf, 1952), pp. 85–86; Sword, *Shiloh: Bloody April*, pp. 434–40; Cohen, *Supreme Command*, pp. 41–48.

22 Jean Smith, *Grant*, pp. 167–205, 284–91, 376–77.

23 Cohen, *Supreme Command*, p. 26; Turner, *Victory Rode the Rails*, pp. 210–23.

24 Archer Jones, *Civil War Command and Strategy*, pp. 93–94; Stephen W. Sears, *Landscape Turned Red: The Battle of Antietam* (New Haven, CT: Ticknor and Fields, 1983), pp. 66–71; Weigley, *Great Civil War*, pp. 147–51.

25 Weigley, *Great Civil War*, p. 151.

26 Reid, *Origins of the American Civil War*, p. 196; Weigley, *Great Civil War*, pp. 151–54.

27 Williams, *Lincoln and His Generals*, pp. 168–78.

28 Quoted in Burlingame, *Abraham Lincoln, A Life*. Vol. 2, p. 407.

29 Burlingame, *Abraham Lincoln, A Life*. Vol. 2, pp. 365–66.

30 Howard Jones, *Union in Peril*, pp. 173–74; James M. McPherson, *Abraham Lincoln and the Second American Revolution* (New York: Oxford University Press, 1991), pp. 33–37.

31 David Brown, *Palmerston: A Biography*, (New Haven, CT: Yale University Press, 2010), pp. 452–55.

32 Archer Jones, *Civil War Command and Strategy*, p. 96; Paludan, *Presidency of Abraham Lincoln*, pp. 142–81; Bensel, *Yankee Leviathan*, pp. 144–45.

33 Herman Hattaway and Archer Jones, *How the North Won: A Military History of the Civil War* (Urbana: University of Illinois Press, 1991), pp. 375–423.

34 McPherson, *Abraham Lincoln*, p. 336; Archer Jones, *Civil War Command and Strategy*, pp. 99–101; Weigley, *Great Civil War*, pp. 231–32.

35 Bruce Catton, *Mr. Lincoln's Army* (Garden City, NY: Doubleday, 1951), p. 96–112.

36 Paludan, *Presidency of Abraham Lincoln*, pp. 208–9; Williams, *Lincoln and His Generals*, pp. 190–94; Catton, *Grant Moves South*, pp. 324–34.

37 Jean Smith, *Grant*, pp. 222–23.

38 J.F.C. Fuller, *Grant and Lee: A Study of Personality and Generalship* (Bloomington: Indiana University Press, 1957), pp. 67–78, 91–93, 256–57; Weigley, *Great Civil War*, pp. 326–29.

39 Weigley, *Great Civil War*, pp. 111–15, 155–58.

40 Ibid., p. 159.

41 Ibid., p. 195.

42 Ibid., p. 194; Williams, *Lincoln and His Generals*, pp. 194–201; Francis Augustin O'Reilly, *The Fredericksburg Campaign: Winter War of the Rappahannock* (Baton Rouge: Louisiana State University Press, 2006).

43 Paludan, *Presidency of Abraham Lincoln*, pp. 1670–79; Burton J. Hendrick, *Lincoln's War Cabinet* (Boston: Little, Brown, 1946).

44 Paludan, *Presidency of Abraham Lincoln*, p. 213; Russell F. Weigley, *History of the United States Army* (Bloomington: Indiana University Press, 1984), pp. 198–210; Fred Albert Shannon, *The Organization and Administration of the Union Army, 1861–1865*. 2 vols.(Gloucester, MA: Peter Smith, 1965), Vol. 1, pp. 295–323, Vol. 2, pp. 103–71; Iver Bernstein, *The New York City Draft Riots* (New York: Oxford University Press, 1990).

45 Paludan, *Presidency of Abraham Lincoln*, p. 191.

46 Weigley, *Great Civil War*, pp. 225–29; Reid, *Origins of the American Civil War*, pp. 269–75; Stephen W. Sears, *Chancellorsville* (Boston: Houghton Mifflin, 1996); Ernest B. Furgurson, *Chancellorsville: The Souls of the Brave* (New York: Alfred A. Knopf, 1992).

47 Weigley, *Great Civil War*, p. 229.

48 Steven E. Woodworth, *Jefferson Davis and His Generals: The Failure of Confederate Command in the West* (Lawrence: University of Kansas Press, 1990), pp. 212–13; Hattaway and Jones, *How the North Won*, pp. 375, 398.

49 Hattaway and Jones, *How the North Won*, pp. 399–401.

50 Ibid., pp. 375–423.

51 Ibid., pp. 341–346; Archer Jones, *Civil War Command and Strategy*, pp. 129–30.

52 Hattaway and Jones, *How the North Won*, pp. 386–87, 402–3.

53 Woodworth, pp. 212–13; Shelby Foote, *Stars in their Courses: The Gettysburg Campaign June–July, 1863* (New York: Modern Library, 1994), pp. 9–10.

54 Edwin B. Coddington, *The Gettysburg Campaign: A Study in Command* (New York: Scribner, 1968), pp. 266–74; McPherson, *Battle Cry of Freedom*, pp. 653–54; Foote, *Stars in their Courses*, pp. 67–68.

55 Weigley, *Great Civil War*, pp. 240–41.

56 Foote, *Stars in their Courses*, pp. 122–33, Weigley, *Great Civil War*, pp. 246–51.

57 Foote., *Stars in their Courses*, pp. 169–244; Weigley, *Great Civil War*, pp. 252–53.

58 Weigley, *Great Civil War*, pp. 271–85; Hattaway and Jones, *How the North Won*, pp. 424–64; John Bowers, *Chickamauga and Chattanooga: The Battles that Doomed the Confederacy* (New York: Harper Collins, 1994).

59 William Tecumseh Sherman, *Memoires of General W.T. Sherman* (New York: Library of America, 1984). p. 365; John F. Marszalek, *Sherman: A Soldier's Passion for Order* (New York: Free Press, 1993), pp. 236–37.

60 Sherman, *Memoires of General W.T. Sherman*.

61 Hattaway and Jones, *How the North Won*, pp. 508–10; Marzalek, *Sherman*, pp. 248–55.

62 William D. Matter, *If It Takes All Summer: The Battle of Spotsylvania* (Chapel Hill: University of North Carolina Press, 1988), pp. 342–49.

63 Weigley, *Great Civil War*, pp. 328–29, 384–96.

64 Catton, *Grant Moves South*, p. 462.

65 David Herbert Donald, *Lincoln* (New York: Simon & Shuster, 1995), p. 499; Weigley, *Great Civil War*, pp. 347–57.

66 Quoted in Weigley, *Great Civil War*, p. 348.

67 Donald, *Lincoln*, pp. 532–47; Paludan, *Presidency of Abraham Lincoln*, pp. 289–90.

68 Mark Grimsley, *The Hard Hand of War: Union Military Policy Toward Southern Civilians, 1861–1865* (New York: Cambridge University Press, 1995), pp. 12–141; Paludan, pp. 179, 299–311; Bensel, pp. 144–45.

69 Albert Castel, *Decision in the West: The Atlanta Campaign of 1864* (Lawrence: University Press of Kansas, 1992), p. 549; Grimsley, *Hard Hand of War*, pp. 168–69; Weigley, *Great Civil War*, pp. 358–63.

70 Grimsley, *Hard Hand of War*, pp. 169–70.

71 McPherson, *Battle Cry of Freedom*, pp. 774–830; Hattaway and Jones, *How the North Won*, pp. 669–71; Mark A. Weitz, *More Damning Than Slaughter: Desertion in the Confederate Army* (Lincoln: University of Nebraska Press, 2005).

72 Hattaway and Jones, *How the North Won*, pp. 675–76.

73 Stig Förster and Jörg Nagler, eds., *On the Road to Total War: The American Civil War and the German Wars of Unification, 1861–1871* (Cambridge, UK: Cambridge University Press, 1997), pp. 1–25.

74 Geoffrey Wawro, *The Franco-Prussian War: The German Conquest of France in 1870–1871* (New York: Cambridge University Press, 2003), p. 265; Michael Howard, *The Franco-Prussian War: The German Invasion of France, 1870–1871* (New York: Collier, 1969), pp. 379–81.

75 Luvaas, *Military Legacy of the Civil War*, pp. 52–57; Arden Bucholz, *Moltke and the German Wars, 1864–1871* (London: Palgrave, 2001), p. 62.

76 Thomas Nipperdey, *Deutsche Geschichte, 1800–1866: Bürgerwelt und starker Staat* (Munich, Germany: C.H. Beck, 1984), pp. 687–714; James J. Sheehan, *German History, 1770–1866* (New York: Oxford University Press, 1989), pp. 865–69; Christopher Clark, *Iron Kingdom: The Rise and Downfall of Prussia, 1600– 1947* (Cambridge, MA: Harvard University Press, 2006), pp. 512–17.

77 Jonathan Steinberg, *Bismarck, A Life* (New York: Oxford University Press, 2011), pp. 13–18; Lothar Gall, *Bismarck: The White Revolutionary*, 2 vols., trans. J.A, Underwood (London: Unwin Hyman, 1986) Vol. 2, pp. 197–218; Gordon A. Craig, *Germany, 1866–1945* (New York: Oxford University Press, 1978), pp. 171–79; David Blackbourn, *The Long Nineteenth Century: A History of Germany, 1780–1918* (New York: Oxford University Press, 1997), pp. 255–56.

78 Quoted in Edward Crankshaw, *Bismarck* (London: Macmillan, 1981), pp. 45–89.

79 Nipperdey, *Deutsche Geschichte, 1800–1866*, pp. 684–85; Steinberg, *Bismarck, A Life*, p. 108; Gall, Vol. 1, pp. 91–130; Crankshaw, *Bismarck*, pp. 45–89; Heinrich August Winkler, *Der lange Weg nach Westen*. 2 vols. (Munich, Germany: C.H. Beck, 2001), Vol. 1, pp. 136–38. Eberhard Kessel, *Moltke* (Stuttgart, Germany: K.F. Koehler, 1957), pp. 87–90.

80 Arden Bucholz, *Moltke, Schlieffen, and Prussian War Planning* (New York: Berg, 1991), pp. 40–41.

81 Sheehan, *German History*, pp. 890–892.

82 Bucholz, *Moltke, Schlieffen, and Prussian War Planning*, pp. 44–45; Gordon Craig, *The Politics of the Prussian Army, 1640–1945* (London: Oxford University

Press, 1955) pp. 180–92; Curt Jany, *Geschichte der Preußischen Armee vom 15. Jahrhundert bis 1914*. 4 vols. (Osnabrück, Germany: Biblio Verlag, 1967), Vol. 4, pp. 236–43; Walter Goerlitz, *The German General Staff, 1657–1945* (New York: Praeger, 1953), pp. 69–102.

83 Alan Sked, *The Decline and Fall of the Habsburg Empire, 1815–1918* (London: Longman, 1989), pp. 187–234.

84 Crankshaw, *Bismarck*, p. 79.

85 Sheehan, *German History*, pp. 892–99; Gall, Vol. 1, pp. 277–83; Steinberg, *Bismarck, A Life*, pp. 226–47; Kessel, *Moltke*, pp. 440–45; Geoffrey Wawro, *The Austro-Prussian War: Austria's War with Prussia and Italy in 1866* (New York: Cambridge University Press, 1996), pp. 44–53.

86 Bucholz, *Moltke, Schlieffen, and Prussian War Planning*, pp. 45–46; Craig, *Politics of the Prussian Army*, pp. 1930–95.

87 Bucholz, *Moltke, Schlieffen, and Prussian War Planning*, p. 46; Wawro, *Austro-Prussian War*, pp. 52–53.

88 Kessel, *Moltke*, p. 447.

89 Gordon A. Craig, *The Battle of Königgrätz: Prussia's Victory over Austria, 1866* (Philadelphia, PA: J.B. Lippincott, 1964), pp. 38–39.

90 Wawro, *Austro-Prussian War*, pp. 75–81.

91 Craig, *Battle of Königgrätz*, p. 79.

92 Dennis Showalter, *The Wars of German Unification* (London: Hodder Arnold, 2004) pp. 180–83.

93 Ibid., pp. 184–87; Wawro, *Austro-Prussian War*, pp. 238–73.

94 Craig, *Battle of Königgrätz*, p. xii; Azar Gat, *A History of Military Thought from the Enlightenment to the Cold War* (New York: Oxford University Press, 2001), p. 337.

95 Craig, *Battle of Königgrätz*, p. 172; Nipperdey, *Deutsche Geschichte, 1800–1866,*, pp. 797–98; Steinberg, *Bismarck, A Life*, pp. 252–57; Gordon R. Mork, "Bismarck and the 'Capitulation' of German Liberalism," *Journal of Modern History* 43, No. 1 (1971), pp. 61–62.

96 Wawro, *Austro-Prussian War*, pp. 286–290; James Q. Whitman, *The Verdict of Battle: The Law of Victory and the Making of Modern War* (Cambridge, MA: Harvard University Press, 2012), pp. 212–15.

97 Showalter, *Wars of German Unification*, p. 212.

98 A.J.P. Taylor, *The Struggle for Mastery in Europe, 1848–1918* (London: Oxford University Press, 1954), p. 210; Denis Brogan, *The Development of Modern France, 1870–1939* (London: Hamish Hamilton, 1967), p. 7; Paul W. Schroeder, "The Lost Intermediaries: The Impact of 1870 on the European System," *International History Review* 6, No. 1 (1984), pp. 1–27.

99 Steinberg, *Bismarck, A Life*, p. 286; Howard, *Franco-Prussian War*, pp. 48–57; David Wetzel, *A Duel of Giants: Bismarck, Napoleon III and the Origins of the Franco-Prussian War* (Madison: University Of Wisconsin Press, 2001), pp. 151–52, 160–61; William Halperin, "The Origins of the Franco-Prussian War Revisited: Bismarck and the Hohenzollern Candidature for the Spanish Throne," *Journal of Modern History* 45, No. 1 (March 1973), pp. 83–91; Josef Becker, ed., *Bismarcks "spanische Diversion" 1870 und der preußisch-deutsche Reichsgründungskrieg*. 2 vols. (Paderborn, Germany: Ferdinand Schöningh, 2003).

100 Howard, *Franco-Prussian War*, p. 56; Arden Bucholz, *Moltke and the German Wars, 1864–1871* (London: Palgrave, 2001), pp. 120–5; Kessel, *Moltke*, p. 109; Robert M. Citino, *The German Way of War: From the Thirty Years War to the Third Reich* (Lawrence: University of Kansas Press, 2005), pp. 117–31.

101 D. Brogan, *Development of Modern France*, p. 17; Henri Ortholan, *L'Armée du Second Empire, 1852–1870* (Paris: Éditions Soteca, 2009); Hew Strachan, *European Armies and the Conduct of War* (London: Routledge, 1983), pp. 78–89.

102 Roger Price, *Napoleon III and the Second Empire* (London: Routledge, 1997); D. Brogan, *Development of Modern France,* pp. 17–18; Howard, *Franco-Prussian War,* pp. 29–39.

103 Arpad F. Kovacs, "French Military Institutions before the Franco-Prussian War," *American Historical Review* 51, No. 2 (1946), pp. 217–35; Richard Holmes, *The Road to Sedan: The French Army 1866–70* (London: Royal Historical Society, 1894), pp. 50–55; John G. Lorimer, "Why Would Military Commanders Study the Franco-Prussian War?" *Defence Studies* 5, No. 1 (2005), pp. 11–15.

104 Geoffrey Wawro, *Franco-Prussian War,* pp. 46–49.

105 Eberhard Kolb, *Der Weg aus dem Krieg: Bismarcks Politik im Krieg und die Friedenanbahnung 1870/71,* (Munich, Germany: R. Oldenbourg, 1989), p. 81.

106 Hazel C. Benjamin, "Official Propaganda and the French Press during the Franco-Prussian War," *Journal of Modern History* 4, No. 2, 1932, p. 217.

107 Lynn M. Case, *French Opinion on War and Diplomacy during the Second Empire* (Philadelphia: University of Pennsylvania Press, 1944), pp. 256–69. See also E. Malcolm Carroll, *French Public Opinion and Foreign Affairs, 1870–1914* (New York: Century Company, 1931), pp. 15–43.

108 Kolb, *Der Weg aus dem Krieg,* pp. 68–69; Howard, *Franco-Prussian War,* pp. 78–79; E. Malcolm Carroll, "French Public Opinion on War with Prussia in 1870," *American Historical Review* 31, No. 4 (1926), pp. 679–700.

109 Wawro., *Franco-Prussian War,* pp. 85–135; Kessel, *Moltke,* pp. 550–53; Bucholz, *Moltke and the German Wars,* pp. 171–73.

110 Wawro., *Franco-Prussian War,* pp. 62–64.

111 Ibid., pp. 152–63.

112 Ibid., pp. 164–85; Citino, *German Way of War,* pp. 186–90.

113 Wawro, *Franco-Prussian War,* 168–85, Howard, *Franco-Prussian War,* pp. 176–82.

114 Wawro, *Franco-Prussian War,* pp. 187–88.

115 Kolb, *Der Weg aus dem Krieg,* pp. 83–112.

116 Kessel, *Moltke,* pp. 562–63; Bucholz, *Moltke and the German Wars,* p. 177.

117 William O'Connor Morris, "The Campaign of Sedan," *English Historical Review* 3, No. 10, 1888, pp. 230–31.

118 Howard, *Franco-Prussian War,* pp. 215–17; Wawro, *Franco-Prussian War,* pp. 220–21.

119 D. Brogan, *Development of Modern France,* p. 31; Gordon Craig, *Germany 1866–1945* (New York: Oxford University Press, 1978), p. 29.

120 J.P.T. Bury, *Gambetta and the Making of the Third Republic* (London: Longman, 1973), pp. 1–8; Jean-Marie Mayeur, *Léon Gambetta. La Patrie et la République* (Paris: Fayard, 2008), pp. 85–132; Wawro, pp. 236–37.

121 Howard, *Franco-Prussian War,* pp. 252–53, 380–81.

122 Crankshaw, *Bismarck,* p. 285.

123 Howard, *Franco-Prussian War,*; Steinberg, *Bismarck, A Life,* pp. 297–98; Kolb, *Der Weg aus dem Krieg,* pp. 304–5.

124 Steinberg, *Bismarck, A Life,* pp. 300–1.

125 Crankshaw, *Bismarck,* p. 287; Gerhard Ritter, *The Sword and the Scepter: The Problem of Militarism in Germany.* 4 vols., trans. Heinz Norden (Coral Gables, FL: University of Miami Press, 1969) Vol. 1, pp. 219–224; Craig, *Politics of the Prussian Army,* pp. 215–216.

126 D. Brogan, *Development of Modern France,* pp. 53–54; J.P.T. Bury and R.P. Tombs, *Thiers, 1797–1877: A Political Life* (London: Allen & Unwin, 1986), pp. 192–97.

127 Craig, *Politics of the Prussian Army,* pp. 204–16.

128 Robert Tombs, *The Paris Commune 1871* (London: Longman, 1999), pp. 20–27; Howard Saalman, *Haussmann: Paris Transformed.* (New York: G. Braziller, 1971); Bury and Tombs, *Thiers,* pp. 204–9.

129 Steinberg, *Bismarck, A Life*, pp. 305–11; Crankshaw, *Bismarck*, pp. 291–97.
130 Dennis E. Showalter, "The Prusso-German RMA, 1840–1871," in *The Dynamics of Military Revolution, 1300–2050*, ed. MacGregor Knox and Williamson Murray (New York: Cambridge University Press, 2001), p. 105; Kolb, *Der Weg aus dem Krieg*, pp. 1–50, 364; Gall, Vol. 1, pp. 355–359.
131 Ritter, *Sword and the Scepter*, Vol. 1, pp. 187–238; Craig, *Politics of the Prussian Army*, pp. 204–216; Beatrice Heuser, *Reading Clausewitz* (London: Pimlico, 2002), pp. 56–62; Hew Strachan, *Carl von Clauswitz's On War: A Biography* (London: Atlantic, 2007) pp. 10–13.
132 Cohen, *Supreme Command*, pp. 47–51; Archer Jones, *Civil War Command and Strategy*, p. 225; Michael Burlingame, ed., *Abraham Lincoln: The Observations of John G. Nicolay and John Hay* (Carbondale: Southern Illinois University Press, 2007), p. 140.
133 U.S. Grant, *Personal Memoirs of U.S. Grant* (New York: C.L. Webster, 1885), pp. 407–8.
134 Michael D. Krause, "Moltke and Grant: A Comparison of their Operational Thinking and Perspective," in Roland G. Foerster, ed., *Generalfeldmarschal von Moltke: Bedeutung und Wirkung* (Munich, Germany: R. Oldenbourg, 1991), p. 131.
135 Ibid., p. 139; J.F.C. Fuller, *Grant and Lee: A Study of Personality and Generalship* (Bloomington: Indiana University Press, 1957), p. 93; See also Donald Stoker, *The Grand Design: Strategy in the U.S. Civil War* (New York: Oxford University Press, 2010), pp. 263–75, 351–54, 367–68.
136 Eric Foner, *Reconstruction: America's Unfinished Revolution, 1863–1877* (New York: Harper & Row, 1988); Paul A.C. Koistinen, *Mobilizing for Modern War: The Political Economy o American Warfare, 1865–1919* (Lawrence: University of Kansas Press, 1997), pp. 58–64.
137 Martin van Creveld, *The Rise and Decline of the State* (New York: Cambridge University Press, 1999), pp. 288–89; Stephen Skowronek, *Building a New American State: The Expansion of National Administrative Capacities, 1877–1920* (New York: Cambridge University Press, 1982), pp. 47–162.
138 Craig, *Germany, 1866–1945*, pp. 61–100; David Blackbourn, *The Long Nineteenth Century: A History of Germany, 1780–1918* (New York: Oxford University Press, 1998), pp. 313–350; Hans-Ulrich Wehler, *Das deutsche Kaiserreich, 1871–1914* (Göttingen, Germany: Vandenhoeck & Ruprecht, 1980), pp. 60–63.
139 Ritter, *Sword and the Scepter*, Vol. 1, p. 161.
140 Craig, *Politics of the Prussian Army*, pp. 226–32.
141 W.O. Morris, "Campaign of Sedan," pp. 209–32.
142 Konrad Canis, "Militärführung und Grundfragen der Außenpolitik in Deutschland 1860 bis 1890," in *Das Militär und der Aufbruch in die Moderne 1860 bis 1890: Armeen, Marinen und der Wandel von Politik, Gesellschaft und Wirtschaft in Europa, den USA sowie Japan*, ed. Michael Epkenhans and Gerhard P. Groß (Munich, Germany: R, Oldenbourg, 2003), pp. 11–12; Gat, *History of Military Thought*, pp. 317–41.
143 B.H. Liddell Hart. *The German Generals Talk* (New York: Morrow, 1948), p. 19.
144 Ibid.
145 Brian Bond, *War and Society in Europe, 1870–1970* (London: Fontana, 1984), p. 15.
146 Krause, "Moltke and Grant," p. 131; Williams, *Lincoln and His Generals*, pp. 313–14; Mark E. Neely Jr., "Was the Civil War a Total War?" in *On the Road to Total War*, Förster and Nagler, eds., pp. 29–51.

4 America, Japan, and the new navalism

Power abhors a vacuum. Between 1898 and 1905 the United States and Japan found it prudent to fill vacuums, the first occasioned by a revolt against the colonial regime of Spain in the Caribbean, the second by the failing hold of China's Qing dynasty on Korea and Manchuria. In each case, competition among established powers for overseas colonies and bases raised concerns about access to foreign resources, markets, and trade routes sufficient to preoccupy governments with establishing, by force of arms, spheres of influence on water and land adjacent to home territory—for the United States, in the Caribbean basin, Cuba, and Panama; for Japan, in the Yellow Sea, Sea of Japan, Korea, and Manchuria. Both the resulting Spanish-American and Russo-Japanese Wars represent pivotal conflicts between declining and emerging powers at the dawn of the twentieth century. Both involved the application of maritime strategy, defined loosely in a classic work of the time as "the principles which govern a war in which the sea is a substantial factor"[1] in landing troops, supplying their extensive land operations, and maintaining incontestable dominance on the seas providing access to the theatre of conflict.

Navalism, the conviction that the possession of an oceanic navy had become an essential attribute of great power status[2] (this subject will be the object of greater attention in Chapter Five), was by 1900 a vogue of strategic thinking that was increasingly compelling after the American and Japanese naval and maritime operations of 1898–1905. Legitimated intellectually by the writings of Alfred Thayer Mahan, it was powered technologically by qualitative changes of ship construction, propulsion, and armament, and driven politically by colonial lobbies and navies competing with other services for their share of national defense budgets. Mahan, a naval officer, lecturer, and president of the United States Naval War College, published *The Influence of Sea Power on History, 1660–1783* in 1890 and followed it two years later with *The Influence of Sea Power on the French Revolution and Empire*. Each maintained that the sea power of England had provided it both with security and a commanding control of ocean lanes sufficient to make it the dominant global power during a period of increasing international commerce. The argument was not novel, but Mahan's lucidity in making the case for it earned him an international readership.[3]

His popularity in Britain was helped by his obvious Anglophilia and the deepening concern of the Royal Navy and sympathetic parliamentarians over naval competition from France, Russia and, above all, Germany.[4] In Germany the forthright commitment to naval power inaugurated in the First Naval Law of 1898 was thought to compensate structural deficiencies in the nation's relative status among other powers. As a latecomer to colonial expansion Germany sought to supplement its military strength as a land power with the construction of a battle fleet powerful enough to inflict serious damage on the Royal Navy and thus compromise Britain's capacity to meet and defeat other enemies. In both Britain and Germany, moreover, governments cultivated popular enthusiasm for the power and prestige of large battle fleets through elaborate public naval reviews.[5] Navalism in the United States featured many similar qualities, yet was more important in terms of its constitutive role in the American view of the twentieth-century world.

A mania born in America

Specifically, Mahan's message to his countrymen became the first article of American global expansionism, a call to the young republic to assert itself in an increasingly predatory international environment. It also spoke to professional ambition. During the 1880s, a generation of American naval officers, troubled by the their career prospects in a service neglected since the Civil War, had sought to articulate a role for naval power as the decisive instrument among the military assets of a nation with unapologetically expansionist designs.[6] If it is true that Mahan's book landed in the next decade "like a bomb in international political, diplomatic, military, and naval circles,"[7] then its detonation was especially welcome in the inner cabinet of President William McKinley. As assistant secretary of the navy to the phlegmatic John Long, Theodore Roosevelt belonged to a group of navalists—including Rear-Admirals Stephen B. Luce and Henry Taylor of the U.S. Naval War College, Professor James R. Soley at the Naval Academy, former Secretaries of the Navy Benjamin Tracy and Hilary Herbert, along with the congressmen who supported them—who sought to redirect American strategic culture from its defensive posture with the creation of a fleet of battleships capable of action far from home. They saw no prudent alternative, as the United States was a transcontinental economy with extensive Atlantic and Pacific approaches, the Caribbean Sea representing the nation's naval center of gravity and key to its maritime frontiers, east and west. American navalists ultimately succeeded in launching the country on a century of expanding sea power due above all to the catalyst of the Spanish-American War.[8]

Coming at a transformative stage in the history of the republic and indirectly a product of American economic radiance, the conflict was short and immensely popular. American economic policy influenced conditions in Cuba, as the tariff of 1894 imposed high duties on the import of its sugar, aggravating economic conditions on the island and hastening the advent of a popular Cuban revolt against Spanish colonial rule. When Cubans launched a war for independence in February 1895, an American diplomatic initiative—and possibly something much stronger—seemed imperative. In 1823, after all, the Monroe Doctrine had asserted an American sphere of interest in stating that "the American continents, by the free and independent condition which they have assumed and maintain, are henceforth not to be considered as subjects for future colonisation by any European powers," and further cautioned that "we should consider any attempt on their part to extend their system to any portion of this hemisphere as dangerous to our peace and safety." President James K. Polk had invoked the doctrine in 1848 in opposition not only to the reconquest of former colonial holdings in the Americas by any European power but also against the cession of territory in the Western Hemisphere to another European power. Polk's interpretation testified to American uneasiness over the fate of the Western territories, which coincided with real and imaginary European encroachment in the Yucatán and the Caribbean. France's Mexican adventures under Napoleon III and Spain's reoccupation of Santo Domingo in 1861–1864 moved the United States again to proclaim Monroe principles during the Civil War years. Although the doctrine became diplomatic dogma in the following decades and was tacitly recognised by Great Britain in the Venezuelan Crisis of 1895–1896, the United States had never been challenged to put muscle behind its hemispheric pretensions.[9] But now, as Spain tried to put down the Cuban rebellion, the conflict became an increasing source of irritation to Washington, especially in light of the destruction of American property and investment on the island. The repression of a popular rebellion meanwhile stirred up public opinion to such a froth of indignation—with the help of the yellow press reporting the real and imagined horrors of the Spanish government's policy of removing Cuban villagers to concentration camps—that progressive sentiment demanded the application of righteous might. News emanating from Cuba was both a shock to the conscience and a cracking good read.[10]

President Grover Cleveland had sought to avoid this by offering to Spain a plan for arbitration, even as the Senate Foreign Relations Committee labored over a resolution to force him to recognise Cuban independence. The resolution was shelved when its existence became known to the press, but the incident served to suspend public opinion in a frenzied state after Cleveland left office and McKinley took the oath. McKinley was no more impatient for war with Spain than Cleveland, but his hand was forced by the destruction of the battleship USS *Maine* in Havana harbour. The *Maine* had been sent to Cuba as a peacekeeping gesture following riots in Havana, and McKinley had extended an invitation for Spanish warships to visit American ports. Even as "Remember the *Maine*" became a popular rallying cry, McKinley made one last attempt at peaceful settlement based on a ceasefire, negotiation, and an end to the concentration camps.

This reasonableness exasperated Theodore Roosevelt, who sought war with Spain, if no worthier opponent were willing, to advance the naval cause. Spain as it turned out refused even to discuss the issue of Cuban independence. When McKinley asked Congress to authorise the use of force to protect American interests, the legislature therefore exceeded him with a joint resolution declaring Cuba sovereign and demanding the withdrawal of Spanish troops. "We intervene not for conquest," cautioned Senator John Spooner of Wisconsin, "we intervene for humanity's sake ... to aid a people who have suffered every form of tyranny and have made a desperate struggle to be free."[11] For a generation of academic, economic, political, and social leadership, some variation of Darwinist outlook made it not just a right but a duty to intervene. The Reverend Joshua Strong's *Our Country*—a summons for the United States to Anglo-Saxonise Mexico and Central and Southern America—had preceded Mahan's books to bestseller status.[12] The principle of humanity thus aligned nicely with the policy of political leaders like Roosevelt, the interests of the navalists, and the principles of Progressivism, as Cuba and Spain's possessions in the Pacific could neither be defended nor captured in the absence of capable naval forces.

The Spanish fleet had never recovered from its joint humiliation with Napoleonic France by the cannons of the Royal Navy off Cape Trafalgar in October 1805, an event cited by Mahan in making the case for American sea power. Trafalgar was also indirectly critical to the gradual encroachment of the United States into the Caribbean, as Spain's loss of its fleet emboldened its colonies to rebellion and hastened the demise of a vast empire in the Americas, the 1890s representing the final stage of its disintegration.[13] Spain therefore recommended itself as an enemy to Roosevelt, who saw a chance to enhance the navy, "in all its majesty and beauty," to be built to a standard worthy of the "honour of America."[14] McKinley gradually yielded to the public, the press, and a Congress increasingly bent on war or any action that would lead to war.

When Spain proposed an unconditional armistice in Cuba yet rejected the administration's condition that this must entail recognition of Cuban sovereignty, the president began to count congressional votes for a war resolution and to craft wording to run up the number. The document read to Congress cited the cause of humanity against cruel and uncivilised practices; expressed an American commercial interest in the island; called for the protection of Cuban citizens and their property; but named "of the utmost importance" the condition of Cuba as "a constant menace to our peace."[15] Elihu Root, later to become Secretary of War but at all times counselor-at-law to whatever administration he served, relieved McKinley of any obligation to intervene yet stressed that he would be violating no divine or international law if he decided to do so and asserted that the Cubans "have a hundred times the cause we had in 1776 or that the English had in 1688."[16]

That the Spanish navy was no longer capable of battle with a first-rank power was revealed in the opening gambit of the war, not in the Caribbean but rather in the Western Pacific, when a second-rate power defeated it with aplomb. Although the United States of 1898 aspired to naval power, it was still far from the goal, and the squadron sent against the Spanish Philippines was no juggernaut. Its cruisers dated to a building program a dozen years old when warships were propelled by a combination of sail and steam, hybrid creatures "born of a past already gone and a future not fully arrived."[17] The U.S. Navy's Asiatic Squadron, under Commodore George Dewey, consisted of the six-year-old protected cruiser *Olympia*, two smaller protected cruisers, *Raleigh* and *Boston*, and the gunboats *Monocacy*, *Petrel*, and *Concord* at anchor in Hong Kong. Neither *Olympia* nor *Monocacy* were battle-ready, so the squadron had to be reinforced by the addition of the *Baltimore* hurriedly dispatched from Honolulu and the revenue cutter *Hugh McCulloch*. Roosevelt had ordered the squadron to Hong Kong from Japan with instructions to stock up on coal; this Dewey did in part by purchasing two British civilian ships outright along with their coal tonnage and accepting the offer of their civilian crews to stay on. Dewey learned that the Spanish navy had some forty warships at Manila with which to oppose him. Yet most of them were gunboats suited to river operations, and, of the half-dozen Spanish cruisers, one was an unarmoured wooden ship. Like the Cubans, the Filipinos were in revolt against a decrepit colonial regime, so that American forces could count on at least a cautious welcome from the local population.

Dewey was furthered aided by the incompetence of the Spanish command.[18] Rear-Admiral Patricio Montojo y Pasarón had an inadequate force at his disposal and indulged himself in a morbid pessimism at the prospects of a successful defense. In the interest of making the best of a bad situation he concluded, logically, that he could engage Dewey's squadron either at Subic Bay, some thirty-five miles north of Manila, or at Manila Bay itself, as in either location the shore batteries could augment the limited firepower of his ships. In preparation for a defense at Subic Bay he ordered one of the bay's two channels closed by the sinking of block ships and the other channel fortified by a minefield and appropriately sited coastal guns. Yet by the time the arrival of the American squadron was imminent, this work had not been completed. Subic Bay still offered the best configuration for confronting Dewey, but the outraged Montojo opted to abandon it in preference for Manila Bay. Here he compounded strategic error with tactical folly by deciding not to position his ships under the cover of the heavy shore guns lining the shoreline of the city of Manila, explaining that this would serve only to bring the city as well as his ships under American fire. Instead, he anchored the ships across Manila Bay, south-west from the city, off Sangley Point and to the north of the Cavite Arsenal, where the Spanish shore batteries were unable to depress their guns sufficiently for short-range fire should it become necessary. In effect, he arrayed his ships less for battle than for dignified execution.[19]

In the meantime, Dewey had sought Montojo at Subic Bay, discovered it abandoned, and set a leisurely speed for Manila, timing his arrival there for the night of April 30. He took his squadron into Manila Bay at midnight in order to measure the vigilance of the shore gunners and suffered no damage in an exchange of fire with a battery his ships managed to silence in a matter of minutes. As May 1 dawned, Dewey then sought the Spanish fleet under the shore guns of Manila and was again disappointed until, turning south, he spotted Montojo's ragged line in the shallow waters in front of the Cavite Arsenal. At 5:15 AM the Spanish ships and shore guns opened fire, kicking off officially the Battle of Manila Bay. At a range of two and a half miles Dewey instructed his ships to "fire as convenient," steamed *Olympia* steadily toward the Spanish, turned west where his maps indicated water becoming dangerously shallow, and was followed at two-hundred-yard intervals by the rest of the squadron, each ship in sequence bringing its port-side guns into action. As the American ships steamed back and forth along the Spanish line sailors on both sides worked amid the deafening gunfire and choking smoke, all of them knowing that failure in getting off the next salvo ahead of their enemy could well mean instant obliteration. After almost two hours of action, Montojo lifted the anchor of his flagship, *Reina Cristina*, and set a course to engage *Olympia*. The entire American line immediately concentrated its guns on the *Reina Cristina*, subjecting it to a devastating barrage of every caliber of shell, one of them exploding in the ship's makeshift hospital, "killing or re-wounding all the patients there and splattering the room with blood."[20] Shortly after Montojo had returned *Reina Cristina* to the Spanish line, two of his torpedo boats made similarly quixotic dashes at Dewey's line—one exploded in a storm of American fire, the other then retired.

At this point Dewey suddenly hankered for breakfast. More accurately, he received a report that *Olympia* had only fifteen rounds left for each of its ten five-inch guns and signaled his squadron to break off action immediately. As the report turned out to be in error—only fifteen rounds per gun had so far been fired; a week's ammunition remained at his disposal—Dewey saved face by ordering breakfast for the squadron's crew. The lull in action permitted Montojo to take stock of the situation, acknowledge it as irretrievable, and order all ships capable of doing so to take refuge in Bacoor Bay behind Cavite. When Dewey resumed the action *Olympia*, *Baltimore*, and *Raleigh* pounded the Spanish shore batteries and *Don Antonio de Ulloa*, the only of Montojo's ships returning fire. This continued for an hour until a white flight was spotted over Cavite. Once the squadron had subdued the remainder of the Spanish fleet, damage reports revealed a lopsided victory for the U.S. Navy: three Spanish ships sunk, six set ablaze, 161 of Montojo's men killed, and 210 wounded, set against slight damage to Dewey's squadron and nine of his men wounded.

Dewey then turned his attention to the city of Manila, squaring up his ships offshore and promising prompt destruction if its shore guns fired upon him. Governor-General Basilio Augustín agreed to their surrender—the commander of the Manila artillery, thus dishonoured, later shot himself in the head—but petulantly refused Dewey the use of the Manila–Hong Kong telegraph line to inform Washington of the American victory.[21] Dewey had the line raised from the bay and severed, opting to send the *McCulloch* to Hong Kong with the news of victory and an urgent call for resupply and sufficient men to assert American control over a new possession in the Western Pacific.

A beachhead for expansion

In the Caribbean, the war's primary theater, naval power was equally critical to the outcome as in the Philippines. The leadership of both the navy and the army was nonetheless remarkably naïve about the demands of expeditionary operations and had devoted little thought to the challenges peculiar to maritime operations.[22] At the time of the declaration of hostilities, the U.S. Army was not in a process of upheaval and modernisation at all analogous to the renaissance of the navy. Its strength stood at 28,747 officers and enlisted men, a pale expression of the martial potential of an industrial nation of 73 million people. Since 1865 the army had been deployed to enforce Reconstruction, quell civil disturbances, and wage a campaign against the tribes of the Great Plains and Far West. It had not known a conventional war in thirty-three years and had not fought a foreign foe in half a century, since the Mexican War of the 1840s. The United States was comparatively slow in strengthening the capacity of its central government to cope with the economic and social rigours of industrial maturity; as a political movement with enthusiasts in both the Democratic and Republican Parties, Progressivism spoke to a broad-based appetite for reform in which government was to assume new regulatory powers. In the 1890s McKinley Republicanism captured the larger electoral dividend of the movement, and the very urban Progressive voters who sought higher wages for workers and more equitable business regulation were also the nationalists who cheered at the chance to kick Spain out of the Caribbean. Their views on expansive foreign policy were often much the same as European nationalists,[23] but they little appreciated the cost involved. The condition of the U.S. Army reflected almost perfectly this popular ignorance.

Moreover, the bellicose patriotism that accrued so naturally to the navy following the destruction of the *Maine* turned into pious constitutionalism when the matter of raising an expeditionary force for Cuba was raised. Secretary of War Russell Alger initially implied that a large army could be fielded by mobilising the existing force and augmenting its numbers with volunteers. A bill to authorise a force of 100,000 men immediately ran into headwinds, coming from congressmen voicing the traditional American distrust of large standing armies and from state governors who feared that if local militia regiments of the National Guard were absorbed into a federal volunteer army, the constitutional right of states to maintain their own militias would be impaired.[24] A compromise permitted the U.S. Army to recruit to a strength of 65,000 for a period of two years, and an additional bill authorised the president to call for volunteers above that ceiling. McKinley issued a call for 125,000 and was rewarded with mass enthusiasm, but provisions to appease state governors included the stipulation that volunteers would retain their local identity by mustering to state regiments with their own officers, the authority to nominate officers to state forces being a source of local patronage for the governors. The raising of this expeditionary force created thereby a decentralised system of recruiting, uneven standards for training, and "too many men chasing too little equipment, weapons and accommodation."[25] The irony was that Congress worried that the War Department sought to force a large and permanent military establishment upon the people, when the Department of the Navy had been laboring in this direction successfully for more than a decade.

Still, the American invasion of Cuba did not want for enthusiastic manpower. Alger estimated that some one million men volunteered in response to the administration's first call. Roosevelt resigned his post to sign up with the army, and former Democratic candidate for the presidency, William Jennings Bryan, accepted a commission with the Third Nebraska Volunteers. Unprepared for the task of assembling and equipping an expeditionary force, yet under pressure to take offensive action against Cuba as soon as possible, Washington improvised the mobilisation. The administrative and logistical ligatures available were simply not up to the sudden and overwhelming demand placed upon them. Consignments arrived without labels indicating their contents; facilities for loading and distribution were inadequate or non-existent; recruits in makeshift camps dealt with poor food and accommodation and such inadequate sanitary conditions that disease, especially typhoid, began to ravage their ranks:

> Government officials bought whatever was available and placed orders for more. Tons of equipment and supplies were soon being transported night and day along the railway tracks, rivers, canals and roads leading to the army bases. The variety and quantity of goods was staggering. This was illustrated by a list which Alger later presented of items which the Quartermaster's Department had either manufactured or purchased during the period from May to August 1898. Among the examples were: 546,338 blankets, 523,203 trousers, 467,705 campaign hats, 153,167 canvas field uniforms, 782,303 shoes, 622,211 dark-blue flannel shirts, 38,963 axes, 34,344 camp-kettles, 64,980 tents, 16,618 horses, 20,183 mules, and 5,179 wagons.[26]

Operational planning too was haphazard. An initial plan for landing a force at Mariel, twenty-five miles west of Havana, was temporarily set aside for the dubious proposition that Havana itself could be taken in a frontal assault by 70,000 men. Nelson Miles, Commanding General of the U.S. Army, was for a time alone in suggesting that the United States make more use of the Cuban insurgents. Miles was able to make contact with the insurgent leader

Calixto García from whose staff he learned that Admiral Pascual Cevera y Topete's Spanish Caribbean Squadron was at Santiago de Cuba on Cuba's south-eastern coast. This information prompted a reappraisal of strategy in which sobriety prevailed, and it was decided that an expeditionary force would depart from Tampa, Florida, land in the vicinity of Santiago de Cuba, and then assist the navy in the destruction of Cevera's fleet in the harbour. Tampa had the advantage of geographic proximity to Cuba, but it had a comparatively small port and was more modestly endowed with railway connections than Charleston, South Carolina, or the Gulf cities of Mobile and New Orleans. These limitations and the pressure to depart quickly produced a chaotic disembarkation. The invasion force languished in Tampa Bay for five days, leaving at last on June 14.[27]

An early American success in the war was the seizure by a battalion of the U.S. Marine Corps of a beachhead at Guantánamo Bay, the defeat of a three-day Spanish counter-attack, and the establishment of a harbour for coaling and supplying. This feat, when compared with the army's logistical tangles, subsequently brought naval reformers to the conclusion that future maritime operations would be well served by making the Marines a permanent expeditionary force.[28] The invasion convoy bound for Cuba was meanwhile the largest expeditionary force yet assembled by the United States, consisting of twenty-six transport vessels and six supply vessels carrying 16,058 men and 819 officers, 959 horses and 1,336 mules—all escorted by the battleship *Indiana*, the cruisers *Detroit* and *Castine,* along with a number of lesser ships. Although the convoy had difficulty holding formation because the capabilities of its ships varied, it arrived unmolested off Santiago de Cuba on June 20.

Major General William Shafter, at the head of the Fifth Army Corps and in command of land operations, thereupon surprised Rear-Admiral William Sampson with the news that he intended not to assault the heights at the harbour entrance but rather to land his force at Daiquirí and to strike an inland route toward Santiago de Cuba to capture the city from the rear. Sampson had assumed that the army would seize the high ground at the mouth of the harbour, supported by the navy's heavy gunfire. Although an element of interservice rivalry was possibly involved in Shafter's decision— the navy had hitherto enjoyed most of the action and glory in this war—it remained within the tactical latitude allotted by the overall operational plan and it offered the virtue of striking the city at its weak point. The logic of the naval blockade of Cuba had been from the start to deprive the Spanish army on the island of resupply by sea; because in the meantime the Cuban insurgents had also challenged the mobility of Spanish troops around the island and denied them access to many of the local resources, Shafter could expect to find a weakened and possibly demoralised Spanish garrison to attack with his fresh troops.

The calculation that a landing at Daiquirí would meet with only modest resistance was well founded. General Arsenio Linares Pomba, the Spanish commander at Santiago de Cuba, had deployed only small detachments along his outer line of defence at Siboney, Daiquirí, and Guantánamo.[29] Between June 22 and 26 Shafter's army was put ashore at Daiquirí after a short naval bombardment forced the small number of defenders to withdraw. This led immediately to the problem of how it was to be supplied for its campaign overland. The lack of good docking facilities and a heavy surf made it impossible for the transports to navigate close to shore, so that supplies had to be loaded onto smaller boats and ferried to the beach. For Shafter the speed of the operation was critical, as he sought to march his army inland and make contact with the enemy before the Cuban climate and disease could ravish its ranks. Haste made waste, and waste provided the unexpected and baleful scenes attending all wars. Heavy artillery intended for attacking the fortifications of Santiago de Cuba was abandoned on the beach; the challenge of getting hundreds of horses and mules ashore was answered by pushing them overboard in the hope they would swim ashore. A major with the Ninth Cavalry wrote, "it is pitiful to see the poor brutes swim from one boat to another. Sometimes they get nearly to the shore, and then turn around and swim to sea."[30]

On their advance toward Santiago de Cuba the Americans laboured in winter-weight wool against tropical heat, insects, and disease. Afternoon rains turned the principal road, the Camino Real, to mud. Their first skirmish with a Spanish force of 1,500 at Las Guasimas in June 24 was of no great military significance yet was unnerving, as the Spanish adopted the tactics of the Cuban insurgents by firing from concealed positions. Americans dropped here and there to the sudden pop of German-made Mauser rifles.[31] The critical engagements came at El Caney and San Juan Hill on July 1. Linares had reinforced the Spanish positions at both locations following the clash at Las Guasimas, yet persisted in the belief that the bay of Santiago de Cuba would face the main assault. As a result, a Spanish force of 520 under General Joaquín Vara del Rey y Rubino defended the fortified village of El Caney against some 6,600 Americans commanded by General Henry Ware Lawton. At San Juan Hill the numerical odds were more balanced—10,400 Spanish and 8,400 Americans—but in both instances the Americans carried the day.

This outcome had little to do with sound planning or crisp execution. Shafter's original plan was to storm the San Juan heights commanding the approaches to Santiago de Cuba and thereupon take the city itself in one stroke. In general terms, the plan was complex enough to confound proper coordination by the staff system Shafter had at his disposal. Whereas the main thrust of his attack was to be on San Juan Hill and the adjacent Kettle Hill, Shafter's knowledge of the terrain and deployment of the Spanish forces moved him to plan two additional secondary assaults, one against El Caney to the north and another at Aguadores, to convince Linares that the antici- pated attack on Santiago de Cuba's harbour had come and thereby discour- age him from reinforcing the San Juan Heights, where Shafter planned his breakthrough. Shafter ordered Brigadier General Henry Lawton to launch an assault with his division against the defenders of El Caney at first light on July 1.

Assuming that Lawton would neutralise El Caney in no more than two hours, Shafter instructed him to thereafter swing his force westward and join the right flank of the main attack on the San Juan Heights. Sound in theory, the plan nonetheless unraveled when Lawton's force encountered stiff resistance from the little Spanish garrison. Outnumbered ten to one, the Spanish managed to maximise the effect of their Mauser rifles by firing upon the assault force from well-entrenched and concealed positions. Lawton had only four small field guns with which to bombard El Caney. Although his regular troops carried a .30 caliber version of the modern Krag-Jörgenson bolt-action rifle, moreover, the Second Massachusetts Volunteers blasted away with 1873-vintage .45 caliber Springfields, which required black powder and belched out such billows of white smoke such that the Spanish were never in doubt to where to settle their sights. The initial attack therefore stalled and "degenerated into a long-range sniping contest."[32] After eight hours Shafter decided that the main issue of the day could be delayed no longer and ordered Lawton to break off at El Caney and take up his position on the American right below the San Juan Heights—yet yielded to Lawton's protest that he was too deeply committed to disengage. Not until mid-afternoon was Lawton able to orchestrate his field guns and infantry for a decisive assault, and the Spanish retreated only when a mere eight of their number were left standing.

An action peripheral to the main objective had imperiled the day. As the fight over El Caney wore on, the troops moving into position for the San Juan attack were encountering, and compounding, problems of their own. The American artillery battery of four 3.2-inch rifles field pieces at El Pozo opened fire at the heights at 8:00 AM, but its smoke permitted the Spanish gunners to calculate range quickly and return fire with sufficient accuracy to silence the American position after only thirty minutes. Tasked now with an imminent uphill assault without artillery support, the 8,000 men moving into position below the heights were then exposed to further peril when a hot-air observation balloon was sent aloft to help coordinate the advance and had the wholly predictable effect of exposing the American line of advance to the Spanish force on the heights. Colonel Leonard Wood later reported that in crossing the San Juan River, "the result was a terrific converging artillery and rifle fire on the ford."[33] An attack originally scheduled for 10:00 AM did not move off until long after noon, while in the meantime the Spanish on the heights poured fire on the Americans below, crouching behind what cover they could find behind ridges and small rises in the ground. At 1:00 PM Lieutenant John D. Miley, General Shafter's aide, seized the initiative. With no order from his superior as to when the men should move off, he instructed the anxious generals around him to take the heights "at all hazards."[34]

The advance over steep and difficult ground upon a well-fortified position could easily have gone very wrong, but for two factors that owed nothing to planning. The absence of artillery support was compensated for by the first factor, when Second Lieutenant John H. Parker was able to get his Gatling gun detachment to within 800 yards of the Spanish positions, so that for some eight critical minutes, three Gatlings ripped up the Spanish at a rate of thirty-six hundred rounds per minute. The ability for the Spanish to continue effective resistance was meanwhile impeded by the second factor. They had located their positions at the top of the hill rather than at its military crest—a point somewhat further down from which they would have an unobstructed view of the entire slope—and were thus unable to see much of the American assault before it was full upon them.[35] As the American infantrymen swarmed up San Juan Hill, dismounted cavalry stormed Kettle Hill, not in the style of mounted charges conjured by the newspapers back home but rather in a breathless scramble under fire up the slopes in waist-high grass. Once the Spanish had fled their trenches and retreated down the reverse side of the slope, the Americans halted on the crest of the heights and, in anticipation of a Spanish counter-attack that never came, threw themselves into the work of strengthening their position. Although Shafter had planned to move on directly against Santiago de Cuba, his troops were in no condition to advance further. It had been a soldier's battle not unlike the Anglo-French victory above the Alma in 1854.

For the day's action the Americans had taken 1,385 casualties against a Spanish total of 593. Only 3,000 of the 15,000-strong American force occupied the position immediately following the assault; they were delirious with exhaustion, had no artillery support, and were thinly strung out along the crest of the San Juan Heights panting for breath.[36] Shafter's plan had been too complex. He could have ignored El Caney or in the alternative pinned down the Spanish garrison there with a much smaller American force and thrown proportionally more troops against the San Juan Heights without awaiting the verdict at El Caney. He could observe El Caney and San Juan from his command post, but he was at considerable distance from either and unable to assess the terrain between them. Age and failing health impeded his personal mobility and stamina, but these limitations could have been remedied with crisp staff work. Instead, he improvised an unwieldy system of messengers and telephone lines for receiving information and issuing orders, so that his troops were robbed of the coordination that comes with genuine command and control. Linares had made his own mistakes, but his troops had disabused the Americans of the assumption that they would crumble at the first sign of determined aggression.[37] They had retreated in good order to better entrenchments around Santiago de Cuba, so the fight was hardly over. A frantic Colonel Roosevelt wrote to Henry Cabot Lodge on July 3 that "the Spaniards fight very hard and charging these entrenchments against modern rifles is terrible;" he pleaded for "every regiment and above all every battery possible," as otherwise "we are within measurable distance of a terrible military disaster."[38]

Even accounting for the Roughrider's gift for hyperbole, this assessment was not wholly unwarranted. The Americans were short of artillery, food, and transportation, while sickness weakened their ranks. The cost of the San Juan engagement so rocked Shafter's confidence, moreover, that on July 2 he asked Admiral Sampson, whom only two weeks earlier he had treated as his junior, to launch a naval attack on the Morro fortress on the eastern side of the entrance to Santiago's harbour and the Socapa batteries on the opposing side. When Sampson declined on the grounds of the risk to his ships and men, Shafter sent an ultimatum to Linares demanding the surrender of the city on pain of bombardment, while simultaneously responding to Washington's demands for news with the unwelcome cable that the defenses of Santiago de Cuba were so strong that he was seriously pondering withdrawal. Alger responded to this alarming evidence of dullness on the sharp edge with a promise of reinforcements and combined it with the remarkable understatement that the effect on public sentiment "would be much better" if Shafter did not fall back. At this point the Spanish interpretation of the engagements at El Caney and the San Juan Heights decided the issue. General Ramón Blanco y Erenas informed Admiral Cevera that his fleet was to sortie the harbour and run the blockade, as the Americans had captured the San Juan Heights and were in a position to attack the entrance to the harbour. In other words, the American strategy for the war was working, even if its execution on land wanted for coherence and conviction. Happily, this meant that the initiative now swung sharply back to the navy.[39]

If the main mission of the navy had been to blockade Cuba and interdict reinforcement or resupply of the Spanish garrison, the squadron brought from Spain under the command of Admiral Pascual Cervara y Topete was to prove obliging. Of six warships, Cervara had no battleships and only four armoured cruisers, the heaviest of which, *Almirante Oquendo* and *Vizcaya*, displaced only 6,890 tons and would face in the worst scenario Sampson's amoured cruisers, *Brooklyn* and *New York*, both of which displaced more than 8,000 tons, and the three battleships, *Indiana*, *Iowa*, and *Oregon*, all of which cleared 10,000 tons. Cervara had initially set course for San Juan, Puerto Rico, but changed his mind and headed for Martinique. When French authorities there denied him the right to coal, he diverted to Curaçao, where Dutch authorities permitted him only forty-eight hours and six hundred tons of fuel. Thereafter he avoided Cienfueos and Havana, because Sampson could easily concentrate his ships and either location, and settled on Santiago de Cuba at the opposite end of the island from Havana. Far from breaking the American blockade, Cervara in effect found a way to include his squadron as part of the besieged Spanish garrison. Indeed, he was able to do this only because the U.S. Navy's Flying Squadron, under the command of Commodore Winfield Scott Schley, had incomplete intelligence on Cervara's movements since he had left Curaçao and was late in setting a course for Santiago de Cuba.[40] By the time Cervara was ordered to run the blockade on July 3, Sampson's North Atlantic Fleet had arrived to reinforce Schley's formation.

Sampson's advantage in firepower alone might have been decisive—18,847 to 6, 014 pounds of broadside—but tactical circumstance enhanced his advantage. Cervara's ships were forced to exit the narrow harbour entrance one at a time, so that most of Sampson's blockading ships were able to fire upon each of Cervara's ships as it emerged. After a quixotic attempt by *Infanta Maria Teresa* to ram *Brooklyn*, Cervara's squadron ran westward along the coast and was completely destroyed for the cost of minor damage to *Brooklyn*, *Texas*, and *Iowa* and one death, against 323 Spanish killed and 151 wounded. Had Cervara not hugged the coast, the carnage would have been much greater; the evidence is that, like Montojo at Manila, he attempted to square honour with humanity.[41] Following two weeks of siege by Shafter's army, Linares surrendered Santiago de Cuba, and on August 12 Spain's representation in Washington agreed to preliminary terms.

Colonial war in the Philippines

As hostilities in Cuba wound down, they graduated to an altogether new stage in the Philippines. Immediately upon Dewey's victory at Manila Bay, the American republic faced its first colonial war. Filipino revolutionaries had launched a revolt against Spanish rule in 1896 but had been defeated by a 28,000-man Spanish army and lost their leader. Following Manila Bay, the remaining rebel leadership returned from exile in Hong Kong, proclaimed the archipelago independent on June 12, 1898, elected a constituent assembly to draft a constitution and declared the Philippine Republic under President Emilio Aguinaldo in January 1899. Because the United States had sought and received help from Filipino insurgents in the effort against Spain, Aguinaldo reasoned that Filipinos were owed an assurance against American rule. This Major General Elwin S. Otis, the U.S. Army's man-on-the-spot, was unable to offer. He lacked the political authority and assumed that propertied Filipinos would actually favour annexation. Nor was he helped by the McKinley administration's ambivalence about the future of the islands, by its insistence that the insurgents submit to the authority of the United States, or by its instructions that the army was to protect only people and property in and around Manila. The first American troops—115 officers and 2,386 enlisted men of what was later designated the Eighth Army Corps—had arrived in the Philippines in June 1898 and were thereafter reinforced only in trickles due to a scarcity of transport; when a third contingent arrived on July 25, the force totaled 10,946 officers and men composed mostly of state militia.

McKinley did not decide on the annexation of the islands until October, and the Senate did not vote in favour until February 6, 1899, the same day it approved the Treaty of Paris ending hostilities with Spain. In the meantime, fighting had already broken out between Aguinaldo's men and the Americans.[42] The instruction that military government be extended as quickly as practicable to the whole archipelago, while the army was to win the "confidence, respect, and affection of the inhabitants," was nevertheless to be the formula for one of the most effective counter-insurgency campaigns conducted by anyone.[43] In the process, the war for the Philippines lasted much longer and cost the United States and the Filipinos many more casualties than the struggle for Cuba, a case of the secondary theatre of the conflict eclipsing in importance the primary theatre.

It began with a nighttime skirmish followed by an advance by 11,000 men under Otis against 20,000 of Aguinaldo's army deployed around Manila, in which Dewey's warships provided artillery support. A simultaneous rising of Aguinaldo supporters on the streets of Manila was easily doused, and the morning of February witnessed a rout of the Filipino forces in which the Americans overran their objectives, whereupon the engagement degenerated into scattered individual actions. In congressional hearings back in Washington, anti-imperialist Senators later tried to determine whether Otis's men had initiated the fighting without provocation so as to aid the administration into stampeding the annexation. Over the following months knowledge among the Filipino insurgents of anti-imperialist sentiment in the United States led them to overestimate its strength and pursue goals they had little chance of achieving.[44]

Reinforcements arrived from the United States, but the onset of spring brought torrential rains, impassable roads, heat exhaustion, and tropical disease. Not until November was Otis able to hazard an offensive with 35,000 men intended to defeat the Filipino army and occupy the main island of Luzon. Technically, the offensive succeeded in scattering Aguinaldo's forces, but the war then entered a difficult guerrilla phase. For Aguinaldo, the virtue of dispersed forces conducting guerrilla operations was that they could avoid any direct contest of firepower with American forces, while the destruction of any one force would not imperil the overall campaign. On the other hand, the fact of a decentralised command made it difficult to coordinate operations across the archipelago; this problem was made worse by the fact that Aguinaldo's army was dominated by the Tagalog people and was regarded with suspicion by the Macabebes, the Illocanos and other ethnic groupings. Still, the guerrillas fought with considerable skill, and, where the U.S. Army appointed Filipinos to official positions in order to integrate them into the new regime, the guerrillas established parallel governing positions in response.

In early 1900 General Arthur MacArthur, father of Douglas MacArthur, took over Otis's command with a determination to coerce respect from the population wherever affection was absent. Specifically, he issued General Orders 100 dating to the Civil War and authorising such "exemplary punishments" as property confiscation, imprisonment, and deportations for any and all who resisted American authority or were seen to support resistance.[45] This legitimated the application of cruelty to operations against guerrillas and sympathisers, including the shooting of prisoners, the burning of villages, and the torturing of suspects; as the guerrillas had long since developed cruelties of their own, the war acquired a new ferocity.

By the end of 1900 MacArthur's army had reached a total strength of 70,000, while the pacification of some provinces permitted a concentration of greater force against remaining guerrilla strongholds. Macabebe, Illocano, and Bicolano recruits assisted, especially as scouts and in gathering intelligence, as the army adjusted quickly to the techniques of the *insurrectos*. At the same time, the U.S. Navy blockaded foreign arms shipments to the guerrillas, closed inter-island trade, and also prevented Aguinaldo from sending troops from Luzon to other islands in the archipelago. While isolating rebel units geographically from each other, the navy facilitated American mobility with an amphibious capacity to land troops anywhere the coast permitted.[46] MacArthur's ruthlessness brought him into conflict with William Howard Taft, appointed by McKinley as civil commissioner and later as governor to the Philippines, who was eager to win the affections of Filipinos and diligent in the effort. Ultimately, their methods proved complementary. As MacArthur punched the guerrillas into a corner and captured Aguinaldo in April 1901, Taft implemented a criminal code, an internal revenue system, incorporation laws, and a districting scheme for an elected assembly. McKinley's administration, and with it his imperial policy, had meanwhile secured reelection in November 1900. For every Progressive voter who recoiled at the thought of a colony in the Philippines, there were two for whom "benevolent assimilation" was a simply a continuation of the expansion of democracy.[47]

For better or worse, the Philippines were thus destined to assume a central role in American strategic thinking well into the twentieth century. The U.S. Navy had taken Midway Atoll in the Pacific back in 1867. In the wake of the Spanish-American War, this was followed by the annexation of Hawaii in 1898. By the outbreak of World War I, Hawaii had been transformed into a major army and navy base for the protection of America's colonial Pacific empire. As strategic vision had hitherto run well ahead of military capacity, it fell to McKinley's successor to fill the gap with a single-minded devotion to the creation of a navy equal to adversaries more formidable than Spain. The Philippines, a serendipitous territorial trophy in the Western Pacific of a war with Spain over Cuba in the Caribbean, projected American naval power into waters of concern to Imperial Japan, an emergent power with its own interpretation of legitimate spheres of interest.

The martial arts of Meiji Japan

There was a certain appropriateness to this turn of events. The United States had first awakened Japan to the implications of naval power with Commodore Perry's visit in 1853. In 1860 Yokoi Shōnan, a mid-ranking scholar-samurai of the late Tokugawa period in Japan, responded to the challenge of Western encroachment in Asia by making a series of policy recommendations to Matsu-daira Shugaku, lord of Echizen. He maintained that "we cannot refuse contacts with the overseas countries that have greatly developed their navigation," and consequently that "a navy is of prime importance in strengthening our military." He argued further that China, endowed with greater territory and resources than Japan, had never been obliged to seek resources overseas or to acquire knowledge from foreigners, as a consequence of which "its arms are weak, and it must suffer indignities from various countries," such as Britain, France, and Russia in particular. More revealing was the observation that after Japan had refused to trade with Britain and Russia, Commodore Perry's war-ships had entered Uraga Bay in 1953 and "unlocked our closed doors." Yokoi further advised that an island nation with few resources should pattern itself after England, whose large navy enabled it to seize foreign territory.[48] Three decades before Mahan's work inaugurated the global vogue of navalism, in other words, Yokoi was making his case to the dying shogunate with a dash of Darwinist reasoning.

By the 1870s Meiji Japan had developed a variant of parliamentary government, a bureaucracy, independent courts, armed forces with universal conscription, and an education system dedicated to literacy and numeracy but also to popular nationalism and emperor worship. Substantive decision-making authority rested with a narrow oligarchy clustered around the emperor, but Meiji paternalism was nothing if not conscientious.[49] The naval enthusiasts of the early Meiji regime were united in extravagant dreams. Cued by the emperor's call in 1868 for the establishment of a strong navy, they thought in terms of a modern, two-hundred-ship armada, the likes of which Japan had never seen. Nor was it likely to, in light of the challenges of a forced march to industrialisation in the absence of natural resources. Japan of the late twentieth century was in many respects a mirror image of the United States. Where the latter had conquered territory on a continental format and grown relentlessly toward mature industrial status between the Civil War and 1900 yet sought only after the war with Spain a navy reflect-ing its wealth, Meiji Japan clearly sought to punch above its weight in naval ambition despite clear disadvantages. Beyond the limits imposed by relative industrial weakness and a shortage of money, material, and men, the army had dominated the civil war that begat the Restoration, and the army initially shaped the Meiji elite's vision of military power.[50]

Nippon Kaigun: A navy for empire

Still, geography alone dictated that the navy's status as an auxiliary force would either be discarded or the Meiji regime would fail in its national mis-sion. A first step was taken in 1872 with the creation of a Navy Ministry, separate from the Military Ministry, under Kawamura Sumiyoshi, but internal revolts continued to direct attention and resources toward the army for most of the decade. Meanwhile, Kawamura and his successor, Naval

Minister Katsu Kaishū, presided over a fleet reflecting the Tokugawa feudal heritage, a collection of ships of every size and configuration.[51] The 1880s witnessed an improved rate of growth along with increased independence for the navy, aided by the influence of the Shimazu clan in the province of Satsuma and imperial patronage. These ties and the navy's long-term plans came upon heavy weather with the flourishing of parliamentary government in the 1890s and the inevitable attack on clique influence. The navy leadership was initially slow to adapt to party politics, but after 1893 Satsuma dominance declined and the navy was forced to adopt administrative and personnel reforms as the price of parliamentary approval for naval expansion. The reforms were overwhelmingly beneficial, imposing a new meritocracy on officers previously seeking command positions through clan connections, so that the naval leadership came to understand and master the arts of legislative politics under the leadership of Yamamoto Gonnohyōe, a reformer in the naval hierarchy in the 1890s, navy minister during the critical years between 1898 and 1906, and prime minister during the early Taishō period of parliamentary democracy.[52] Initially, Japan acquired military technology through licensing agreements with European manufacturers, as its naval yards lacked the capacity to build large warships. Meiji policy was to study the foreign imports with a mind to domesticating arms production as quickly as possible.[53]

Even an improved navy lacked the legitimacy that comes only from fortune in the contest of arms, and international circumstance of the late nineteenth century indicated that Japanese naval power would have to develop a maritime vocation. Japan's immediate concern, after all, was not the waxing of American naval power but rather with the waning of the Qing dynasty in China and its implications for Japanese influence in Korea and Manchuria. Japanese conquests at the expense of China thus became integral to a comprehensive plan of modernisation and industrialisation. In 1894, a rebellion in Korea following the assassination of its pro-Japanese reformist prime minister prompted both China and Japan to intervene militarily. After helping to defeat the rebellion, however, Japan refused to withdraw its forces and instead invited China to institute reforms in Korea in order to buttress its hold as the suzerain power on the peninsula. Qing rejection of this advice, as well as of the notion that Japan had any legitimate interest in Korea, led to a war declared officially on August 1, 1894, in which Japan chalked up an easy triumph. Its navy destroyed eight of the twelve ships in the Chinese Beiyang fleet; its army advanced and captured Port Arthur on the Liaotung Peninsula by late November. After the fall of Weihaiwei in February 1895, Japanese armies continued their advance into Manchuria. This prompted China to sue for peace.[54] Japan's victory was rightly viewed as vindication of the modernisation programs of the state-building Meiji reformers, but the navy gained more from the war than any other institution apart from the imperial household itself.[55] Still viewed it as the junior service, it had begun to emerge as a serious rival to the army, and funding flowed more freely.

This was because the final outcome of the war with China was much less satisfying than expected and, if anything, intensified Japanese strategic insecurity while stoking nationalist resentment. The Treaty of Shimonoseki, which awarded Japan Formosa, the Pescadores, and the Liaotung Peninsula with its excellent harbour at Port Arthur, alarmed Tsar Nicholas II. The Russian court sought the ice-free waters of Port Arthur and such access to nominally Chinese territory as would enable it to take full advantage of Qing decline. Nicholas was able to convince both France and Germany that Japan's advance was a threat to their own interests in the region, and their collective diplomatic pressure was sufficient to force Japan to return Port Arthur and its Liaotung hinterland. National indignation at European bullying deepened determination to build naval capacity, while the Boxer Uprising in China intensified both concern over Qing decline and further European predations on the mainland in the wake of the Boxers' defeat.[56]

These worries were then wholly vindicated by subsequent Russian behaviour in signing a convention with China over Manchuria yet failing to abide by its commitment to withdraw some 200,000 troops from the region. It was immediately evident that St. Petersburg had overplayed its diplomatic hand when Austria, Britain, Germany, Italy, and the United States all urged China to resist additional Russian demands over Manchuria; whereas in 1895 the European powers could agree that Japanese power in Asia should be limited, by 1900 they were more troubled by Russian presumption. "Presumption" was indeed the correct word, insofar as Japan had already taken steps to ensure Russia's military and diplomatic isolation. The Anglo-Japanese Alliance of 1902 stipulated that each signatory would remain neutral if the other should find itself at war but also that each would come the aid of the other if a third power were to come to the aid of the enemy. It secured for Britain an ally in the Far East to help contain Tsarist ambition and gave to Japan the assurance that whatever military steps it ventured to take to thwart the Russian advance in Manchuria and Korea would not be opposed by the world's preeminent naval power.[57]

In principle, the decision-making structure of the ruling oligarchy in Japan placed the Emperor Meiji at its apex. In substance the deliberations of the *genrō* (retired elder statesmen who remained advisors to the emperor), the ministers of state, the military leadership, and the Privy Council established a policy line in his name. In 1901, however, the *genrō*, who had dominated the premiership since 1885, were unable to form a cabinet to succeed the fourth cabinet of Ito Hirobumi and were eclipsed by a succeeding generation who established the first cabinet of Count Katsuru Taro. Moreover, the Sino-Japanese War and its aftermath accelerated a trend toward compromise between the oligarchs and party politicians in the Diet, where members without executive responsibility voiced public resentment over the meager returns of the war with China, filtered by nationalist societies, such as the Genyōsha, along with chauvinist academics and journalists.[58] The Genyōsha's leadership strata included the mining entrepreneur Hiraoka

Kōtarō and the ultranationalist Tōyama Mitsuru. Together with a press that waxed more bellicose as it became more popular, these activists buttressed the position of hardliners within the oligarchy, but their primary significance was in the cultivation of popular support for assertive diplomacy.[59]

By 1904 such diplomacy had vastly more steel behind it than a decade earlier. Whereas the treaty of 1902 guaranteed the non-intervention of the Royal Navy in any conflict with Russia, British shipyards supplied the bulk of Japan's massive orders for ship construction. On the eve of the war with Russia, the Imperial Navy had six battleships less than ten years old, seven armoured cruisers, and seven protected cruisers of the same age. Under Yamamoto, Japan sought the fastest, most heavily armed and armoured capital ships in the world to compensate for the numerical superiority of foreign fleets.[60] Japanese naval education meanwhile was beginning to show signs of tactical sophistication and independent thought. The Meiji government had sought and received British tutelage for the early generations of naval officers. Lieutenant Commander Archibald Douglas headed instruction at the Naval Academy at Tsukii for many years and left a British imprint on Japanese naval culture. Lieutenant Commander L.P. Willan taught gunnery and tactics, and Captain John Ingles influenced everything from the Japanese appreciation of modern naval technology to tactical advances, naval professionalism, the naval applications of science, and the organisation of fleets.

Yet far and away the greatest influence at the Naval Staff College was Akiyama Saneyuki, a naval intellectual very much in the mold of Mahan, who had spent two years in the United States. There he approached Mahan directly for advice on his naval education and wrote to Assistant Secretary of the Navy Theodore Roosevelt for abstracts of courses offered at the Naval War College. When Sampson first blockaded and then destroyed Cervara's Spanish squadron off Santiago de Cuba, Akiyama had been present as a foreign observer. At the staff college Akiyama took care to import the latest Western ideas on naval arms and combined them with Chinese and Japanese tradition. His effort raised the level of professionalism at the college dramatically, while his ideas on engagement and decisive battle informed Japanese naval war planning for generations.[61]

In 1904 the Meiji oligarchy dovetailed its war-planning with its diplomacy toward St. Petersburg in such a way as to give its strategy for establishing a presence on the Asian mainland all the advantages of coherence that timing and circumstance could offer. Japan's last gesture, proffered January 13, 1904, was an offer to declare Manchuria beyond its sphere of interest if Russia would do the same for Korea. For want of a reply, on February 4 the Japanese ambassador informed his hosts in St. Petersburg that time had run out. Thereafter, naval operations formed the bookends of the conflict, permitting Japan in the first instance to land sufficient troops to wage a land war, then in the last convincing Russia that Japanese naval power in support of those troops was beyond the capacity of Russia to defeat.[62] The oligarchy reasoned that the coming struggle was of existential importance, to be prosecuted with the utmost determination. Japan therefore made a formal declaration of war on February 10. But the navy had sailed on February 6, and during the night of February 8–9 Japanese destroyers launched a torpedo attack on Russian ships anchored at Port Arthur.

Japanese troops meanwhile occupied Fusan, Masamp, and Chinhae Bay on the south coast of Korea, while the navy supported the landing of troops at the port of Chemulpo (present-day Inchon) on the west coast. The Combined Fleet's commander, Admiral Heihchirō Tōgō, had sent the destroyers against the Russian fleet at Port Arthur, while the Second Fleet under Vice-Admiral Sotokichi Uryu took four cruisers to escort merchant vessels carrying 3,000 troops to the Chemulpo landing.[63]

The attack on Port Arthur sought to prevent the main Russian squadron—six battleships and six cruisers—from leaving the harbour to challenge the Japanese seizure of the waters of the Yellow Sea and Korea Bay. The first shots of the war were actually fired at Chemulpo, where the Japanese cruisers *Asama* and *Chiyoda*, with the help of sixteen torpedo boats, put the Russian cruiser *Yaryag* and the gunboat *Koreyets* out of action. The destroyer attack on the Russian squadron at Port Arthur was followed up by an attack by battleships and armoured cruisers on February 9. The balance of damage favoured the Japanese fleet, although the engagement was hardly decisive. Instead, Russian incompetence and timidity, in choosing to keep its Port Arthur squadron within the covering range of the shore batteries, ensured that Japanese command of the sea would not for the time being be contested seriously. Although Japanese strategy has been criticised because its failure to destroy the Port Arthur squadron obliged the Combined Fleet to impose a protracted blockade,[64] the Imperial Navy nonetheless had control of the sea around Korea and Liaotung Peninsula while the invading army was put ashore. Over time, the shock registered in the preemptive move against Port Arthur became part of Japanese national mythology and the doctrine of surprise a cornerstone of military strategy until its reappearance in the skies over Pearl Harbor in 1941.[65]

With the Russian navy at least temporarily neutralised, Japan was able to transport troops over water to the theatre of war and supply them with ease and speed, as both geography and national infrastructure now came into play. The Japanese merchant marine, which had grown from 167,000 in gross tonnage in 1893 to 626,745 at the war's outbreak, included many new and fast steamers of more than 5,000 tons. Additionally, Japan had advantages of seaborne access to Korea similar to those enjoyed by the United States in transporting troops to Cuba, with the difference that its coastline directly across from Korea was studded with fine harbours connected directly with garrisons in the interior by rail, while the Inland Sea provided a supplementary line of communications from center of the main island to its western extremity.[66] Nothing now presented an obstacle to the Imperial Army's presence in strength in Korea, a necessary condition as it faced not a small colonial garrison on a neighboring island but the largest army of Europe on the mainland of Asia.

Chemulpo was used to land troops in Korea until the spring thaw permitted the use of more northerly locations; by late afternoon on February 9, the army had four battalions of its 12th Division safely ashore, and subsequently Haiju to the north was open as an additional landing point. By March 10, the Japanese cavalry had proceeded inland to occupy Anju on the north-east corner of Korea Bay, where it was joined by a battalion of infantry the following day and three more battalions a week later. Meanwhile, Chinampo, still further north up the Korean coast, was chosen for the disembarkation of the remaining troops of the Japanese First Army, even as ice there was breaking up, because the long march from landing points to the south could thereby be avoided.[67] The warming temperatures that had freed the Korean coast for the landings also turned the Korean roads to mud, thus slowing progress northward. General Tamemoto Kuroki, commander of the First Army, was able to mitigate the problem by taking to the coastal road rather than interior routes and designating a fourth port, Rikaho, as an additional landing supply base. This meant that by the time the First Army met the Tsar's forces for the first major land engagement of the war at the Yalu River in late April it could bring to bear three divisions, composed of 2,000 cavalrymen, 28,000 infantry, and 128 field guns, including some brand new Krupp 4.7-inch howitzers, against the Russian Eastern Detachment of 5,000 cavalry, 15,000 infantry, and only 60 guns.

This balance of forces did not reflect the strategic depth of the adversaries. In 1904 the manpower of the Japanese army stood at 850,000, but the standing army had only 380,000 troops at it disposal; active Russian strength meanwhile totaled over a million men backed by reserves of over two million. Why then did the disparity of strength tilt in Japan's direction in the only place and time where numbers truly mattered, at the Yalu River in the spring of 1904? Beyond Japanese determination to seize the initiative by moving quickly, there were three principal reasons for the comparatively weak Russian showing. In combination they made the Tsarist government's policy on the Russian Far East ambiguous, its attitude to the prospect of war with Japan casual, and the prosecution of the war uncertain.

First among them was the nature of late Tsarism itself. When Nicholas II came to the throne in 1894, he inherited a policy championed by his finance minister, Sergei Witte, according to whom the needs of Russia's continuing industrialisation and imperial opportunity beckoning in the Far East and the Pacific could be met by the construction of a Trans-Siberian Railroad and a Chinese Eastern Railroad through Manchuria. Whereas Witte deemed the projects inherently wholesome, others saw them as vehicles for a predatory annexation of territory in China's borderlands at the expense of the failing Qing or a path for Russia to turn away from the West and reclaim its Asian cultural heritage.[68] The Tsar's East Asian diplomacy was thus a mirror reflecting the contradictory visions of assorted nationalist ideologues.[69]

Additionally, Nicholas presided over a nation in pre-revolutionary turmoil. In the decades between the Napoleonic Wars and the Crimean conflict the victorious Romanov dynasty enjoyed and phase of stability and legitimacy that suited its conservatism about absolutist prerogative. Defeat in the Crimea in 1856, however, undermined Romanov prestige while exposing the cost to Russia's empire of its society's failure to modernise abreast of competitors such as Britain and France. The challenge facing Romanov rule thereafter "was that it was impossible to ignore the demands either of external military security or of internal political stability and that these demands pulled hard in opposite directions."[70] For the Tsarist army of the early twentieth century this was quite palpably true, insofar as domestic unrest routinely resulted in its deployment in defeating revolt on one front or another of what amounted to an internal theater of war in town and country.[71] It is possible that by 1894, when Nicholas II inherited the throne, no Tsar could have met the challenge, but in Nicholas the nation had an autocrat not wholly dedicated to the cause and out of his depth in effort, more responsible than any single figure for an unnecessary war with Japan. Remarkably incurious about the vast territories and many peoples he ruled, he had no prime minster and no cabinet, but might be convinced that a small war smartly won would transcend domestic grievances in moment of national togetherness. "A soft haze of mysticism," Witte noted, "refracts everything he beholds and magnifies his own functions and person."[72] Russian Tsarism held that Nicholas II not only symbolised centuries of labour in shaping the Russian peoples and their territories into one vast empire and powerful state but also that he personified the achievement and was indispensable, politically and administratively, to its preservation.[73] The lack of a personal conception of autocratic rule—what is was and what it perhaps ought to be—meant that Nicholas aggravated rather than leavened the idiosyncrasies of the sprawling administrative structure about him.

Russian administrative incontinence was the product of a history in which the development of law reflected the separate evolution of the state and its people. Yet the state "sought to regulate every detail of social life for its own purposes and in its own image."[74] A system dating to Nicholas I and initially intended to enhance the accountability of Tsarism exposed Nicholas II to regular written reports by his senior servitors, each narrowly focused upon matters exclusive to their respective departments yet often detailed and dealing with matters as trivial as tax deferments. Even the State Council, the highest deliberative body, was composed of ministers and former senior bureaucrats mired in administrative minutiae to a degree that impaired collective consideration of larger issues or the management of unanticipated events. Nicholas was in effect the personnel director of a vast bureaucracy and personal referee for 130 million subjects, his policy "little more than the sum of innumerable ad hoc decisions."[75]

Far from an optimal arrangement for the foreign policy of any great power at the turn of twentieth century it was especially problematic for

Russia, where diplomacy was traditionally divided into distinct European and Asian spheres, with subordinate status awarded to the latter.[76] In the late stages of the diplomatic exchange with Meiji Japan Russian policy-making was even more disorganised than the usual "clique-war without rules" that typically prevailed at the court of St. Petersburg.[77] Nicholas subordinated the coherence of his Asian policy to a personnel change designed to free himself of the overbearing influence of Witte, who opposed a belligerent posture with Japan, by cutting him out of Finance and replacing him with E.D. Pleske, a banker with no political acumen. He sought simultaneously to placate resentful rivals. Specifically, he created a Far Eastern governorship and appointed Admiral E.I. Alekseev to head the office in Port Arthur, depriving Witte and his minister of war, A.N. Kuropatkin, of any direct authority in relations with Japan, while placing Alekseev geographically and administratively in the middle of the crisis. Nicholas thereby short-circuited policy-making deliberations among Witte, Kuropatkin, and Foreign Minister Count V.N. Lamzdorff and created the impression in Tokyo that Nicholas II had set Russian policy on a collision course. In truth, the he barely knew his way around the ship of state.[78]

Nicholas was reportedly incredulous when the Japanese navy opened hostilities. Over the preceding months his government had been badly served by its intelligence services regarding Japanese capabilities and intentions, yet not so badly served that due attention to available information would have failed to create a sense of urgency.[79] A misreading of evidence as to the imminence of conflict then compromised Russian conduct of it. Ever since the overthrow of the Treaty of Shimonoseki the two sides had discussed a sphere-of-influence agreement over Korea and Manchuria. Frustration with St. Petersburg's delays over a final formula, even as Russian troops remained in Manchuria, had in fact convinced the Japanese oligarchy of Russia's bad faith and the prudence of taking action. Yet even as the two armies converged on the Yalu River, the Tsar's government continued to believe that Japanese intentions were possibly confined to Korea and gave explicit directions to Admiral Eugene Alexeiev to undertake no overt action against the Japanese as long as they remained on Korean soil south of the Yalu. Alexeiev, for whom a war with an Asian upstart was hardly to be taken seriously, was himself happy to believe that Kuroki's army would halt at the Yalu. Even Kuropatkin, who appreciated the situation better than most, was committed to an initial defensive posture and the possible necessity of trading space for time.[80]

The losses of limited war

Russia could benefit from the superior strength of its army only if it could mobilise quickly, yet in 1904 the Trans-Siberian Railway buoyed imperial spirits much more effectively than it transported troops. The line from European Russia to Harbin and from Harbin southward to Mukden and

Liaoyang was broken at Lake Baikal, across which men and supplies had to be ferried. Even when a track around the lake was completed in September 1904, the line could initially handle only six pairs of trains daily; in optimum conditions the 5,000-mile haul could be completed in fifteen days, but a forty-day journey was more usual. By the end of the year the railway was handling nine to ten trains daily and had carried 410,000 troops, 93,000 horses and 1,000 guns. A typical Russian army corps required 267 trains to reach the front. Russia's lack of infrastructure to meet its needs, much less its ambitions, were thus felt first-hand in this massive logistical problem,[81] a result of which was that Japan's opening naval operations paid an enormous strategic dividend. Having seized control of the waters off Korean's east coast, the efficiency of its merchant marine turned the war into a local conflict at a point when Russia had only two of its twenty-nine army corps east of the Urals.

The advantage was felt first at the Yalu River. In contemplation of landing the Second Army at Dalny on the Liaotung Peninsula, thus isolating and capturing Port Arthur, the Japanese command urged Kuroki to cross the Yalu against all Russian opposition and move into Manchuria in such force as to require Kuropatkin's urgent attention. In approaching the Yalu Kuroki had already partly accomplished this task. Kuropatkin warned Major-General Kashtalinski, commanding the Russian Eastern Detachment at the Yalu, not to risk decisive action against superior forces. Because Kuroki had superior forces, in other words, he was to be stalled but not stopped in crossing into Manchuria; thereafter there would ample opportunity to delay his advance through the territory between the Yalu and the town of Liaoyang further north. With a limited number of troops at his disposal and the Japanese First Army at large in Manchuria, this meant that Kuropatkin would be in no position to concentrate forces to oppose the landing of the Japanese Second Army at Dalny.[82]

The Battle of the Yalu River achieved only the slightest of delays. Kuroki's efforts to dislodge the Russians from the Manchurian bank of the river began in earnest on April 25 and concluded in overwhelming success on May 2. Although the Russian decision to engage the Japanese at the Yalu was sound strategically, the troops available were few and Russian tactics squandered their potential for effective defense. Lieutenant-General M.I. Zasulich made no attempt to conceal his positions and spread his troops too thinly in a linear defense of some seven battalions and sixteen guns flung out over six miles. The level of the Yalu and Ai Rivers being low, Kuroki greatest challenge was to get his troops across a series of shallow channels and sandy islands more quickly than Russian firepower could bleed off their numbers. This he met by building a decoy bridge over main channel to draw fire and reveal the Russian artillery positions, meanwhile preparing nine portable bridges capable of spanning the narrower channels some eight miles upstream on the Russian left flank. By day Kuroki took elaborate measures to camouflage his intentions; by night he moved troops and guns into positions for operations at dawn. By 5:30pm on May 1 the fight was over. Losses on both sides were light—1,036 Japanese killed or wounded against 2,700 Russians killed, wounded or captured—but its shock to Russian and boost to Japanese morale was immense. A small engagement crisply executed preserved the initiative for the Japanese army, and Japan's creditors in London and New York were impressed enough to offer further financing of the war.[83]

As the First Army crossed into Manchuria, the Second managed its landing only sixty miles east of Port Arthur on May 5. The amphibious operation, along 3,000 yards of shore near Pitzuwo, required a fleet of seventy transports to carry the troops and almost as many destroyers and torpedo boats to protect them. Despite strong winds and high seas the landings continued day and night, each transport leaving independently for Japan immediately upon clearing its load. At high tide the troops used wharves built by engineers and civilian carpenters from Japan; at low tide lighters were grounded and the troops waded ashore. On May 8 General Oku Yasukata landed with his command headquarters. By the night of May 13 all three divisions of the Second Army were safely ashore. The last group of transports was accompanied by a cable ship laying a line from Korea, establishing direct telegraphic communication with imperial headquarters in Tokyo.[84]

Oku's force now threatened to cut off Port Arthur's garrison from any relief by Russian forces in Manchuria. As a preliminary defense against a now imminent siege of the city, the East Siberian Rifles were able to position only 4,000 men and 65 guns against Oku's 35,000 men and 215 guns across a narrow isthmus at Nanshun. Following a brief a struggle—in which Oku suffered an alarming 4,300 casualties, mostly to machine-guns—the Russians retired in the direction of Port Arthur. Yet for Oku, the city was not the issue of the moment. This was now left to the Third Army under General Nogi Maresuke, while the General Nozu Michitsura's Fourth Army, landed at Tukushan, was to join Oku and proceed north to join Kuroki's First Army against Kuropatkin for the main land engagements of the war.

These were at Liaoyang and Mukden, necessarily discussed together as they were two episodes of a single campaign now prosecuted to force the war quickly to a decision—a goal sought as fervently by the government in Tokyo as by its armies on the fertile plains and rough mountains of Manchuria. As the three Japanese armies in Manchuria converged south of Liaoyang in July 1904, Field Marshal Iwao Oyama arrived to assume overall command. This change reflected the size of the combined armies and the scale of their operations over broad territory, but it also testified to an urgent awareness that the passage of time favoured the enemy. The extraordinary efforts devoted to improving the railway reinforcement and supply of the Tsar's armies was beginning to tilt the numerical balance in Manchuria in Russia's favour; by late August Kuropatkin had concentrated 135,000 infantry and 12,000 cavalry to meet Oyama's 115,000 infantry and 4,000 cavalry. Upon his departure Oyama promised to take charge of the fighting in Manchuria on the understanding that the oligarchs would know when to stop the war.[85]

The Battle of Liaoyang only postponed that day. In some respects the first great engagement of the twentieth century with masses of men moving over wide territory against weapons of unprecedented lethality, it began on August 26 when Oku's Second Army struck against the outer belt of well-prepared defenses on Kuropatkin's western flank while Nodzu's Fourth Army hit the Russian center. The main effort, a gigantic sweep by Kuroki on the Russian eastern flank was generally successful, but the orderly retreat of the Russians to inner lines of prepared defenses thwarted the envelopment Oyama sought. Russian counter-attacks in the center and west meanwhile threatened the Second Army and Oyama's headquarters. Fearing encirclement from the east, Kuropatkin ordered a general retirement in the direction of Mukden on September at precisely the moment when more aggressive tactics might have turned the struggle in his favour. He had suffered 3,611 killed and 14,301 wounded yet inflicted 5,537 killed and 18,063 wounded on Oyama.[86] It would all have to be done again.

To make matters worse, Nogi's early attempts to capture Port Arthur had failed, so that the men and material expected from an easy victory there would not be available to Oyama in Manchuria. Tōgō's Combined Fleet had thwarted a breakout by the Russian squadron in a running battle in the Yellow Sea, but a lack of aggressive tactics resulted in its return to harbour rather than its destruction. The oligarchs in Tokyo were now under pressure from the expectations of imminent victory among nationalists and the general population and the reality that factories in Japan could not keep pace with the expenditure of munitions from expanded operations, even as four new field divisions and forty-eight reserve battalions had to be raised by extending the service period of second reservists. Russia could now reinforce its army in Manchuria at a rate and to a level that Japan could not match. In is true that Russia's railway lifeline was extremely vulnerable in light of its extension deep into the zone of conflict. Over 50,000 men were required to defend it between the Urals and Manchuria, while another 25,000 protected it within Manchuria. Chinese Hunhutze guerrillas made ninety attacks on the line between Mukden and Tiehling in just one month. By February 1905 the length of the Chinese Eastern Railway still in Russian hands required 31,000 men, or twenty-five men per mile, to secure it.[87] Without a convincing Japanese defeat of Kuropatkin's army, nonetheless, continued hostilities advantaged Russia.

Baron Kaneko Kentarō had been sent as special envoy to the United States shortly after the outbreak of hostilities. Based on a series of conversations with President Theodore Roosevelt in which the baron explained the extent—and more crucially the limits—of Japan's intentions, the government had by July 1904 already drafted a set of conditions for peace that assumed the fall of Port Arthur and a decisive battle at Liaoyang.[88] The Tsar's government now took measures to reverse the tide of military fortune, in the short-term with a counter-offensive at Sha-ho between Liaoyang and Mukden and in the long-term by dispatching the Russian navy's Baltic squadron to relieve Port Arthur. It is a comment on how costly the war had become that engagements such

Sha-ho and San-de-pu—in each of which defensive firepower claimed thousands of casualties—are treated as hiccups on the road to Mukden. This is because the Russian counteroffensive failed to reverse the Japanese advance toward the climactic struggle. Although the Oyama's armies were running low on supplies, Kuropatkin's were running low on morale. In appreciation of this Japan's creditors upped their ante by £12 million in November 1904 even as Port Arthur continued to hold out. Not until frustration with Nogi prompted Oyama to place his own Chief-of-Staff, Kodama Gentarō, in overall command did the effort at Port Arthur progress beyond medieval siege-craft with modern weapons. Even after the capture of 203-Metre Hill on November 30, from which the shelling of the town and its harbour could be directed, the Russian garrison of Port Arthur did not surrender until January 2, 1905, by which time it had taken 31,000 against nearly 58,000 Japanese casualties. The losses to dysentery and beri-beri brought the total closer to 91,000, with the result that Oyama was unable to match the strength Kuropatkin's force at Mukden even after the Third Army joined him from Port Arthur, and the 1st Reserve Division and the 11th Division further reinforced his numbers. He had almost 200,000 infantry, 7,350 cavalry, and 992 artillery pieces with which to overcome 275,000 infantry, 16,000 cavalry and 1,219 guns.[89]

From preliminary skirmishes on February 19 and the Russian evacuation of the town three weeks later Mukden evolved into the largest battle to date, involving nearly a half-million men along some hundred miles of contested front. At the points of most intense contact defensive firepower promptly asserted a role that foreshadowed the Somme in 1915:

> Towards midday the Japanese brought up reserves and hurled themselves against Beresnev Hill in a fresh series of assaults, but their fury was equaled by the determination of the Russians, who time and again raised themselves from their trenches in order to search the dead ground with their fire and drove the attackers down the hill. Nevertheless, the Japanese persisted in spite of the increasing fire from the defenders, the explosion of the *fougasses* and the difficulty of the *abattis*, through which they had to force their way. At last, when hope of penetrating the defence had almost been abandoned, a little group of five men made good their ascent to the summit and for a moment stood silhouetted against the skyline. Then a reinforcing section struggled up, followed by others, the men tumbling over the corpses of their comrades in the eagerness to close with the Russians and a furious bayonet struggle ensued.[90]

Common as such engagements were, it was neither the doggedness of the Japanese nor the stubbornness of the Russian infantry that determined the outcome at Mukden. The Russian command had come to understand Japanese strategy and had taken enormous efforts to counter it, but operational shortcomings and tactical errors limited their impact on the fighting. Inadequate coordination among the Russian generals and poor control of their units across the ground between the mountains to the south-east and the Hun River to the south-west left the initiative with Oyama. Kuropatkin's advantage in cavalry counted for nothing, as the Cossacks ordered to scout Japanese movements in the west were unaggressive in the execution and slow to realise the direction of the Japanese thrust. Lateral movement of Russian units, as Kuropatkin first gave and then countermanded orders, only reduced the number resisting the Japanese pressure along the front generally, so that Oyama's armies were able to break through at any number of points. Orderly retirement degenerated into flight.

Even where the Russian retreat was orderly, Nogi's troops were able to deploy along the embankment of the railway line and pour rifle and artillery fire into the Russian columns withdrawing to the north. Japanese forces entering Mukden on March 10 were able to capture some 20,000 Russian prisoners, yet failed Oyama again in the effort to encircle and annihilate Kuropatkin's remaining strength, partly because their own was approaching exhaustion. Mukden had cost the Russians about almost 90,000 casualties or a third of their numbers, but Japanese casualties ran to 75,000, a quarter of their strength. Oyama had won a great victory even as his armies approached the limits of their ability.[91]

He therefore urged his government to give its "careful consideration" to bringing the nation's foreign policy goals into "harmony" with the circumstance of its army in the field. The military leadership generally had no objection to mild terms for peace; indeed, it thought Prime Minister Katsura and the *genro* distressingly slow to approach President Roosevelt about mediation. On Roosevelt's recommendation to Baron Kaneko that Japan indicate its terms for peace, the Katsuro cabinet had drafted a decision by April 21 that included reparation for Japan's war expenses, a demand its military deemed foolish.[92] By this time Russian Baltic fleet was completing its long voyage to the theater of war, so that the Tsar adhered publicly to a continuing troop build-up in Manchuria while agreeing to secret peace negotiations.

The fortunes of war now touched upon the longevity of his regime, and the Baltic Fleet was a metaphor for its state of repair.[93] Seven and half months at sea and 18,000 nautical miles had covered the ships' hulls with moss and barnacles, its crews were ravaged by tropical diseases and exhausted by the labour and choked by the dust of coaling, its commander, Rear-Admiral Zinovi Rozhdestvenski, irritable and occasionally delusional.[94] Renamed the Second Pacific Squadron, it was not so much engaged as ambushed by Tōgō's Combined Fleet. Tōgō led his warships out of the strategic post of Chinhae Bay on the south coast of Korea to fall upon Rozhdestvenski's fleet as it was about to emerge from Tsushima Strait on May 27. Only superficially were the two battle fleets equal in capability. Although each had four modern battleships and Rozhdestvenski had older capital ships in addition, Tōgō had eight modern armoured cruisers against Rozhdestvenski's one. The Russian squadron had distinct advantage in 10 and 12-inch guns, but the Combined Fleet's secondary armament more than compensated for this by contributing to an overall greater firepower. Additionally, Rozhdestvenski's older ships, slower by virtue of design and

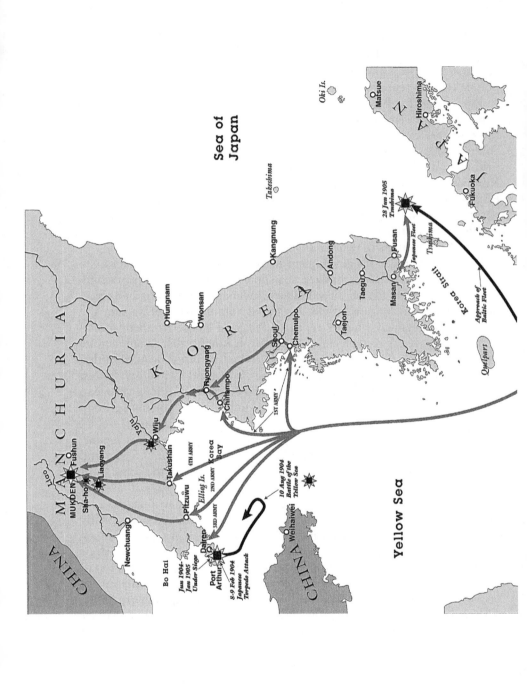

propulsion, were encumbered by tons of coal, while Tōgō 's faster ships were made faster still when he ordered any coal superfluous to the coming battle thrown overboard.

Superior speed, aided by the coordination of the ships made possible by better use of wireless communications, made Tsushima a series of Japanese manoeuvres around the Russian squadron's plodding progress to the north-east and then north-west. Most critical to the outcome, however, was Tōgō's approach to the encounter, involving a risky turn of his entire line into the fire of the Russian fleet in order to prevent its escape and to engage it at close range while running a parallel course.[95] Although Rozhdestvenski opened fire first and scored worthy hits—striking Tōgō's flagship *Mikasa* sixteen times and forcing the armoured cruiser *Asama* to fall out of the line—once the exchange began in earnest from a range of some 5,500 metres, a volume of nearly a thousand shells per minute ensued that ultimately cost the Russian navy five battleships, four cruisers, and five destroyers. When Rozhdestvenski attempted to turn his ships away to the starboard, Tōgō used his speed to pull ahead on the outside of the turn, maintain his range, and continue to pour shells into the Russian line. Japanese explosives technology also made a difference, as Tōgō's guns used the *furoshiki* shell whose thin jacket, Shimose powder, and Ijuin fuse caused it to detonate with tremendous force upon impact with any feature of an enemy ship. A member of Rozhdestvenski's staff later wrote:

> Iron ladders were crumpled up into rings, and guns were literally hurled from their mountings. Such havoc could never be caused by simple impact of a shell, still less by the splinters. It could only be caused by the force of the explosion [...] In addition to this there was the unusual high temperature and liquid flame of the explosion which seemed to spread over everything. I actually watched a steel plate catch fire from a burst. Of course the steel did not burn, but the paint on it did. Such practically incombustible material such as hammocks and rows of boxes drenched with water flared up in a moment. At times it was impossible to see anything with glasses owing to everything being so disturbed with the quivering of the heated air.[96]

As Tōgō's fleet closed to within 3,000 metres and changed to armour-piercing rounds, the Russian formation quickly lost all coherence. After only twenty minutes, Russian command and communications unraveled, the battle degenerated into a series of individual actions, and the Japanese gunners devoted themselves to the vocation of destruction. As night came, Japanese destroyers and torpedo boats attacked under darkness the remaining Russian ships limping for Vladivostok. By noon of the following day, thirty-four of the thirty-eight ships Rozhdestvenski commanded had been sunk, scuttled, captured, or interned. Tōgō had lost three torpedo boats, taken moderate damage to three capital ships, and seen eight destroyers and torpedo boats temporarily disabled—and chalked the greatest naval triumph since Trafalgar.[97]

The oligarchy therefore wasted no time seeking Roosevelt's help in converting it into a diplomatic triumph. Roosevelt was a superb mediator: informed, patient, understanding, and objective. But he could not be entirely disinterested. The recent victory of his own country over Spain and the acquisition of the Philippines had engaged his interest in the Western Pacific as never before, and the efficiency with which the little Island Empire had humiliated Russia, notes his biographer, "made him wonder what future expansion Japan was capable of."[98]

Naval strategy and the great Pacific war

That thought no doubt informed Roosevelt's mediation at Portsmouth, but possibly more important was Japan's eagerness to have a treaty. Portsmouth essentially froze the strategic situation that had resulted from Mukden, Japan winning the southern half of Sakhalin, a concession on the Kwantung Peninsula, including Port Arthur and the rights to the South Manchurian Railway. Although it was in large part the failure to extract an indemnity from Russia that ignited nationalist rage back in Japan, the Meiji oligarchy had been uncharacteristically foolish in raising this expectation in the first place. Rather, it was the Russian retention of the northern half of Sakhalin as well as control over the Kharbin-Changchun Railway in northern Manchuria that failed to reflect the balance of military performance in a war in which Japan had won every major engagement. The oligarchy blamed Roosevelt for the disappointing outcome, but the clouding of relations between Japan and the United States after 1905 had as much to do with restrictions placed on Japanese immigration by American states and municipalities as with disappointment at Portsmouth.

Still, if Russia's continuing presence in northern Manchuria diverted Japan's attention from more southerly latitudes this could only benefit the United States. When Roosevelt wondered whether the immigration issue might yet provoke a crisis with Japan and observed that "in the event of war we would be operating far from our base," the exposed position of the Philippines was on his mind—as was *Satsuma*, a dreadnought under construction at the Yokosaku naval arsenal.[99] Between 1898 and 1905 the United States and Japan had with remarkable speed conducted naval and maritime operations and fought limited wars to establish spheres of interest in regional waters and adjacent territories. Although America's emergence was in some respects more consequential, Roosevelt could appreciate better than most that Japan's was more sensational.

Internationally, Japan's victory stoked the zeal of naval enthusiasts who could only admire the fashion in which a weaker power had levered strategic advantage from its naval and maritime capacity. Governments felt compelled to grapple with technological, economic, and political challenges inherent in preparing battle fleets for future Tsushimas. Few felt more vindicated in their ambitions for national naval power than Roosevelt, who saw the tentative lessons of Manila and Santiago Bay confirmed in spectacular fashion, grasped the consequences for international affairs, and exploited them immediately in pressing on Congress the cause of battleship construction. Although the Royal Navy revolutionised battleship design in favour of all-big-gun configurations with the launch of HMS *Dreadnought* in 1906, the USS *Michigan* was in many respects as advanced, and approval of its construction in 1905 had already committed the United States to the international naval arms race.[100]

Japan's triumph testified simultaneously to an awareness of the limits of military power—particularly in the Meiji oligarchy's pursuit of optimum diplomatic conditions for initiating and terminating hostilities. The border between war and peace being more usually obscure during the diplomatic phase leading to a conflict, each conditions the other, and opportunism pervades the relationship.[101] Opportunism in the years between the Triple Intervention and the attack on Port Arthur in 1904 gave Japan its first triumph in the coming conflict in the Anglo-Japanese treaty of 1902. Julian Corbett, among the most influential naval strategists of the time, observed that possibly only in England was there an appreciation of what an island nation might achieve against a stronger continental adversary. Whereas England's military performance on the European continent traditionally depended on an orchestration of coalition warfare, for Japan the treaty of 1902 had the effect of eliminating the complicating factor of alliances and isolating the struggle to a contest of the fighting ability of the two belligerents.[102] The Meiji government thereafter made the conflict a popular war. By contrast, the "heart of Russia was never stirred," the specter of revolution haunting the Tsarist state and influencing its army's operations for the duration.[103]

Corbett was nonetheless critical of Japan's abandonment of the principles of limited war, a flaw he attributed to the influence of German doctrine over the Japanese army and the pursuit of decisive battle to culminate in a Jena or a Sedan.[104] By most measures the Japan faced by Russia in 1904 was a remarkable example of a successful state modernisation, whose emergence was of itself of global significance. Victory provided proof of the vitality of the nation and the prescience of its state by defeating a European power in Asia where Europeans had hitherto seemed invincible, the battlefield.[105] Yet at Liaoyang, Mukden, and Port Arthur the Imperial Army had demonstrated a willingness to accept high casualties in the attempt to secure a clear decision. Port Arthur had claimed 59,000 officers and men killed, wounded, or missing, along with another 34,000 hospitalised with illness. Having sacrificed two sons to the war with Russia, Nogi and his wife later committed ritual suicide partly as atonement for the thousands sacrificed at his command.

Rage from the Japanese public at the terms of the Portsmouth peace initially turned inward against the Meiji government, but the denial of a manifest destiny for which the nation had paid in blood and treasure would later be directed against the United States. Major General Tanaka Giichi, who in 1907 helped to develop a new Imperial National Defence Policy, cited the ¥2 billion and the blood of 230,000 men in making the case for what amounted to moral as well as an economic claim to Manchuria and ridiculed as shameless countrymen who would abandon the claim.[106] The Imperial Navy's comparative standing was hugely improved by the war, but naval planners such as Akiyama drew lessons from Tsushima concerning fleet concentration and decisive engagement that later influenced designs for war in the Central Pacific with baleful consequences. In short, the Japanese army and navy cultivated myths about Russo-Japanese war that subsequently degenerated into strategic pathologies.[107] The oligarchy that had pondered soberly the prospects and perils of war with Russia and arrived at a realistic diplomatic and military strategy was a product of the Meiji state's transition to modernity; the *genrō* were themselves products of a feudal society determined to overcome feudal obstructions to the creation of a strong state and modern economy. Neither they nor their sobriety were replicated in succeeding generations for whom aggressive Japanese nationalism was a mass movement rather a state project.[108]

Satsuma symbolised the determination of the Meiji state to overcome the technical problems and fiscal limitations to the construction of a formidable instrument of war. In the process the Imperial Navy had become a lobby capable of persuading politicians and civilians to assume the enormous fiscal burden of sustained commitment. The great victory at Tsushima achieved a qualitative leap in the navy's political fortunes when in October 1905 Tōgō's return occasioned a massive fleet review attended by some 150,000 spectators. As the Meiji regime gave way to Taishō parliamentary democracy, the navy's public relations and lobbying effort on behalf of continued expansion adapted to the changes in the budgetary process. New prestige and lobbying skill inevitably led to serious rivalry with the Imperial Army. *Satsuma* was nonetheless a pre-dreadnought design, and the greater portion the materials in its manufacture were from foreign suppliers. It was not until 1909 that the Kure Navy Yard laid down Japan's first dreadnought, *Settsu*, and Japan's greatest warship of the pre–World War I era, the 27,000-ton *Kongo*, was built by the British firm Vickers.[109]

By contrast, the United States had all the resources it needed to build a first-class battle fleet. Steel came from the Bethlehem and Carnegie works in Pennsylvania; ordnance from Pennsylvania but also from the Gatling Gun Company and the Colt factory in Hartford (Connecticut). Projectiles were made by Crucible Steel in Newark (New Jersey) and Miami Cycle and Manufacturing Company in Middletown (Ohio); while warships took shape not only at Cramp and Sons in Philadelphia (Pennsylvania) and Newport News (Virginia) but also at Moran Brothers in Seattle (Washington), the Union Iron Works of San Francisco (California), and the Columbia Iron Works of Baltimore (Maryland). Bethlehem Steel Corporation, established in 1904, quickly became a major supplier of the national arsenal. Still, the national commitment to the navy was politically circumstantial, dependent on the Roosevelt administration's expansive foreign policy, allies in Congress to vote appropriations for warship construction, and the links between the navy and industry to build a durable lobby able to ride out the boom and bust of political fad.[110] There was no American equivalent of *kokutai*, the notion of a "national essence" with an almost mystical claim on obedience to the state's cause. One aspect of the Progressive era whose enthusiasms Roosevelt rode so well was imperialist, but another was anti-imperialist, even pacifist, and subscribed to the idea that a colonial regime in the Philippines was as un-American as monarchy.

The war with Spain had temporarily impressed Congress with the need for naval power. The launch of *Dreadnought* prompted Roosevelt to caution the House Naval Committee that the United States must build comparable warships or relinquish its position in both oceans. When Congress responded with authorisation for only one new capital ship, Roosevelt countered with a demand for no fewer than four and set off a bitter legislative battle.[111] When the Japanese immigration issue turned into a diplomatic crisis in the summer of 1907, his discussions concerning the disposition of American warships with Secretary of the Navy Victor Metcalf, Captain Richard Wainright of the General Board, and Colonel W.W. Wotherspoon, acting president of the Army War College, were leaked to the *New York Herald* and began the public debate about possibly radical changes to naval policy that culminated in the world cruise of the sixteen battleships later referred to as the Great White Fleet.[112] The navy had been considering such an exercise for two years, but Roosevelt saw an opportunity to combine assertive diplomacy, preventive strategy, and technical training with a pageant of power to fire the public imagination. Fleet reviews in Britain and Germany were now regular events involving ever more spectacular displays of imperial swagger, but the tentative nature of American navalism called for something novel.[113] The Great White Fleet's fourteen-month and 45,000-mile world tour became a political and diplomatic triumph. It produced improvements in engineering reliability and fuel conservation and demonstrated that the U.S. Navy's battle fleet could steam to the Western Pacific and arrive in fit condition to engage an enemy formation. Naval planners reduced their estimates of the time required to mount operations against Japan from 120 to 90 days and decided that the main American naval base in the Pacific should be located at Pearl Harbor.[114] What is more, the reception accorded the U.S. Navy in Yokohama was more than polite, it was determinedly warm, as domestic unrest over the tax burden of military and naval expansion forced the Japanese government of Saionji Kimmochi onto a course of fiscal retrenchment and diplomatic rapprochement. In the Root-Takahira Agreement of 1908 the United States acknowledged Japan's vital interest in Korea in exchange for an affirmation that Japan had no designs on the Philippines.

Relentless pressure on Congress enabled Roosevelt to transform the big stick from a metaphor to a gray steel instrument of American power. During his presidency the United States launched fourteen battleships; in the thirty-seven months between April 2, 1902, and May 1, 1905, American shipyards laid down no fewer than twelve ships and achieved an acceleration of the average building time of one year per ship.[115] The political constituency for naval appropriations prospered as the industrial base of naval construction broadened. At the same time, Roosevelt sought to capitalise on support for a policy of strength from Pacific-coast states to make the case for the Pearl Harbor base, as "the key to the Pacific," not in anticipation of any immediate crisis with Japan but rather "with a view to the emergencies that there is a reasonable chance may arise within the next decade or two."[116] To this he added an appeal to Congress for additional defense appropriations as would permit a battle fleet to be retained in the Pacific in defence of the Pearl Harbor facility. The new navy required new facilities to see to its passage and provision, but such facilities would themselves be indefensible unless the fleet itself was increased in size. Roosevelt's aggressive leadership on the issue began to transform the very nature of American politics itself, raising the presidency above the legislative branch and cultivating a popular appetite for a strong executive that anticipated the war administrations of Woodrow Wilson and Franklin Roosevelt.[117]

The operations of 1898–1902 were an important phase in the modernisation of the U.S. Army as well, increasing its size to 125,000 regulars and volunteers and changing its composition by weeding out older officers unequal to the rigors of war while providing battalion or regimental command to younger officers who welcomed them. The Colonial Army of the Philippines survived until World War II and was an imperial force in virtually the same way as was the British army in India, claiming an affection among those posted there bordering on the romantic. Yet as early as 1906 many American strategists doubted the defensibility of the archipelago, so that the navy's efforts between 1908 and 1912 to promote a major fleet base there failed. Indeed, had Japan found reason to strike at the Philippines at the time, the defeats sustained by the United States would have ranged between grave and disastrous.[118] America's war in Cuba had been a modest affair compared to Japan's invasion of Korea and Manchuria, its maritime operations amateurish, and its way of war in the new century was only half-way to invention. In the 1930s, political crisis in Japan produced both an army preoccupied with expansion on the Asian continent and a navy determined to eject all foreign presences from the waters of the Western Pacific. The wars conducted in 1898 and 1904–1905 had made the United States and Japan safer from threats of other great powers yet increased their exposure to each other. Both would require vastly more powerful navies, capable of placing and sustaining large numbers of troops on foreign shores over oceanic distances on a scale that war had never witnessed.[119]

Notes

1 Julian S. Corbett, *Principles of Maritime Strategy* (London: Longmans, Green, 1911) p. 13.
2 The definition comes from the glossary of John Keegan, *The Price of Admiralty*, London: Hutchinson, 1988; London: Pimlico, 1993).
3 Philip A. Crowl, "Alfred Thayer Mahan: The Naval Historian," in *Makers of Modern Strategy from Machiavelli to the Nuclear Age*, ed. Peter Paret (Princeton, NJ: Princeton University Press, 1986), pp. 444–77.
4 Keegan, *Price of Admiralty*, p. 101; William L. Langer, *The Diplomacy of Imperialism, 1890–1902* (New York: Knopf, 1968), pp. 415–44; Mark Russell Shulman, *Navalism and the Emergence of American Sea Power, 1882–1893* (Annapolis, MD: Naval Institute Press, 1995); Lisle A. Rose, *Power at Sea: The Age of Navalism, 1890–1918* (Columbia: University of Missouri Press, 2007); Paul M. Kennedy, *The Rise of Anglo-German Antagonism, 1860–1914* (London: Allen & Unwin, 1980).
5 Jan Rüger, *The Great Naval Game: Britain and Germany in the Age of Empire* (New York: Cambridge University Press, 2007) pp. 201–17.
6 Dirk Bönker, "Zwischen Bürgerkrieg und Navalismus: Marinepolitik und Handelsimperialismus in den USA 1865 bis 1890," in *Das Militär und der Aufbruch in die Moderne,* ed. Michael Epkenhans and Gerhard P. Groß (Munich: R. Oldenbourg Verlag, 2003), pp. 93–115.
7 Lisle Rose, *Power at Sea,* p. 3.
8 George Baer, *One Hundred Years of Sea Power: The U.S. Navy, 1890–1990* (Stanford, CA: Stanford University Press, 1993), pp. 9–48.
9 Walter LaFeber, *The New Empire: An Interpretation of American Expansion, 1860–1898. 1963* (Ithaca, NY: Cornell University Press, 1987); Frederick Merk, *The Monroe Doctrine and American Expansionism* (New York: Knopf, 1966); Dexter Perkins. *A History of the Monroe Doctrine* (Boston: Little, Brown, 1963).
10 Walter A. McDougall, *Promised Land, Crusader State: The American Encounter with the World since 1776* (Boston: Houghton Mifflin, 1997), pp. 110–11; Frank Freidel, *The Splendid Little War* (New York: Dell, 1958), pp. 10–11; Sean Dennis Cashman, *America in the Age of the Titans: The Progressive Era and World War I* (New York: New York University Press, 1988), p. 7; Walter Mills, *The Martial Spirit: A Study of Our War with Spain* (Boston: Houghton Mifflin, 1931), pp. 42–43.
11 Quoted in Mills, *The Martial Spirit*, pp. 110–11; H.W. Brands, *TR: The Last Romantic* (New York: Basic Books, 1997), pp. 321–29.
12 Warren Zimmerman, *First Great Triumph: How Five Americans Made Their Country a World Power* (New York: Farrar, Straus and Giroux, 2002), pp. 35–34.
13 A.T. Mahan, *The Influence of Sea Power upon History* (New York: Hill and Wang, 1957 [1890]), p. 41; Charles J. Esdaile, *Spain in the Liberal Age: From Constitution to Civil War, 1808–1939* (Oxford: Blackwell, 2000), pp. 186–205.
14 Brands, *TR*, p. 321.
15 J.D. Richardson, ed., "McKinley's War Message," in *A Compilation of the Messages and Papers of the Presidents, 1789–1897*, Vol. 10, pp. 139–50. Available at http://onlinebooks.library.upenn.edu/webbin/gutbook/lookup?num=13893.
16 Quoted in Philip C. Jessup, *Elihu Root*, 2 vols. (New York: Dodd, 1938), Vol. 1, p. 197.
17 G.J.A. O'Toole, *The Spanish War: An American Epic* (New York:. Norton, 1984), p. 177.
18 Ivan Musicant, *Empire by Default: The Spanish-American War and the Dawn of the American Century* (New York: Henry Holt, 1998); James M. McCaffrey,

Inside the Spanish-American War: A History Based on First-Person Accounts (Jefferson, NC: McFarland, 2009), pp. 8–9; Brands, *TR*, p. 326.

19 Musicant, *Empire by Default*, pp. 210–21.

20 McCaffrey, *Inside the Spanish-American War*, p. 16.

21 Ibid., p. 18; Musicant, *Empire by Default*, pp. 229–30.

22 Brian McCallister Linn, "The U.S. Military and Expeditionary Warfare," in *Battles Near and Far: A Century of Overseas Deployment*, ed. Peter Dennis and Jeffrey Grey (Canberra, Australia: Army History Unit, Department of Defence, 2005), pp. 80–81.

23 Martin van Creveld, *The Rise and Decline of the State* (New York: Cambridge University Press, 1999), pp. 288–89; James MacGregor Burns, *The Workshop of Democracy* (New York: Alfred A. Knopf, 1985), pp. 234–49.

24 Joseph Smith, *The Spanish-American War: Conflict in the Caribbean and the Pacific* (New York: Longman, 1994), pp. 98–99.

25 Ibid., pp. 99–100.

26 Ibid., p. 105.

27 Ibid., pp. 106–17.

28 Linn, "U.S. Military and Expeditionary Warfare," pp. 81–82; Jack Shulimson, "Marines and the Spanish-American War," in *Crucible of Empire: The Spanish-American War and Its Aftermath*, ed. James C. Bradford, pp. 141–47 (Annapolis, MD: Naval Institute Press, 1993).

29 David F. Trask, *The War with Spain in 1898* (New York: Macmillan, 1981), pp. 203–8; Smith, *Spanish-American War*, pp. 130–31.

30 Smith, *Spanish-American War*, p. 214.

31 Gerald F. Linderman, *The Mirror of War: American Society and the Spanish-American War* (Ann Arbor: University of Michigan Press, 1974), p. 104.

32 McCaffrey, *Inside the Spanish-American War*, pp. 94–95; Trask, *War with Spain*, pp. 236–37.

33 Quoted in Joseph Wheeler, *The Santiago Campaign 1898* (Boston: Lamson, Wolffe, 1898), p. 72.

34 Ibid., pp. 103–5. Miley's own account, remarkably self-effacing, was published in 1899. See John D. Miley, *In Cuba with Shafter* (New York: Scribner, 1899), pp. 101–28.

35 Trask, *War with Spain*, p. 242.

36 Ibid., p. 244; O'Toole, *Spanish War*, p. 319.

37 Trask, *War with Spain*, pp. 234–35, 244–46; Smith, *Spanish-American War*, p. 141.

38 Quoted in H.W. Brands, ed., *The Selected Letters of Theodore Roosevelt* (New York: Cooper Square Press, 2001) p. 193.

39 Trask, *War with Spain*, p. 259; Smith, *Spanish-American War*, pp. 145–47.

40 David F. Trask, "The Battle of Santiago," in *Great American Naval Battles*, ed. Jack Sweetman (Annapolis, MD: Naval Institute Press, 1998), pp. 202–3.

41 Ibid., pp. 209–14.

42 Brian McCallister Linn, *The Philippine War, 1899–1902* (Lawrence: University of Kansas Press, 2000), pp. 3–29.

43 Ibid., pp. 30–31; Max Boot, *The Savage Wars of Peace: Small Wars and the Rise of American Power* (New York: Perseus Books, 2002), pp. 99–128.

44 Linn, *The Philippine War*, pp. 42–53; John M. Gates, "Philippine Guerrillas, American Anti-Imperialists, and the Election of 1900," *Pacific Historical Review* 46, no. 1, 1977, pp. 51–64.

45 Linn, *The Philippine War*, p. 213.

46 Linn, *The Philippine War*, p. 325; Glenn Anthony May, *Battle for Batangas: A Philippine Province at War* (New Haven, CT: Yale University Press, 1991).

47 Gates, "Philippine Guerrillas," pp. 61–64; Stuart Creighton Miller, *"Benevolent Assimilation": The American Conquest of the Philippines, 1899–1903*. (New Haven, CT: Yale University Press, 1982), p. 3; H.W. Brands, *Bound to Empire: The United States and the Philippines* (New York: Oxford University Press, 1992), p. 61; William E. Leuchtenburg, "Progressivism and Imperialism: The Progressive Movement and American Foreign Policy," *Mississippi Valley Historical Review* 39, No. 3, 1952, pp. 483–504.

48 Quoted in William Theodore de Bary, Carol Gluck, and Arthur E. Tiedemann, eds., *Sources of Japanese Tradition*. 2 vols. (New York: Columbia University Press, 2005), Vol. 2, p. 645–47.

49 W.G. Beasley, *The Meiji Restoration* (Stanford, CA: Stanford University Press, 1972); Shumpei Okamoto, *The Japanese Oligarchy and the Russo-Japanese War* (New York: Columbia University Press, 1970); van Creveld, *Rise and Decline of the State*, p. 323.

50 J. Charles Schenking, *Making Waves: Politics, Propaganda, and the Emergence of the Imperial Japanese Navy, 1868–1922* (Stanford, CA: Stanford University Press, 2005) pp. 10–12.

51 Ibid., pp. 15–18.

52 Ibid., pp. 26–77.

53 Jonathan A. Grant, *Rulers, Guns, and Money: The Global Arms Trade in the Age of Imperialism* (Cambridge, MA: Harvard University Press, 2007), pp. 134–44.

54 S.C.M. Paine, *The Sino-Japanese War of 1894–1895: Perceptions, Power, and Primacy* (Cambridge, UK: Cambridge University Press, 2003).

55 Schencking, *Making Waves*, p. 105.

56 William T. Rowe, *China's Last Empire: The Great Qing* (Cambridge, MA: Belknap Press, 2009), pp. 233–46.

57 Richard Connaughton, *Rising Sun and Tumbling Bear: Russia's War with Japan* (London: Cassell, 2003), pp. 11–36; Immanuel C.Y. Hsü, *The Rise of Modern China*. (New York: Oxford University Press, 2000), pp. 398–404; Ian H. Nish, *The Anglo-Japanese Alliance: The Diplomacy of Two Island Empires, 1894–1907* (London: Athlone Press, 1966).

58 Okamoto, *Japanese Oligarchy*, pp. 11–40, 49–50.

59 Ibid., pp. 57–102.

60 Lisle Rose, *Power at Sea*, pp. 97–98.

61 David C. Evans and Mark R. Peattie, *Kaigun: Strategy, Tactics, and Technology in the Imperial Japanese Navy, 1887–1941*. (Annapolis, MD: Naval Institute Press, 1997), pp. 11–13, 67–74; H.P. Willmott, *The Last Century of Sea Power*. 2 vols. (Bloomington: University of Indiana Press, 2009), Vol. 1, p. 125.

62 Willmott, *Last Century of Sea Power*, Vol 1, p. 76.

63 The Combined Fleet (the Japanese First and Second Fleets) consisted of six battleships, ten cruisers, forty destroyers, and forty smaller vessels.

64 Willmott, *Last Century of Sea Power*, Vol 1, p. 81.

65 Ibid. pp. 79–81.

66 *Official History (Naval and Military) of the Russo-Japanese War*, 3 Vols. (London: Historical Section of the Committee of Imperial Defence, 1910) Vol. 1, p. 45.

67 Ibid., pp. 71–72.

68 Dietrich Geyer, *Russian Imperialism: The Interaction of Domestic and Foreign Policy, 1860–1914* (New York: Berg, 1987); Theodore von Laue, *Sergei Witte and the Industrialization of Russia* (New York: Columbia University Press, 1963); Donald Rayfield, *The Dream of Lhasa: The Life of Nikolay Przhevalsky (1839–88) Explorer of Central Asia* (Athens: Ohio University Press, 1976).

69 David Schimmelpenninck van der Oye. *Toward the Rising Sun: Russian Ideologies of Empire and the Path to War with Japan* (DeKalb: Northern Illinois University Press, 2001), pp. 196–211.

70 Dominic Lieven, *Nicholas II. Emperor of all the Russians* (London: John Murray, 1993), pp. 6–7.

71 Dietrich Beyrau, *Militär und Gesellschaft im vorrevolutionären Russland* (Cologne, Germany: Böhlau Verlag, 1984), pp. 436–37.

72 Denis A. Warner and Peggy Warner, *The Tide at Sunrise: A History of the Russo-Japanese War, 1904–1905* (New York: Charterhouse, 1974), pp. 56–80. Witte quoted in Raymond A. Esthus, "Nicholas II and the Russo-Japanese War," *Russian Review* 40, No. 4 (1981), pp. 396–97.

73 Andrew M. Verner, *The Crisis of Russian Autocracy: Nicholas II and the 1905 Revolution* (Princeton, NJ: Princeton University Press, 1990), pp. 70–103.

74 Ibid., p. 49.

75 Ibid., p. 46.

76 A.V. Ignat'ev, "The Foreign Policy of Russia in the Far East at the Turn of the Nineteenth and Twentieth Centuries," in *Imperial Russian Foreign Policy,* ed. Hugh Ragsdale (New York: Cambridge University Press, 1930, pp. 247–67.

77 Beyrau, *Militär und Gesellschaft*, p. 447.

78 Geyer, *Russian Imperialism*, pp. 212–13.

79 Bruce W. Menning, "Miscalculating One's Enemies: Russian Military Intelligence before the Russo-Japanese War," *War in History* 13, No. 2 (2006), pp. 141–70.

80 Ibid., "Miscalculating One's Enemies," pp. 163–64; Warner and Warner, *Tide at Sunrise*, p. 256; Connaughton, *Rising Sun and Tumbling Bear*, p. 67.

81 J.N. Westwood, *Russia Against Japan: A New Look at the Russo-Japanese War* (Albany: State University of New York Press, 1986), pp. 122–23; Connaugton, pp. 29–30; Beyrau, *Militär und Gesellschaft*, p. 442.

82 D. Warner and P. Warner, *Tide at Sunrise*, pp. 253–54.

83 Ibid., pp. 256–69; Connaughton, *Rising Sun and Tumbling Bear*, pp. 74–87. Morinosuke Kajima, *The Diplomacy of Japan, 1894–1922.* 2 vols. (Tokyo: Kajima Institute of International Peace, 1976), Vol. 2, p. 124.

84 *Official History*, pp. 137–38; Evans and Peattie, *Kaigun: Strategy, Tactics, and Technology*, p. 101.

85 Okamoto, *Japanese Oligarchy*, pp. 101–2.

86 D.Warner and P. Warner, *Tide at Sunrise*, pp. 353–573; David T. Zabecki, "Liao-Yang: Dawn of Modern Warfare," *Military History* 16, No. 5 (December 1999), pp. 54–61.

87 Evans and Peattie, *Kaigun: Strategy, Tactics, and Technology*, pp. 102–7; Connaugton, p. 115; *Official History*, Vol. 3, p. 814.

88 Kajima, Vol. 2, pp. 201–28; Okamoto, *Japanese Oligarchy*, pp. 105–17.

89 D. Warner and P. Warner, *Tide at Sunrise*, pp. 427–66.

90 *Official History*, pp. 277–79. A *fougasse* is an improvised morter; an *abattis* is a field obstacle consisting of the branches of trees laid in a row, with the sharpened tops directed toward the enemy.

91 D. Warner and P. Warner, *Tide at Sunrise*, pp. 473–80.

92 Okamoto, *Japanese Oligarchy*, pp. 109–19; Kajima, pp. 228–34.

93 Verner, *Crisis of Russian Autocracy*, p. 192.

94 D. Warner and P. Warner, *Tide at Sunrise*, pp. 481–93.

95 Evans and Peattie, *Kaigun: Strategy, Tactics, and Technology*, pp. 126–27.

96 Quoted in Julian S. Corbett, *Maritime Operations in the Russo-Japanese, 1904–1905.* 2 vols. (Annapolis, MD: Naval Institute Press, 1994), Vol. 2, p. 249; Evans and Peattie, *Kaigun: Strategy, Tactics, and Technology*, p. 63.

97 Willmott, Vol. 1, pp. 115–19; Evans and Peattie, *Kaigun: Strategy, Tactics, and Technology,* pp. 116–24. See also H.W. Wilson, *Battleships in Action.* 2 vols. (Toronto, ON: Ryerson Press, 1926), Vol. 1, pp. 240–65.
98 Edmund Morris, *Theodore Rex* (New York: Random House, 2001), p. 397.
99 Ibid., p. 485.
100 Ronald H. Spector, *At War at Sea: Sailors and Naval Combat in the Twentieth Century* (New York: Penguin, 2001), pp. 1–21; Lisle Rose, *Power at Sea,* pp. 124–27; Carl Cavanagh Hodge, "A Whiff of Cordite: Theodore Roosevelt and the Transoceanic Naval Arms Race, 1897–1909," *Diplomacy & Statecraft* 19, no. 4, pp. 712–731; Matthew M. Oyos, "Theodore Roosevelt and the Implements of War," *Journal of Military History* 60 (1996), pp. 631–55.
101 Geoffrey Blainey, *The Causes of War* (New York: Free Press, 1988), p. 173.
102 Corbett, *Principles of Maritime Strategy,* p. 74.
103 Corbett, *Maritime Operations,* Vol. 2, p. 397.
104 Corbett, *Principles of Maritime Strategy,* pp. 80–81.
105 van Creveld, *Rise and Decline of the State,* p. 323.
106 Yoshihisa Tak Matsusaka, *The Making of Japanese Manchuria, 1904–1932* (Cambridge, MA: Harvard University Press, 2001), pp. 180–82.
107 Willmott, Vol. 1, pp. 124–25.
108 Beasley, *Meiji Restoration,* pp. 405–24; Okamoto, *Japanese Oligarchy,* pp. 230–32.
109 Schencking, *Making Waves,* pp. 110–12, 223–28; Evans and Peattie, *Kaigun: Strategy, Tactics, and Technology,* pp. 159–61.
110 Benjamin Franklin Cooling, *Gray Steel and Blue Water Navy: The Formative Years of America's Military-Industrial Complex, 1881–1917* (Hamden, CT: Archon Books, 1979), p. 168; Kenneth Warren, *Bethlehem Steel: Builder and Arsenal of America* (Pittsburgh, PA: University of Pittsburgh Press, 2008), pp. 84–101.
111 Harold Sprout and Margaret Sprout, *The Rise of American Naval Power, 1776–1918* (Princeton, NJ: Princeton University Press, 1939), p. 264.
112 James R. Reckner, *Teddy Roosevelt's Great White Fleet* (Annapolis, MD: Naval Institute Press, 1988), pp. 10–11.
113 Morris, *Theodore Rex,* p. 494.
114 Reckner, *Teddy Roosevelt's Great White Fleet,* p. 161.
115 Willmott, Vol. 1, p. 56.
116 Charles E. Neu, *An Uncertain Friendship: Theodore Roosevelt and Japan, 1906–1909* (Cambridge, MA: Harvard University Press, 1967), pp. 224–25.
117 Lewis L. Gould, *The Presidency of Theodore Roosevelt* (Lawrence: University of Kansas Press, 1991), pp. 271–301.
118 Brian McCallister Linn, *Guardians of Empire: The U.S. Army in the Pacific, 1902–1940* (Chapel Hill: University of North Carolina Press, 1997); William Reynolds Braisted, *The United States Navy in the Pacific, 1897–1909* (Austin: University of Texas Press, 1958), p. 243; Edward S. Miller, *War Plan Orange: The U.S. Strategy to Defeat Japan in the Pacific, 1897–1945* (Annapolis, MD: Naval Institute Press, 1991).
119 Corbett, *Principles of Maritime Strategy,* p. 101; Russell F. Weigley, *The American Way of War: A History of United States Military Strategy and Policy* (Bloomington: Indiana University Press, 1973) p. 189.

5 Militarism and the modern state, 1890–1914

The wars discussed in Chapters 3 and 4, from the American Civil War to the Russo-Japanese War, represent the bookends of change wrought by major military conflict to the international system between the 1860s and 1914. The American Civil War and the Franco-Prussian War brought forth two reconstituted and powerful nation-states, each destined to become major antagonists of the global conflicts of the twentieth century. Whereas the unification of Germany under Prussia at direct cost to France was felt immediately as a fundamental shift in the balance of power, geographic distance and the domestic preoccupations of the Gilded Age kept the United States from an assertive role in international affairs for a quarter of a century after 1865.[1]

More important than the delay in the realisation of American military power, however, was the specific form of its initial iteration and its contribution to competition among the established and emerging powers after 1890. The post–Civil War U.S. Army enjoyed none of the prestige accorded the German military after 1871; its numbers were reduced, its commands decentralised, its mission redirected toward the pacification of the tribes of the Great Plains, until the army "seemed never to have left the simpler past."[2] By contrast, the naval profession was comparatively free of the social stigma inflicted on standing armies in the United States since the Revolution. It had no role in constabulary duty on the frontier, suffered no opprobrium for occupation in the South, and bore no tarnish from deployment in labour disputes. Although it was no more immune from American cultural suspicion of the uniformed services, in the expansive and optimistic commercial atmosphere of the second half of the century the U.S. Navy articulated a mission for itself in the furthering and protection of overseas trade that by 1898 made it the primary agent of American power abroad with an embryonic military-industrial political economy to support it. In the process, American naval thought exerted a profound influence on the strategic reasoning of other powers that accelerated the pace and raised the stakes of great power competition with the onset of the New Imperialism.[3]

To say that Meiji Japan's debut as a top tier military power in 1904–1905 was an international sensation is an understatement. Exerted not against a decrepit Spanish Empire in the Americas but at cost to a Tsarist Russia engaged in domestic reform and territorial expansion in Central Asia and the Far East, it underscored how quickly a modernising military-industrial state with a coherent strategy could overturn the regional balance of power in its favour. Coming upon the heels of America's acquisition of the Philippines it could only heighten concerns in Washington about further Japanese expansion beyond the new colony in Manchuria. Involving not only successful maritime operations on Chinese and Korean coasts but also the most decisive battle fleet engagement since Trafalgar, Japan's emergence moved both Washington and London to make arrangements for their own positions in the Western Pacific, in part through diplomacy and appeasement, in part through contingency planning and outright alliance at a time when technological progress gave new heat to the naval aspect of intensified competition among the imperial powers.[4] The alpha navalist of the United States himself, President Theodore Roosevelt, deemed the British Empire the "great guaranty of the peace of the world," and Japan's victory at Tsushima yielded an astonishing dividend to Britain in return for a modest diplomatic investment. In a few short years Britain competed successfully in the naval arms race but also consolidated its position strategically through arrangements with France and Russia. "That left the Germans," notes John Darwin's history of the British Empire,[5] and it is to Germany's uniquely problematic role in the New Imperialism of the late nineteenth century that comparative discussion of war and the modern state seventy-five years following Napoleon's defeat inevitably turns.

The new imperialism

A classic study of modern Great Power competition within and beyond Europe dates the Age of Empire to 1875.[6] Others note accelerating activity in the last decade of the century.[7] A rapid increase in the global population and technological innovations such as railways and telegraphic communications simultaneously made human society demographically larger and geographically smaller. A new commercially viable cross-fertilisation of cultures was made possible by this process. In 1875 Arthur Lazenby Liberty opened a shop at 218A Regent Street in London, which became the home of Art Nouveau in England. Liberty imported silks from the East and later porcelain, ceramics, fans, screens, wallpapers, swords, mats, lacquer ware, lanterns, bronzes, and wall masks from Japan. When Japan banned the wearing of swords in 1876, many Japanese metalworkers diversified into cutlery and kitchenware featuring motifs altogether novel and extraordinarily appealing to English customers.[8] Rarely was strategic vision the author of overseas expansion. More usually, new colonial possessions were acquired on an ad hoc basis according to opportunity or commercial ambition, national strategy struggling to catch up to the expansion and the new advantages or vulnerabilities it implied. Private colonial initiatives—from Cecil Rhodes' diamond mining in South Africa to the serial filibuster expeditions of William

Walker in Central America and King Leopold's Congo—were common.[9] We have already seen how British and French imperialism groped forward in south-central Asia and northern Africa in the 1830s, so it is reasonable to think of the New Imperialism as partly a renovation of earlier efforts. Britain's position on the Cape of Good Hope was a windfall of the Napoleonic Wars, and the British settler bridgehead in South Africa was initially feeble. But any navy positioned on the African cape had both a base of operations for Atlantic and Indian Oceans and a base of supply for operations inland. Decades later Rhodes's commercial ambition for the South Africa Company drove the Cape-to-Cairo vision for Britain's position in South Africa as much as any single factor, just as Robert Goldie's did for the Royal Niger Company in West Africa. In South Africa resistance to northern expansion led to wars with African peoples that had little international impact and wars with the Boer trekker republics that led to a diplomatic crisis with Germany and a wave of anti-war protest in Britain.[10] For Belgium, France, Germany, and Italy, the 1880s inaugurated an era of frantic colonial acquisition. By 1914 the total land area of all European colonies had doubled. Although Asian possessions were usually the most valuable, European expansion was far and away at its most spectacular in Africa.[11]

Next to Britain, France was the most significant Great Power presence in Africa. A crisis of Anglo-French competition at Fashoda on the Nile in 1898, like the Anglo-German confrontation over the Boer War, testified to the potential for conflict among the European powers from frictions distant from Europe and European public consciousness. But few countries were more insecure for their position in Europe and their status internationally than was France following its defeat by Prussia in 1871. Far from blunting French nationalism, the humiliation of that year quickened the zeal of governments of the left and right of the Third Republic to compensate French power in the international arena for its loss of territory and prestige in Europe. Léon Gambetta, the champion of republicanism and popular resistance in 1871, became in equal part a nationalist and revanchist who viewed colonialism as France's passport to durable greatness. His instincts on Africa became competitive to the point of recklessness. In the 1880s his insistence that France should have absolute equality with the British in Egypt precipitated a small crisis with Gladstone's government in London. Gambetta's nationalism was eclipsed only by that of Jules Ferry, another republican who routinely brought a Darwinian spirit into parliamentary debate:

> Gentlemen, in Europe as it is today, in this competition of the many rivals we see rising up around us, some by military or naval improvements, others by the prodigious development of incessant population growth; in a Europe, or rather in a universe such as this, a policy of withdrawal or abstention is simply the high road to decadence! Nations in our time are great only through activity; it is not by "peaceful radiant light of their institutions" that they are great in these times. [...]Spreading light

without acting, without taking part in the affairs of the world, staying clear of all European alliances and viewing all expansion into Africa or the Orient as a trap, a misadventure—for a great nation to live this way is, believe me, to abdicate and, in less time than you may think, to sink from the first rank to the third and fourth.[12]

The comparatively free trade policies of the Second Empire were therefore discarded in favour of traditional mercantilism. Because France was a late starter in industrialisation, a new colonial empire in which French goods would have preferential right of entry would, so went the argument, benefit national industries and the welfare of the working classes alike.[13] Even politicians unexcited by the prospect of governing distant peoples could appreciate the importance of overseas resources to a mature industrial society and an increasingly democratic political system.

British commitment to free-trade principles remained officially intact, but the worry that other great powers might have fewer scruples about protectionism was ever present. As commercial expansion was slowed by falling export prices and lower rates of growth after 1875, the French thrust from Senegal into the African interior could only deepen anxiety. By the 1890s a "firm line" on British policy in West Africa meant determined penetration from the Gold Coast into the interior to divert the French presence toward the lighter soils of the desert—along with brutal elimination of indigenous resistance in the process. Steam technology and shallow draft vessels facilitated upstream navigation of African rivers; early versions of machine-gun technology were deployed against the Ashanti in West Africa and the Zulu in South Africa.[14]

Yet superior weapons were no guarantee of success in Africa any more than they had been earlier in Algeria or Afghanistan. European soldiers and civilians fell as often to disease as to spears, and innovative African tactics could offset technological advantages. When Britain annexed the Transvaal to its South African possession in 1877, it met with organised resistance from the Zulu kingdom under chief Cetewayo. An invasion force of 5,000 British and 8,000 native troops under Lord Chelmsford carrying Martini-Henry rifles faced 40,000 Zulu armed chiefly with *assegais*, short spears that could be thrown or used as swords. At Isandhlwana in January 1879 the well-trained and disciplined Zulu force neutralised the British firepower advantage with coordinated tactics that used the terrain to conceal numbers and movements. Achieving complete surprise they annihilated the British centre column, consisting of 900 British and more than 500 native levies. Attempting to follow up the victory with an attack on the British base at Rorke's Drift, they were defeated by the volley fire of fewer than a hundred British soldiers. When Chelmsford sought a decisive engagement by marching on the Zulu capital, Ulundi, he deployed his force in a large hollow square with cavalry sheltered inside, against which successive Zulu assaults fell "in heaps, as though they had been tipped out of carts" to rifle volleys, as well as machine-gun and canister fire.[15] Against the massed defensive firepower, Zulu valour at Ulundi proved as futile as Russian valour at Inkerman. Overconfidence and contempt for the enemy equally attended the misadventures of the French military against the Muslim empire of Touré Samori in the Western Sudan. Simultaneously fighting wars of conquest against fellow Africans, even as French military encroachment increased in the 1880s, Samori developed a toolkit of flexible tactics and strategy. Lieutenant Colonel Gustave Humbert, who led a campaign against Samori in 1891, was slow to realise that initial lack of resistance testified not to weakness but rather to calculated refusal to meet the French in a set-piece battle and to wage a protracted guerrilla campaign. When Samori chose to fight at a time and place of his own choice, his men used European repeating rifles with devastating effect. Following a bloody engagement at Diamanko, Humbert was forced to concede that Samori's forces were the strongest he had faced and that they fought "exactly like Europeans"—their edge being in fact that they didn't.[16]

Bismarck's Germany was a latecomer to the race for colonies, not least of all due to Bismarck himself. The chancellor regarded colonialism as a business for other nations that would hopefully divert enough of their attention and energies away from Europe where Germany's position was—industrial and military strength notwithstanding—inherently vulnerable. This attitude he famously summed up to a colonial enthusiast by observing that "your map of Africa is very fine, but my map of Africa is here in Europe. Here is Russia and here is France and here we are in the middle."[17] Yet this sobriety was increasingly out of step with the heady nationalist romanticism of his countrymen in the last quarter of the century—a country in which Richard Wagner's *Ring* cycle of operas was given its first full performance in 1876, and Richard Strauss's tone poem, *Ein Heldenleben*, continued the tradition of heroic self-dramatisation in 1897. The *Kunstpolitik* of racialist ideologues like Julius Langbehn mixed cultural theories of authentic Germanism with intellectualised anti-Semitism and the notion that Germany had a mission to defy the democratic and cosmopolitan warp of modernity.[18]

Bismarck's change of heart on the colonial issue is more likely explained by opportunistic pragmatism in dealing with contending pressures in domestic politics and foreign affairs. By the 1880s, some of Bismarck's conservative supporters held that colonies were fast becoming an economic necessity, while others observed that the vision of a colonial empire aroused sufficient popular enthusiasm to be of electoral advantage. Admittedly, the Reichstag presented no check on executive authority present in the British or French parliaments, but elections to them were a measure of public sentiment powerful enough that popular imperialism might deter opposition to policies on related and unrelated issues. In spite of tariff legislation passed in 1879, Bismarck was advised that a return to protectionism alone was unlikely to revitalise a German industry hungry for new markets unless commercial policy were given an entirely new direction. The electoral fortunes of the

Social Democratic Party, the most influential exponent of Marxist politics in Western Europe, continued to wax in the face of laws prohibiting most of its activities, so that a failure to conjure a convincing answer to the industrial overproduction might well nurture the working class discontent on which it thrived. Lobbies such as the *Kolonialverein* and the *Gesellschaft für deutsche Kolonisation* defended their imperial enthusiasm in the language of economic prosperity in one instance, international prestige and national unity in the next. Academics Gustav Schmoller and Heinrich von Treitschke outbid the rhetoric of Jules Ferry with the warning that an overseas colonial presence was a matter of national life and death. The Scots physician and lawyer Robert Munro later argued that the Prussian state had always been naturally attuned to Darwinism's stress on incessant competition among species.[19]

Bismarck's instincts told him that the appropriate policy could mollify grievances and sooth neuroses at home, even as powers were balanced abroad. It was thus the heretic of German colonialism who declared the official protection of the Reich over Lüderitzland, the founding of German South West Africa in April 1884—promptly followed by Togo—and, in February 1885, of German East Africa. The first of these gave the British Cape Colony a new and unwanted German neighbor; the latter placed a Germany colony in the path of the Cairo-to-Cape railway envisioned by Cecil Rhodes in the 1890s to connect Egypt and the Mediterranean with the Cape.[20] Bismarck even parlayed Germany's colonial coming-out into gains for nationalist parties in the 1884 Reichstag elections and significant diplomatic concessions at the Berlin Conference of 1884–1885, a multilateral negotiation crafted to make the scramble for Africa into a partition of Africa.[21] What matters here is that, for all their national peculiarities, British, French, and German imperialism came to share a view of a world that, in words of Élie Halévy in his history of nineteenth-century England, "maintains the balance of species at the cost of a never-ending struggle."[22]

Having compared lofty sentiments, the delegates of thirteen European countries, with the United States in an observer role, settled in for three and a half months of bargaining in Berlin that drew or confirmed borders in Africa, including the Belgian Congo. They also declared the Congo and Niger Rivers open to free trade and divided Lower Guinea between France and Germany. They gave Gabon to France and the Congo to Belgium and confirmed German claims to Tanganyika and South West Africa along with Britain's claim to Egypt. Bismarck steered clear of challenging British vital interests in the Lower Niger and in return secured free trade access to the Congo Basin. The most important agreement obliged all the signatories to make formal notification, having established effective territorial control, of any new protectorates or colonies. Its effect was to force Britain to establish direct control over territories it had hitherto governed at arm's length.[23]

Bismarck's brief career in colonial policy gave German imperialism an improvised quality, but this was not half so consequential—for Germany and Europe—as the improvised nature of the German state itself. Following Bismarck's dismissal by Wilhelm II in 1890 Germany's foreign policy lost his characteristic caution and became progressively more erratic. It is important to remember that Wilhelm II came to the throne by a combination of the incoherence of the constitution of 1871, which made the King of Prussia also the German Kaiser, and of accident, when Wilhelm I's heir, Friedrich III, died of throat cancer only three months into his reign. The relationship between Wilhelm I and his chancellor had been skewed in favour of the latter from the outset by force of personality alone, Bismarck routinely prevailing in quarrels over policy with rages and threats of resignation. Thus, Wilhelm I had been content to remain a Prussian king, and, when Frederick III passed, the office of the emperor "was like a house in which most of the rooms had never been occupied."[24] Wilhelm II moved into a vacuum of personalised authority, realist statesmanship, and intellect left behind with Bismarck's dismissal. His chancellor, Count Leo Caprivi, had none of Bismarck's qualities, and the balance of power between emperor and chancellor was reversed. Regardless of their very different paths in political development, Britain and France were by 1900 vastly more democratic polities than either had been in 1800 or even 1850, and the functions of government in each were fundamentally different from those of Germany, a Prussian kingdom dominating a German Empire with executive prerogative concentrated in a monarchy unrestrained by parliamentary authority. British Prime Minister Lord Salisbury, who could never be counted among Bismarck's admirers, nonetheless thought his demise "an enormous calamity," and enough has since be written about Wilhelm II's personality to judge his coronation as possibly the most fateful development of the late nineteenth century.[25]

This because the publication of Alfred Thayer Mahan's thoughts on sea power exerted a profound influence on the governments of all the major powers during the 1890s, the young Kaiser's prominent among them. Mahan balked at reducing sea power to naval capacity and included seaborne commerce and shipping as assets "from which alone a military fleet naturally and healthily springs."[26] Speaking in the first instance to the national interest of the United States, Mahan linked industry, markets, marine capacity and naval power together in a strategic philosophy that made mercantilist imperialism and naval might virtually synonymous. In a critical passage Mahan held that "the due and control of the sea is but one link in the chain of exchange by which wealth accumulates; but it is the central link, which lays under contribution other nations for the benefit of the one holding it, and which history seems to assert, most surely of all gathers to itself riches."[27] The implications of such a philosophy in the charged international environment of the 1890s were obvious, as it gave coherence and intellectual sheen to the inarticulate impulses and neuroses already troubling the international competition in which the scramble for Africa represented only the primary theatre. For the United States it represented a logical strategic extension of Manifest Destiny, a statement of the self-evident imperative that a continental power with Atlantic, Caribbean, and Pacific frontiers must necessarily be a sea power. To the dominant power of the time, Great Britain, it explained its dominance; to an emergent power such as Germany it posed a choice between respect gained with the calling card of a powerful navy or subservience in the absence thereof. When William Gladstone, no friend of armaments, declared Mahan's second volume, *The Influence of Sea Power upon the French Revolution and Empire*, "the book of the age," he was merely predicting the resonance of its message.[28]

The interoceanic naval arms race

Since the 1860s, when Britain had pondered intervention in the American Civil War and questioned whether the Royal Navy's seagoing warships could prevail against the firepower of Union iron-clad monitors and heavy shore batteries in American coastal waters, the awareness that technological innovation might offset Britain's international edge in naval power had preoccupied successive governments. The alliance of Britain and France against Russia of the Crimean War had been a fleeting moratorium on naval competition between them; after 1857, Napoleon III's empire, restored to full great-power dignity, commenced a full mobilisation of its military and naval resources. France now had an army of 102 divisions and two foreign legions that were battle-hardened and could be deployed anywhere from Algeria across the Mediterranean to Indochina around the world. More disturbing for the Admiralty was the naval power France was developing to tie together her land, sea, and maritime capabilities. The era of the wooden navy that Britain had so completely dominated in the wake of Trafalgar was now over; France was in the vanguard of many new technologies in ship construction and weaponry, from Paixhans exploding shells to screw-propelled ships and armour-plated batteries.[29] Ships such as HMS *Warrior* and HMS *Black Prince* were the response. Even if London and Paris could reach an entente on naval competition such as might save them money and simultaneously speak to the liberal spirit of the time that saw in new weapons a predisposition to belligerence, the emergence of a German naval power in the 1890s cancelled all bets on fiscal thrift.

Germany was by the 1890s the most dynamic economy and society in Europe, but it is critical to remember that the liberal spirit of reform and progress there was even more closely linked to patriotic zeal than in either Britain or France. An early instalment in the advocacy of what became *Weltpolitik* under Wilhelm II was articulated by the sociologist and political economist Max Weber in his inaugural lecture at Albert-Ludwigs University in Freiburg, wherein Weber argued that Germany could not continue to progress against the deadweight of Prussian authoritarianism unless and until it tackled, like England and France before it, the mission of becoming a world power.[30] Wilhelm was interested in another variety of progress in which Germany's evolution from European to world power could be the catalyst for the transformation of Prussian autocracy into a nationalist German monarchy. The germ of the idea was initially circulated by Georg Müller, at the time a corvette captain but later to become Chief of the Kaiser's Naval Cabinet, in a memorandum to the Kaiser's brother condemning Caprivi's foreign policy goal of consolidating Germanys' position on the European continent as wholly inadequate to a world "now dominated by the economic struggle."[31] The memo was not an official document, "but the ideas that are considered in it with such breathtaking insouciance," writes Wilhelm's biographer, became "absolutely characteristic" of the spirit and substance of German foreign policy under the new Kaiser.[32]

In this international environment generally, and the German context specifically, the dissemination of Mahan's ideas were bound to have profound resonance for two interrelated reasons. First, unlike Clausewitz's *On War*, an uncompleted manuscript struggling mightily to combine an analysis of Napoleonic warfare with a general theory of war, Mahan's *Influence* was a forthright and vigorous effort in policy advocacy on behalf of American sea power, combining enough historical sweep and scholarly rigour to elicit the attention of naval enthusiasts anywhere. Second, *On War* appeared in the comparatively quiet period of the German *Vormärz* and was first translated into French in 1851 and English in 1873. It was, and is, well known but little read and usually subject to partisan interpretation, "the Real Clausewitz sterilised and almost disappearing behind mountains of scholarly talk."[33] Mahan's books were released into a charged national and international context, were promptly translated into German, French, Japanese, Russian, Italian, Spanish, and Swedish, and were enthusiastically seized upon by naval enthusiasts everywhere, because they "defined, focused, and gave clear direction to the ideas and notions already held by many of them."[34] For the impulses behind *Weltpolitik* they meant nothing less than the reorientation of Germany, traditionally a land power, toward to the development of blue water naval power. Although it is tempting to trace this radical change to the growth of German industry along with the intensified competition for colonies, the scale and persistence of the Second Reich's naval build-up "were most decisively influenced by the personal interest, not to say obsession, of the Kaiser."[35]

The germ of the international navalism of the 1890s, a subspecies of militarism defined earlier, is to be found in Mahan's assertion that history had demonstrated that:

> [i]t is not the taking of individual ships or convoys, be they few or many, that strikes down the money power of a nation; it is the possession of that overbearing power on the sea which drives the enemies flag from it, or allows it to appear only as a fugitive; and which by controlling the great common, closes the highways by which commerce moves to and from the enemy's shores.[36]

In short, only with the possession of a great battle fleet could a great power stake a claim, *inter pares*, to a presence on the global common. As much as a powerful army, a great navy was a requirement of a modern state. Admittedly, there were contending schools of thought ranging from cruiser warfare and commerce raiding to amphibious and maritime capabilities, but the conviction that a battle fleet capable of annihilating an enemy fleet was crucial to the outcome of future war is what animated the interoceanic naval arms race of 1890–1914.[37]

Germany's contribution to it was by far the most disturbing to the balance of power, as it was accompanied by gratuitous diplomatic blunders in one instance and calculated menace in the next. The failure to renew Bismarck's 1887 Reinsurance Treaty with Russia—consenting several times before refusing, without ever having grasped its significance—is an example of the authoritarian capriciousness the Kaiser routinely brought to weighty matters of state. If Bismarck's appreciation of Germany's inherent vulnerability—France on one flank, Russia on the other—had combined prudence with cynicism in hedging bets in Eastern Europe, how could it be in Germany's strategic interest to abandon a policy of assurance to Russia in the absence of provocation from its government? The long-term cost of the error was to open the door to an understanding between France and Russia while increasing Germany's dependency on Austria in the east.[38] Between 1891 and 1894 republican France and autocratic Russia responded, capping a series of military consultations with a formal defensive alliance. In 1894 *Weltpolitik* then began its rolling blunder in another direction. Antagonism with Britain over colonies and spheres of interest in East Africa was accompanied by increases in Germany's navy budget to provide for more ship construction, a modest yet substantial beginning to naval modernisation that implied a challenge to British naval supremacy.[39] Once having pushed Russia into an understanding with France, it could hardly be in Germany's strategic interest even to ponder a naval arms race with Britain.

Yet the pedigree of German navalism was only one part strategic. When militarism is viewed as the use of military power for domestic political goals or for an aggressive foreign policy to an extent that a sober sense of the national interest is lost, then it has a special yet not exclusive application to Germany. Most of the European powers and Japan adopted some variation of conscription on Prussia's successful example in 1871 and had come to value a large standing army, not only as a vital component of national security but also as "an instrument for developing social cohesion and political docility in the masses."[40] As a subspecies of popular militarism, the navalism of the 1890s had a particularly political function in Wilhelmine Germany. The army, having emerged from the victory of 1871 "in a nimbus of glory" had ever since been a central institution of the Second Reich, woven deeply into the fabric of the society around it; because the army was above all a Prussian institution, Wilhelm saw the navy both as a genuinely national symbol of German power and as the instrument of an assertive foreign policy that would enhance the international prestige and domestic popularity of his reign. As a very public monarch who took care to be filmed or photographed in uniform when the occasion afforded, Wilhelm sought to conflate naval power with *Weltpolitik* and identify both with his person and the legitimacy of his regime. In this effort imperial lobbies such as the German Fleet Association and public relations office of the *Reichsmarineamt* were of invaluable assistance in making navalism both a keystone of foreign policy and the fashionable opinion of the informed public.[41] The dissemination of Mahan's publications served to stress the centrality of trade to German industry, the importance of colonies to commerce, and the dependence of both on the navy. They lent intellectual sheen to arguments favoring a greater share of the defence budget for the navy, while within the navel profession, his prescriptions for battle fleets imposed limits on dissenting opinion from within officer corps. Mahan's naval thought exercised so many political and cultural functions vital to the Wilhelmine state as to amount to the New Testament of German militarism.[42]

In Mahan's homeland it encountered a very different politico-cultural and constitutional context and nurtured a version of militarism adapted to the demands of an American republic in the first flush of great power ambition. The U.S. Navy of the early 1880s was a pale representation of American industrial and technological capacity, with hardly any vessels fit for warfare and few for normal cruising. Modest change came with the presidency of Chester Arthur in 1885, when Secretary of the Navy William Chandler established the Naval War College, and the college's first president, Commodore Henry Luce, found in Mahan both an instructor of officers in the arts of naval warfare and an architect for American naval philosophy. In 1888 a three-cornered dispute over the Samoan Islands in the South Pacific—involving American, British, and German warships—ended diplomatically yet underscored for Americans the fact that their interests were transoceanic in a world radically shrunken by new naval technologies. It was in this atmosphere, well before the war with Spain, that Mahan's first volume neared publication.[43]

So the United States had the rudiments of an emerging naval-technocratic elite, connected socially to the financial and industrial interests critical to the construction of a battle fleet at the moment when Mahan's books gave it urgency and coherence as a national imperative.[44] The development of the naval power by the United States was more constitutive of national strategic outlook than in Germany, the latter already endowed with a large army whose social prestige had no equal among the other powers, yet was forced to compete with the navy both for resources and influence over Germany's competing, and less coherent, strategic perspectives. When the rapid advance of American industry began to demand more administrative capacity for a society founded on limited government, the resulting Progressive movement of the 1890s incorporated the navy into the larger project of building a leviathan worthy of a great industrial power. When the provincial military virtues of the early republic began to yield to reality it was navy appropriations that laid the foundations of the American military-industrial complex and basis of American strategic outlook.[45] Although it is true that American and German naval officers "operated within the same universe of military-operational thought and practice"—not least of all due to the prevalence of Mahan's ideas—the U.S. Navy articulated a vastly more optimistic and expansive vision of the national future in which global sea power was Manifest Destiny.[46] How could it be otherwise for nation so distant from great power conflicts zones yet endowed with Atlantic, Pacific, and Caribbean coastlines?

Germany's contrast to Britain was no less striking and much more important. To begin with, there was the ideological gulf between Germany and the Liberal government of William Gladstone, in charge of Britain's affairs at the time. Even before the clash of 1870, Gladstone's government sought to save money on Britain's military budget and to preserve peace on the continent by promoting arms limitations. For Bismarck the idea of limiting the capacity of the Prussian army as it progressed toward the fulfilment of the national mission was out of the question, a point he made clear to Gladstone's foreign secretary. The episode illustrates how a naval power like Britain, under any government, regarded a large army as only circumstantially justified, whereas for Prussia just such an army had been seen since Napoleon as a means of survival. The personal gulf between Gladstone and Bismarck was even more marked, as the pacifist streak and parsimonious temper of British liberalism regarded as "a distasteful excrescence upon the body politic of any nation" that which was held by Prussia's leaders to be "the most essential instrument of state and nationhood."[47] Conservatives and others who opposed Gladstone's policy of restraint were galled that Bismarck's wars were reconstituting the European equilibrium with little or no comment, much less initiative, from Britain, but they were not agreed about the prudent response. Hence, Britain's diplomatic inclination of this period was a policy of appeasement, acknowledging and satisfying grievances of rival powers through compromise as a legitimate principle of foreign policy.[48] There had never been anything inevitable about Anglo-German antagonism, but after 1890 mounting antipathy was somewhere between a probability and a certainty.

Governments Conservative and Liberal understood that Germany's colonial ventures of the 1880s were a sham crafted to stroke the latent Anglophobia of public opinion to buttress domestic support. When in the 1890s the Kaiser's misty vision of *Weltpolitik* took on the concrete form—first in the appointment of Alfred von Tirpitz in 1897 to head the Reich Navy Office, then in the First and Second Navy Bills of 1898 and 1900—Britain was compelled to respond with countermeasures. By 1899 Britain was at war with the Boer republics of South Africa, so that a German navy constituted, as Tirpitz's navy was, to threaten British home waters while Royal Navy ships attended to far-flung imperial commitments required a change in both diplomacy and in naval policy. Any lingering doubts about this at Westminster were eroded by small but symbolic aggravations to national sensibilities, such as the seizure of Kioachou in China by German warships, a personal bagatelle of the Kaiser, or the seizure by British cruisers of German vessels on the suspicion of supplying the Boers despite Berlin's official neutrality.[49] By 1902 Britain had prevailed in its most controversial colonial war without direct German inference. Yet it had also altered priorities to apply appeasement to the United States in the Caribbean in the face of American triumph in the Spanish-American War, and alliance with Japan to permit a redeployment of naval assets from Asian to North Sea waters. In 1903–1904 it added détente-entente with France after nearly coming to blows at Fashoda on the Nile in 1898, and in 1907 the Anglo-Russian Convention settling spheres of interest claims in Central Asia. But above all, Britain had made a commitment to find the fiscal resources for increased naval spending and a radical modernisation of warship design.[50]

Beginning in the 1890s all the major powers constructed ironclad warships. Britain had passed the Naval Defence Act setting the "two-power standard" according to which the Royal Navy's strength should equal that of the next two largest navies combined, at the time those of France and Russia. France began building pre-dreadnoughts in 1889, Russia in 1892; between 1890 and 1905 they launched a combined total of thirty-eight. The first warship of this class in the U.S. navy was the USS *Indiana* laid down in 1891 and completed in 1895, but by 1907 twenty-three more had been added. The larger *Virginia* class displaced 15,000 tons, the *Vermont* class 17,600 tons. Japan ordered two *Royal Sovereign* class warships from British shipyards in 1893 and added four of the *Majestic* class in 1896.[51] The First Naval Law of 1898 committed Germany to the construction of nineteen battleships, while the Second Naval Law in 1900 set the bar at thirty-eight. The number of ships alone challenged Britain's two-power standard, but under Tirpitz German naval strategy also developed a "risk fleet theory," according to which, in the event of war, Britain would not be in a position to concentrate its fleet against Germany in the home waters of the North Sea and simultaneously meet the burden of the defence of a worldwide empire; because the German navy would need only to inflict enough damage to compromise the Royal Navy's ability to meet and defeat other enemies, Britain would never risk a major naval engagement with Germany. Even in victory, the theory concluded, the potential damage to Britain's overall strategic position would be prohibitive.[52] The theory was overdetermined by a wishful thinking that counted on the cooperation of the prospective adversary. The most thoughtful treatment of Germany's naval dilemma of this period concludes that the only prospective solution to British mercantilist war against Germany would have been diplomatic, a community of interest among secondary maritime powers to offset British naval hegemony.[53]

Anglo-French entente alone made Tirpitz's risk theory less credible, but the Royal Navy reforms wrought by Sir John Fisher as First Sea Lord complicated the terms, accelerated the pace, and raised the costs of the naval arms competition generally. Fisher introduced changes to the reserve system, recalled ships from far-flung stations and retired obsolete ships to save money for new designs, consolidated the Channel and Home fleets, introduced torpedo-firing destroyers–and fought successfully for a greater share of the national budget. The development of "flotilla defence" permitted Britain to station significant naval forces on the outer marches of the Empire, supported by a network of bases and coaling facilities, without exposing itself to invasion over home waters. Fisher sought additionally to revolutionise capital ship design by promoting the construction of battle cruisers, heavily armed yet lightly armoured, fast enough to catch enemy warships and powerful enough to destroy them by bringing them to action at long range with state-of-the art fire control such as would permit them to strike without being struck in return. Fisher's most radical innovation was the steam-turbine-powered battle cruiser *Invincible*. It had 17,250 tons displacement, was 567 feet long and 78 feet wide, had eight twelve-inch guns, and was capable of twenty-five knots. His most consequential innovation nonetheless was the adoption of the all-big-gun *Dreadnought* class of battleship. At 18,100 tons of displacement, 527 feet of length by 82 feet of width and carrying ten twelve–inch guns with no secondary batteries, yet capable of only twenty-one knots, the first *Dreadnought* was slower than *Invincible* but was launched first and captured the headlines. More important than the launch of new ships was the comprehensiveness of Fisher's reforms, which scrapped expenditures peripheral to the navy's fighting power, recalled much of its strength to home waters, and with the new ships added a competition in technological quality to the race of numbers, thereby increasing the cost to all states of staying in the naval arms race.[54] Germany responded to the *Dreadnought* challenge by laying down the 18,500-ton SMS *Nassau*, armed with twelve eleven–inch guns, in 1907 and followed up with the heavier *Helgoland, Moltke,* and *Kaiser* classes in 1908, 1909, and 1910.[55] Although Fisher's reforms and the *Dreadnought* revolution were not focused exclusively on meeting Germany's challenge, together they caught Germany in the unfavorable fiscal circumstance of the 1907 recession, pushing its rising naval expenditure against the cost of an already enormous army. Worse still, Fisher's "recall of the legions" called the bluff of risk fleet theory by implying that Britain would indeed weaken imperial defence to buttress its strength in home waters.[56]

Risk theory had always been a questionable substitute for greater naval capacity that at times became a mere subterfuge for Tirpitz in making the case for successive navy bills. Under his leadership German navalism had become above all an instrument of belligerent propaganda, yet moved the British from apprehension over *Weltpolitik* in the 1890s toward diplomatic and military preparations for a conflict with Germany after 1904.[57] What was true of Tirpitz—namely, that he had used "determination, luck, cunning, and trickery" to secure massive fiscal resources in the effort, losing sight of what the effort was for—was at least partly true of Fisher.[58] For both, the navalist vogue created its own momentum of ambition, as the fascination with new technologies and the determination to turn them to advantage made Mahan's vision a preordination of decisive sea battle.[59]

Diplomacy and strategy

Placed in a context broader than the waters between the Heligoland and the Thames Estuary, it quickly becomes apparent that the Anglo-German naval arms race drew the strands of international imperial rivalries around the world ever tighter to focus on Europe and the prospect of a great power war for the first time since 1815. An examination of the two decades leading to World War I reveals the progressive isolation of Germany, with Britain as the primary agent in the process—not in the articulation of a single strategic vision but rather in prudent, piecemeal responses to a series of episodes, opportunities, and provocations that collectively suggested the wisdom of measures to contain German power. Incrementally, these measures acquired a strategic coherence not unlike that developed likewise in increments by Castlereagh a century earlier. Once more Britain, now a European and world power one step removed by geography from a European land war, was forced by its position on the periphery of the main theatre of conflict to develop its relationship with actual and potential allies on the continent from a broad perspective linking naval and land power. Pondered together with the provisions the United States, at great distance from the future theatre of conflict, found expedient in bolstering its immediate and future security, it becomes apparent that a primary factor in the evolution of "Anglo-Saxon" grand strategy was the need to combine force with diplomacy in influencing the course of a conflict at a distance from it, to connect all the parts to the whole—to see the forest and the trees.[60]

The clash of British and French imperialist interests in 1898 at Fashoda on the Upper Nile in Africa ended in a humiliating climb-down for France, yet also marked the beginning of a reorientation in French foreign policy that led to the Entente of 1904. Under the influence of the *Jeune École*, the French navy was equipped with fast, powerful ships for commerce raiding, not for a battle fleet slugfest with the Royal Navy.[61] In the latter scenario France would surely have lost and would have had to abandon its position on the Mediterranean where it was also troubled by the emergence of the Italian navy. French Foreign Minister Théophile Delcassé therefore sought to improve Franco-Italian relations with a mind to Italy's possible orientation in a future conflict. Because France's Entente partner was by 1909 engaged with the challenge posed to its North Sea position by Germany, the possible withdrawal of Royal Navy ships from the Mediterranean left France less than comfortable about its position. France promised its Entente partner that it would help protect British interests in the Mediterranean, yet could not be fully confident that its own Nineteenth Army Corps could be transferred safely from northern Africa to metropolitan France in the event of a general European war. Italy played a double game between the Entente and the Central Powers in the decade before 1914, but the plausible application of Anglo-French sea power against it sobered its leadership on the cost of any commitment to the Central Powers to an extent that advantaged the Entente strategically.[62]

So, although the crisis embittered French nationalists, for Delcassé the lesson of Fashoda was to "not let the reach exceed the grasp" and to somehow secure an agreement with the superior naval power—to not forget the wound of 1871 because of the scratch of 1898. For his part, Wilhelm believed that the Anglo-French crisis would lead to war and thus to a strengthening of Germany's position so long as Germany possessed the battle fleet that France did not.[63] Coming in the midst the Dreyfus Affair, the great crisis of French politics at the turn of the century, Fashoda deepened the sense of national humiliation. But the Dreyfus case ultimately laid bare the corruption of the French army and strengthened the republican and socialist left in France. It matured France politically by revealing even to moderate conservatives how a state-within-a-state could warp not only elementary justice but also a realistic assessment of the national interest.[64]

Among the factors adding steel to Britain's position at Fashoda had been the approach of colonial war in South Africa. The Boer Republic of Transvaal in particular resented the British immigrant *Uitlanders* as self-appointed standard-bearers of progress; the Boer population generally set itself against the British claim to supremacy in South Africa, casually asserted in 1815 but now critical to its strategic interests and world power status.[65] Coming when it did and proceeding as it did, the Boer War was thus for Britain a special kind of trauma. Specifically, Boer forces assumed the offensive in October 1899 and set the British army on its heels with some remarkable early successes at Mafeking, Kimberley, Talana Hill, and Nicholson's Nek. The British Army of 1899 was completely unprepared for the conflict before it. It could inflict only negligible losses on Boer defenders occupying entrenched positions, and suffered high casualties when launching frontal assaults on Boer forces armed with smokeless repeating rifles, especially when in concealed positions. As the Boers were usually mounted, they could break off the engagement at any point and dissolve into the veldt to fight again on another occasion. At Stormberg, Magersfontein, and Colenso, British forces were repeatedly bested by more determined opponents skilled in mobile tactics. The impact of these events was to set off a storm of public fury in Britain and a shock wave of Anglophobia across the Continent, "precipitated by the war, and prolonged by Britain's failure to win it."[66]

Field Marshal Viscount Roberts and his chief of staff, Viscount Kitchener, began a massive program of army reorganisation to raise a sizable force of mounted infantry and cavalry supplemented by light horse regiments drawn from those parts of the Empire with frontier settler populations such as Australia, Canada, and New Zealand. As British resolved stiffened and troop numbers increased, the Boer tactics of hit and run with small commando units never evolved into a strategy to win the conflict.[67] Benefiting from the arrival of large numbers of reinforcements and use of the railways to move and supply them deep in Boer territory, Roberts began to restrict Boer mobility while moving to the offensive. In March Roberts took Bloemfontein, the capital of the Orange Free State, and in May Redvers Buller, the victim of earlier reverses, defeated the Boers at Glencoe and Dundee in Natal. Once a force of cavalry and mounted infantry under General Bryan Mahon had relieved Mafeking, Roberts was free to invade the Transvaal. He captured Johannesburg on May 31 and the capital, Pretoria, on June 5, before uniting with Buller's forces at Vlakfontein on July 4.

Yet the fall of Boer capitals marked only the end of the "conventional" phase of the war. For eighteen months Kitchener struggled against the Boer commandos and some 10,000 Cape Afrikaners, now rebel British subjects, who joined them. British troops laid miles of barbed wire and built networks of blockhouses in order to further restrict mobility. Ultimately, Kitchener turned to a harsh "scorched earth" policy not unlike that of Napoleon in Spain, involving the burning of Boer crops and farmhouses, wholesale slaughter of their livestock, and imprisonment of their women and children in concentration camps where some 20,000 died of disease and malnutrition. By the time Boer resistance collapsed, the war had cost British and imperial forces approximately 22,000 dead (7,882 killed in combat, the remainder by disease), and another 22,000 wounded, compared to approximately 6,000 Boers killed and 24,000 taken prisoner. As almost a half million men had been needed to subdue Boer forces no greater than 40,000 at any one time; the experience demanded reforms to the British army over the years following. The Boer War was the greatest crisis of late Victorian imperialism, troubling the increasingly liberal conscience of British public opinion; a march in Pretoria was one thing, "a messy, inconclusive war of attrition, punctuated by defeats and compromised by barbarism was quite another."[68] The Boer War cast a cloud over the public mood of even the most confident of the Great Powers, the latest increment of a cumulative unease:

> British militarism—although "softer" than the Prussian variety—became perceptibly more strident in the generation before World War 1. As specialists have shown, it grew from deep historical roots: from the Victorian cults of muscular Christianity and public school Spartanism to the martial ingredients of nonconformity and working class radicalism; from the racial and imperial insecurities evoked by the Crimean War and Indian Mutiny to the war scares of the later century and Britain's pathetic performance during the Boer War.[69]

Viewed from this perspective the understanding with France in 1904 takes on a quality of urgency. Appropriately, Charles Petty-Fitzmaurice, Lord Lansdowne, who had been secretary of war under Salisbury as the Boer War began and suffered much of the criticism for its initial humiliations, took the initiative. In his new post as foreign secretary, Lansdowne persuaded the French government into a settlement of imperial disputes—most notably in Egypt, where the British position had been a sore point in relations since the 1880s, and Morocco, "whose proximity to French Algeria made its external connections a matter of intense concern to governments in Paris."[70]

It was therefore especially foolhardy of Germany to test the mettle behind the Entente in 1905, when Wilhelm visited Tangiers and assured the Sultan of support against France's efforts to enforce a reform program in Morocco and extend its influence over the territory. Contrived to split the Entente with a bluster of German intervention, it encouraged Britain to view the Moroccan crisis not as a colonial issue but rather as a European and naval-strategic issue. The "military conversations" with France initiated by the Conservative government of Arthur Balfour were given new importance by Edward Grey, foreign secretary of the succeeding Liberal cabinet, to the extent that Anglo-French consultation began to approximate war planning. At the ensuing international conference at Algeciras, convened at Germany's insistence to resolve the issue, Berlin's delegation was isolated in large part because Grey was determined that British interests be regarded as "virtually identical" with those of France. Events from Fashoda to Transvaal to Tangiers thus had the effect of steering naval thought in an anti-German direction.[71]

Popular Anglophobia in Germany during the Boer War, adroitly exploited by its government to secure more naval spending, was of itself a factor in London's investment in the Entente, especially as the African Cape was among Fisher's five strategic keys to Britain's empire, along with Dover, Gibralter, Alexandria, and Singapore.[72] Germany's actions in its own African colony, German South West Africa (virtually next door to Britain's possession, the Cape) can only have hardened London's resolve. Between 1904 and 1907 General Lothar von Trotha, an experienced officer who had seen service in German East Africa and in the Boxer Rebellion, led a campaign against the Herero and Nama peoples on behalf of German settlers, defeating the main Herero force at the Waterberg River in August 1904 and driving the survivors into the desert where many died of starvation. The Nama and Herero then fought a running guerilla war against which von Trotha unleashed a campaign of reprisal of genocidal proportions. There was indeed public outrage at this barbarism back in Germany, but it was in a fundamentally weaker position than comparable protest in Britain, where opposition was not denigrated a priori as unpatriotic. For its part British outrage at von Trotha's actions was genuine enough—though compromised by hypocrisy—but the sheer fury of the repression testified to the deep insecurity of German foreign policy at its highest level and a view held by the Kaiser and his narrow circle of advisors in a "lawless world of state jackals bent on destroying one another."[73] Berlin's determination to prevail in its colony was out of all proportion to its importance, the product of a *Weltpolitik* lacking a strategic coherence proportional to its energy and increasingly governed by impulse. Although Britain's attitude toward German power had never been inevitably hostile, its naval preparations and serial diplomatic responses inflicted a preemptive measure of defeat on Germany:

> In objective terms it was evident by 1908/09 that Germany would fall behind, that the "Tirpitz Plan" had failed, that Germany could not alter the balance of forces. But neither the gradual realisation of the extraordinary advantage the British fleet had won through the entente with France (the concentration of the fleet in the North Sea, while France covered the Mediterranean), nor the relief vis-à-vis Russia in other waters and the actual or potential alliance with new world powers such as Japan and the United States, none of that altered Germany's unaccountable confidence of being able to win or at least finish the naval arms race with relative success. Britain too, as it was clearly winning, indeed had won, the bloodless war, was unable or unwilling to find a way out of the confrontation and normalise its superior position with accommodation, was bound by alliance policy and imperial obligations."[74]

Britain was less bound than any other power. Its prospective ally and Germany's foe, France, shared with Germany a folkloric militarism based in large part on the maintenance of huge standing armies and the highly visual presence of the military in daily life. However, it is not true that the two countries were in "lockstep" so far as the influence of military on national policy was concerned.[75] France was a fundamentally more mature society politically if less advanced economically. It had wrestled with the legacies of Bonapartism and republicanism, had repeatedly yielded to the seductions of the former, yet following the defeat of 1871 tilted increasingly toward the latter with a minimal consensus "around the idea of a law-based state, constitutional government, basic civil and political freedoms, and a certain basic notion on 'being French' which celebrated both the local and national character of national unity."[76] The turbulent years of the Third Republic witnessed serial political dramas—from the Boulanger crisis of the late 1880s to the Panama scandal of 1892, the Dreyfus Affair of 1894–1906 and *l'Affaire des Fiches* in 1904–1905—and in the course of them threw up proto-fascist movements such as Charles Maurras' *Action française*. But the climax of these in the Dreyfus case, not simply a legal scandal but a politico-cultural convulsion, decided the struggle for the republic and achieved a domestication of the army that German civilian authority never genuinely attempted.[77] In the Affair as in other instances, Radicals and Socialists, from George Clemençeau to Jean Jaurès, led the fight politically and were able to bring about both a subordination of military to civil authority more durable than any since 1815 along with significant reform and reorganisation of the army itself. Jaurès sought to address France's manpower disadvantage relative to Germany by promoting a more prominent role for reservists in army reorganisation and advocating defensive warfare. Joseph Joffre, whose military career benefited so significantly from the army reforms that he emerged Commander in Chief in 1914, cultivated a faith in offensive initiative. Although the reforms were incomplete by the time France faced war with Germany, the army of 1914 was a fundamentally superior force to that of 1870 and, as result of the diplomatic consequences of Germany's *Weltpolitik* since 1890, did not face war alone.[78] If Britain was bound to anyone, it was bound to France; now a stable parliamentary democracy, France was Britain's natural partner.

The French republican and socialist left in the two decades before World War I found no true partner in Germany, tributes to internationalist solidarity notwithstanding. The tragedy of the European socialism in the twenty years before 1914 was that it was so dominated by the *Sozialdemokratische Partei Deutschlands* (SPD) and its interpretation of Marxist ideology. Able to survive laws prohibiting its activity dating to Bismarck's chancellorship, the SPD of the 1890s developed extraordinary organisational skills in cultivating an ever-growing working class vote for its candidates in elections to the Reichstag. Because the Reichstag was not a sovereign parliament exercising consequential authority over the political executive, German Socialists were excused from collaboration with the other parties of the left and centre-left in determining how such authority might be exerted. This meant that the SPD was by 1912 the largest of the parties in the Reichstag, supported by more than a third of the electorate, yet had never formed a government or an electoral alliance with any of the parties of the left or centre which were genuinely committed to democratic constitutional reform. Instead, its leadership advised that the party remain aloof from such collaboration, and its growing vote seemed to vindicate the prudence of this policy. Meanwhile, the dominant and increasingly orthodox Marxist reasoning of its chief ideologue, Karl Kautsky, maintained in effect that cooperation with the other parties was irrelevant, because the industrial capitalism that delivered ever more votes to the party would inevitably produce its own demise and deliver political power as well. This policy fought off challenges from within the party—from revisionists advocating alliance with the liberals and radicals demanding revolutionary activism—under the sterile slogan that the SPD was a revolutionary party by virtue of its existence.[79] Theoretical discourse on the nature of capitalism and imperialism was the primary vocation of German Socialism, a glue that kept the party a united yet an oddly apolitical organisation. Since it explained why the Wilhelmine Reich and the society it governed were doomed, it became popular among its membership to say that the best foreign policy was no foreign policy at all. This belief of "scientific socialism" in the inevitability of revolutionary change driven by impersonal historical forces was the source of German Socialism's "negative integration" into German politics and society, isolated both from other forces favouring democratic change and from any responsibility of public office.[80] Much as militarist nationalism was the opiate of the German Right, Marxist determinism sedated the political imagination of the German Left.

Without crediting too much the nature of the political regime involved, it is noteworthy how nuanced were the relations among the Western democracies relative to the Anglo-German gyre of mutual suspicion even in the midst of the interoceanic arms race. The coming-out of naval power in Mahan's homeland, the United States, became the work of Theodore Roosevelt, beginning with his service as under secretary of the navy in the administration and continuing through his career as McKinley's successor in the presidency to 1909.

To Roosevelt the national challenge was in the first instance a matter of naval capacity catching up to the strategic exposure of the United States following its easy triumph over Spain, the projection of American power into the Caribbean, and acquisition of a colony in the Western Pacific. America of the Progressive Age was in most respects his natural political element; the left of the political spectrum responded to the expansive role of government Roosevelt applied to domestic affairs, the right to his assertive foreign policy with its own variant of Social Darwinism based on the "strenuous life" Roosevelt sought from himself and his countrymen.

On the matter of American power on the world stage, naval policy scrambled ideological categories, carrying the tide of public opinion because it expressed a new spirit of revitalised democracy.[81] The "big stick" for which his foreign policy became noted was wielded more often against Congress than foreign adversaries in extracting ever-greater appropriations for naval construction. As a result, American shipyards laid down twelve battleships between April 1902 and May 1905; during Roosevelt's administration the United States launched no fewer than fourteen, achieving in the process an acceleration of construction tempo of a cut of more than a year per ship. Moreover, American naval planners had anticipated *Dreadnought* and the revolution in battleship configuration it started. USS *Michigan*, approved in 1905, was in some respects more, in others less, advanced than *Dreadnought*. The first American warship to combine all-big-gun armament with turbine propulsion was USS *Delaware*. The *Delaware* class ships that followed displaced 20,000 tons and featured ten twelve–inch guns.[82] The disposition of American naval forces between Atlantic and Pacific waters was as important as their absolute numbers, a dilemma for which the construction of the Panama Canal connecting the Caribbean backyard with the Pacific was only a partial solution, especially as fleet concentration was an imperative of Mahan's strategic thought. A meeting with the naval leadership over the issue in 1907 ultimately culminated in the world cruise of the sixteen battleships later referred to as the Great White Fleet. One part diplomatic pageantry and one part imperial swagger, the cruise was additionally a technical-logistical exercise to determine the time in which a large fleet could sail to distant waters and arrive in fit condition to fight—a matter made urgent by the condition of the Russian Baltic Fleet at Tsushima. Naval planners reduced by a quarter their estimate of the time required to mount operations against Japan, decided that the main American naval base in the Pacific should be located in Hawaii at Pearl Harbor, and drafted War Plan Orange as a tentative blueprint for prospective conflicts with Japan in the Central and Western Pacific.[83] The conflict with Spain had thus been as constitutive of the American military thinking as the Civil War, the beginning of an effort to overcome the tyranny of distance entirely by developing the capability not merely to deploy a battle fleet on the British model but also "to place on foreign shores and support over oceanic distances large numbers of soldiers."[84]

Yet these provisions did not close the gap between existing naval capacity and the exposure of the United States in the naval arms race. Relations with Japan were strained, not only over Japan's disappointment with the Treaty of Portsmouth but also over "yellow peril" anti-immigration agitation in California and the state's egregious mistreatment of even its Americanised Japanese citizens. The Root-Takahira Agreement of 1908, confirming Japan's position in Korea in return for a pledge that Japan had no designs on the Philippines, mitigated tensions somewhat, but the size and power of Japanese capital ships, now built in Japanese shipyards, made them among the best in the world.[85] It is ironic, then, that among the reasons for Roosevelt's decision to divide the fleet between the Atlantic and Pacific—and to devote greater attention to the latter—was Germany's naval presence around Samoa going back to the 1880s, the visit of a German warship at Manila Bay following Dewey's victory, and Wilhelm's seizure of Kioachou in China.[86]

In the pivotal waters of the Caribbean, the United States had therefore to redeem the hemispheric claim of the Monroe Doctrine, yet leaven boldness with discretion. When Britain and Germany, joined later by Italy, blockaded Venezuela, seized its navy, and bombarded the fort of Puerto Cabello in punishment for Venezuela's delinquency in meeting financial obligations, Roosevelt condemned the Anglo-German action with the argument that Berlin sought to poison Anglo-American relations by involving Britain in gunboat bullying in the Americas. The Balfour government countered that British actions intended no offense to the Monroe Doctrine, as no country was more anxious than Britain that the United States defend its principles. When Venezuelan president Cipriano Castro proposed arbitration of the dispute, Roosevelt supported the proposal and sent a fleet of warships to Venezuelan waters to underscore his position while lamenting that Britain had permitted itself to be used by Germany in the affair. To Berlin he conveyed the message that any violation of the Monroe Doctrine by way of territorial acquisition in South America would mean war with the United States. There was at the time a trans-Atlantic social and cultural rapprochement that middle-brow opinion embraced as Anglo-Saxon racial fraternity from which the president was not wholly immune, but above all Roosevelt's ruthless pragmatism compelled him to view the Royal Navy for the time being as the guarantor of America's Atlantic security. From London's perspective the United States now looked "less like an imperial rival and more like a forceful, determined super-dominion."[87]

Mutual concern about Germany, in other words, favored a rosy view on the Anglo-American relations. Under these circumstances Britain and the United States adopted a circumstantial posture on the Hague Conventions of 1899 and 1907 governing arms limitations and the peaceful settlement of international disputes. It is worthwhile noting here that Tsar Nicholas II initiated the diplomacy to convene discussion of these wholly prudent goals and that they represented a revival of ideas initially circulated by Britain and Russia following the Napoleonic Wars, motivated as much by the fiscal burden of military expenditure of the era as by any other principle. The first Hague conference managed an anodyne resolution that arms reduction was desirable and that the conferees would study it. The second was promoted by Roosevelt, at the time seeking pacifist votes in his 1904 reelection campaign, but it concentrated on the peaceful settlement of disputes and set aside the question of arms reductions—a change Russia welcomed following its recent defeat by Japan and objections by the Tsar's General Staff to any restrictions on rearmament.

Popular pacifist movements were more influential in Britain and the United States—naval powers with fundamental strategic advantages afforded by geography and societies less burdened by the militarism associated with large standing armies—than they were in Europe or in Japan. The Liberal government of Henry Campbell-Bannerman elected in 1906 therefore suggested international discussion on arms limitations, but based the initiative on a fundamental confidence in British naval supremacy and a desire to divert expenditure to domestic social reforms. A proposal dressed up in pacifist and humanitarian principles, yet so nakedly self-interested, received a predictable sneer from Germany, where Tirpitz and his Kaiser had worked too hard to build a battle fleet to ever countenance its restriction by an international agreement. For their part, Germany's Austrian allies were even more resistant to the idea, Emperor Franz Josef suggesting that arms limitation would only popularise anti-militarism. The Tsar's government had meanwhile come full circle; it is a testimony to how the militarism of the pre-1914 decades had so warped national political discourse that the Tsar's foreign minister, Alexander Izvolsky, derided arms limitation as an "idea of just Jews, socialists, and hysterical women."[88]

Planning for, planning on, war

The remark is also illustrative of the poor intellectual quality of policy formulation and decision making abiding in the upper reaches of European governments—most especially in Vienna, St. Petersburg, and Berlin—and the "endless capacity for unreality" that transformed the July Crisis of 1914 into World War I.[89] This condition was most consequential in the German government. Its chancellor, Prince Bernhard von Bülow, in charge of the day-to-day business of the executive, was alternately incompetent or negligent in handling his monarch, a state of affairs that led in 1908 to Germany's humiliation, and nearly a constitutional crisis, when London's *Daily Telegraph* published the text of an indiscrete and incendiary Wilhelm interview had given on the great issues of the times. When the text triggered a wave of public indignation across Germany—even calls for his abdication—Wilhelm sulked that he had been the victim of a conspiracy connecting his chancellor with international Jewry to deprive him of his throne. Bülow's successor in the chancellery, Theobald von Bethmann-Hollweg, was an able and industrious civil servant, yet had no experience in foreign affairs.[90]

Between the Austrian annexation of Bosnia-Herzogovina in 1908 and Europe's last summer of peace in 1914, the Kaiser's government continued to steer Germany's foreign policy with a combination of feigned insouciance and frantic impulse. There had been several anti-Ottoman revolts in the Balkans in the first half of the nineteenth century, and Ottoman decline in Northern Africa had led indirectly to the opportunism that took France into Algeria in 1830. But in the 1850s Russia's predations on Ottoman territory had drawn in Britain and France, again with a measure of opportunism, into the Crimea in a war of greater duration and carnage than anyone had anticipated. The Balkan Crisis of 1875 began in Bosnia-Herzegovina as a peasant revolt against Ottoman taxation and progressed to Serbian and Croatian demands for outright freedom and thence to the Russo-Turkish War of 1877–1878 in which Romania and Serbia became Russian allies. When the Treaty of San Stefano imposed humiliating terms on Turkey— guarantees for the autonomy of the Bulgarian principality, independence of Montenegro, Serbia, and Romania, and ceded self-administration to Bosnia and Herzegovina—British and Austrian protests had prompted German Chancellor Bismarck to host an international conference at Berlin to mediate a revision. In doing so he was motivated by the dictum articulated only the year before that it was in Germany's primary interest to make itself useful enough to other powers that a coalition against Germany could never be in their interest. The actual substance of a Balkan settlement was irrelevant. Bismarck's initiative had the merit of avoiding a European war over the Balkans and enhancing Germany's prestige temporarily, but in the effort he agreed to a reassurance treaty with Austro-Hungary that became a terminal burden to German foreign policy.[91]

Following the Berlin conference, armed resistance to Habsburg rule in Bosnia-Herzegovina was usually crushed by military force, and the provinces were governed by Austro-Hungarian civil servants and officers. The formal annexation of the provinces in 1908, however, provoked Serbian nationalists, who sought to unite the provinces to Serbia, to new paroxysms of rage in which many clamored for war against Vienna. And yet the first two Balkan crises leading to military conflict in 1912 and 1913 were fought principally over control of the Ottoman provinces in Macedonia and Thrace, the first by the Balkan League of Bulgaria, Serbia, Greece, and Montenegro forcing the Turks to give up all their European possessions west of the Enos-Media line, the second over the territorial spoils of the first, especially in Macedonia, and at great cost to Bulgaria.[92] After 1908 there was widespread acceptance that a general war arising from an Austro-Russian confrontation over the future of Serbia was probable. In 1911 the configuration that such a war might take on was evident the Moroccan Crisis, in which Berlin demanded the French Congo as compensation for France's declaration of a protectorate over Morocco. The appearance of the German gunboat *Panther* in the port of Agadir, another gratuitous provocation contrived to intimidate France and drive a wedge in the Entente instead prompted from British Chancellor of the Exchequer David Lloyd George the bellicose Mansion House speech citing Britain's historic role in redeeming continental nations from national extinction. Radicals in Lloyd George's party were horrified, but the Tories purred approval and the *Times* printed a violent attack on Germany's foreign policy. The journalist and publisher C.P. Scott observed that Germany sought a European dominance "not far removed from the Napoleonic."[93]

The bluster of Berlin's actions, continuing demands of the naval race, and France's enduring hostility to Germany now had the cumulative effect of giving the Entente partners common interests far beyond Morocco, extending from the diplomatic to the military, and shunting them from an understanding over colonial rivalries to an alliance for a European war. Whether British policy was the circling-in of Germany in Central Europe or circling-out of Germany from world affairs, Germany had connived in its own isolation.[94] An interpretation of World War I as in the first instance as the Third Balkan War[95] is therefore entirely compatible with another that cites the Austro-German relationship as prominent among the "structural" features that transformed the Third Balkan War into World War I. Because one of the groups violently opposed to Habsburg rule, Young Bosnia (*Mlada Bosna*), managed to assassinate the Habsburg heir, Francis Ferdinand, in the Bosnian capital of Sarajevo on June 28, 1914, the diplomatic crisis that followed is properly viewed as a series of initiatives that incrementally foreclosed on the chances that a regional crisis might be confined to a regional war. The determination to do so has to be doubted. Three weeks before Sarajevo, Wilhelm had predicted not only the imminence of the third chapter of the Balkan Wars but a role for Germany in it.[96]

In particular it was the Austrian government's failure, having decided to punish Serbia for an assassination perpetrated by ethnic Serbs, to act promptly and unilaterally that required Germany to take a position on a wider conflict. Bethmann Hollweg and the foreign secretary, Gottlieb von Jagow, appreciated better than anyone else in Berlin the implications of Russia being drawn into a Balkan war and therefore the prudence of restraining Austria while cooperating with Britain according to a common plan to guarantee European peace. In the event, no collective deliberation and strategic thinking guided German policy in Berlin or consultation with Vienna;

instead, the infamous "blank cheque" Wilhelm II so casually issued to Vienna's representatives for whatever actions they might take to "eliminate Serbia as a power-political factor in the Balkans" tied the fortunes of the most powerful state in Europe to what Jagow regarded as "an Atridite dynasty" in the throes of accelerating disintegration.[97] Although the failure to avert a European war by confining the Third Balkan War to the Balkans can be traced to "the near-collective failure of statecraft by the rulers of Europe," no decisions were taken in the other capitals of Europe in the days following Sarajevo comparable in consequence to those taken in Vienna and Berlin.[98] With St. Petersburg's response to the crisis, the triangle of incompetent government atop the three monarchies was completed:

> These gigantic empires staggered under the vast weight of their pre-modern constitutional arrangements that could not meet the demands of a modern state. The existence of different power centres, frequently in competition with each other, and the absence of responsible governments, in the sense of an executive responsible to the public or parliament for its actions, prevented the formulation of coherent foreign policy strategies at Vienna, Berlin, and St. Petersburg."[99]

Germany's support for Austria was in large part a calculated bet that Russia would not intervene on behalf of brother-Slavs at a risk of war to itself, especially if Austria acted quickly—while international outrage at the murder of Austrian royalty was fresh—and achieved diplomatic or military *faits accomplis* that could not be easily reversed. Instead, the theatre of the forty-eight hour ultimatum delivered to Serbia on July 23, almost a month after the assassination, received agreement from Serbia on most but not all of its demands. It also prompted Belgrade to mobilise its forces on July 26, even before filing a reply, on the prudent calculation that Vienna intended military action in any event. At this point, the British foreign minister, Edward Grey, a veteran of successful arbitration during the Balkan wars, proposed an international conference to which France and Russia agreed. Vienna rebuffed outright any submission of an issue of national honour to the opinion of other governments, an absurd posture given that its redemption was dependent on German steel. Austria also mobilised and made hostilities with Serbia official on July 28. Austria thus had the war it sought, but Grey hoped that a wider conflict could yet be averted if Germany would agree to mediation and constrain its ally—a notion his advisors, Eyre Crowe and Arthur Nicolson, correctly thought was based on an assumption of goodwill in Berlin that was only circumstantially available. What Germany sought was British neutrality in the event of a wider war, a delay in any possible Russian mobilisation, and to keep Britain and France inactive as Austria retrieved its chestnuts from the fire.[100]

From this point plans for the mobilisation of armies were integral to the diplomatic dance. As Austria's forces were divided into three concentrations—the largest to the north in Poland against Russia, the smallest in the south against Serbia, with a swing group to reinforce either of these—the commitment of the swing group against Serbia to hasten its defeat would leave Austria exposed to Russia in the north. Because Serbia's tiny army outnumbered Austria's strength in the south and operational prudence alone required that the swing group be directed against it, Austria had no business attacking Serbia if success were dependent on Russian inaction.[101] Because Austria posed no threat to Russia, Russian mobilisation could be justified only on the grounds of honoring its commitment to Serbia, not on the grounds of strategic precaution. Since its humiliation by Japan in 1904–1905, however, the Tsarist regime had undertaken significant steps to improve the performance of its army, including a faster timetable for the army's mobilisation, along with railroad construction to speed its deployments both within Russia's vast territory and to the frontiers of the empire. Although its rearmament program was not yet complete, Russia was in a much higher state of readiness than in 1904 and did not see the Balkan crisis as any more an Austrian than a German affair, "since Austria was deemed to be the stalking horse for a malevolent German policy."[102]

This perception was general enough among the Tsar's ministers that those with portfolios as dissimilar as foreign affairs (Sergei Sasonov) and agriculture (Alexander Krivoshein) advised Nicholas II that fear of revolution at home could no longer be an excuse for inaction abroad and that war might be the catalyst of national unity—a line of reasoning with which neither Chief of General Staff Vladimir Sukhomlinov nor Navy Minister Ivan Grigorovich took issue. A council of ministers on July 24 therefore agreed to ask Vienna to postpone its ultimatum deadline by forty-eight hours and to urge Belgrade to be conciliatory but also to prepare the districts of Kiev, Odessa, Moscow, and Kazan for mobilisation. Thus, Russia's response to the crisis combined military with diplomatic posture from the beginning. Whether one traces the Tsar's hesitation in this procedure to personal fecklessness or a justified premonition of disaster, his cancellation of mobilisation followed by an order for partial mobilisation in those districts facing only Austria, thereby to encourage German restraint, met with fury from the military command, as "Russia had only one plan for mobilisation" and "the last thing the General Staff needed was to have a wrench thrown in the machinery at the very outset of the process."[103] On July 30, 1914, the Russian army numbered 1.4 million men and 40,000 officers, but at mobilisation it grew to 4.5 million men and doubled its number of officers. Once the order for the mobilisation of an army so large had been given there was little time left to prevent the Third Balkan Crisis from becoming World War I.

Where Russia had planned for war, Germany had planned on it. There was now a good deal of justified nervousness shared by the Kaiser, his chancellor, and the foreign office that manifested itself in last-minute attempts to get Russia to delay or limit its mobilisation and/or to get a pledge of neutrality from Britain in the event of a now near-certain war with France and Russia. But Lloyd George had made plain Britain's position on a Franco-German conflict back in 1911, and Grey reiterated it to the Commons in a speech following Berlin's failed ultimatum on Russian mobilisation and its subsequent declaration of war on July 29, its ultimatum to Belgium on August 2, and its declaration of war on France on August 3, in which he reminded MPs of British interests, honour, obligations, and "long-standing friendship with France."[104] The German General Staff had never doubted Britain's position in a continental war, but had in fact doubted that such a war could be avoided; it is a measure of how thoroughly Germany's political leadership and foreign office had been colonised intellectually by its military leadership that in the eleventh hour Chancellor Bethmann Hollweg sought not to stop the Austro-German war but rather to enhance Germany's prospects in a general conflict. It may or may not be that the "prevailing spirit of militarism and Social Darwinism in Wilhelmine Germany" made this turn of events inevitable, but it is undeniable that the combination of Germany's foreign policy since 1890 and the extraordinary influence given the military in its articulation had brought upon Germany a war it was unlikely to win.[105]

Although Germany's comparative guilt for the war that ended the Great Power peace of 1815 and destroyed much of European civilisation in the process will continue be an object of debate, concern here is not with guilt but rather with strategic calculation. It has been the argument of this concluding chapter that the diplomacy and arming of Wilhelmine Germany had by 1914 produced an overwhelming coalition against its war aims every bit as powerful as the coalition that ultimately defeated Napoleon a century before, with the difference that the coalition was largely in place before hostilities even commenced. A great deal of scholarship has dealt with the role of war plans and mobilisation timetables in stampeding diplomatic events in the summer of 1914,[106] and a school of scholarship has tended to view Germany's war plan in particular as a creature of purely military calculation bereft of political reason.[107] Since the triumph over France in 1871 Germany's military hierarchy had also adhered to Helmuth Moltke's notion of the strict separation of military operations from political "interference," and it was appropriate that the younger Moltke, since labelled "the Lesser," found himself at the apex of the Wilhelmine military hierarchy when Germany again invaded France. But the *Weltpolitik* that had incrementally but relentlessly put Germany at a strategic disadvantage by 1907 had been the work of the Kaiser and his political leadership, a leadership that by 1914 had been familiar with Germany's war plans—their diplomatic, and hence strategic, implications—for more than a decade when the July Crisis proceeded down to the short strokes. Even discounting a British declaration of war, those plans accepted and provided for simultaneous operations against France in the West and Russia in the East. The assumption that Russia would be slow to mobilise turned out to be dangerously erroneous, but the derivative assumption that the preponderance of German strength should therefore be hurled against France to deliver an early knock-out punch remained theoretically valid.

Whatever the controversy over the origin of and revisions to the so-called Schlieffen Plan for the invasion of France through Belgium, by the end of July Germany's policy no longer distinguished between the deployment of forces and the initiation of offensive operations, so that European peace was steamrollered in Belgium by the imperative of a lighting victory over France at any cost.[108] The plan reflected Germany's foreign policy as a whole in its "desperate attempt to reconcile Germany's great strength and ambitions with her relative inferiority vis-à-vis the Entente coalition;" its scale exceeded the limits of German's strength just as *Weltpolitik* had for a quarter century.[109] Whatever the original conception of the plan drafted by Alfred von Schlieffen, chief of the German General Staff from 1891 to 1905, and subsequent revisions and modification made by Moltke as his successor, Germany's vision for France's defeat in 1914 was of a massive envelopment of Allied forces in Belgium and Northern France by six German armies swinging west and south to bring about a decisive engagement east of Paris within six weeks. France was thus to be out of the war before Britain could adequately reinforce Allied strength, whereupon Germany's armies in the West could be redeployed to meet Russia's armies in the East.

Similar in design to Napoleon's envelopment of the Austrians at Ulm, in the execution the invasion of France featured no comparable operational celerity. Logistically, the German invasion was a disaster by the end of the last week in August, the biggest drain on German strength being the distance and direction of the advance itself. The fact that the invasion began to unravel in early September may to some degree be chalked to the uncertainty of Moltke's leadership in its early stages, but the sheer scale of the operations challenged their cohesion, as coordinating the movement of six separate armies proved beyond the communications capacity of Moltke's headquarters, even as physical cohesion of some units began to fall apart from exhaustion. In the first two days of September, in fact, communications were so poor that Moltke was not even certain of the position of the First and Second Armies responsible for the wide, arching flanking movement of the German right wing.[110] And if France's war plan, Plan 17, initially played directly to Germany's advantage by launching an offensive into the lost departments of Alsace and Lorraine, it was fundamentally a blueprint for the concentration of French armies in anticipation of counter-attack once the direction and strength of the invaders had been determined. When the larger pattern of German advances became apparent it is not going too far to say that General Joffre read the Schlieffen Plan like a book and was able to redeploy his forces, along with the small but potent British Expeditionary Force (BEF), with superior communications behind interior lines of defence. When the First Army under Alexander von Kluck altered its direction of advance from a south-westerly to a south-easterly direction in order to close up any gap with the Second Army under Karl von Bülow, effectively shifting the operational plan from one of envelopment from the Allied left to one of breakout in the Allied centre, Joffre was able to threaten both the western flank of the German right and to march the BEF into the gap between the two German armies. The resulting First Battle of the Marne was the most consequential of the war:

> The French had "fixed" the Germans in the east and manoeuvred to strike against them in the west; the Germans initial victories had been valueless because they neither fixed nor destroyed their opponents, but left them free to manoeuvre and fight again. The immediate consequences were political. France and the French were saved: without that the Entente would have no base for continuing operations in Western Europe. Italy was confirmed in its decision to be neutral, in the unwisdom of honouring its commitment to the Triple Alliance. The longer-term effects were strategic. Germany had failed to secure the quick victory on which its war plan rested. From now on it was committed to a war on two fronts. With hindsight some would say that Germany had already lost the war.[111]

The German army dismissed thirty-three generals due to the failure at the Marne, and press releases misled the public concerning the facts and likely consequences of what had happened. Given the army's social prestige and the myth of its infallibility, this is not surprising, but the army command in effect lied to itself as well when it refused to reappraise its strategic logic underpinning the war plan, even once Moltke was replaced by the Prussian minister of war, Eric von Falkenhayn. Like Moltke, Falkenhayn was cut from an institutional and intellectual cloth that held the plan of 1914 to be the last word in military thinking. Debate spun around operational options for saving it rather than a reappraisal of its reasoning.[112] Where Moltke led the army to the Marne, von Falkenhayn would take it to Verdun and the Somme.

The stalemated bloodbath for which the nightmare of the following four years has since been remembered was something close to a certainty once the initial German offensive had been halted. Because the forces on the Western Front were more or less balanced—about 2 million French against 1.7 million Germans—neither side enjoyed a significant edge. The German army had better heavy artillery, but Anglo-French forces had better field artillery. Germany had fielded a higher percentage of reservists, but they were better trained than the French reservists; whatever advantage this gave the Germans was offset by the presence of the BEF and over a hundred Belgian battalions. The Western allies, moreover, had a better ratio of troops with recent battle experience, and it is noteworthy that the professionals the BEF had deployed to meet the von Kluck's army on the German right wing, many of whom had fought in the Boer War, knew to dig entrenchments, the better to rake the Germans advancing over the flat, marshy meadows along the Mons-Condé Canal with defensive fire.[113] Upon its check at the

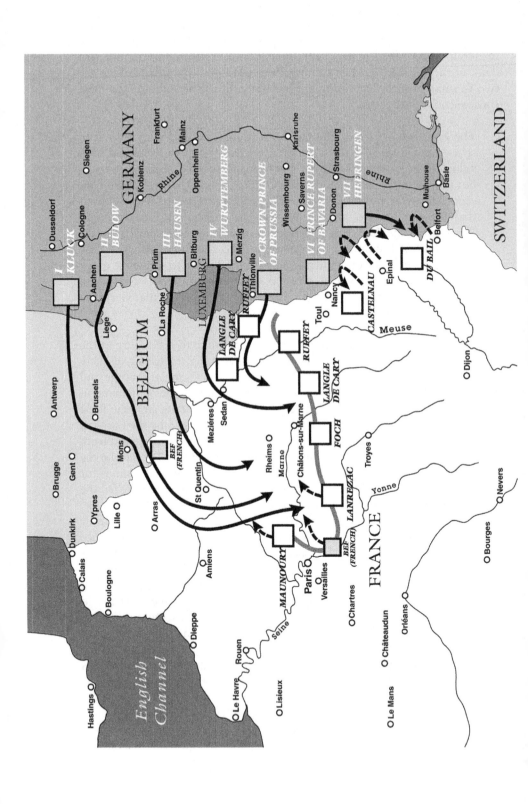

Marne, the German army too dug in order to defend its hard-won positions, so entrenchment quickly became a generalised feature of the Western Front between the English Channel and the Swiss border. Even after the German army's rout of the Russians at Tannenberg in East Prussia, August 26–30, 1914—the product not of a master plan but of an innovated offensive-defensive manouevre—trench warfare was not general but common on the Eastern Front. Tannenberg generated a myth of Napoleonic operational brilliance, but Russia was yet far from beaten.[114] By mid-September, just weeks into the fighting, the pattern of the war was in place. The German army had fought into France but not on to Paris; it had neither enveloped the Entente armies nor been enveloped by them. Germany had beaten Russia in East Prussia, yet Russia had beaten Germany's Austro.-Hungarian allies. Although the war in the east was more fluid than in the west, it did not produce a strategic shift in fortunes one way or the other. The underlying operational and tactical reasons for the stagnation that gripped both fronts by December 1914 were thus very different—but the war was stagnant nonetheless. Within three months, what began as the Third Balkan War extended hostilities to and/or drew forces from the Middle East, Africa, Asia, Australia, and Canada. And if by 1917 modern war was too much for Tsarist Russia and Germany was able to grind out a Carthaginian peace with its Bolshevik successor, the addition of the United States to the Entente cause on the Western Front neutralised its strategic dividend.[115]

Even with the armistice of 1918, World War I was inconclusive and so unsatisfying to the Western powers, the successor states of Tsarist, Habsburg, and Ottoman imperialism and Germany's Weimar Republic, that it was fought all over again, in 1939–1945. But the World Wars are altogether another chapter in the history of modern war, distinct from the developments that that linked the Napoleonic era with the crisis of peace in July 1914.

Notes

1 Dirk Bönker, "Zwischen Bürgerkrieg und Navalismus: Marinepolitik und Handelsimperialismus in den USA 1865 bis 1890," in *Das Militär und der Aufbruch in die Moderne 1860 bis 1890: Armeen, Marinen und der Wandel von Politik, Gesellschaft und Wirtschaft in Europa, den USA sowie Japan*, ed. Michael Epkenhans and Gerhard Groß (Munich, Germany: R. Oldenbourg Verlag, 2003), p. 93.
2 Russell F. Weigley, *History of the United States Army* (Bloomington: Indiana University Press, 1984), pp. 265–67.
3 Rolf Hobson, *Imperialism at Sea: Naval Strategic Thought, The Ideology of Sea Power and the Tirpitz Plan, 1875–1914* (Boston: Brill, 2002) pp. 110–53; Bönker, pp. 95–115; Paul A.C. Koistinen, *Mobilizing for Modern War: The Political Economy of American Warfare, 1865–1919* (Lawrence: University of Kansas Press, 1997), pp. 1–57.
4 Jürgen Osterhammel, *The Transformation of the World: A Global History of the Nineteenth Century*, trans. Patrick Camiller (Princeton, NJ: Princeton

University Press, 2014), p. 445; Yoshihisa Tak Matsusaka, *The Making of Japanese Manchuria, 1904–1932* (Cambridge, MA: Harvard University Press, 2001), pp. 120–25; Sidney Pash, *The Currents of War: A New History of American-Japanese Relations. 1899–1941* (Lexington: University of Kentucky Press, 2014), pp. 13–30.

5 John Darwin, *Unfinished Empire: The Global Expansion of Britain* (London: Bloomsbury Press, 2012), p. 329.

6 Eric Hobsbawm. *The Age of Empire, 1875–1914*. (New York: Vintage, 1989).

7 Osterhammel, *Transformation of the World*, pp. 392–468; C.A. Bayly, *The Birth of the Modern World, 1780–1914* (Oxford: Blackwell, 2004), pp. 247–82, 451–87; H.L. Wessling, *The European Colonial Empires, 1815–1919*, trans. Diane Webb (Harlow, UK: Pearson/Longman, 2004), pp. 121–46.

8 Victor Arwas, *Art Nouveau: From Macintosh to Liberty, The Birth of a Style* (London: Andreas Papadakis, 2000), pp. 90–91.

9 Osterhammel, *Transformation of the World*, pp. 443–45.

10 Heinrich August Winkler, *Geschichte des Westens*, 2 Vols (Munich, Germany: C.H. Beck, 2012) I, p. 880; John Darwin, *The Empire Project: The Rise and Fall of the British World System, 1830–1970* (Cambridge, UK: Cambridge University Press, 2009), pp. 49–50.

11 Wesseling, *European Colonial Empires*, p. 147.

12 Jules Ferry, *Discours et opinions de Jules Ferry*, 7 vols., ed. Paul Robiquet (Paris: Colin, 1897), Vol. 5, p. 199–200, 210–11, 215–16, 217–18; Wesseling, *European Colonial Empires*, pp. 132–33; Thomas Pakenham, *The Scramble for Africa: White Man's Conquest of the Dark Continent from 1876–1912* (New York: Harper Collins, 1991), pp. 128–31; *Discours et opinions de Jules Ferry,* 7 vols., ed. Paul Robiquet (Paris: Colin, 1897), Vol. 5, p. 199–200, 210–11, 215–16, 217–18.

13 Denis Brogan, *The Development of Modern France, 1870–1939* (London: Hamish Hamilton, 1967) p. 218.

14 P.J. Cain and A.G. Hopkins, *British Imperialism, 1688–2000* (London: Pearson, 2002) pp. 329–31; Daniel Headrick, *The Tools of Empire: Technology and European Imperialism in the Nineteenth Century* (New York: Oxford University Press, 1981), pp. 101–3; Alan Lloyd, *The Drums of Kumasi: The Story of the Ashanti Wars* (London: Longman, 1964).

15 Saul David, *Zulu: The Heroism and Tragedy of the Zulu War of 1879* (New York: Penguin, 2005), p. 348; Michael Barthorp, *The Zulu War: Isandhlwana to Ulundi* (London: Weidenfeld & Nicolson, 2002); Ian Castle, *Zulu War, 1879* (Westport, CT: Greenwood Publishing, 2005).

16 A.S. Kanya-Forstner, *The Conquest of the Western Sudan: A Study in French Military Imperialism* (New York: Cambridge University Press, 1969), pp, 186–87; Yves Person, "Guinea-Samori," in *West African Resistance: The Military Response to Colonial Occupation*, ed. Michael Crowder, (London: Hutchinson, 1971), pp. 11–43; Brian J. Peterson, "History, Memory and the Legacy of Samori in Southern Mali, 1880–1898," *Journal of African History* 49, No. 2 (2008), pp. 261–79.

17 Quoted in Gordon Craig, *Germany, 1866–1945* (New York: Oxford University Press, 1978) pp. 116–17.

18 Thomas Nipperdey, *Deutsche Geschichte, 1866–1918: Machtstaat vor Demokratie* (Munich, Germany: C.H. Beck, 1992), pp. 304–5; Fritz Stern, *The Politics of Cultural Despair: A Study in the Rise of the Germanic Ideology* (Berkeley: University of California Press, 1961), pp. 116–80.

19 Heinrich August Winkler, *Der lange Weg nach Westen*, 2 vols. (Munich, Germany: C.H. Beck, 2000), Vol. 1, p. 251; Paul Crook, *Darwinism, War and History* (Cambridge, UK: Cambridge University Press, 1994), p. 158.

20 Craig, *Germany, 1866–1945,* p. 119; Hans-Ulrich Wehler, *Bismarck und der Imperialismus* (Cologne, Germany: Kiepenheuer & Witsch, 1969).
21 Pakenham, *Scramble for Africa,* pp. 239–54; Stig Förster, Wolfgang J. Mommsen, and Ronald Robinson, *Bismarck, Europe, and Africa: The Berlin Africa Conference 1884–1885 and the Onset of Partition* (London: Oxford University Press, 1988).
22 Élie Halévy, *A History of the English People in the Nineteenth Century.* 6 vols., trans. E.I. Watkin (London: Ernest Benn, 1961), Vol. 5,. pp. 20–21.
23 Cain and Hopkins, *British Imperialism, 1688–2000,* pp. 303–39.
24 Christopher Clark, *Iron Kingdom: The Rise and Fall of Prussia, 1600–1947* (Cambridge, MA: Belknap, 2006), pp. 587–89; John C.G. Röhl, *The Kaiser and his Court: Wilhelm II and the Government of Germany* (Cambridge, UK: Cambridge University Press, 1996).
25 Paul M. Kennedy, *The Rise of Anglo-German Antagonism, 1860–1914* (London: Allen & Unwin, 1980), p. 204.
26 A.T. Mahan, *The Influence of Sea Power upon History, 166–1783* (Boston: Little, Brown, 1890; reprint New York: Dover, 1987), p. 28.
27 Ibid., p. 226.
28 William E. Livezey, *Mahan on Sea Power* (Norman: University of Oklahoma Press, 1947), p. 59.
29 Howard J. Fuller, *Empire, Technology and Seapower: Royal Navy Crisis in the Age of Palmerston* (London: Routledge, 2013), pp. 76–79, 231–45; Rebecca Berens Matzke, *Deterrence through Strength: British Naval Power and Foreign Policy under Pax Britannica* (Lincoln: University of Nebraska Press, 2011).
30 Winkler, *Der lange Weg nach Westen,* Vol. 2, p. 266.
31 John C.G. Röhl, *Wilhelm II: The Kaiser's Personal Monarchy, 1888–1900,* trans. Sheila De Bellaigue (New York: Cambridge University Press, 2004), pp. 934–35. John C.G. Röhl, *Germany without Bismarck: The Crisis of Government in the Second Reich, 1890–1900* (Berkeley: University of California Press, 1967), pp. 162–63.
32 Röhl, *Wilhelm II,* p. 936.
33 Azar Gat, *A History of Military Thought from the Enlightenment to the Cold War* (New York: Oxford University Press, 2001), p. 254; Hew Strachan, *Carl von Clausewitz's On War: A Biography* (London: Atlantic, 2007), pp. 1–27.
34 Gat, *History of Military Thought,* p. 454; Philip A. Crowl, "Alfred Thayer Mahan: The Naval Historian," in *Makers of Modern Strategy from Machiavelli to the Nuclear Age,* ed. Peter Paret (Princeton, NJ: Princeton University Press, 1986), pp. 444–77.
35 Gat, *History of Military Thought,* p. 455.
36 Mahan, *Influence of Sea Power,* p. 138.
37 William L. Langer, *The Diplomacy of Imperialism, 1890–1902* (New York: Knopf, 1968), pp. 425–42; Beatrice Heuser, *The Evolution of Strategy: Thinking War from Antiquity to the Present* (New York: Cambridge University Press, 2010), p. 224.
38 Röhl, *Wilhelm II,* pp. 342–43; Nipperdey, *Deutsche Geschichte, 1866–1918,* p. 622.
39 Hobson, *Imperialism at Sea,* pp. 216–46; Patrick J. Kelly, *Tirpitz and the Imperial German Navy* (Bloomington: Indiana University Press, 2011), pp. 105–28.
40 Stig Förster, *Der doppelte Militarismus: Die deutsche Heeresrüstungspolitik zwischen Status-quo-Sicherung und Aggression, 1890–1913* (Stuttgart, Germany: Franz Steiner Verlag, 1985), p. 6; Brian Bond, *War and Society in Europe, 1870–1970* (London: Fontana, 1984; reprint Montréal, PQ: McGill-Queen's University Press, 1998), p. 32.

41 Clark, *Iron Kingdom*, pp. 590–602; Wilhelm Deist, *Flottenpolitik und Flottenpropaganda: Das Nachrichtenbureau des Reichsmarineamtes, 1897–1914* (Stuttgart, Germany: Deutsche Verlags-Anstalt, 1976), pp. 71–29; Eckart Kehr, *Battleship Building and Party Politics in Gremany, 1894–1901* (Chicago, IL: University of Chicago Press, 1973).

42 Deist, *Flottenpolitik und Flottenpropaganda*, p. 89.

43 Dudley W. Knox, *A History of the United States Navy* (New York: Putnam, 1936), pp. 318–39; Mark Russell Shulman, *Navalism and the Emergence of American Sea Power* (Annapolis, MD: Naval Institute Press, 1995), p. 43; George W. Baer, *One Hundred Years of Sea Power: The U.S. Navy, 1890–1990* (Stanford, CA: Stanford University Press, 1993), pp. 9–48; Harold Sprout and Margaret Sprout, *The Rise of American Naval Power, 1776–1918* (Princeton, NJ: Princeton University Press, 1939; reprint Annapolis, MD: Naval Institute Press, 1990), p. 240.

44 Peter Karsten, *The Naval Aristocracy: The Golden Age of Annapolis and the Emergence of Modern American Navalism* (New York: Free Press, 1972), pp. 277–325; William M. McBride, *Technological Change in the United States Navy, 1865–1945* (Baltimore, MD: Johns Hopkins University Press, 2000), pp. 8–37.

45 Stephen Skowronek, *Building a New American State: The Expansion of National Administrative Capacities, 1877–1920* (New York: Cambridge University Press, 1982), pp. 42–43, 86–87; Paul A.C. Koistinen, *Mobilizing for Modern War* (Lawrence: University of Kansas Press, 1997), pp. 56–57.

46 Dirk Bönker, *Militarism in a Global Age: Naval Ambitions in Germany and the United States before World War I* (Ithaca, NY: Cornell University Press, 2012), pp. 302–10.

47 Kennedy, *Rise of Anglo-German Antagonism*, pp. 20–21.

48 Ibid., pp. 22–37. See also Paul M. Kennedy, "The Tradition of Appeasement in British Foreign Policy, 1865–1939," *British Journal of International Studies* 2, No. 3 (1976), pp. 195–215.

49 Kennedy, *Rise of Anglo-German Antagonism*, pp. 231–55; Charles Stephenson, *Germany's Asia-Pacific Empire: Colonialism and Naval Policy, 1885–1914* (Woodbridge, UK: Boydell & Brewer, 2009) pp. 17–30; Patrick J. Kelly, *Tirptiz and the Imperial German Navy* (Bloomington: Indiana University Press, 2011), pp. 129–202; Volker Berghahn, *Der Tirpitz-Plan: Genesis und Verfall einer innenpolitischen Krisenstrategie unter Wilhelm II* (Düsseldorf, Germany: Droste, 1971).

50 Nipperdey, *Deutsche Geschichte, 1866–1918*, pp. 660–61; Kennedy, *Rise of Anglo-German Antagonism*, pp. 251–88; William N. Tilchin, *Theodore Roosevelt and the British Empire: A Study in Presidential Statecraft* (New York: St. Martin's, 1997); Ian H. Nish, *The Anglo-Japanese Alliance: The Diplomacy of Two Island Empires* (London: Athlone, 1966); Christopher Andrew, *Théophile Delcassé and the Making of the Entente Cordiale* (New York: St. Martin's, 1968); Jon Tetsuro Sumida, *In Defence of Naval Supremacy: Finance, Technology and British Naval Policy, 1899–1914* (London: Unwin Hyman, 1989).

51 James L. George, *History of Warships: From Ancient Times to the Twenty-First Century* (Annapolis, MD: Naval Institute Press, 1998), pp. 89–90.

52 Hobson, *Imperialism at Sea*, pp. 215–95; Kelly, *Tirptiz and the Imperial German Navy*, pp. 195–202; Holger H. Herwig, *Luxury Fleet: The Imperial German Navy, 1888–1918* (London: Allen & Unwin, 1980), pp. 36–37; Jonathan Steinberg, *Yesterday's Deterrent: Tirpitz and the Birth of the German Battle Fleet* (London: Macdonald, 1965), pp. 20–21; Charles H. Fairbanks Jr., "The Origins of the *Dreadnought* Revolution: A Historiographical Essay," *International History Review* 13, No. 2 (1991), pp. 221–440.

53 Hobson, *Imperialism at Sea*, p. 329.
54 Nicholas A. Lambert, *Sir John Fisher's Naval Revolution* (Columbia: University of South Carolina Press, 1999); Paul Kennedy, *The Rise and Fall of British Naval Mastery* (London: Allen Lane, 1976; reprint London: Penguin, 2001), p. 218.
55 Siegfried Breyer, *Schlachtschiffe und Schlachtkreuzer, 1905–1970* (Munich, Germany: J.F. Lehmanns Verlag, 1970), pp. 283–94.
56 David Stevenson, *Armaments and the Coming of War: Europe, 1904–1914* (Oxford, UK: Clarendon Press, 1996), pp. 100–2; Hew Strachan, *The First Word War*, 2 vols. (Oxford: Clarendon Press, 2001), pp. 17–18; Holger H. Herwig, "The German Reaction to the *Dreadnought* Revolution," *International History Review*, 13, no. 2 (1991), pp. 221–40.
57 Livezey, *Mahan on Sea Power*, pp. 273–74.
58 Kelly, *Tirptiz and the Imperial German Navy*, p. 466.
59 Ibid., p. 199; Nicholas A. Lambert, *Sir John Fisher's Naval Revolution*, p. 167; Herwig, "The German Reaction to the *Dreadnought* Revolution," p. 275.
60 Richard Hart Sinnreich, "Victory by Trial and Error: Britain's Struggle against Napoleon," in Williamson Murray and Richard Hart Sinnreich, eds., *Successful Strategies: Triumphing in War and Peace and Antiquity to the Present* (New York: Cambridge University Press, 2014), pp. 155–88; Heuser, *Evolution of Strategy*, pp. 216–47.
61 Jean Meyer and Martine Acerra, *Histoire de la Marine française des origines à nos jours* (Rennes, France: Éditions Ouest-France, 1994), pp. 273–308; Theodore Ropp, *The Development of a Modern Navy: French Naval Policy, 1871–1904* (Annapolis, MD: Naval Institute Press, 1987), pp. 306–59.
62 Jon K. Hendrickson, *Crisis in the Mediterranean: Naval Competition and Great Power Politics, 1904–1914* (Annapolis, MD: Naval Institute Press, 2014), p. 117; M.B. Hayne, *French Foreign Office and Origins of the First World War, 1898–1914* (Oxford University Press, 1993); Marco Rimanelli, *Italy between Europe and the Mediterranean* (Peter Lang, 1970; Laurence Sondhaus, *The Habsburg Empire and the Sea: The Naval Policy of Austro-Hungary, 1867–1918* (West Lafayette, IN: Purdue University Press, 1989).
63 Brogan, *Development of Modern France*, p. 322–26; Kennedy, *Rise of Anglo-German Antagonism*, pp. 236–37; Darrell Bates, *The Fashoda Incident of 1898: Encounter on the Nile* (New York: Oxford University Press, 1984).
64 Brogan, *Development of Modern France*, pp. 357–87.
65 Darwin, *Empire Project*, p. 219.
66 Thomas Pakenham, *The Boer War* (New York: Random House, 1979; reprint Perennial, 2001), pp. 257, 347–57.
67 V.G. Kiernan, *Colonial Empires and Armies, 1815–1960* (1982; repr. Montréal, PQ: McGill-Queen's University Press, 1998), pp. 92–93.
68 Darwin, *Empire Project*, p. 247.
69 Crook, *Darwinism, War and History*, p. 80.
70 Darwin, *Empire Project*, p. 260.
71 Kennedy, *Rise of Anglo-German Antagonism*, pp. 275–82; Douglas Porch, *The Conquest of Morocco* (New York: Farrar, Straus and Giroux, 1982), pp. 137–45; Strachan, *First World War*, Vol. 1, pp. 16–19; Eugene N. Anderson, *The First Moroccan Crisis, 1904–1906* (Hamden: Archon, 1966).
72 Paul Kennedy, *Strategy and Diplomacy: Eight Studies* (London: Allen & Unwin, 1983) pp. 129–60.
73 Isabel V. Hull, *Absolute Destruction: Military Culture and the Practices of War in Imperial Germany* (Ithaca, NY: Cornell University Press, 2005, pp. 187–93; Helmut Bley, *South-West Africa under German Rule, 1894–1914* (Evanston, IL: Northwestern University Press, 1971); Jon Bridgman. *The Revolt of the Hereros* (Berkeley: University of California Press, 1981).

74 Nipperdey, *Deutsche Geschichte, 1866–1918*, pp. 668–71.
75 Jakob Vogel, "Military, Folklore, *Eigensinn*: Folkloric Militarism in Germany and France, 1871–1914," *Central European History* 33, no. 4, 2000, pp. 487–504. By the same author, see also *Nationen im Gleichschritt: Der Kult der "Nation in Waffen" in Deutschland und Frankreich, 1871–1914* (Göttingen, Germany: Vandenhoeck & Ruprecht, 1997).
76 Sudhir Hazareesingh, *From Subject to Citizen: The Second Empire and the Emergence of Modern French Democracy* (Princeton, NJ: Princeton University Press, 1998), p. 320.
77 Dennis Brogan, *Development of Modern France*, pp. 183–87; Jean-Denis Bredin, *The Affair: The Case of Alfred Dreyfus*, trans., Geoffrey Mehlman (New York: George Braziller, 1986); Zeev Sternell, *La Droite Révolutionnaire* (Paris: Seuil, 1978).
78 David Ralston, *The Army of the Republic: The Place of the Military in the Political Evolution of France, 1871–1914* (Cambridge, MA: MIT Press, 1967), pp. 203–376; Robert A. Doughty, *Pyrrhic Victory: French Strategy and Operations in the Great War* (Cambridge, MA: Harvard University Press, 2005), pp. 4–45.
79 Nipperdey, *Deutsche Geschichte, 1866–1918*, pp. 104–9, 554–72; Carl Cavanagh Hodge, *The Trammels of Tradition: Social Democracy in Britain, France, and Germany* (Westport, CT: Greenwood, 1994), pp. 16–21.
80 Susanne Miller, *Burgfrieden und Klassemkampf: Die deutsche Sozialdemokratie im Ersten Weltkrieg* (Düsseldorf, Germany: Droste, 1974) p. 33; Dieter Groh, *Negative Integration und revolutionärer Attentismus* (Frankfurt am Main, Germany: Ullstein, 1973).
81 J. Simon Rofe, "Preparedness and Defense: The Origins of Theodore Roosevelt's Strategy for the United States on the International Stage," in *A Companion to Theodore Roosevelt*, ed. Serge Ricard, (Chichester, UK: Wiley-Blackwell, 2011), p. 81; Edmund Morris, *Theodore Rex*, (New York: Random House, 2001), p. 420; Sean Dennis Cashman, *America in the Age of the Titans: The Progressive Era and World War I* (New York: New York University Press, 1988).
82 H.P. Willmott, *The Last Century of Sea Power*. 2 vols. (Bloomington: Indiana University Press, 2009), Vol. 1, p. 56; Breyer, *Schlachtschiffe und Schlachtkreuzer*, pp. 208–18.
83 Carl Cavanagh Hodge, "A Whiff of Cordite: Theodore Roosevelt and the Interoceanic Naval Arms Race, 1897–1909," *Diplomacy & Statecraft* 19, No. 4 (2008), pp. 712–31; James R. Reckner, *Teddy Roosevelt's Great White Fleet* (Annapolis, MD: Naval Institute Press, 1988), pp. 220–23, 161; Edward S. Miller, *War Plan Orange: The U.S. Strategy to Defeat Japan, 1897–1945* (Annapolis, MD: Naval Institute Press, 1991), pp. 1–38.
84 Russell F. Weigley, *The American Way of War: A History of United States Military Strategy and Policy* (Bloomington: Indiana University Press, 1973), pp. 188–89; Williamson Murray, "US Naval Strategy and Japan," in *Successful Strategies*, ed. Williamson Murray and Richard Hart Sinnreich, pp. 280–313.
85 Morris, *Theodore Rex*, pp. 482–85; Sidney Pash, *The Currents of War: A New History of American-Japanese Relations, 1899–1941* (Lexington: University of Kentucky Press, 2014), pp. 19–20; David C. Evans and Mark R. Peattie, *Kaigun: Strategy, Tactics, and Technology in the Imperial Japanese Navy, 1887–1941* (Annapolis, MD: Naval Institute Press, 1997), pp. 153–67.
86 Baer, *One Hundred Years of Sea Power*, pp. 36–37.
87 Darwin, *Empire Project*, p. 267; Kennedy, *Rise of Anglo-German Antagonism*, pp. 256–61; Kenneth Bourne, *Britain and the Balance of Power in North America, 1815–1908* (Berkeley: University of California Press, 1967); P.P. O'Brien, *British*

and *American Sea Power: Politics and Policy, 1900–1936* (Westport, CT: Praeger, 1998); William N. Tilchin, *Theodore Roosevelt and the British Empire: A Study in Presidential Statecraft* (New York: St. Martin's, 1997).

88 Stevenson, *Armaments and the Coming of War*, pp. 105–9; Kelly, *Tirptiz and the Imperial German Navy*, pp. 276–79.

89 Thomas Otte, *July Crisis: The World's Descent into War, Summer 1914* (Cambridge, UK: Cambridge University Press, 2014), p. 511.

90 Craig, *Germany, 1866–1945*, pp. 283–85; John C.G. Röhl, *Kaiser Wilhelm II: A Concise Life* (Cambridge, UK: Cambridge University Press, 2014), pp. 110–15; Katharine Anne Lerman, *The Chancellor as Courtier: Bernhard von Bülow and the Governance of Germany, 1900–1909* (New York: Cambridge University Press, 1990), pp. 221–27.

91 Winkler, *Geschichte des Westens*, Vol. 1, pp. 856–60; Craig, *Germany, 1866–1945*, pp. 110–16.

92 Christopher Clark, *The Sleepwalkers: How Europe Went to War in 1914* (New York: Harper Collins, 2012), pp. 251–58; Edward J. Erickson, *Defeat in Detail: The Ottoman Army in the Balkans, 1912–1913* (Westport, CT: Praeger, 2003); Richard C. Hall, *The Balkan Wars, 1912–1913: Prelude to the First World War* (London: Routledge, 2000).

93 Peter Rowland, *Lloyd George* (London: Barrie & Jenkins, 1975), pp. 250–52.

94 Samuel R. Williamson Jr., *The Politics of Grand Strategy: Britain and France Prepare for War, 1904–1914* (London: Ashfield, 1990), pp. 167–204; Geoffrey Barraclough, *From Agadir to Armageddon: Anatomy of a Crisis* (London: Weidenfeld & Nicholson, 1982). Paul W. Schroeder, "World War I as Galloping Gertie: A Reply to Joachim Remak," *Journal of Modern History* 44, no. 3 (1972), p. 329.

95 Joachim Remak, "1914–The Third Balkan War: Origins Reconsidered," *Journal of Modern History* 43, no. 3 (1971), pp. 353–66; Otte, *July Crisis*, pp. 9–47.

96 Röhl, *Kaiser Wilhelm II*, p. 149; Schroeder, "World War I as Galloping Gertie," p. 343; Clark, *Sleepwalkers*, pp. 242–312; Alexander Watson, *Ring of Steel: Germany and Austria-Hungary in World War I* (New York: Basic Books, 2014), p. 25; Geoffrey Wawro, *A Mad Catastrophe: The Outbreak of World War I and the Collapse of the Habsburg Empire* (New York: Basic Books, 2014), pp. 56–64.

97 Otte, *July Crisis*, pp. 94–101, 509; Wawro, *Mad Catastrophe*, pp. 108–10; John Keegan, *The First World War* (London: Hutchinson, 1998), pp. 48–52.

98 Otte, *July Crisis*, pp. 116, 507.

99 Otte, *July Crisis*, p. 512.

100 Ibid., pp. 262–385; Clark, p. 430; Strachan, pp. 79–80; Keegan, *First World War*, p. 60; Zara Steiner, *The Foreign Office and Foreign Policy, 1898–1914* (Cambridge, UK: Cambridge University Press, 1969), pp. 155–57.

101 Keegan, *First World War*, p. 60; Wawro, *Mad Catastrophe*, pp. 120–28.

102 Clark, pp. 474–75; Strachan, pp. 81–83.

103 Strachan, p. 83; David R. Stone, *The Russian Army in the Great War: The Eastern Front, 1914–917* (Lawrence: University of Kansas Press, 2015), pp. 29–31; Joshua A. Sanborn, *Imperial Apocalypse: The Great War and the Destruction of the Russian Empire* (Oxford, UK: Oxford University Press, 2014), p. 22.

104 Otte, *July Crisis*, p. 495.

105 Strachan, pp. 87–90; Otte, *July Crisis*, pp. 508–24; Imanuel Geiss, "The Outbreak of the First World War and German War Aims," *Journal of Contemporary History* 3, No. 3 (1966), pp. 75–91; Walter Goerlitz, *History of the German General Staff, 1657–1945* (New York: Praeger, 1953), pp. 143–56.

106 Strachan, pp. 163–207; Keegan, *First World War*, pp. 24–47.

107 Gerhard Ritter, *The Schlieffen Plan: Critique of a Myth*, trans. Andrew and Eva Wilson (New York: Praeger, 1958).
108 Otte, *July Crisis,* pp. 442–43; Terence Huber, *Inventing the Schlieffen Plan: German War Planning, 1871–1914* (New York: Oxford University Press, 2002); Holger H. Herwig, "Germany and the Short War Illusion: Toward a New Interpretation, *Journal of Military History* 66, No. 3 (2002), pp. 681–93; Terence M. Holmes, "The Reluctant March on Paris: A Reply to Terence Zuber's 'The Schlieffen Plan Reconsidered," *War in History* 8, No. 2 (2001), pp. 208–32.
109 Gat, *History of Military Thought,* p. 366.
110 Strachan, pp. 208–43; Keegan, *First World War,* pp. 71–22; Max Hastings, *Catastrophe 1914: Europe Goes to War* (New York: Knopf, 2014), pp. 313–42.
111 Strachan, p. 261; Doughty, *Pyrrhic Victory,* pp. 85–97.
112 Strachan, p. 262, Goerlitz, *History of the German General Staff,* p. 164.
113 Strachan, p. 207; Keegan, *First World War,* pp. 97–100.
114 Strachan, pp. 322–35; Norman Stone, *The Eastern Front, 1914–1917* (London: Hodder & Stoughton, 1975), p. 92, pp. 66–69; Prit Buttar, *Collision of Empires: The War on the Eastern Front in 1914* (Oxford: Osprey, 2014), pp. 148–202.
115 Stone, *The Eastern Front,* p. 92; Strachan, pp. 373, 1113–39.

Epilogue

Although the argument of the final chapter of this book has been that the Great War of 1914–1918 was by no means inevitable, the conclusion is that it was nonetheless probable—if not in its fact then certainly in its form. Looking back on the war in an address to the Royal Institute in March 1926, the Cambridge historian J. Holland Rose conceded that "it may seem impertinent for a civilian to venture on these criticisms of the military art" but that he had yet to have an explanation from a prominent admiral or general of the "devastating deadlock to which modern warfare on a grand scale has been reduced." Rose's remarks were a study of the courtesy one profession feels it owes to another, for as a scholar of the Napoleonic era and much of what followed, he knew many of the answers, yet insisted that "history would abdicate one of her functions if she did not examine the causes of the mass-wastage into which mass-warfare has degenerated." Rose noted, for example, that dominance of artillery and machine guns on the Western Front in 1914 had led to all and more of the clogging effects foretold by Jomini a century earlier.[1] Jomini's conclusions about operations were actually more instructive, especially where he stressed that when military operations are crafted to take advantage of genuine strategic advantage while effectively concealing intent, a military campaign can expect success—possibly without a major engagement. But if adversaries are more or less equally matched in terms comparative strength and knowledge of each other's intent, "there will result one of those stupendous tragedies like Borodino, Wagram, Waterloo, Bautzen, and Dresden."[2] The Marne, the Somme, and Verdun were to be added to those place-names.

In the Napoleonic Wars, France's adversaries were at a loss to know what was happening to them until 1809, when they began to reform and adapt in successful imitation the Napoleonic way of war. A sober acceptance of France's strategic strengths and vulnerabilities, such as Napoleon never cultivated, would have ended the career of conquest earlier with France in strategically sustainable circumstance and might possibly have preserved the superiority of French arms for decades. Instead, the modern French state under Napoleon, having defended the Revolution against it enemies, became primarily an instrument of martial coercion supplemented occasionally and instrumentally by diplomacy, a political expression of "all the tenacious mental characteristics of the young Corsican *caporal*,"[3] undone in the end by Europe's nationalist uprising and Castlereagh's patient strategic vision. In 1914, by contrast, the arts of mass warfare had been studied by all the Great Powers and cultivated to an encrusted orthodoxy, so German arms in 1914 possessed none of the shock of Austerlitz in 1805. And Britain had this time produced coherent strategic decisions in advance of the conflict, not only in the months before and the weeks after the July Crisis but also over the years of *Weltpolitik*'s evolution from a theoretical to actual threat to Britain's security.[4]

Over the period between the dawn of Napoleonic warfare and the July Crisis, from Valmy to Verdun, the most revealing aspect of modern war was the conception and execution of increasingly complex *operations* and in the service of, or absence of, strategic thought. Whereas early Napoleonic campaigning served a strategic purpose—by offering France a more defensible peace—the superiority of Napoleonic operations ultimately outran strategic purpose. The primary purpose of Napoleonic France, the first modern state, having thereafter become aggressive warfare, all of Europe's other powers were obliged, political regime notwithstanding, for the sake of survival to make military might integral to their own claim on modernity. Among the most striking aspects of the military power of the modern state—what Finer means by military power as the "syndrome of modernity"[5]—was the extent to which it rationalized itself and was only rarely applied with coherent strategic purpose. Indeed, the casualness with which France and Britain resorted to armed coercion in Algeria and Afghanistan in the 1830s is quite remarkable; in both cases ambitious expeditionary campaigns were undertaken in expression as much of political impulse as strategic calculation. Neither was what Clausewitz had in mind in defining war as a *continuation of political discourse*, yet in both cases the course of the conflict was profoundly influenced by waxing and waning of domestic political support. Initially cabinet wars, both had greater domestic political consequences than anticipated at their conception, in part because parliamentary accountability was beginning to assert itself as a feature of the democratic modern states. The Anglo-French campaign against Tsarist Russia in the Crimea then demonstrated both a high degree of operational coordination between the allies, a combined logistical capacity fundamentally superior to Tsarist forces fighting on their soil, and significant edge in the use of more advanced small arms as well. The British and French governments did not prosecute the war without a strategic plan—naval, maritime, and land operation were coherent and complementary—but their military commanders abandoned the operational plan following the Battle of Alma and inflicted on their troops a longer and unnecessarily squalid ordeal. Soldiers perished as often from disease as from Russian bullets, but the extensive Allied trench works at Sevastopol at the height of the siege was a tribute to the battlefield dominance of defensive firepower.

Defensive firepower of a mass, range, and lethality that attacking Napoleonic infantry never faced was present in, and critical to, the outcome of every major engagement of the American and German wars of national unity. In the late stages of the American Civil War, trenches were an increasingly common feature of the landscape, as the Confederacy had little left but defensive firepower to answer the might of the Union armies closing the ring around it. That the effectiveness of small arms and artillery improved significantly in the five year interval between the Union invasion of the South and the Prussian invasion of France is evident in the higher casualty rate of latter. Both conflicts witnessed the incorporation of the civilian population into the military struggle, in America as collateral damage in the Union assault on Southern society, in France as a frantic response to the threat of a threat of a popular insurgency. That Lincoln was less ruffled by this aspect of modern war than was Bismarck was a product of the differing political nature of the wars: France had only to be defeated, the Confederacy had to be destroyed. Although the Union and Prussian armies both prosecuted the war with strategies involving impressive operational coordination of multiple armies facilitated by railway transport, the American political and military command was superior even over a protracted conflict. When Bismarck's short, sharp war refused to conclude tidily, the conflicting priorities of the civilian and military leadership came out into the light. From 1864 to 1871 Bismarck's conviction that Germany could prevail sequentially against diplomatically isolated adversaries was vindicated. For his part, Moltke had looked "into the Gorgon visage of a wholly new kind of war;"[6] the German General Staff that later replaced his studied intuition with bureaucracy and contingency planning came to believe that it had mastered it. No chancellor after Bismarck was able to ensure that war plans were subordinated to and consistent with state policy.[7]

In all the wars reviewed here the development of the modern state trailed behind the evolution of modern war; politics often ran well ahead of strategic sobriety, and governments resorted war to as an expedient rather than a strategic interest. This was certainly true of the United States, when the splendid little war with Spain found the U.S. Army embarrassingly unprepared to fight a geriatric Spanish Empire offshore in Cuba, even as the modernising U.S. Navy projected an American presence into the Western Pacific. The first article of American foreign policy was of navalism's promise that only a first-class battle fleet could answer the needs of a great industrial and commercial power in world of predatory imperialism. Japan's war with Russia was in most respects the supreme contrast to the Spanish-American War: carefully planned combined naval, maritime and land operations awaited only the optimum diplomatic moment for the Meiji oligarchy to spring the trap. Yet for all the impressive skill with which land and sea operations realised a coherent strategic plan, Japan was as anxious to secure a peace in 1905 as Prussia had been in 1871. In every major engagement, the Japanese army had bested its adversary, but at tremendous cost. The Union's bloodiest three days at Gettysburg cost it 23,000 casualties; in just one day at Gravelotte-Saint-Privat, Prussia lost 19,000 men; in three weeks at Mukden Japan lost over 75,000. Tsushima appeared to confirm with éclat the arguments of navalists around the world, just as the American and Japanese wars impressed upon everyone the fact of that world's new smallness.

The naval race was only the most visible manifestation of the general arms race and the diffusion of new technologies that accompanied it. Not only did genuine strategic thought fail to keep pace with growth of armies and navies, it is obvious that for the most part it was abandoned altogether. Only Britain's time-honoured convention of fighting wars-in-coalition—and the positive response it elicited from France—testifies to an inkling of what a general European war might entail. But it was no more than an inkling. And where all the major conflicts of the latter half of the nineteenth century involved a striking asymmetry of strength, preparedness, or strategic coherence between victor and vanquished, after 1900 the possession of new technologies and the progress in operational planning was so general that the two sides of the 1914 conflict cancelled each other out. Thus, the arms race itself did not undermine the peace but was rather "an outward manifestation of an underlying disorder."[8] This disorder, Finer's syndrome of the modern, involved the militarisation of political reasoning at the highest instances of civilian authority in all the combatant nations.[9] And it extended far beyond the cabinet rooms, so that even when the hope of bringing the conflict to swift decision was dashed, European societies continued "to mobilise for total war and eventually to commit the totality of their young manhood to mutual and existentially pointless slaughter."[10] The modern states of the nineteenth century failed to develop a modern strategy for the military power they had developed. Where they succeeded only too well was in cultivating sufficient levels of political support—indeed popular enthusiasm—and a stoic faith in ultimate triumph among the combatant peoples of 1914 to drive them to soldier on, literally, to the exhausted stalemate of 1918.

Notes

1 J. Holland Rose, *The Indecisiveness of Modern War and Other Essays*, (London: G. Bell, 1927), p. 48.
2 Baron de Jomini, *The Art of War*, trans. G.H. Mendell and W.P. Craighill (Radford, VA: Wilder Publications, 2008), p. 248.
3 J. Holland Rose, *The Revolutionary and Napoleonic Era, 1789–1815*, (Cambridge, UK: Cambridge University Press, 1935), p. 370.
4 Thomas Otte, *July Crisis: The World's Descent into War, Summer 1914* (Cambridge, UK: Cambridge University Press, 2014), p. 514; Samuel R. Williamson Jr., *The Politics of Grand Strategy: Britain and France Prepare for War, 1904–1914*, (London: Ashfield Press, 1990), pp. 328–42; John Gooch, "The Weary Titan: Strategy and Policy in Britain," in *The Making of Strategy: Rulers, States, ad War*, ed. Williamson Murray, MacGregor Knox, and Alvin Berstein (New York: Cambridge University Press, 1994), pp. 278–306.

5 S.E. Finer, *The History of Government from the Earliest Times.* Vol. 3, *Empires, Monarchies, and the Modern State* (New York: Oxford University Press, 1997), III pp. 1481–82.

6 Walter Goerlitz, *History of the German General Staff, 1657–1945* (New York: Praeger, 1953), pp. 93–102.

7 Brian Bond, *War and Society in Europe, 1870–1970* (London: Fontana, 1984; reprint Montréal, PQ: McGill-Queen's University Press, 1998), p. 59.

8 David Stevenson, *Armaments and the Coming of War: Europe, 1904–1914* (Oxford, UK: Clarendon Press, 1996), p. 417.

9 Ibid., p. 421.

10 Keegan, p. 426.

Select bibliography

Adkins, Roy. *Trafalgar: The Biography of a Battle* (London: Little, Brown, 2004).

Ageron, Charles-Robert. *Modern Algeria: A History from 1830 to the Present*, Trans. Michael Brett (London: Hurst & Company, 1991).

Aldrich, Robert. *Greater France: A History of French Overseas Expansion* (London: Macmillan, 1996).

Anderson, Eugene N. *The First Moroccan Crisis, 1904–1906* (Hamden: Archon, 1966).

Andrew, Christopher. *Théophile Delcassé and the Making of the Entente Cordiale* (New York: St. Martin's, 1968).

Azan, Paul. *L'Armée d'Afrique, de 1830 à 1852* (Paris: Librairie Plon, 1936).

———, ed. *Par l'épée et par la charrue: Écrits et discours de Bugeaud* (Paris: Presses universitaires de France, 1948).

Baer, George W. *One Hundred Years of Sea Power: The U.S. Navy, 1890–1990* (Stanford, CA: Stanford University Press, 1993).

Barker, A.J. *The War Against Russia, 1854–1856* (New York: Holt, Rinehart and Winston, 1970).

Barraclough, Geoffrey. *From Agadir to Armageddon: Anatomy of a Crisis* (London: Weidenfeld & Nicholson, 1982).

Barthorp, Michael. *Heroes of the Crimea: The Battles of Balaclava and Inkerman* (London: Blandford, 1991).

———. *The Zulu War: Isandhlwana to Ulundi* (London: Weidenfeld & Nicolson, 2002).

Baumgart, Winfried. *The Crimean War, 1853–1856* (New York: Oxford University Press, 1999).

Bayly, C.A. *The Birth of the Modern World, 1780–1914* (Oxford, UK: Blackwell, 2004).

Bears, Edward C. *The Vicksburg Campaign*. 3 vols. (Dayton, OH: Morningside, 1995).

Beasley, W.G. *The Meiji Restoration* (Stanford, CA: Stanford University Press, 1972).

Becker, Josef, ed. *Bismarcks "spanische Diversion" 1870 und der preußisch-deutsche Reichsgründungskrieg.* 2 vols. (Paderborn, Germany: Ferdinand Schöningh, 2003).

Bennoune, Mahfoud. *The Making of Contemporary Algeria, 1830–1987* (New York: Cambridge University Press, 1988).

Bensel, Richard Franklin. *Yankee Leviathan: The Origin of Central State Authority in America, 1859–1877* (New York: Cambridge University Press, 1990).

Bergeron, Louis. *France Under Napoleon*, trans. R.R. Palmer (Princeton, NJ: Princeton University Press, 1981).

Berghahn, Volker. *Der Tirpitz-Plan: Genesis und Verfall einer innenpolitischen Krisenstrategie unter Wilhelm II* (Düsseldorf, Germany: Droste, 1971).

Bertaud, Jean-Paul. *The Army of the French Revolution: From Citizen-Soldiers to Instrument of Power*, trans. R.R. Palmer (Princeton, NJ: Princeton University Press, 1988).

———. *Valmy: La démocratie en armes* (Paris: Éditions Julliard, 1970).

Bertier de Sauvigny, Guillaume de. *The Bourbon Restoration*, trans. Lynn Case (Philadephia: University of Pennsylvania Press, 1966).

Bew, John. *Castlereagh: A Life* (New York: Oxford University Press, 2012).

Beyrau, Dietrich. *Militär und Gesellschaft im vorrevolutionären Russland* (Cologne, Germany: Böhlau Verlag, 1984).

Biddle, Stephen. *Military Power: Explaining Victory and Defeat in Modern Battle* (Princeton, NJ: Princeton University Press, 2004).

Black, Jeremy. *Rethinking Military History* (Abingdon, UK: Routledge, 2004).

———. *European Warfare, 1660–1815* (New Haven, CT: Yale University Press, 1994).

Blackbourn, David. *The Long Nineteenth Century: A History of Germany, 1780–1918* (New York: Oxford University Press, 1997).

Blanning, T.C.W. *The Origins of the French Revolutionary Wars* (London: Longman, 1986).

Bley, Helmut. *South-West Africa Under German Rule, 1894–1914* (Evanston, IL: Northwestern University Press, 1971).

Bond, Brian. *War and Society in Europe, 1870–1970* (London: Fontana, 1984; reprint Montréal, PQ: McGill-Queen's University Press, 1998).

Bönker, Dirk. *Militarism in a Global Age: Naval Ambitions in Germany and the United States before World War I* (Ithaca, NY: Cornell University Press, 2012).

Boot, Max. *The Savage Wars of Peace: Small Wars and the Rise of American Power* (New York: Perseus Books, 2002).

Bourne, Kenneth. *Britain and the Balance of Power in North America, 1815–1908* (Berkeley: University of California Press, 1967).

Bowden, Scott. *Napoleon's Grande Armée of 1813* (Chicago, IL: Emperor's Press, 1990).

Bowers, John. *Chickamauga and Chattanooga: The Battles that Doomed the Confederacy* (New York: Harper Collins, 1994).

Bradford, James C., ed. *Crucible of Empire: The Spanish-American War and Its Aftermath* (Annapolis, MD: Naval Institute Press, 1993).

Braisted, William Reynolds. *The United States Navy in the Pacific, 1897–1909* (Austin: University of Texas Press, 1958).

Brands, H.W. *Bound to Empire: The United States and the Philippines* (New York: Oxford University Press, 1992).

———. *TR: The Last Romantic* (New York: Basic Books, 1997).

Bredin, Jean-Denis. *The Affair: The Case of Alfred Dreyfus*, trans. Geoffrey Mehlman (New York: G. Braziller, 1986).

Bret, Patrice. *L'État, l'armée, la science: L'invention de la recherche publique en France (1763–1830)* (Rennes, France: Presses universitaires de Rennes, 2002).

Brewer, John. *The Sinews of Power: War, Money and the English State, 1688–1783* (Cambridge, MA: Harvard University Press, 1988).

Bridgman, Jon. *The Revolt of the Hereros* (Berkeley: University of California Press, 1981).

Broers, Michael. *Europe under Napoleon* (London: I.B. Taurus, 2015).

———. *Napoleon, Soldier of Destiny* (New York: Pegasus, 2014).

Brogan, Denis. *The Development of Modern France, 1870–1939* (London: Hamish Hamilton, 1967).

Brogan, Hugh. *Alexis de Tocqueville, A Life* (New Haven, CT: Yale University Press, 2006).

Brower, Benjamin Claude. *A Desert Named Peace: The Violence of France's Empire in the Algerian Sahara* (New York: Columbia University Press, 2009).

Brown, David. *Palmerston and the Politics of Foreign Policy, 1846–55* (Manchester, UK: Manchester University Press, 2002).

———. *Palmerston, A Biography* (New Haven, CT: Yale University Press, 2010).

Brown, Howard G. *War, Revolution, and the Bureaucratic State: Politics and Army Administration in France 1791–1799* (Oxford, UK: Clarendon Press, 1995).

Bruce, Robert V. *Lincoln and the Tools of War* (Urbana: University of Illinois Press, 1989).

Brunner, Otto. Werner Conze, Reinhart Koselleck, eds. *Geschichtliche Grundbegriffe.* 8 vols. (Stuttgart, Germany: Klett-Cotta, 1978).

Bucholz, Arden. *Moltke and the German Wars, 1864–1871* (London: Palgrave, 2001).

———. *Moltke, Schlieffen, and Prussian War Planning* (New York: Berg, 1991).

Burlingame, Michael. *Abraham Lincoln, A Life.* 2 vols. (Baltimore, MD: Johns Hopkins University Press, 2008).

Burns, James MacGregor. *The Workshop of Democracy* (New York: Alfred A. Knopf, 1985).

Bury, J.P.T. *Gambetta and the Making of the Third Republic* (London: Longman, 1973).

Bury, J.P.T., and R.P. Tombs. *Thiers, 1797–1877: A Political Life* (London: Allen & Unwin, 1986).

Buttar, Prit, *Collision of Empires: The War on the Eastern Front in 1914* (Oxford, UK: Osprey Publishing, 2014).

Cain, P.J., and A.G. Hopkins. *British Imperialism, 1688–2000* (Harlow, UK: Pearson Education, 2002).

Calwell, C.E. *Small Wars, Their Principles and Practice* (London: H.M.S.O, 1906; reprint Lincoln: University of Nebraska Press, 1996).

Carroll, E. Malcolm. *French Public Opinion and Foreign Affairs, 1870–1914* (New York: Century Company, 1931).

Case, Lynn M. *French Opinion on War and Diplomacy during the Second Empire* (Philadelphia: University of Pennsylvania Press, 1944).

Cashman, Sean Denis. *America in the Age of the Titans: The Progressive Era and World War I* (New York: New York University Press, 1988).

Castel, Albert. *Decision in the West: The Atlanta Campaign of 1864* (Lawrence: University Press of Kansas, 1992).

Castle, Ian. *Zulu War, 1879* (Westport, CT: Greenwood, 2005).

Catton, Bruce. *Grant Moves South* (Boston: Little, Brown, 1960).

———. *Mr. Lincoln's Army* (Garden City, NJ: Doubleday & Company, 1951).

Cecil, David. *Lord M. or the Later Life of Lord Melbourne* (London: Arrow Books, 1962).

Chakravarty, Suhash. *From Khyber to Oxus: A Study in Imperial Expansion* (New Delhi: Orient Longman, 1976).

Chamberlain, M.E. *British Foreign Policy in the Age of Palmerston* (London: Longman, 1980).

Chambers, James. *Palmerston, The People's Darling* (London: John Murray, 2004).

Chandler, David G. *The Campaigns of Napoleon* (New York: Scribner, 1966).

Citino, Robert M. *The German Way of War: From the Thirty Years War to the Third Reich* (Lawrence: University of Kansas Press, 2005).

Clark, Christopher. *Iron Kingdom: The Rise and Fall of Prussia, 1600–1947* (Cambridge, MA: Belknap Press, 2006).

———. *The Sleepwalkers: How Europe Went to War in 1914* (New York: Harper Collins, 2012).

Clausewitz, Carl von. *On War*, ed. and trans. Michael Howard and Peter Paret (Princeton: Princeton University Press, 1976).

Clayton, Anthony. *France, Soldiers and Africa* (London: Brassey's Defence Publishers, 1988).

Coddington, Edwin B. *The Gettysburg Campaign: A Study in Command* (New York: Scribner, 1968).

Cohen, Eliot A. *Supreme Command: Soldiers, Statesmen, and Leadership in Wartime* (New York: Free Press, 2002).

Collingham, H.A.C. *The July Monarchy: A Political History of France, 1830–1848* (London: Longman, 1988).

Colmar, Wilhelm Leopold, baron von der Goltz. *Von Roßbach bis Jena und Auerstedt: Ein Beitrag zur Geschichte des preussischen Herres* (Berlin: Ernst Friedrich und Sohn, 1906).

Connaughton, Richard. *Rising Sun and Tumbling Bear: Russia's War with Japan* (London: Cassell, 2003).

Cooke, James J. *New French Imperialism, 1880–1910: The Third Republic and the Colonial Mission* (Hamden, CT: Archon Books, 1973).

Cooling, Benjamin Franklin. *Gray Steel and Blue Water Navy: The Formative Years of America's Military-Industrial Complex, 1881–1917* (Hamden, CT: Archon Books, 1979).

Corbett, Julian S. *The Campaign of Trafalgar*. 2 vols. (London: Longmans, Green & Co., 1919).

———. *Maritime Operations in the Russo-Japanese, 1904–1905*, 2 vols. (Annapolis, MD: Naval Institute Press, 1994).

———. *Principles of Maritime Strategy* (London: Longmans, Green, 1911).

Craig, Gordon A. *The Battle of Königgrätz: Prussia's Victory over Austria, 1866* (Philadelphia, PA: J.B. Lippincott, 1964).

———. *Germany, 1866–1945* (New York: Oxford University Press, 1978).

———. *The Politics of the Prussian Army 1640–1945* (New York: Oxford University Press, 1964).

Crankshaw, Edward. *Bismarck* (London: Macmillan, 1981).

Curtiss, John Shelton. *Russia's Crimean War* (Durham, NC: Duke University Press, 1979).

Dallas, Gregor. *The Final Act: The Roads to Waterloo* (New York: Henry Holt, 1996).

Darwin, John. *The Empire Project: The Rise and Fall of the British World System, 1830–1970* (New York: Cambridge University Press, 2009).

———. *Unfinished Empire: The Global Expansion of Britain* (London: Bloomsbury Press, 2012).

Daumas, Eugène. *The Ways of the Desert*, trans. Sheila M. Ohlendorf (Austin: University of Texas Press, 1971),

David, Saul, *Zulu: The Heroism and Tragedy of the Zulu War of 1879* (New York: Penguin, 2005).

Deist, Wilhelm. *Flottenpolitik und Flottenpropaganda: Das Nachrichtenbureau des Reichsmarineamtes, 1897–1914* (Stuttgart, Germany: Deutsche Verlags-Anstalt, 1976).

Dennis, Peter, and Jeffrey Grey, eds. *Battles Near and Far: A Century of Overseas Deployment* (Canberra, Australia: Army History Unit, Department of Defence, 2005).

Donald, David Herbert. *Lincoln* (New York: Simon & Schuster, 1995).

Doughty, Robert A. *Pyrrhic Victory: French Strategy and Operations in the Great War* (Cambridge, MA: Harvard University Press, 2005).

Drea, Edward J. *Japan's Imperial Army: Its Rise and Rise and Fall, 1853–1945* (Lawrence: University of Kansas Press, 2009).

Duckers, Peter. *The Crimean War at Sea: The Naval Campaigns against Russia, 1854–56* (Barnsley, UK: Pen & Sword, 2011).

Duffy, Christopher. *Borodino and the War of 1812* (New York: Scribner, 1973).

Dupree, Nancy Hatch. "The Question of Jalalabad during the First Anglo-Afghan War," *Asian Affairs* 6, no. 1 (1975), pp. 45–60.

Durand, Henry Marion. *The First Afghan War and Its Causes* (London: Longmans, Green, 1879).

Elting, John R. *Swords Around a Throne: Napoleon's Grande Armée* (New York: Free Press, 1988).

Englund, Steven. *Napoleon: A Political Life* (Cambridge, MA: Harvard University Press, 2004).

Epkenhans, Michael, and Gerhard Groß, eds. *Das Militär und der Aufbruch in die Moderne 1860 bis 1890: Armeen, Marinen und der Wandel von Politik, Gesellschaft und Wirtschaft in Europa, den USA sowie Japan* (Munich, Germany: R. Oldenbourg Verlag, 2003).

Erickson, Edward J. *Defeat in Detail: The Ottoman Army in the Balkans, 1912–1913* (Westport, CT: Praeger, 2003).

Esdaile, Charles J. "De-Constructing the French Wars: Napoleon as Anti-Strategist," *Journal of Strategic Studies* 31, No. 4 (2008), pp. 515–52.

———. *The Peninsular War: A New History* (London: Penguin, 2003).

———. *Spain in the Liberal Age: From Constitution to Civil War, 1808–1939.* (Oxford, UK: Blackwell, 2000).

Evans, David C., and Mark R. Peattie. *Kaigun: Strategy, Tactics, and Technology in the Imperial Japanese Navy, 1887–1941* (Annapolis, MD: Naval Institute Press, 1997).

Evans, Martin. *Algeria: France's Undeclared War* (New York: Oxford University Press, 2012).

Eyre, Vincent. *Journal of an Afghan Prisoner* (London: Routledge & Kegan Paul, 1976; original edition published 1843 under the title *The Military Operations at Cabul*)).

Farwell, Byron. *Queen Victoria's Little Wars* (New York: Norton, 1972).

———. *Stonewall: A Biography of General Thomas J. Jackson* (New York: Norton, 1992).

Fellman, Michael. *Inside War: The Guerrilla Conflict in Missouri during the American Civil War* (New York: Oxford University Press, 1989).

Ferry, Jules. *Discours et Opinions de Jules Ferry.* 7 vols., ed. Paul Robiquet (Paris: Armand Colin, 1897).

Figes, Orlando. *The Crimean War, A History* (New York: Metropolitan Books, 2010).

Finer, S.E. *The History of Government from the Earliest Times.* Vol. 3, *Empires, Monarchies, and the Modern State* (New York: Oxford University Press, 1997).

Foerster, Roland G., ed. *Generalfeldmarschal von Moltke: Bedeutung und Wirkung* (Munich, Germany: R. Oldenbourg Verlag, 1991).

Foner, Eric. *Free Soil, Free Labor, Free Men: The Ideology of the Republican Party before the Civil War* (New York: Oxford University Press, 1995).

———. *Reconstruction: America's Unfinished Revolution, 1863–1877* (New York: Harper & Row, 1988).

Foote, Shelby. *Stars in their Courses: The Gettysburg Campaign June–July, 1863* (New York: Modern Library, 1994).

Förster, Stig. *Der doppelte Militarismus: Die deutsche Heeresrüstungspolitik zwischen Status-quo- Sicherung und Aggression, 1890–1913* (Stuttgart, Germany: Franz Steiner Verlag, 1985).

Förster, Stig, Wolfgang J. Mommsen, and Ronald Robinson. *Bismarck, Europe, and Africa: The Berlin Africa Conference 1884–1885 and the Onset of Partition* (Oxford, UK: Oxford University Press, 1988).

Fortescue, J.W. *A History of the British Army.* 13 vols. (London: Macmillan, 1927).

Fraser, Ronald. *Napoleon's Cursed War: Popular Resistance in the Spanish Peninsular War* (London: Verso, 2008).

Freedman, Lawrence. *Strategy, A History* (New York: Oxford University Press, 2013).

Freidel, Frank. *The Splendid Little War* (New York: Dell, 1958).

Fuller, Howard J. *Empire, Technology and Seapower: Royal Navy Crisis in the Age of Palmerston* (London: Routledge, 2013).

Fuller, J.F.C. *Grant and Lee: A Study in Personality and Generalship* (Bloomington: Indiana University Press, 1957).

———. *War and Western Civilization, 1832–1932: A Study of War as a Political Instrument and the Expression of Mass Democracy* (London: Duckworth, 1932).

Furgurson, Ernest B., *Chancellorsville, 1863: The Souls of the Brave* (New York: Alfred A. Knopf, 1992).

Gall, Lothar. *Bismarck: The White Revolutionary.* 2 vols., trans. J.A. Underwood (London: Unwin Hyman, 1986).

Gallaher, John G. *The Iron Marshal: a Biography of Louis N. Davout* (Carbondale: Southern Illinois University Press, 1976).

Gardiner, Robert, ed. *The Campaign of Trafalgar, 1803–1805* (Annapolis, MD: Naval Institute Press, 1997).

Gat, Azar. *A History of Military Thought: From the Enlightenment to the Cold War* (New York: Oxford University Press, 2001).

George, James L. *History of Warships: From Ancient Times to the Twenty-First Century* (Annapolis, MD: Naval Institute Press, 1998).

Geyer, Dietrich. *Russian Imperialism: The Interaction of Domestic and Foreign Policy, 1860–1914* (New York: Berg, 1987).

Gibbs, Peter. *The Battle of Alma* (London: Weidenfeld & Nicolson, 1963).

Glover, Michael. *Wellington as Military Commander* (London: B.T. Batsford, 1968).

Godechot, Jacques. *The Counter-Revolution: Doctrine and Action, 1789–1804*, trans. Salvator Attanasio (New York: Howard Fertig, 1971).

Goerlitz, Walter. *History of the German General Staff, 1657–1945* (New York: Praeger, 1953).

Goetz, Robert, *1805 Austerlitz: Napoleon and the Destruction of the Third Coalition* (London: Greenhill, 2005).

Goldfrank, David M. *The Origins of the Crimean War* (London: Longman, 1994).

Gould, Lewis L. *The Presidency of Theodore Roosevelt* (Lawrence: University of Kansas Press, 1991).

Grant, Jonathan A. *Rulers, Guns, and Money: The Global Arms Trade in the Age of Imperialism* (Cambridge, MA: Harvard University Press, 2007).

Gray, Colin S. *The Leverage of Sea Power: The Strategic Advantage of Navies in War* (New York: Macmillan, 1992).

———. *Modern Strategy* (New York: Oxford University Press, 1999).

Greaves, Rose Louise. *Persia and the Defence of India, 1884–1892* (London: Athlone Press, 1959).

Greenhill, Basil and Ann Giffard. *The British Assault on Finland, 1854–1855* (Annapolis, MD: Naval Institute Press, 1988).

Grimsley, Mark. *The Hard Hand of War: Union Military Policy Toward Southern Civilians, 1861–1865* (New York: Cambridge University Press, 1995).

Groh, Dieter. *Negative Integration und revolutionärer Attentismus* (Frankfurt am Main, Germany: Ullstein, 1973).

Gueniffey, Patrice. *Bonaparte*, trans. Steven Rendall (Cambridge, MA: Belknap Press, 2015).

Halévy, Élie. *A History of the English People in the Nineteenth Century*. 6 vols., trans. E.I. Watkin (London: Ernest Benn, 1961).

Hall, John R. *The Bourbon Restoration* (London: Alston Rivers, 1909).

Hall, Richard C. *The Balkan Wars, 1912–1913: Prelude to the First World War* (London: Routledge, 2000).

Hansen, Ernst Willi, Gerhard Schreiber, and Berndt Wegner, eds. *Politischer Wandel, organisierte Gewalt und nationale Sicherheit: Beiträge zur neuern Geschichte Deutschlands und Frankreichs* (Munich, Germany: R. Oldenbourg Verlag, 1995).

Harding, D.F. *Small Arms of the East India Company, 1600–1856*. 4 vols. (London: Foresight Books, 1997).

Hastings, Max. *Catastrophe 1914: Europe Goes to War* (New York: Alfred A. Knopf, 2014).

Hattaway, Herman, and Archer Jones, *How the North Won: A Military History of the Civil War* (Urbana: University of Illinois Press, 1991).

Hayne, M.B. *The French Foreign Office and Origins of the First World War, 1898–1914* (Oxford, UK: Clarendon Press, 1993).

Hays, Sam W. *James K. Polk and the Expansionist Impulse* (New York: Longman, 1997).

Hayward, Jack. *Fragmented France: Two Centuries of Disputed Identity* (New York: Oxford University Press, 2007).

Hazareesingh, Sudhir. *From Subject to Citizen: The Second Empire and the Emergence of Modern French Democracy* (Princeton, NJ: Princeton University Press, 1998).

———. *The Legend of Napoleon* (London: Granta, 2004).

Headrick, Daniel. *The Tools of Empire: Technology and European Imperialism in the Nineteenth Century* (New York: Oxford University Press, 1981).

Heathcote, T.A. *The Afghan Wars, 1839–1919* (Staplehurst, UK: Spellmount, 2003).

Hendrick, Burton J. *Lincoln's War Cabinet* (Boston: Little, Brown, 1946).

Hendrickson, Jon K. *Crisis in the Mediterranean: Naval Competition and Great Power Politics, 1904–1914* (Annapolis, MD: Naval Institute Press, 2014).

Herman, Arthur. *To Rule the Waves: How the British Navy Shaped the Modern World* (New York: Harper Collins, 2004).

Herwig, Holger H. "The German Reaction to the *Dreadnought* Revolution," *International History Review* 13, no. 2 (1991), pp. 221–40.

———. "Germany and the Short War Illusion: Toward a New Interpretation, *Journal of Military History* 66, no. 3 (2002), pp. 681–93.

———. *Luxury Fleet: The Imperial German Navy, 1888–1918* (London: Allen & Unwin, 1980).

Heuser, Beatrice. *The Evolution of Strategy: Thinking War from Antiquity to the Present* (New York: Cambridge University Press, 2010).

———. *Reading Clausewitz* (London: Pimlico, 2002).

Hevia, James. *The Imperial Security State: British Colonial Knowledge and Empire-Building in Asia* (New York: Cambridge University Press, 2012).

Hilton, Boyd. *A Mad, Bad, and Dangerous People: England, 1793–1846* (Oxford, UK: Clarendon Press, 2006).

Hobsbawm, Eric. *The Age of Empire, 1875–1914* (New York: Vintage, 1989).

Hodge, Carl Cavanagh. *The Trammels of Tradition: Social Democracy in Britain, France, and Germany* (Westport, CT: Greenwood, 1994).

Holmes, Richard. *The Road to Sedan: The French Army 1866–70* (London: Royal Historical Society, 1894).

Holt, E. *The Carlist Wars in Spain* (London: Putnam, 1967).

Hopkirk, Peter. *The Great Game: On Secret Service in High Asia* (London: John Murray, 1990).

Horricks, Raymond. *Marshal Ney: The Romance and the Real* (London: Archway Publishing, 1988).

Horward, Donald D. *The Battle of Bussaco: Masséna vs. Wellington* (Tallahassee: Florida State University, 1965).

Howard, Michael. *The Franco-Prussian War: The German Invasion of France, 1870–1871* (New York: Collier, 1969).

———. *War in European History* (New York: Oxford University Press, 1976).

Hsü Immanuel Chung-Yueh. *The Rise of Modern China* (New York: Oxford University Press, 2000).

Huber, Terence. *Inventing the Schlieffen Plan: German War Planning, 1871–1914* (New York: Oxford University Press, 2002).

Hull, Isabel V. *Absolute Destruction: Military Culture and the Practices of War in Imperial Germany* (Ithaca, NY: Cornell University Press, 2005).

Ingle, Harold N. *Nesselrode and the Russian Rapprochement with Britain, 1836–1844* (Berkeley: University of California Press, 1976).

Ingram, E. *The Beginning of the Great Game in Asia, 1828–1834* (Oxford, UK: Clarendon, 1979).

James, Lawrence. *The Iron Duke: A Military Biography of Wellington* (London: Weidenfeld & Nicolson, 1992).

———. *Raj: The Making and Unmaking of British India* (New York: St. Martin's Griffin, 1997).

Jany, Curt. *Geschichte der Preußischen Armee vom. 15 Jahrhundert bis 1914*. 4 vols. (Osnabrück, Germany: Biblio-Verlag, 1967).

Jessup, Philip C. *Elihu Root*. 2 vols. (New York: Dodd, Mead,1938).

Johnson, Paul. *Napoleon* (New York: Penguin, 2002).

Johnson, Wesley G., ed. *Double Impact: France and Africa in the Age of Imperialism* (Westport, CT: Greenwood Press, 1985).

Joll, James. *The Second International, 1889–1914* (London: Weidenfeld & Nicolson, 1955).

Jones, Archer. *The Art of War in the Western World* (Urbana: University of Illinois Press, 2001).

———. *Civil War Command and Strategy: The Process of Victory and Defeat* (New York: Free Press, 1992).

Jones, Howard. *Union in Peril: The Crisis over British Intervention in the Civil War* (Chapel Hill: University of North Carolina Press, 1992).

Jordan, David. *The History of the French Foreign Legion, from 1831 to the Present Day* (Guilford, CT: Lyons Press, 2005).

Julien, Charles-André. *Histoire l'Algérie contemporaine*. 2 vols. (Paris: Presses universitaires de France, 1964).

Kagan, Frederick W. *The End of the Old Order: Napoleon and Europe, 1801–1805* (Cambridge, MA: Da Capo Press, 2006).

Kaiser, David. *Politics and War: European Conflict from Philip II to Hitler* (Cambridge, MA: Harvard University Press, 2000).

Kajima, Morinosuke. *The Diplomacy of Japan, 1894–1922*. 2 vols. (Tokyo: Kajima Institute of International Peace, 1976).

Kanya-Forstner, A.S. *The Conquest of the Western Sudan: A Study in French Military Imperialism* (Cambridge, UK: Cambridge University Press, 1969).

Karsten, Peter. *The Naval Aristocracy: The Golden Age of Annapolis and the Emergence of Modern American Navlism* (New York: Free Press, 1972).

Keay, John. *The Honourable Company* (London: Harper Collins, 1991).

Keegan, John. *The American Civil War: A Military History* (New York: Vintage, 2009).

———. *The Face of Battle* (London: Jonathan Cape, 1976).

———. *The First World War* (London: Hutchinson, 1998).

———. *The Price of Admiralty* (London: Hutchinson, 1988; London: Pimlico, 1993).

Kelly, Patrick J. *Tirptiz and the Imperial German Navy* (Bloomington: Indiana University Press, 2011).

Kennedy, Paul, M. *The Rise and Fall of British Naval Mastery* (London: Allen Lane, 1976; London: Penguin, 2001).

———. *The Rise of Anglo-German Antagonism, 1860–1914* (London: Allen & Unwin, 1980).

———. *Strategy and Diplomacy: Eight Studies* (London: Allen & Unwin, 1983).

Kessel, Eberhard. *Moltke* (Stuttgart, Germany: K.F. Koehler, 1957).

Kiernan, V.G. *Colonial Empires and Armies, 1815–1960* (London: Fontana, 1982; Montreal, PQ: McGill-Queen's University Press, 1998).

———. *European Armies from Conquest to Collapse, 1815–1960* (Leicester, UK: Leicester University Press: 1982).

Kissinger, Henry. *A World Restored: Metternich, Castlereagh and the Problems of Peace, 1812–1822* (London: Weidenfeld & Nicolson, 1957).

Knox, Dudley W. *A History of the United States Navy* (New York: Putnam, 1936).

Knox, MacGregor, and Williamson Murray, eds. *The Dynamics of Military Revolution, 1300–2050* (New York: Cambridge University Press, 2001).

Koistinen, Paul A.C. *Mobilizing for Modern War: The Political Economy of American Warfare, 1865–1919* (Lawrence: University of Kansas Press, 1997).

Kolb, Eberhard. *Der Weg aus dem Krieg: Bismarcks Politik im Krieg und die Friedenanbahnung 1870/71* (Munich, Germany: R. Oldenbourg Verlag, 1989).

LaFeber, Walter. *The New Empire: An Interpretation of American Expansion, 1860–1898* (Ithaca, NY: Cornell University Press, 1987).

Lambert, Andrew D. *The Challenge: America, Britain and the War of 1812* (London: Faber and Faber, 2012).

———. *The Crimean War: British Grand Strategy against Russia, 1853–56* (Farnham, UK: Ashgate, 2011).

Lambert, Nicholas A. *Sir John Fisher's Naval Revolution* (Columbia: University of South Carolina Press, 1999).

Langer. William L. *The Diplomacy of Imperialism, 1890–1902* (New York: Alfred A. Knopf, 1968).

Lawday, David. *Napoleon's Master: A Life of Prince Talleyrand* (London: Jonathan Cape, 2006).

Lawson, Philip. *The East India Company: A History* (New York: Longman, 1993).

Lefebvre, Georges. *The Directory,* trans. Robert Baldick (London: Routledge & Kegan Paul, 1964).

Léonard, Émile G. *L'Armée et ses problèmes au XVIIIe siècle* (Paris: Librairie Plon, 1958).

Lerman, Katharine Anne. *The Chancellor as Courtier: Bernhard von Bülow and the Governance of Germany, 1900–1909* (New York: Cambridge University Press, 1990).

Liddell Hart, B.H. *The German Generals Talk* (New York: Morrow, 1948).

———. *The Real War, 1914–1918* (Boston: Little, Brown, 1930).

———. *Strategy* (New York: Meridian, 1991).

Lieven, Dominic. *Nicholas II: Emperor of all the Russians* (London: John Murray, 1993).

———. *Russia Against Napoleon: The True Story of the Campaigns of War and Peace* (New York: Viking, 2009).

Linderman, Gerald F. *The Mirror of War: American Society and the Spanish-American War* (Ann Arbor: University of Michigan Press, 1974).

Linn, Brian McCallister. *Guardians of Empire: The U.S. Army in the Pacific, 1902–1940* (Chapel Hill: University of North Carolina Press, 1997).

———. *The Philippine War, 1899–1902* (Lawrence: University of Kansas Press, 2000).

Livezey, William E. *Mahan on Sea Power* (Norman: University of Oklahoma Press, 1947).

Lloyd, Alan. *The Drums of Kumasi: The Story of the Ashanti Wars* (London: Longman, 1964).

Low, Charles Rathbone, ed. *The Afghan War, 1838–1842: From the Journal and Correspondence of the late Major-General Augustus Abbott* (London: Richard Bentley, 1879).

Luttwak, Edward N. *Strategy: The Logic of War and Peace* (Cambridge, MA: Harvard University Press, 1987).

Luvaas, Jay. *The Education of an Army: British Military Thought, 1815–1940* (Chicago, IL: University of Chicago Press, 1964).

———. *The Military Legacy of the Civil War: The European Inheritance* (Lawrence: University of Kansas Press, 1988).

Lynn, John A. *The Bayonets of the Republic: Motivation and Tactics in the Army of Revolutionary France, 1791–94* (Chicago, IL: University of Chicago Press, 1984).

Lyons, Martyn. *France under the Directory* (London: Cambridge University Press, 1975).

Magraw, Roger. *France 1815–1914: The Bourgeois Century* (London: Fontana, 1983).

Mahan, A.T. *The Influence of Sea Power upon History, 1660–1783* (Boston: Little, Brown, 1890; New York: Dover, 1987).

Marshall-Cornwall, James. *Napoleon as Military Commander* (London: B.T. Batsford, 1967).

Marszalek, John F. *Sherman: A Soldier's Passion for Order* (New York: Free Press, 1993).

Matsusaka, Yoshihisa Tak. *The Making of Japanese Manchuria, 1904–1932* (Cambridge, MA: Harvard University Press, 2001).

Matter, William D. *If It Takes All Summer: The Battle of Spottsylvania* (Chapel Hill: University of North Carolina Press, 1988).

Matzke, Rebecca Berens. *Deterrence through Strength: British Naval Power and Foreign Policy under Pax Britannica* (Lincoln: University of Nebraska Press, 2011).

Maude, Frederic N. *The Jena Campaign 1805* (London: Swan Sonnenschein, 1909).

May, Glenn Anthony. *Battle for Batangas: A Philippine Province at War* (New Haven, CT: Yale University Press, 1991).

Mayeur, Jean-Marie. *Léon Gambetta. La Patrie et la République* (Paris: Fayard, 2008).

McBride, William M. *Technological Change in the United States Navy, 1865–1945* (Baltimore, MD: Johns Hopkins University Press, 2000).

McCaffrey, James M. *Inside the Spanish-American War: A History Based on First-Person Accounts* (Jefferson, NC: McFarland, 2009).

McCarthy, Justin. *The Ottoman Turks: An Introductory History to 1923* (New York: Longman, 1998).

McDonough, James Lee. *Shiloh–In Hell before Night* (Knoxville: University of Tennessee Press, 1984).

McDougall, Walter A. *Promised Land, Crusader State: The American Encounter with the World since 1776* (Boston: Houghton Mifflin, 1997).

McNeill, William H. *The Pursuit of Power: Technology, Armed Force, and Society since A.D. 1000* (Chicago, IL: University of Chicago Press, 1982).

McPherson, James M. *Abraham Lincoln and the Second American Revolution* (New York: Oxford University Press, 1991).

McPherson, James M. *Battle Cry of Freedom: The Civil War Era* (Oxford, UK: Oxford University Press, 1988).

Mead, Walter Russell. *Special Providence: American Foreign Policy and How It Changed the World* (New York: Alfred A. Knopf, 2001).

Mercer, Patrick. *Give Them a Volley and Charge!: The Battle of Inkerman, 1854* (Staplehurst, UK: Spellmount, 1998).

Merk, Frederick. *The Monroe Doctrine and American Expansionism* (New York: Alfred A. Knopf, 1966).

Meyer, Jean, and Martine Acerra. *Histoire de la Marine française: des origines à nos jours* (Rennes, France: Éditions Ouest-France, 1994).

Meyer, Karl E., and Shareen Blair Brysac. *Tournament of Shadows: The Great Game and the Race for Empire in Central Asia* (Washington, DC: Counterpoint, 1999).

Miley, John D. *In Cuba with Shafter* (New York: Scribner, 1899).

Miller, Edward S. *War Plan Orange: The U.S. Strategy to Defeat Japan in the Pacific, 1897–1945* (Annapolis, MD: Naval Institute Press, 1991).

Miller, Stuart Creighton. *"Benevolent Assimilation": The American Conquest of the Philippines, 1899–1903* (New Haven, CT: Yale University Press, 1982).

Miller, Susanne. *Burgfrieden und Klassemkampf: Die deutsche Sozialdemokratie im Ersten Weltkrieg* (Düsseldorf, Germany: Droste, 1974).

Mills, Walter. *The Martial Spirit: A Study of Our War with Spain* (Boston: Houghton Mifflin, 1931).

Montagnon, Pierre. *La Conquête de l'Algérie, les germes de la discorde, 1830–1871* (Paris: Pygmalion–Gérard Watelet, 1986).

Moon, Joshua. *Wellington's Two-Front War: The Peninsular Campaigns at Home and Abroad* (Norman: University of Oklahoma Press, 2011).

Morris, Edmund. *Theodore Rex* (New York: Random House, 2001).

Morriss, Roger. *The Foundations of British Maritime Ascendancy: Resources, Logistics and the State, 1755–1815* (New York: Cambridge University Press, 2011).

Mostert, Noël. *The Line upon a Wind: The Greatest War Fought at Sea under Sail, 1793–1815* (London: Vintage, 2008).

Muir, Rory. *Britain and the Defeat of Napoleon, 1807–1815* (New Haven, CT: Yale University Press, 1996).

Murray, Williamson, MacGregor Knox, and Alvin Bernstein, eds. *The Making of Strategy: Rulers, States, and War* (New York: Cambridge University Press, 1994).

Murray, Williamson, and Richard Hart Sinnreich, eds. *Successful Strategies: Triumphing in War and Peace from Antiquity to the Present* (New York: Cambridge University Press, 2014).

Murray, Williamson, Richard Hart Sinnreich, and James Lacey, eds. *The Shaping of Grand Strategy: Policy, Diplomacy, and War* (New York: Cambridge University Press, 2011).

Musicant, Ivan. *Empire by Default: The Spanish-American War and the Dawn of the American Century* (New York: Henry Holt, 1998).

Nafziger, George F. *Napoleon's Invasion of Russia* (New York: Ballantine, 1988).

Neu, Charles E. *An Uncertain Friendship: Theodore Roosevelt and Japan, 1906–1909* (Cambridge, MA: Harvard University Press, 1967).

Nevins, Allan Nevins. *Ordeal of the Union.* 4 vols. (New York: Collier, 1992).

Nipperdey, Thomas. *Deutsche Geschichte, 1800–1866: Bürgerwelt und starker Staat* (Munich, Germany: C.H. Beck, 1984).

———. *Deutsche Geschichte, 1866–1918: Machtstaat vor Demokratie* (Munich, Germany: C.H. Beck, 1992).

Nish, Ian H. *The Anglo-Japanese Alliance: The Diplomacy of Two Island Empires* (London: Athlone Press, 1966).

Norris, J.A. *The First Afghan War, 1838–1842* (New York: Cambridge University Press, 1967).

O'Brien, P.P. *British and American Sea Power: Politics and Policy, 1900–1936* (Westport, CT: Praeger, 1998).

Okamoto, Shumpei. *The Japanese Oligarchy and the Russo-Japanese War* (New York: Columbia University Press, 1970).

Olsen, John Andreas, and Martin van Creveld, eds. *The Evolution of Operational Art: From Napoleon to the Present* (New York: Oxford University Press, 2011).

Oman, Charles. *A History of the Peninsular War*, 2 vols (London: Greenhill Books, 1903).

Onuf, Peter S. *Jefferson's Empire: The Language of American Nationhood* (Charlottesville: University Press of Virginia, 2000).

O'Reilly, Francis Augustin. *The Fredericksburg Campaign: Winter War of the Rappahannock* (Baton Rouge: Louisiana State University Press, 2006).

Ortholan, Henri. *L'Armée du Second Empire, 1852–1870* (Paris: Éditions Soteca, 2009).

Osterhammel, Jürgen. *The Transformation of the World: A Global History of the Nineteenth Century* Trans. Patrick Camiller (Princeton, NJ: Princeton University Press, 2014).

O'Toole, G.J.A. *The Spanish War: An American Epic* (New York: Norton, 1984).

Otte, Thomas. *July Crisis: The World's Descent into War, Summer 1914* (Cambridge, UK: Cambridge University Press, 2014).

Outram, James. *Rough Notes on the Campaign in Sinde and Afghanistan in 1838–9* (Bombay, India: American Mission Press, 1840).

Padfield, Peter. *Maritime Power and the Struggle for Freedom: Naval Campaigns That Shaped the Modern World, 1788–1851* (New York: Overlook Press, 2003).

Paine, S.C.M. *The Sino-Japanese War of 1894–1895: Perceptions, Power, and Primacy* (Cambridge, UK: Cambridge University Press, 2003).

Pakenham, Thomas. *The Boer War* (New York: Random House, 1979; New York: Perennial, 2001).

———. *The Scramble for Africa: White Man's Conquest of the Dark Continent from 1876 to 1912* (New York: Harper Perenniel, 1992).

Paludan, Phillip Shaw. *The Presidency of Abraham Lincoln* (Lawrence: University of Kansas Press, 1994).

Paret, Peter, *Clausewitz and the State: The Man, His Theories and His Times* (Princeton, NJ: Princeton University Press, 1985).

———, ed. *Makers of Modern Strategy from Machiavelli to the Nuclear Age* (Princeton, NJ: Princeton University Press, 1986).

Pash, Sidney. *The Currents of War: A New History of American-Japanese Relations. 1899–1941* (Lexington: University of Kentucky Press, 2014).

Perkins, Dexter. *A History of the Monroe Doctrine* (Boston: Little, Brown, 1963).

Pfanz, Harry. *Gettysburg: The Second Day* (Chapel Hill: University of North Carolina Press, 1987).

Porch, Douglas. *The Conquest of Morocco* (New York: Farrar, Strauss and Giroux, 1982).

———. *Counterinsurgency: Exposing the Myths of a New Way of War* (New York: Cambridge University Press, 2013).

———. *The French Foreign Legion: A Complete History of the Legendary Fighting Force* (New York: Skyhorse Publishing, 2010).

Price, Roger. *The French Second Empire: An Anatomy of Political Power* (New York: Cambridge University Press, 2001).

———. *Napoleon III and the Second Empire* (London: Routledge, 1997).

Quimby, Robert S. *The Background of Napoleonic Warfare: The Theory of Military Tactics in Eighteenth-Century France* (New York: Columbia University Press, 1957).

Quinn, Frederick. *The Overseas French Empire* (Westport, CT: Praeger, 2000).

Ragsdale, Hugh, ed. *Imperial Russian Foreign Policy* (New York: Cambridge University Press, 1993).

Ralston, David. *The Army of the Republic: The Place of the Military in the Political Evolution of France, 1871–1914* (Cambridge, MA: MIT Press, 1967).

Rauchensteiner, Manfried. *Kaiser Franz und Erzherzog Carl: Dynastie und Heerwesen in Österreich, 1796–1809* (Munich, Germany: R. Oldenbourg Verlag, 1972).

Rayfield, Donald. *The Dream of Lhasa: The Life of Nikolay Przhevalsky (1839–1888) Explorer of Central Asia* (Athens: Ohio University Press, 1976).

Reckner, James R. *Teddy Roosevelt's Great White Fleet* (Annapolis, MD: Naval Institute Press, 1988).

Reid, Brian Holden. *The Origins of the American Civil War* (New York: Longman, 1996).

Reinhard, Marcel. *Le Grand Carnot* (Paris: Hachette, 1952).

Ricard, Serge, ed. *A Companion to Theodore Roosevelt* (Chichester, UK: Wiley-Blackwell, 2011).

Rimanelli, Marco. *Italy between Europe and the Mediterranean: Diplomacy and Naval Strategy from Unification to NATO, 1800s–2000* (New York: Peter Lang, 1997).

Ritter, Gerhard. *The Schlieffen Plan: Critique of a Myth*, trans. Andrew Wilson and Eva Wilson (New York: Praeger, 1958).

———. *Staatskunst und Kriegshandwerk: Das Problem des "Militarismus" in Deutschland*. 4 Vols. (Munich, Germany: R. Oldenbourg Verlag, 1968).

———. *The Sword and the Scepter: The Problem of Militarism in Germany*. 4 vols., trans. Heinz Norden (Coral Gables, FL: University of Miami Press, 1969).

Roberts, Andrew. *Napoleon the Great* (London: Allen Lane, 2014).

———. *Salisbury, Victorian Titan* (London: Phoenix, 2000).

———. *Waterloo: Napoleon's Last Gamble* (New York: Harper Perennial, 2005).

Robertson, Ian C. *Wellington Invades France: The Final Phase of the Peninsular War, 1813–1814* (London: Greenhill, 2003).

Robiquet, Paul, ed. *Discours et opinions de Jules Ferry*. 7 vols. (Paris: Armand Colin, 1897).

Rodger, N.A.M. *The Command of the Ocean: A Naval History of Britain* (New York: Norton, 2005).

Röhl, John C.G. *Germany without Bismarck: The Crisis of Government in the Second Reich, 1890–1900* (Berkeley: University of California Press, 1967).

———. *The Kaiser and His Court: Wilhelm II and the Government of Germany*, trans. Terence F. Cole (Cambridge: Cambridge University Press, 1996).

———. *Kaiser Wilhelm II: A Concise Life*, trans. Sheila de Bellaigue (Cambridge, UK: Cambridge University Press, 2014).

———. *Wilhelm II: The Kaiser's Personal Monarchy, 1888–1900*, trans. Sheila de Bellaigue (New York: Cambridge University Press, 2004).

Ropp, Theodore. *The Development of a Modern Navy: French Naval Policy, 1871–1904* (Annapolis, MD: Naval Institute Press, 1987).

Rose, J. Holland. *The Indecisiveness of Modern War and Other Essays* (London: G. Bell, 1927).

———. *The Personality of Napoleon* (New York: Putnam, 1912).

———. *Pitt and Napoleon: Essays and Letters* (London: G. Bell, 1912).

———. *The Revolutionary and Napoleonic Era, 1789–1815* (Cambridge, UK: Cambridge University Press, 1935).

Rose, Lisle A. *Power at Sea: The Age of Navalism, 1890–1918* (Columbia: University of Missouri Press, 2007).

Rosenau, James N., Kenneth W. Thompson, and Gavin Boyd, eds. *World Politics: An Introduction* (New York: Free Press, 1976).

Rothenberg, Günther E. *The Art of Warfare in the Age of Napoleon* (Bloomington: Indiana University Press, 1978).

———. *The Napoleonic Wars* (London: Cassell, 1999).

Rüger, Jan. *The Great Naval Game: Britain and Germany in the Age of Empire* (New York: Cambridge University Press, 2007).

Saalman, Howard, *Haussmann: Paris Transformed* (New York: G. Braziller, 1971).

Sanborn, Joshua A. *Imperial Apocalypse: The Great War and the Destruction of the Russian Empire* (Oxford, UK: Oxford University Press, 2014).

Schenking, J. Charles. *Making Waves: Politics, Propaganda, and the Emergence of the Imperial Japanese Navy, 1868–1922* (Stanford, CA: Stanford University Press, 2005).

Schroeder, Paul W. *The Transformation of European Politics, 1763–1848* (New York: Oxford University Press, 1994).

Scott, H.M. *The Birth of a Great Power System, 1740–1815* (London: Pearson, 2006).

Sears, Stephen W. *Chancellorsville* (Boston: Houghton Mifflin, 1996).

———. *Landscape Turned Red: The Battle of Antietam* (New Haven, CT: Ticknor and Fields, 1983).

———. *To the Gates of Richmond: The Peninsula Campaign* (New York: Ticknor and Fields, 1992).

Seaton, Albert. *The Crimean War: A Russian Chronicle* (London: B.T. Batsford, 1977).

Semmel, Stuart. *Napoleon and the British* (New Haven, CT: Yale University Press, 2004).

Shannon, Fred Albert. *The Organization and Administration of the Union Army, 1861–1865.* 2 vols. (Gloucester, MA: Peter Smith, 1965).

Sheehan, James J. *German History, 1770–1866* (New York: Oxford University Press, 1989).

Sherman, William Tecumseh. *Memoires of General W.T. Sherman* (New York: Library of America, 1984).

Showalter, Dennis E. *The Wars of German Unification* (London: Hodder Arnold, 2004).

Shulman, Mark Russell. *Navalism and the Emergence of American Sea Power* (Annapolis, MD: Naval Institute Press, 1995).

Siborne, William. *The Waterloo Campaign, 1815* (Westminster, UK: Archibald Constable, 1900).

Simms, Brendan. *The Impact of Napoleon: Prussian High Politics, Foreign Policy and the Crisis of the Executive, 1797–1806* (New York: Cambridge University Press, 1997).

Singer, Barnett, and John Langdon. *Cultured Force: Makers and Defenders of the French Colonial Empire* (Madison: University of Wisconsin Press, 2004).

Sked, Alan. *The Decline and Fall of the Habsburg Empire, 1815–1918* (London: Longman, 1989).

Skowronek, Stephen. *Building a New American State: The Expansion of National Administrative Capacities, 1877–1920* (New York: Cambridge University Press, 1982).

Smith, Jean Edward. *Grant* (New York: Simon & Schuster, 2001).

Smith, Joseph. *The Spanish-American War: Conflict in the Caribbean and the Pacific* (New York: Longman, 1994).

Snow, Peter. *To War with Wellington: From the Peninsula to Waterloo* (London: John Murray, 2010).

Sondhaus, Laurence. *The Habsburg Empire and the Sea: The Naval Policy of Austro-Hungary, 1867–1918* (West Lafayette, IN: Purdue University Press, 1989).

Spector, Ronald H. *At War at Sea: Sailors and Naval Combat in the Twentieth Century* (New York: Penguin, 2001).

Sprout, Harold, and Margaret Sprout. *The Rise of American Naval Power, 1776–1918* (Princeton, NJ: Princeton University Press, 1939).

Stamm-Kuhlman, Thomas. *König in Prueßens großer Zeit: Friedrich Wilhelm III. der Melancholiker auf dem Thron* (Berlin: Siedler Verlag, 1992).

Steinberg, Jonathan. *Bismarck: A Life* (New York: Oxford University Press, 2011).

———. *Yesterday's Deterrent: Tirpitz and the Birth of the German Battle Fleet* (London: Macdonald, 1965).

Steiner, Zara. *The Foreign Office and Foreign Policy, 1898–1914* (Cambridge, UK: Cambridge University Press, 1969).

Sternell, Zeev. *La Droite révolutionnaire* (Paris: Seuil, 1978).

Stevenson, David. *Armaments and the Coming of War: Europe, 1904–1914* (Oxford, UK: Clarendon Press, 1996).

Stoker, Donald. *The Grand Design: Strategy in the U.S. Civil War* (New York: Oxford University Press, 2010).

Stone, David R. *The Russian Army in the Great War: The Eastern Front, 1914–1917* (Lawrence: University of Kansas Press, 2015).

Stone, Norman. *The Eastern Front, 1914–1917* (London: Hodder and Stoughton, 1975).

Strachan, Hew. *Carl von Clausewitz's On War: A Biography* (London: Atlantic Books, 2007).

———. *European Armies and the Conduct of War* (London Routledge, 1983).

———. *The First Word War*. 2 vols. (Oxford, UK: Clarendon Press, 2001).

———. *From Waterloo to Balaclava: Tactics Technology, and the British Army, 1815–1854* (New York: Cambridge University Press, 1985).

Sullivan, Anthony Thrall. *Thomas-Robert Bugeaud: France and Algeria, 1784–1849: Politics, Power, and the Good Society* (Hamden, CT: Archon Books, 1983).

Sumida, Jon Tetsuru. *In Defence of Naval Supremacy: Finance, Technology, and British Naval Policy, 1899–1914* (London: Unwin Hyman, 1989).

Sutherland, D.M.G. *The French Revolution and Empire: The Quest for Civic Order* (Oxford, UK: Blackwell, 2003).

———. *France 1789–1815: Revolution and Counterrevolution* (New York: Oxford University Press, 1986).

Sweetman, Jack, ed. *Great American Naval Battles* (Annapolis, MD: Naval Institute Press, 1998).

Sweetman, John. *Balaclava 1854: The Charge of the Light Brigade* (London: Greenwood Publishing, 2005).

Sword, Wiley. *Shiloh: Bloody April* (New York: William Morrow, 1974).

Taylor, A.J.P. *The Struggle for Mastery in Europe, 1848–1918* (London: Oxford University Press, 1954).

Telp, Claus. *The Evolution of Operational Art, 1740–1813: From Frederick the Great to Napoleon* (London: Cass, 2005).

Thiers, M. Adolphe. *History of the French Revolution*, trans. Thomas W. Redhead (London: A. Fullarton, 1845).

Tilchin, William N. *Theodore Roosevelt and the British Empire: A Study in Presidential Statecraft* (New York: St. Martin's, 1997).

Tilly, Charles. *The Vendée* (Cambridge, MA: Harvard University Press, 1964).

Tombs, Robert. *The Paris Commune 1871* (London: Longman, 1999).

Tone, John Lawrence. *The Fatal Knot: The Guerilla War in Navarre and the Defeat of Napoleon in Spain* (Chapel Hill: University of North Carolina Press, 1994).

Trask, David F. *The War with Spain in 1898* (New York: Macmillan, 1981).

Turner, George Edgar. *Victory Rode the Rails: The Strategic Place of Railroad in the Civil War* (Lincoln: University of Nebraska Press, 1992).

Vagts, Alfred. *A History of Militarism: Civilian and Military* (New York: Free Press, 1937).

van Creveld, Martin. *The Rise and Decline of the State* (New York: Cambridge University Press, 1999).

———. *Supplying War: Logistics from Wallenstein to Patton* (New York: Cambridge University Press, 2004).

van der Oye, David Schimmelpenninck. *Toward the Rising Sun: Russian Ideologies of Empire and the Path to War with Japan* (DeKalb: Northern Illinois University Press, 2001).

Vandervort, Bruce. *Wars of Imperial Conquest in Africa, 1830–1914* (Bloomington: Indiana University Press, 1998).

Verhey, Jeffrey. *The Spirit of 1914: Militarism, Myth, and Mobilization in Germany* (New York: Cambridge University Press, 2000).

Verner, Andrew M. *The Crisis of Russian Autocracy: Nicholas II and the 1905 Revolution* (Princeton, NJ: Princeton University Press, 1990).

———. *Nationen im Gleichschritt: Der Kult der "Nation in Waffen" in Deutschland und Frankreich, 1871–1914* (Göttingen, Germany: Vandenhoeck & Ruprecht, 1997).

Von Laue, Theodore H. *Sergei Witte and the Industrialization of Russia* (New York: Columbia University Press, 1963).

Walter, Dierck. *Preußische Heeresreformen 1807–1870: Militärische Innovationen und der Mythos der "Roonschen Reform"* (Paderborn, Germany: Verlag Ferdinand Schöningh, 2003).

Waltz, Kenneth N. *Man, the State and War: A Theoretical Analysis* (New York: Columbia University Press, 1954).

Warner, Denis A., and Peggy Warner. *The Tide at Sunrise: A History of the Russo-Japanese War, 1904–1905* (New York: Charterhouse, 1974).

Warner, Oliver. *Trafalgar* (London: B.T. Batsford, 1959).

Warren Gordon H. *Fountain of Discontent: The Trent Affair and the Freedom of the Seas* (Boston: Northeastern University Press, 1981).

Warren, Kenneth. *Bethlehem Steel: Builder and Arsenal of America* (Pittsburgh, PA: University of Pittsburgh Press, 2008).

Warschauer, Robert. *Studien zur Entwicklung der Gedanken Lazare Carnots über Kriegführung, 1784–1793* (Berlin: Verlag E. Eberling, 1937).

Watson, Alexander. *Ring of Steel: Germany and Austria-Hungary in World War I* (New York: Basic Books, 2014).

Watson, S.J. *Carnot* (London: Bodley Head, 1954).

Wawro, Geoffrey. *The Austro-Prussian War: Austria's War with Prussia and Italy in 1866* (New York: Cambridge University Press, 1996).

———. *The Franco-Prussian War: The German Conquest of France in 1870–1871* (New York: Cambridge University Press, 2003).

———. *A Mad Catastrophe: The Outbreak of World War I and the Collapse of the Habsburg Empire* (New York: Basic Books, 2014).

Weber, Eugen. *Peasants into Frenchmen: The Modernization of Rural France, 1870–1914* (Stanford, CA: Stanford University Press, 1976).

Webster, Charles. *The Foreign Policy of Palmerston, 1830–1841*. 2 vols. (London: G. Bell, 1951).

Wehler, Hans-Ulrich. *Das deutsche Kaiserreich, 1871–1914* (Göttingen, Germany: Vandenhoeck & Ruprecht, 1980).

———. *Bismarck und der Imperialismus* (Cologne, Germany: Kiepenheuer & Witsch, 1969).

Weigley, Russell F. *The Age of Battles: The Quest for Decisive Warfare from Breitenfeld to Waterloo* (Bloomington: Indiana University Press, 1991).

———. *The American Way of War: A History of United States Military Strategy and Policy* (Bloomington: Indiana University Press, 1973).

———. *A Great Civil War: A Military and Political History* (Bloomington: Indiana University Press, 2000).

———. *History of the United States Army* (Bloomington: Indiana University Press, 1984).

Weitz, Mark A. *More Damning Than Slaughter: Desertion in the Confederate Army* (Lincoln: University of Nebraska Press, 2005).

Wentker, Hermann. *Zerstörung der Großmacht Rußland? Die britischen Kriegsziele im Krimkrieg* (Göttingen, Germany: Vandenhoeck & Ruprecht, 1993).

Wessling, H.L. *The European Colonial Empires: 1815–1919*, trans. Diane Webb (Harlow, UK; Pearson Longman, 2004).

Westwood, J.N. *Russia against Japan: A New Look at the Russo-Japanese War* (Albany: State University of New York Press, 1986).

Wheeler, Joseph. *The Santiago Campaign, 1898* (Boston: Lamson, Wolffe, 1898).

Whitman, James Q. *The Verdict of Battle: The Law of Victory and the Making of Modern War* (Cambridge, MA: Harvard University Press, 2012).

Wilkinson, Henry Spencer. *Command of the Sea and Brain of the Navy* (London: Archibald Constable, 1894).

Williams, T. Harry. *Lincoln and His Generals* (New York: Alfred A. Knopf, 1952).

Williamson, Samuel R. Jr. *The Politics of Grand Strategy: Britain and France Prepare for War, 1904–1914* (London: Ashfield Press, 1990).

Willmott, H.P. *The Last Century of Sea Power*. 2 vols. (Bloomington: University of Indiana Press, 2009).

Wills, Garry. *Lincoln at Gettysburg: The Words That Remade America* (New York: Simon & Schuster, 1992).

Wilson, H.W. *Battleships in Action*. 2 vols. (Toronto, ON: Ryerson Press, 1926).

Winkler, Heinrich August. *Geschichte des Westens, von den Anfängen in der Antike bis zum 20. Jahrhundert*. 2 vols. (Munich, Germany: C.H. Beck, 2012).

———. *Der lange Weg nach Westen*. 2 vols. (Munich, Germany: C.H. Beck, 2001).

Wohlfeil, Rainer. *Spanien und die deutsche Erhebung* (Wiesbaden, Germany: Franz Steiner Verlag, 1965).

Wood, Gordon S. *Empire of Liberty: A History of the Early Republic, 1789–1815* (New York: Oxford University Press, 2009).

Woodham-Smith, Cecil. *The Reason Why* (London: Penguin, 1991).

Woodworth, Steven E. *Jefferson Davis and His Generals: The Failure of Confederate Command in the West* (Lawrence: University of Kansas Press, 1990).

Yapp, M.E. *Strategies of British India: Britain, Iran, and Afghanistan, 1798–1850* (New York: Oxford University Press, 1980).

Zegger, Robert E. *John Cam Hobhouse: A Political Life, 1819–1852* (Columbia: University of Missouri Press, 1973).

Zeldin, Theodore. *France 1848–1945: Politics and Anger* (New York: Oxford University Press, 1979).

Zimmerman, Warren. *First Great Triumph: How Five Americans Made Their Country a World Power* (New York: Farrar, Straus and Giroux, 2002).

Index